The Yearbook of Psychoanalysis and Psychotherapy

The YEARBOOK of
PSYCHOANALYSIS AND PSYCHOTHERAPY

Editor-in-Chief: **ROBERT LANGS, M.D.**, *New York, New York*

Associate Editors, Clinical Research:

Stuart Hauser, M.D., Ph.D.
Boston, Massachusetts

Peter H. Knapp, M.D.
Boston, Massachusetts

Editorial Board

DR. MAURICIO ABADI
Argentina-Buenos Aires

CHRISTOPHER BOLLAS
London, England

RON BROWN, M.D.
Montreal, Quebec, Canada

J. ALEXIS BURLAND, M.D.
Bala Cynwyd, Pennsylvania

STANLEY CATH, M.D.
Belmont, Massachusetts

THEODORE DORPAT, M.D.
Seattle, Washington

MERTON GILL, M.D.
Chicago, Illinois

PETER GIOVACCHINI, M.D.
Winnetka, Illinois

EUGENE GOLDBERG, M.D.
New York, New York

LEO GOLDBERGER, Ph.D.
New York, New York

WILLIAM GOODHEART, M.D.
San Francisco, California

MARTIN GREENE, D.S.W.
Great Neck, New York

C. JESS GROESBECK, M.D.
Sacramento, California

JAMES GROTSTEIN, M.D.
Beverly Hills, California

ALAN JACOBS, M.D.
New York, New York

M. MASUD R. KHAN, M.A.
London, England

LEON KUPFERSTEIN, M.D.
New York, New York

EDWARD LEADER, M.D.
Atlanta, Georgia

ADAM LIMENTANI, M.D.
London, England

MARC LUBIN, Ph.D.
Chicago, Illinois

RENE MAJOR, M.D.
Paris, France

WILLIAM MEISSNER, M.D.
Cambridge, Massachusetts

ROY MENDELSOHN, M.D.
St. Louis, Missouri

STANLEY OLINICK, M.D.
Washington, D.C.

JEROME OREMLAND, M.D.
San Francisco, California

ANNA ORNSTEIN, M.D.
Cincinnati, Ohio

HERBERT PARDES, M.D.
Potomac, Maryland

JAMES RANEY, M.D.
Seattle, Washington

HERBERT ROSENFELD, M.D.
London, England

RICHARD RUSSELL, M.D.
Pittsburgh, Pennsylvania

PETER SCHUSTER, M.D.
Vienna, Austria

HAROLD SEARLES, M.D.
Washington, D.C.

MORTON SHANE, M.D.
Los Angeles, California

OZZIE SIEGEL, Ph.D.
Great Neck, New York

SAMUEL SLIPP, M.D.
New York, New York

VAMIK D. VOLKAN, M.D.
Charlottesville, Virginia

ROY WHITMAN, M.D.
Cincinnati, Ohio

ERNEST S. WOLF, M.D.
Chicago, Illinois

The Yearbook of Psychoanalysis and Psychotherapy

Volume 1/1985

Edited by
ROBERT LANGS, M.D.
and the Editorial Board

NEWCONCEPT press, inc.
Emerson   New Jersey

Copyright © by Newconcept Press, Inc.

All rights reserved. No part of this book may be reproduced in any form, by photostat, microform, retrieval system, or any other means, without the prior written permission of the publisher, Newconcept Press, Inc., Emerson, N.J. 07630.

ISBN 0-931231-04-3
ISSN 8756-4998

Printed in the United States of America
10 9 8 7 6 5 4 3 2 1

CONTENTS

Editorial Board ii
Editorial Statement ix
Contributors xi

PART I: WOMEN'S ISSUES IN THERAPY

1/ Feminist Values and Psychoanalysis:
The Patient's Curative Capacities /3

LINDA KANEFIELD, M.S.

2/ *Discussion Paper:* Psychotherapy: Egalitarian Values and
Transference /25

MALKAH T. NOTMAN, M.D.

3/ The Effect of the Therapist's Gender on the
Transference /33

NANCY MANN KULISH, Ph.D.

4/ *Discussion Paper:* Theoretical and Technical
Considerations of Cross-Gender Transferences with Male
Patients /63

PHYLLIS TYSON, Ph.D.

5/ Early Developmental Processes and Adult Intimate
Violence /77

LINDA JEAN STROTHMAN, A.M., A.C.S.W.

6/ *Discussion Paper:* Culture and Development in Adult
Family Violence /119

SHIRLEY COOPER, M.S.

PART II: THE CLINICAL SITUATION

7/ The First Session /125

ROBERT LANGS, M.D.

8/ Latent and Manifest Effects of Audiorecording in Psychoanalytic Psychotherapy /151

ELIZABETH MURRAY FRICK, Psy.D.

9/ *Discussion Paper:* A Critique of Robert Langs's Conceptions of Transference, Evidence by Indirection, and the Role of the Frame /177

MERTON M. GILL, M.D.

10/ Frame Deviations and Dreams in Psychoanalytic Psychotherapy /189

FRANK P. TROISE, A.C.S.W.

11/ *Discussion Paper:* The Therapist Undisguised in Dreams and Reduction of Resistance /201

JOSEPH M. NATTERSON, M.D.

12/ The Onset of Unconscious Perception /209

ROY M. MENDELSOHN, M.D.

13/ *Discussion Paper:* On a Scientific Method for Psychoanalysis /241

J. ALEXIS BURLAND, M.D.

14/ Narcissim, Object Relatedness, and Drive-Conflict Issues /247

JAMES BEATRICE, Ph.D.

15/ *Discussion Paper:* Is Narcissus a Myth? /273

PETER L. GIOVACCHINI, M.D.

PART III: CLINICAL TOPICS

16/ A Proposed Revision of the Psychoanalytic Concept of the Death Instinct /299

JAMES S. GROTSTEIN, M.D.

17/ *Discussion Paper:* Instinct, Structure, and Personal Meaning /327

THOMAS H. OGDEN, M.D.

18/ Recent Findings and New Directions in Child Psychiatry /335

MELVIN LEWIS, M.B., B.S., F.R.C.Psych., D.C.H.

19/ *Discussion Paper:* Psychoanalysis, Science, and Child Psychiatry /359

JOSEPH H. BEITCHMAN, M.D.

20/ Murder, Frenzy, and Madness—The Logistics of Humiliations: Notes on Dostoevsky and *The Idiot* /371

M. MASUD R. KHAN

21/ Psychosomatic Symptoms and Latent Psychotic States /381

HERBERT ROSENFELD, M.D., F.R.C.Psych.

Author Index /399
Subject Index /405

STATEMENT BY THE EDITOR-IN-CHIEF

The Yearbook of Psychoanalysis and Psychotherapy is dedicated to the clinical practice of psychoanalytically oriented treatment modalities. It will publish clinically based papers that make original contributions of importance to practicing psychotherapists and those engaged in research into the psychotherapeutic process. A discussion format will be used as a means of encouraging debate and clarification and to stress controversial issues and clinical problems. Unsolicited contributions to the *Yearbook* are most welcome. We are pleased to have been chosen as the official journal of the Society for Psychoanalytic Psychotherapy, and we will do our utmost to maintain the highest standards of scholarship, originality, and clinical relevance.

Robert Langs, M.D.
for the Editorial Board

CONTRIBUTORS

JAMES BEATRICE, Ph.D
Currently in private practice in psychoanalytic psychotherapy for adults and children. 4024 Ibis Street, San Diego, California 92103.

JOSEPH H. BEITCHMAN, M.D., M.P.H., F.R.C.P. (C), D.A.B.P.N.
Director of a program for preschoolers with developmental and psychiatric problems, Dr. Beitchman is involved in clinical research and teaching at The Royal Ottawa Hospital and has a pending appointment as Associate Professor and Director of The Child and Family Studies Unit at The Clarke Institute of Psychiatry, University of Toronto. Department of Psychiatry, Royal Ottawa Hospital, 1145 Carling Avenue, Ottawa, Ontario K1Z 7K4.

J. ALEXIS BURLAND, M.D.
Training and Supervising Analyst, Philadelphia Psychoanalytic Institute. Clinical Professor of Psychiatry and Human Behavior, Jefferson Medical College, Philadelphia. 15 Colwyn Lane, Bala Cynwyd, Pennsylvania 19004.

SHIRLEY COOPER, M.S.
Clinical Professor of Social Work, Department of Psychiatry, University of California, San Francisco. Former Child Clinical Services Director, Department of Psychiatry, Mount Zion Hospital and Medical Center, San Francisco. Private practice. 1988 Bush Street, San Francisco, California 94115.

ELIZABETH M. FRICK, Psy. D.
Associate, Department of Psychiatry and Behavioral Sciences, Northwestern University Medical School. Faculty, Postgraduate Program in Psychoanalytic Psychotherapy, The Illinois School of Professional Psychology. Director, Partial Hospitalization Services, Chemical Dependence Program, Northwestern Memorial Hospital. Private practice. 1210 Astor Street, Chicago, Illinois 60610.

MERTON M. GILL, M.D.
Professor of Psychiatry, University of Illinois Medical Center, Chicago. Supervising Analyst and faculty member, Institute for Psychoanalysis, Chicago. Department of Psychiatry, University of Illinois Medical Center, Box 6998, Chicago, Illinois 60680.

PETER L. GIOVACCHINI, M.D.
Clinical Professor, Department of Psychiatry, University of Illinois College of Medicine. Private practice of Psychoanalysis. 270 Locust Road, Winnetka, Illinois 60093.

JAMES S. GROTSTEIN, M.D.
Associate Clinical Professor of Psychiatry, UCLA. Training and Supervising Analyst, Los Angeles Psychoanalytic Institute. Attending Staff Physician, Cedars-Sinai Medical Center, and Director of the Interdisciplinary Group for Advanced Studies in Psychotic, Borderline, and Narcissistic Disorders. 9777 Wilshire Boulevard, Beverly Hills, California 90212.

LINDA KANEFIELD, M.S.
Doctoral candidate, Department of Psychology, University of Massachusetts, Amherst. Clinical Psychology Intern, Saint Elizabeths Hospital, Washington, D.C. 6513 Westmoreland Avenue, Takoma Park, Maryland 20912.

M. MASUD R. KHAN, M.A., D.Litt.
Member of the Institute of Psychoanalysis, London. Director of the Sigmund Freud Copyrights. Foreign Editor of *Nouvelle Revue de Psychoanalyse*. Former editor of the International Psycho-Analytical Library, and a Consultant Associate Editor for the *International Journal of Psycho-Analysis* and the *International Review of Psycho-Analysis*. Flat 7, 24 Palace Court, London W2 4HU, England.

NANCY MANN KULISH, Ph.D.
Clinical instructor, Department of Psychiatry, Wayne State University, Detroit. Research cndidate, Michigan Psychoanalytic Institute. Private practice. 29260 Franklin, Southfield, Michigan 48034.

ROBERT LANGS, M.D.
Program Director, Lenox Hill Hospital Psychotherapy Program, New York City. Founder of the Society for Psychoanalytic Psychotherapy, Dr. Langs is a practicing and supervising psychotherapist and psychoanalyst and is Editor-in-chief of *The Yearbook of Psychoanalysis and Psychotherapy*. 30 East 60th Street, New York City, New York 10022.

MELVIN LEWIS, M.B., B.S. (London), F.R.C.Psych., D.C.H.
Professor of Pediatrics and Psychiatry and Director of Medical Studies, Child Study Center, Yale University School of Medicine. Attending Physician in Pediatrics and Psychiatry, Yale-New Haven Hospital, New Haven. Editor, *Journal of the American Academy of Child Psychiatry*. Yale University Child Study Center, 230 South Frontage Road, New Haven, Connecticut 06510.

ROY M. MENDELSOHN, M.D.
Child Psychoanalyst. Member, American Psychoanalytic Association. Fellow, American Psychiatric Association. Fellow, American Orthopsychiatric Association. Alumnus, Menninger School of Psychiatry. 404 South Clay Avenue, St. Louis, Missouri 63122.

JOSEPH M. NATTERSON, M.D.
Training Analyst, Southern California Psychoanalytic Institute. Clinical Professor of Psychiatry, UCLA School of Medicine. Attending Psychiatrist, Cedars-Sinai Medical Center, Los Angeles. 9911 West Pico Boulevard, Los Angeles, California 90035.

MALKAH T. NOTMAN, M.D.
Training and Supervising Psychoanalyst, Boston Psychoanalytic Institute. Clinical Professor of Psychiatry, Tufts University School of Medicine. Director of Psychotherapy for the Department of Psychiatry, New England Medical Center. Formerly Director of Consultation-Liaison Psychiatry in Obstetrics and Gynecology at Beth Israel Hospital, Boston, and Harvard Medical School. Box 1007, 171 Harrison Avenue, Boston, Massachusetts 02111.

THOMAS H. OGDEN, M.D.
Assistant Clinical Professor of Psychiatry, University of California, San Francisco School of Medicine. Faculty, Department of Psychiatry, Children's Hospital, San Francisco. Private practice. 1721 Scott Street, San Francisco, California 94115.

HERBERT ROSENFELD, M.D., F.R.C. Psych.
Member of the British Psychoanalytic Society, Dr. Rosenfeld is in private practice as H.A.R. psychoanalyst in London and is also engaged in H.A.R. teaching, training, and supervising analysts from other countries as well as from the U.K. 18 Burgess Hill, London NW2 2DA, England.

LINDA JEAN STROTHMAN, A.M., A.C.S.W.
Director, Constance Morris House of Des Plaines Valley Community Center of Hull House Association, Summit, Illinois. Clinical Consultant, Lifespan, Des Plaines, Illinois. Former Clinical Consultant to Uptown Hull House Woman Abuse Action Program, Chicago. Former Post Master's Clinical Social Work Fellow, Mt. Zion Hospital, San Francisco. Private practice. 55 East Washington, Room 1521, Chicago, Illinois 60602.

FRANK P. TROISE, A.C.S.W.
Director, Lynbrook Consultation and Referral Service, Lynbrook, New York. Private Practice in Psychoanalytic Psychotherapy. 10 Union Avenue, Lynbrook, New York 11563.

PHYLLIS TYSON, Ph.D.
Assistant Clinical Professor, Department of Psychiatry, University of California, San Diego, School of Medicine. Faculty, San Diego Psychoanalytic Institute. Adjunct Faculty, California School of Professional Psychology. Private practice, child and adult psychoanalysis. 3252 Holiday Court, La Jolla, California 92037.

The Yearbook of Psychoanalysis and Psychotherapy

I
WOMEN'S ISSUES IN THERAPY

1/
Feminist Values and Psychoanalysis: The Patient's Curative Capacities
Linda Kanefield, M.S.

> . . . I do not have to love you
> As I loved her,
> To be devastated, but,
> Angel and surgeon of the psyche,
> I am free to love you now
> Outside all the myths,
> The confused dreams,
> Beyond all the barriers,
> In the warm natural light
> Of simple day.
> I am allowed to give you
> Unstrained, flowing,
> Wise-infant
> To wise-mother love.
>
> You broke the spell;
> You with your whippets around you
> Like some lady in a tapestry
> Said to the unicorn,

An earlier version of this paper was presented at the meetings of the American Psychological Association, Los Angeles, California, August 1981. I am grateful to Alexandra Kaplan and Harold Jarmon for their ideas and encouragement. Others who thoughtfully commented on earlier drafts of this paper are Norman Schneider, Bonnie Strickland, Sandra Levy, Nathan Kravis, and Robert Langs.

The lines from "The Action of Therapy" from *Selected Poems of May Sarton,* edited by Serena Sue Hilsinger and Lois Brynes, are reprinted by permission of W. W. Norton & Company, Inc. Copyright (c) 1978 by May Sarton.

"If the child needs the mother,
The mother needs the child."
So be it.

—May Sarton, "The Action of Therapy,"
Selected Poems of May Sarton

This paper argues for a reconciliation of feminist values and psychoanalytic psychotherapy. Toward this goal, it traces an aspect of psychoanalytic technique that stems from the object relations and interpersonal schools, and is also consistent with feminist ideology: the patient's acting unconsciously as therapist or supervisor to the therapist. The underlying constructive aim is examined both developmentally, in the wish to be of use to the mother, and as it occurs in psychotherapy, in the patient's capacity to be of use to the therapist. Within this psychoanalytic perspective, recognition of the therapist's humanness and fallibility acknowledges the patient's reparative powers and active participation in the process of change, this recognition permits a fuller actualization of feminist values in the psychoanalytic relationship.

INTRODUCTION

Until the 1970s, the discourse between psychoanalysis and feminists consisted essentially of irreconcilable debate. Responding to Freud's early views on the development of femininity and female sexuality, many feminists saw psychoanalysis as a theory that justified and perpetuated the subjugation of women (de Beauvoir, 1952; Friedan, 1965; Firestone, 1970; Millett, 1970). With Juliet Mitchell's *Psychoanalysis and Feminism* (1974) and the two separate collections and commentaries on women and analysis edited by Jean Baker Miller (1973) and Jean Strouse (1974; see also Howell, 1981), however, reevaluations and reconsiderations of psychoanalysis took root. Feminists began to approach psychoanalysis as a comprehensive theory raising crucial questions about relations between the sexes, and about the acquisition and meaning of these relations within the individual and within the culture. Freud's theories were recognized as poignantly central to the issues that could ultimately free people to change themselves and their world.

Welcome as this recent confirmation of the productive interface of psychoanalytic theory and feminism may be, there has been little amplification of the implications of this union for the practice of psychoanalytic psychotherapy. Until recently, the evolution of psychoanalytic theory and its relevance to therapeutic practice since Freud's founding contributions have also been neglected in feminist critique. In particular, adherents of the object relations school of psychoanalysis have much to offer to a more comfortable merging of psychoanalytic therapy and feminism.

Like traditional or classical Freudian psychoanalytic theory, object relations theory provides and elaborates a developmental framework for making sense of complex unconscious, intrapsychic conflict. Object relations theorists, however, often deemphasize Freud's instinct theory and highlight instead the significance of the earliest primary relationship for psychological growth. By extension, these theorists espouse the view that psychopathology is not solely intrapsychic, but is both genetically based and presently experienced in the context of interpersonal relationships.[1] For feminists who have struggled to defy Freud's (1925) proclamation of women's natural physical and moral inferiority, and for those feminists who have resisted analysis of that defiance to protect themselves and their ideas in their battle in an unsympathetic social structure, the object relations perspective provides a pathway for retaining the richness of psychoanalysis: if psychological development and pathology rest in part on interpersonal relations, then interpersonal connections to others and connections to society, as well as intrapsychic pathology, are relevant to understanding women.

My argument is that a reconciliation of feminist values and certain aspects of psychoanalytic theory and therapy can contribute significantly to the liberation of both women and men. Toward this goal, I shall focus on how the patient acts unconsciously as therapist or supervisor to the therapist. This aspect of psychoanalytic technique, which stems from the object relations and interpersonal schools of psychoanalysis, is consistent with feminist ideology. As we shall see, from a developmental perspective, the patient's capacity to be of use to the therapist originates in the wish to be of use to the the mother. Within the psychoanalytic perspective, it is recognition of the therapist's humanness and fallibility that acknowledges the patient's own reparative powers and allows the patient's active participation in the process of change. Such a stance provides for a fuller realization of feminist values in the psychoanalytic relationship.

---

[1] Even among those who write and practice within the object relations school, there is considerable ambiguity and diversity concerning the relative roles of intrapsychic and interpersonal components of psychopathology, as well as the relative roles of genetic and environmental determinants of psychopathology. Most simplistically, views range from those of Melanie Klein—whose conceptualization of the active unconscious fantasies and ideas representing inborn instincts that interact with environmental reality is closest to Freud's discussion of instincts—to those of Fairbairn, who posits that instincts are important only insofar as they are relationship-seeking. See Segal (1974) and Fairbairn (1954).

FEMINIST VALUES AND PSYCHOANALYTIC THERAPY

In its striving for political, economic, educational, and interpersonal equality for women and men, the feminist movement upholds, as must any social movement of its scope, a wide variety of personal and collective values. Arguments by separatists—or, conversely, by those who reject all notions of difference between the sexes—have often obscured the complexity of the different strengths and vulnerabilities that women and men face interpersonally and intrapsychically in the developmental process. Nevertheless, feminists, particularly those concerned with psychological development, largely agree that men have constructed most of the predominant psychological theories, which construe women's development as incomplete and devalue women's capacities for interpersonal empathy and relatedness (Gilligan, 1982). In this view, patriarchally based injustices compromise such feminist (and also humanitarian) values as interpersonal honesty, appreciation and trust in empathic understanding, respect for autonomous and independent strength as well as dependent needs, and mutuality in healthy adult interdependence. Not surprisingly, feminist critics have attacked psychoanalytic therapy in both sophisticated and stereotyped ways.

For example, the therapeutic relationship in psychoanalysis or psychoanalytically oriented psychotherapy—in which the therapist can be viewed as healthy, powerful, objective, and omniscient, and the patient as sick, dependent, emotionally confused, and even submissive—has been described as one that re-creates the patriarchal structure of Western culture. Because the psychoanalytic therapy relationship is hierarchical in nature and fosters dependency, it is indicted for creating yet one more demand for women to depend on, and defer to, authority (Foucault, 1965; Chesler, 1971a, 1971b, 1972; Steiner, 1971; Franks, 1979; Rohrbaugh, 1979). Not only do mental health professionals have different definitions of mental health for men and women (Broverman et al., 1970), but traditional therapists have been criticized for working within a relationship that implicitly encourages and perpetuates dependency, passivity, and reliance on dominant authority for help, and thereby violates therapeutic goals of empowering, trusting, and respecting patients. Linking the institutions of psychotherapy and marriage, Chesler contends that both are vehicles of social control and oppression of women, mirroring and supporting a sexist hierarchy in each other (1971a, 1971b, 1972). This position is given added credence by the fact that most psychiatric patients, whether documented by community studies, private doctors' records, first hospital admissions, private or public outpatient psychiatric centers, are women (Gove and Tudor, 1973), while most therapists are men (Chesler, 1971b). This demographic finding highlights, in microcosm, the extent to which educational and professional opportunities have been more available to men than to women in our society, and it sets the stage for potential misuse and misconstrual of the imbalance of power and status between a therapist and a patient seeking help.

It has been suggested that there are incompatible differences in the styles and goals of psychoanalytically oriented therapy and feminist or radical tenets that espouse egalitarian values and the empowerment of women (Steiner, 1971; Rawlings and Carter, 1977; Rohrbaugh, 1979). Since therapist neutrality is interpreted as cutting off the expression of negative feelings, as depriving the patient of feedback and information about the therapy process, and as securing and maintaining the therapist's power, some feminists, according to Rohrbaugh, "insist that traditional psychotherapies always involve a destructive power relationship that keeps women dependent and helpless" (1979, p. 434). Indeed, such criticism has provided the impetus for the development of feminist and radical therapy (Agel, 1971; Kaplan, 1976; Thomas, 1977; Franks, 1979). And it has propelled some to rethink psychoanalytic concepts from a feminist perspective to regain the richness and breadth that the theory offers (Miller, 1973; Mitchell, 1974; Strouse, 1974; Chodorow, 1978; Eichenbaum and Orbach, 1982; Kanefield, 1983).

Although the psychoanalytic therapy relationship can become an arbitrarily or rigidly hierarchical one, many of the feminist critics tend to conceptualize the therapeutic process simplistically and to ignore those central aspects of psychoanalytic theory and technique which can be consistent with feminist aims. Under the guise of egalitarian values, many feminists have confused pathological dependent relationships, fostered by cultural as well as by psychological needs, with healthy dependency that permits satisfying adult mutuality. With the goal of empowering women by trusting the accuracy and truthfulness of what they have to say about themselves, and in an effort to avoid the reductionism of stereotyped conceptualizations, many feminist critics of psychoanalytic therapy have failed to distinguish between conscious and unconscious communication. Such a distinction between manifest and latent content is crucial to the therapeutic task; as will be discussed later, it has implications for all notions of trust, respect, equality, and understanding within the therapeutic relationship. Although some feminists have advocated a supposedly egalitarian and fully reciprocal relationship between therapist and patient, in which all information and feelings are mutually shared (Rawlings and Carter, 1977), this framework seems unrealistic in the light of a patient's request for expert help, and a therapist's capacity to give it. Moreover, one must consider the unconscious implications of this apparent manifest equality.

It is a misinterpretation of the psychoanalytic therapeutic process to construe an imbalance of power or therapist neutrality as necessarily detrimental to the patient. If proper attention is paid to the interpersonal aspects of psychopathology and the actual therapeutic interaction, then, when distortions in perception, conflicts between patient and therapist, or emotional blocks to therapeutic progress arise, the therapist is obligated to consider the ways in which she or he, as well as the patient, may be actively contributing to the situation. In essence, this focus on the interpersonal lays the groundwork for a translation of the feminist goals of respect and empowerment to the level and appreciation of unconscious communication.

Beginning with traces in Freud's writings (1910, 1912a, 1937), and later in formulations by the interpersonal psychiatrists, Sullivan (1970) and Fromm-Reichmann (1950), and most recently and explicitly in the work of Searles (1979), Greenson (1971), and Langs (1976, 1978, 1982a), there has been a growing emphasis on the role of the therapist in reenacting and comprehending the patient's pathology. None of the theorists to be discussed in this paper entirely abandons the central role of intrapsychic processes in psychological development; and while all depart from Freud in their greater emphasis on the interpersonal aspects of psychological development, they vary greatly on this controversial dimension, and so do not represent a single, unified position. Nevertheless, and despite its lack of acceptance by the mainstream of classical psychoanalysis, the view that emotional difficulties are both intrapsychic and interpersonal difficulties is a prominent one today. And this view demands that adequate analysis of a patient's thoughts, feelings, and mental processes take place within an interpersonal relationship open to investigation.

My own position is in agreement with the belief that psychopathology arises in part in early significant relationships and is transferred by the patient and to some extent by the therapist to the psychotherapy context. Somewhat parallel to the controversy surrounding the degree of emphasis on the interpersonal components of psychopathology is the dispute over the meaning and use of countertransference (see Little, 1951; Zetzel, 1956), which, in this paper, is defined as the pathological or inappropriate responses aroused in the therapist. Concomitant with the perspective that stresses the role of interpersonal aspects of pathology is the view that countertransference responses, if unanalyzed by the therapist, can lead to misinterpretation and problems in the therapeutic process, but, if properly analyzed and understood, can be used as a sensitive and powerful therapeutic tool. This conceptualization of therapy as a bipersonal field (Langs, 1976), where both therapist and patient have interacting emotional responsiveness, begins to bridge the gap between a misconstrual of traditional therapy and feminist values. After briefly acknowledging the historical origins of such a perspective, I shall explore the ways in which patients enable therapeutic work to progress and help create a productive therapeutic working alliance by unconsciously acting as therapists or supervisors to their therapists.

TRANSFERENCE, NONTRANSFERENCE, AND COUNTERTRANSFERENCE

In his early papers on technique, Freud (1910) considers the extent to which a therapist can overcome her or his countertransference as key to the management of the patient's analysis. Here, Freud uses "countertransference" to refer to the analyst's problematic unanalyzed and distorted responses to the patient; hence, the need to overcome it. He advocates self-analysis on a continuing and deepening basis while working with patients, even stating that lack of success in self-analysis precludes any successful treatment of patients. In analysis, Freud contends, "we must reckon not only with the structure of the patient's ego but the personal characteristics of the analyst" (1937, p. 265). He thus provides the justification for considering the active and dynamic unconscious of two individuals in the therapy setting. Although he alerts our attention, Freud does not develop this kernel that implicates the importance of this two-person relationship; his theory is primarily an instinct theory and he concentrates on the patient's transference.

With the neo-Freudians, such as Sullivan, Fromm-Reichmann, and Searles in this country, and the object relation theorists, including Fairbairn (1954) and Winnicott (1965) in England (see also Whitaker and Malone, 1953; Alexander, Eisenstein, and Grotjar, 1966), a major shift away from classical Freudian psychoanalysis, toward comprehending psychopathology as both an intrapsychic and interpersonal phenomenon, occurred.[2] Consequently, the patient-therapist relationship has become increasingly acceptable to many psychoanalysts as the new arena for expressing and working through intrapsychic and interpersonal pain. The

---

[2]This theoretical shift marks an important divergence from classical Freudian psychoanalytic practice, with its emphasis on oedipal conflict and triangular relationships, and its focus on neurosis. Many of the ideas of Searles, Fairbairn, and Winnicott arise from work with psychotic, borderline, or narcissistically disturbed patients. These more seriously disturbed individuals were initially considered unsuitable for analysis by Freud because of their potential for severe regression and because of the salience of preoedipal concerns. The acceptance of seriously disturbed patients for analysis, and the consequent emphasis on preoedipal issues of intimacy, dependency, and dyadic relationships in therapy, stems mainly from the work of the British object relation theorists and those in this country (Otto Kernberg, Heinz Hartmann, and Robert Langs, for example) who build on their ideas. For a theoretical and historical discussion of these changes, see Guntrip (1971) and Balint (1968).

process of the patient-therapist interaction, rather than simply the content of patient communications, is magnified in importance; in this way the therapist as well as the patient is exposed and vulnerable to analysis and emotion. Little (1951) describes the exquisite interaction of transference and countertransference in the bipersonal context of therapy:

> . . . transference and countertransference are not only syntheses by the patient and analyst acting separately, but, like the analytic work as a whole, are the result of a joint effort. We often hear of the mirror which the analyst holds up to the patient, but the patient holds one up to the analyst too, and there is a whole series of reflections in each, repetitive in kind, and subject to continual modification. The mirror in each case should become progressively clearer as the analysis goes on, for the patient and analyst respond to each other in a reverberative kind of way, and increasing clearness in one mirror will bring the need for a corresponding clearing in the other [p. 37].

The notion of the analyst as participant-observer (Sullivan, 1970), contributing actively to the relationship with the patient, not only mandates that the analyst's countertransference experiences be understood and dealt with as they interfere with the therapy, but that they be "a helpful instrument in understanding otherwise hidden implications in a patient's communications" (Fromm-Reichmann, 1950, p. 6).

Feminist criticism has considered the centrality of the relationship in therapy as potentially abusive, particularly when attention to the relationship has focused entirely on the transference or the patient's distortion of the therapy. The fantasies and patterns of relating that have proved troublesome to a patient become accessible to the therapist's scrutiny as they are re-created in the transference distortions, and so analysis of the pathological transference is clearly at the crux of helping people within any psychoanalytic perspective. However, the sole concentration on genetic interpretations arising from the distorted transference component of the patient-therapist relationship, which dominates much of classical psychoanalysis, is problematic.

Indeed, numerous analysts address the salience of the real, nontransference dimensions of the psychoanalytic situation. Fairbairn (1958), who teaches that instincts are crucial only insofar as they are relationship-seeking, stresses that the real relationship that unfolds between therapist and patient constitutes a major factor in the healing process. Just as it is the total primary relationship between a child and parent that forms a child's developing personality, he writes, it is the total relationship with the analyst, and not simply the transference distortions, that permits significant personality change in the patient.

It is the therapist's responsibility to interpret appropriate, healthy nontransference perceptions and reactions which might otherwise be attributed to the pathological transference. Greenson writes that "to facilitate the full flowering and ultimate resolution of the patient's transference reactions, it is essential in all cases to recognize, acknowledge, clarify, differentiate, and even nurture the nontransference or relatively 'transference-free' reaction between patient and therapist" (1969, p. 361; see also 1965). He considers that it is the appropriate, nondistorted elements of the patient's perceptions of the therapist that permit the development of a solid working alliance, without which interpretation and resolution of the patient's pathology would be impossible. All relations with others, including the therapist, are mixtures between what is real and what is fantasy, what is appropriate and what is distorted, what is correct perception and what is inappropriate, what is nontransference and what is transference (Little, 1951; Greenson, 1965, 1969, 1971; Langs, 1976, 1978). Only when the therapist is capable of making these distinctions nondefensively can the patient begin to take in, or introject, those healthy aspects of the therapist that facilitate effective functioning.

Neglect of the real relationship in therapy, Greenson (1971) explains, is not only defensive, but also destructive to the patient because it jeopardizes adequate analysis of the pathological transference. Clearly, there are analysts and therapists who do not agree with Greenson, and others who have erred in this way. Nevertheless, the argument here is that denial of nontransference or countertransference is, in practice, tantamount to impairing a patient's reality testing, undermining her or his self-esteem, and possibly leaving the patient with a sense of craziness, instead of perceptiveness. Such ignorance on the part of the therapist has been called "anti-analytic procedure" by Greenson (1969, p. 366) and referred to as "misalliances" and "bastions" by Langs (1975b, 1976). What is involved is an interactional avoidance of material by both therapist and patient; more specifically, the focus may be on listening to manifest content, rather than decoding the latent, unconscious material that is communicated in symbolic, metaphorical, or derivative form.

Discussion of the nontransference and countertransference dimensions of the therapeutic interaction is relevant to an integration of feminist values and psychoanalytic therapy as it represents a specific translation of the essence of some of the broader feminist criticisms of psychoanalytic technique. Appropriate and helpful utilization of these aspects of the therapeutic relationship often depends on the therapist's apparent neutrality, since this neutrality makes it most possible for the therapist to skillfully separate the patient's pathological fantasies from her or his healthy perceptions, and to separate the therapist's own feelings and conflicts from those of the patient. The therapist's apparent neutrality, however, is often consciously experienced by the patient as a powerful and authoritarian withholding by the therapist. This is particularly the case for individuals whose experience has taught them to expect or fear such imbalances of power within relationships. For this reason, many feminists, who maintain a belief in the potential of women to know what is best for themselves, have criticized this therapeutic approach as one that forces a patient to submit detrimentally to the therapist's situationally defined power. This is a misconception, however, resting on a failure to distinguish conscious and superficial self-knowledge from the patient's more richly illuminating, personally idiosyncratic, and truth-revealing, unconscious encoded perceptions and communications (Langs, 1979, 1982a, 1982b). True respect for the patient requires appreciation of the depth of the patient's capacity to understand and communicate unconsciously.

As Langs (1976, 1978, 1982a) persuasively articulates, the patient's integrity and wisdom can be respected and worked with in psychoanalytic therapy. Langs encourages appreciation and use of the patient's unconscious sensitivity, creativity, and perceptiveness. He writes of his intention "to allow the patient . . . to teach us some of the fundamental techniques related . . . to the development of the therapeutic relationship and the bipersonal field in which it takes place" (1976, p. 15; see also DeRacker, 1961). In an atmosphere where the patient is permitted to say whatever comes to mind, where the sessions are allowed to unfold accordingly, and where the therapist maintains the framework of the therapy and patiently provides a safe holding environment for the patient's feelings, the therapist must have the well-placed faith that the patient will unconsciously know what is best.

THE PATIENT'S CURATIVE CAPACITIES

With extraordinarily rich communications, patients reveal that they want their deepest feelings understood. The therapist, if listening properly, will hear not only material to compose an interpretation, but also an indication when there is deviation from this goal (Langs, 1978). Winnicott writes, "The principle is that it is the patient and only the patient who has the answers" (1969, p. 87). Through trust and respect, the therapist appreciates the patient's ability to aid in the healing process, and the patient's health-seeking strengths lead her or him to unconsciously act as therapist or supervisor to the therapist. Therapists who recognize this unconscious relational quality demonstrate an aspect of psychoanalytic therapy consistent with feminist ideology: the patient's reparative capacity and active participation in the process of change are acknowledged; patients are empowered, arbitrary authority reduced, and mutuality enhanced.

Freud, despite the paucity of his writings on psychoanalytic technique and his inability to explicate all of his insights, planted the seed of virtually every issue that arises in psychoanalysis today. He warned against the therapist's self-disclosures, claiming:

> this technique makes him less able than ever to overcome the deeper resistances, and in the more severe cases it invariably fails on account of the insatiability it arouses in the patient, who then tries to reverse the situation, finding the analysis of the physician more interesting than his own [1912b, p. 124].

Embedded in Freud's words is a reference to the possible curative motives of the patient—a potential too often neglected in the medical model of healthy doctor and sick patient. Freud leaves a fuller exposition of the patient's capacity to give to the therapist for others to explore. This is unfortunate because omission of this potential role inversion has contributed to the disempowerment of patients in psychotherapy and to misconceptions of the therapeutic process. The underlying constructive intention, the developmental wish to help the mother, proceeds in psychotherapy as the patient's ability to be of use to the therapist. Acknowledgment of the patient's unconscious curative capacity, as well as the therapist's humanness and fallibility, endorses a realization of feminist values of mutuality and respect within the psychoanalytic therapy relationship.

Fairbairn (1940, 1941) argues that the most profound knowledge an individual must acquire is that she or he has the capacity to receive love without being annihilated and the ability to give love without destroying the recipient. The second of these capacities is most relevant to this discussion. To feel that one's love is not accepted by the parent is to learn that one lacks what is good to give (M. Klein, 1937; Fairbairn, 1941; Searles, 1975). Akin to this sense is the feeling that one's love is bad and destructive—a predicament so terrible that it threatens the child's ability to love at all. In an effort to protect the caretaker on whom they are dependent, children sometimes withdraw from object relating, and consequently do not get what they need. Without the ability to give, a person is incapable of genuinely receiving (Winnicott, 1954–1955, 1963).

According to Winnicott, in relating to the mother in the feeding process, the infant is aware of depleting her at the breast, of emptying her through greed, of creating a hole in the mother. Perception of this destructiveness gives rise to a personal sense of guilt, alleviated only when the child believes that she or he can fill in the hole that has been created. Development of this optimism requires that the mother recognize her child's capacity for concern, the potency of the love that she is given, and be able to accept it. For the child to make reparation for this "depletion," an adult must be present to receive and accept the infant's love. The baby's anxiety—called depressive anxiety by Melanie Klein (1935a, 1935b), Winnicott (1954), and others (Segal, 1974)—is a reaction to consuming and losing the mother, and it is tolerated and modified only by the confidence that the child can meaningfully contribute to the mother. It is this developmental achievement that subsequently permits a more liberated risk-taking in the expression of instincts, and thereby fosters growth and maturity.

Just as it is imperative that someone external to the self accept one's love in ordinary growth, so it is in the evolving therapeutic relationship (Winnicott, 1954–1955, 1963). Therapists must see in their patients, and patients must see in themselves, the patient's immense capacity for compassion and helpfulness. This is crucial to the patient's sense of usefulness as a human being. Many patients come to therapy with the devastating sense of having failed as people because their parents did not permit them to make constructive contributions. This sense of uselessness, of impotence and disapproval, can only be supplanted if the pain of being unable to give to all-knowing and seemingly needless parents is not re-created in the therapy (Singer, 1971; Searles, 1975).

In the spirit of these aims, Singer (1971) discusses his willingness to let his patients aid him in a way that he claims does not interfere with the therapeutic unfolding of their relationship, but brings the patient's strengths to the immediacy and intimacy of the therapy. However, Singer errs significantly in his efforts because he responds only to the direct and overt helpfulness he hears in his patients' communications. Singer believes he is allowing his patients to feel genuinely useful to him when he tells them of his wife's serious illness that has kept him from his work and accepts their consolation, advice, and even reassurance. Because his illustrations pertain only to his patients' conscious attempts at soothing and healing, he simplifies and misconstrues the depth of the patients' unconscious constructive attempts that are under consideration here.

For example, Singer writes of one patient's immediate and manifestly helpful response to his self-revelation. "She eagerly informed me about the outstanding authorities on my wife's illness and intimated that she might be able to get us an entree to one of them, a man indeed quite prominent but, since he was semi-retired, difficult to reach. At the same time she insisted with great self-confidence that my wife was going to be 'all right,' that she knew this as a fact" (1971, p. 59). Even this very brief glimpse of the therapeutic interaction reveals clues to the latent meaning of such overt helpfulness and the likelihood of an unconscious collusion between therapist and patient (Langs, 1982a). In the context of a reunion after her therapist's hitherto unexplained absence, it is probable that the patient entered the session with conscious and unconscious fantasies, feelings, and perceptions triggered by this disruption. Evidently, Singer did not give his patients the opportunity to expose their own responses to the situation before launching into his own agenda. In effect (and he raises and dismisses similar concerns himself), by sharing his own material initially, and by responding to the patient's conscious reactions graciously, but without interpretation of their more disguised meanings, Singer creates an atmosphere that is probably only superficially therapeutic. Singer either cuts off or does not listen to the more idiosyncratic and dynamically meaningful responses from his patients, perhaps protecting himself from their rageful or hostile feelings of abandonment, betrayal, or helplessness at a time when he too may have felt the need to ward off his own painfully similar feelings.

Although Singer does not offer enough specific clinical material to make elaborate speculations, it is possible that embedded in the patient's reference to the difficult-to-reach, half-retired expert, is an accurate perception of Singer himself, at least in part unavailable to attend to his patient. Her insistence that Singer's wife will be all right may reflect a desperate mobilization of her own resources when she can no longer trust her therapist's caretaking, as well as a possibly overdetermined,[3] but currently appropriate wish to have her therapist's caretaking role reinstated. The overtly helpful, but actually rather unrealistic and platitudinous types of response Singer has evoked from his patients, in all likelihood demonstrate their efforts to collude with him in creating a barrier to the more disturbing impressions of what has occurred.

That children must become convinced of their capacity to give to others is implicit in Winnicott's notion of the mirroring role of the mother in child development (1967). Before distinguishing between the self and the mother, and imperative to the process of this separation, infants need to experience a sense of omnipotence, a belief that the mother is subjectively created by the self. The idea of mirroring metaphorically captures the process by which infants look at the mother's face and see themselves, thus establishing the experience of getting back what one gives. The process of looking, being seen, and being assured of one's own existence depends, in normal development, on the presence of a parent who is willing to allow her or himself to be taken as an image of the baby. In therapy, this process rests on the analyst's willingness to do the same—by providing a secure framework in which the therapist can receive and contain all the material that the patient communicates, by listening to the

---

[3]Overdetermined, possibly, because of her propensity toward "longing for magical gratification of dependent needs for nurturance" [p. 59], which Singer describes.

patient's unconscious and encoded messages, and by conveying her or his understanding with sensitivity and timely interpretations that are linked dynamically to the therapeutic relationship.

Searles suggests that all individuals have psychotherapeutic strivings and that any thwarting of one's capacity to love the other, to help the other to fulfill her or his psychological and human potential, hinders one's own healthy development. He writes that it is:

> ... not merely that the patient wants to give therapy to, as well as receive therapy from his doctor. ... I am hypothesizing that the patient is ill because, and to the degree that, his own psychotherapeutic strivings have been subjected to such vicissitudes that they have been rendered inordinately intense, frustrated of fulfillment or even acknowledgment, admixed therefore with unduly intense components of hate, envy, and competitiveness; and subjected, therefore, to repression. In transference terms, the patient's illness expresses his unconscious attempt to cure the doctor [1975, p. 95].

Intrinsic to this notion is a powerful self-curative effort. In the infant, this striving serves to create a mother who is integrated, competent, and mature enough to properly parent; who can provide, in Winnicott's (1954, 1960) terms, good-enough mothering and a holding environment. In the patient, this endeavor assures that one will have a therapist who can contain anxiety, hold one's loving and destructive feelings, and hence firmly maintain the therapeutic framework in a way that allows the therapist to aid the patient properly.

The need to make one's parent good enough is so pervasive that, as Searles tells us, a person will postpone "individuation, in the service of functioning symbiotically as therapist to one or another of his family members, or to all collectively in a family symbiosis" (1975, p.98). This aspect of parent-child relationships, referred to as "parentification" (Boszormenyi-Nagy and Spark, 1973), is adaptive when it permits the child appropriately to learn about responsibility and helpfulness, and simultaneously relieves the parent of some burdens (Karpel, 1976). This relational reversal disrupts, rather than contributes to, healthy development when parents are incapable of responsible parenting, thus rendering fruitless the child's attempt to contribute effectively to the family. In such situations, the child's loyalty and concern for the parent's psychological stability intensify the child's sense of guilt for insufficiently parenting the parent and augment the motivation to continue to make restitutive gestures.

Although there is ordinarily a conflict between the desire to be mature and fulfill one's individuality and the wish to remain in infantile symbiosis with the mother, this bind takes on pathological qualities when the parentified child, in expressing her or his deep love and loyalty to the mother, sacrifices individual maturity to aid the mother's functioning (Searles, 1973). It is the child's compulsion to create a healthy mother, as well as the felt duty to be helpful to her, that fuels this regressive process. Distressingly, an impairing cycle is subsequently produced: the mother rejects the child's reparative contributions, thereby failing to become a good-enough mother and rendering the child helpless to express her or his capacity for concern.

The most debilitating guilt a person may have to endure stems from this earlier inability to complement the fragmented mother's ego, to be effective in efforts to enhance the mother's maturity. Powerless to provide her- or himself with a proper and whole model for positive identification, the child ultimately sacrifices her or his own individuality to repair this perpetual state. This sacrifice of independence, says Searles, accounts for the most severe regression seen in schizophrenia; it reveals not simply a means to cope with an outer reality that may be unbearable, but involves the actual psychological introjection of the unhealthy parts of the mother in order to heal her. Unconsciously, then, the child introjects "those most deeply ill components of mother and subsequent mother-transference figures—by taking those components into himself and trying thus to free her (and her successors) from the burden of them" (1973, p. 178).

Similarly, the patient strives to create "a constructive model for identification" in the therapist to allow the therapist to function and to facilitate the patient's own further maturation. With sensitivity and comprehension, Searles further elaborates on the importance of empowering patients by recognizing their human psychotherapeutic strivings. He stresses that therapists must implicitly accept the reciprocal symbiotic dependency, crucial to healthy adult relatedness, that unfolds between therapist and patient as it existed between mother and infant. "An understanding of the nature of the therapeutic symbiosis requires that one grasp something of the extent to which the patient is himself devoted to functioning as a therapist to his officially designated analyst" (1973, p. 174). Translated into technique, such an implicit acceptance of the reciprocal dependency within the therapeutic relationship requires that the therapist be capable of distinguishing transference distortions from accurate nontransference perceptions, silently benefit from the patient's unconscious communications about the therapist's inappropriate contributions to the therapeutic relationship, and thus provide a safe holding environment in which the patient can reveal her or his deepest self. Implicit acknowledgment that the patient can behave therapeutically on behalf of the therapist is a value indispensable to a successful therapy, and crucial in promoting mutuality within the psychoanalytic mode.

Clinical Illustration

The case of M. illustrates the complexity of such thematic curative efforts. A 33-year-old woman, M. had a long history of depression and anxiety. She had previously been in therapy for seven years, and she entered this therapy because her current anxiety was so debilitating that it precipitated her withdrawal from professional school. Unclear about career or educational goals, M. remained closely tied to her parents, virtually unable to decide anything for herself without first considering her parents' reactions, even though she recognized the disparity between their values and ideas and her own. Her fear of taking chances, of broadening the rigid roles her parents had defined, left her anxious and often stagnant in relationships.

The conscious and unconscious levels to M.'s wishes to be helpful wove a continuous thread in her therapy. M. linked her pervasive self-doubts to her "sense that I can't take care of them [her parents], can't make their lives happier by doing things in my own life." She called herself "invisible," forever trying to share her helpful, constructive feelings with her mother and inevitably being thwarted in her efforts. "She physically pushed me away as if I was no use to her. I felt I had some capacity to console her, even if I was only a child."

Within the relatively safe therapeutic environment, where M. was permitted to say whatever came to her mind, and the therapist provided a reliable, consistent, and secure hold, M. began to experience herself in new ways. Triggered by incidents within the therapeutic relationship, M.'s fears that her caring feelings would be destructive, intrusive, and burdensome came to the fore and were explored. Through interpretations of M.'s varied communications that her strong feelings for the therapist would be unacceptable, M. implicitly learned that her feelings were not cut off, not rejected, and not intrusive. The therapist's capacity to allow herself to be deeply aided and loved by the patient led to M.'s conscious and unconscious satisfaction that her loving, reparative feelings and gestures could be received by another adult; her autonomy was enhanced.

Ten months into the therapy, and with neither conscious nor unconscious indications that were discerned by the therapist prior to her announcement, M. decided to discontinue therapy. To her therapist, M.'s termination initially seemed an abrupt, premature flight from her deepening dependency. In their last session the therapist, making use of M.'s references to her previous therapist and to her mother, interpreted M.'s fear that she, the therapist, would be like M.'s mother and previous therapist—unable to let M. go even when she was ready, making it necessary for M. to escape. Although this was largely an accurate view of what had occurred, the therapist, through self-analysis and supervision, later became aware of the components of M.'s fear that were reality-based. The therapist realized the extent to which she had perceived M. as an indispensable teacher and had unconsciously burdened M. with her own wishes and expectations that M. continue therapy. She recognized the degree to which her own countertransference issues around attachment and separation led to her unconscious view of M. as an extension of herself and made it difficult for her to keep from joining M. in a pathological fusion.

M. had been reluctant to loosen her tie to her mother: she was afraid of betraying her, of depriving her of her primary and most meaningful role of mothering, and even associated her autonomous strivings with destroying her mother. Much as she was aware that her mother relied on her to be a mother, M. perceived that she had become important to her therapist. Ironically, it was M.'s ability to leave her therapist—this time, not needing to sacrifice her autonomy to make her therapist/mother a better caretaker, and without unrealistic fears of emptying her—that demonstrated M.'s growth within the therapy.

Distortion vs. Healing

The therapist's genuine acceptance of the patient's reparative feelings, as they are expressed in encoded communications, is complicated not just by the therapist's capacity to recognize her or his own deep and healthy dependence on the patient, but also because many patients, especially the more seriously disturbed ones of whom Searles and the object relation theorists write, have sacrificed their independence in the service of their parents' needs and enter therapy with the expectation that the therapist will demand the same of them. Although the focus in this paper has been to demonstrate how the therapist must not repeat the parental pattern that defeated the patient's autonomous growth either by denying or taking advantage of her or his need for the patient, or by denying the patient's unconscious curative efforts, it is important not to overlook the patient's pathological contributions to this process in the therapy. Many of these patients on a conscious level, but more important, unconsciously, find it painfully difficult to trust that the therapist tries to listen to them and understand. Regardless of the therapist's caring and skill, they may either experience intense mistrust of the therapist or undermine and deny the therapist's understanding. Only when the therapist has been diligent in distinguishing accurate perceptions from transference distortions, can she or he adequately interpret the distorted component of such unconsciously communicated distrust.

Extending the healthy aspects of the patient's caretaking even further, Langs (1976) asserts that because patients want to be healthy, they will cure the therapist if the therapist's pathology impedes the way for the therapist to do the curing. By the unconscious interactional mechanism of introjective identification, patients take into themselves the therapist's illness and venture to cure the therapist "so that a healthier analyst can eventually be born out of the patient" (Searles, 1975, p. 127; see also Whitaker and Malone, 1953). Concurrently, in order to be therapeutically beneficial to the therapist, and to themselves, patients will project those aspects of themselves that are relatively strong onto the therapist.

THE THERAPIST'S HUMANNESS AND FALLIBILITY

In addition to appreciating the reality components of the therapeutic relationship and the richly curative elements of the patient's unconscious curative efforts on behalf of the therapist, a fuller consideration of the therapist's responsibilities is crucial to a blending of feminist values and psychoanalytic therapy. Langs, building on the theorists cited thus far, most nearly approximates Freud's original statement by his persistent focus on the therapist's role in the process. While he attends to the hopefulness and optimism buried in the patient's therapeutic strivings, he directs his concentration to the negative aspects of the therapy that dictate a temporary role reversal of patient and therapist. With technical sophistication, Langs enlarges the notion of the patient's healing capacities to encompass the patient's supervisory attempts to alert therapists to their unconsciously hurtful and seductive comments and to their therapeutic frame violations. Because he constructs an elaborate listening and validating process for hearing the patient's accurate perceptions of the therapist and censures much of the analytic work done today as undynamic and potentially destructive, he raises important questions about the helpfulness of therapy. Langs empowers the patient by respecting an unconscious curative helpfulness, by appreciating the patient's autonomous resources, and by acknowledging the mutuality inherent in the therapeutic relationship; in this way, he contributes significantly to the implementation of a feminist psychoanalytic therapy.

While a therapist's humanness allows her or him to be helpful to a patient, it also makes fallibility inevitable. Langs (1975a) credits patients with remarkable unconscious sensitivity in detecting and reacting significantly to the therapist's errors in conceptualization, understanding, technique, or personal countertransference problems. Similarly, Little writes, "a patient may quite well become aware of real feelings in his analyst even before the analyst himself is fully aware of them" (1951, p. 39). It is the therapist's task to bring these feelings into consciousness, despite their being "the very thing to which he has himself the greatest resistance. Analysts often behave unconsciously exactly like the parents who put up a smoke-screen, and tantalize their children, tempting them to see the very things they forbid them seeing" (p. 38).

Although a patient is unlikely to consciously express awareness of the therapist's errors, the associations that follow an error may contain, in disguised form, reference to it in themes of insensitivity, ineptness, unhelpfulness, or blindness in other people. Admittedly, these themes do not always refer to the therapist's errors since distortions of and angry attacks on the therapist are also likely to be transference-related and demand interpretation as such. When such communications do pertain to the therapist's errors, they indicate not only a personal and idiosyncratic response to the therapist's failure to understand, but also contain the optimistic effort to bring the error to the therapist's attention so that the therapeutic task may ensue. Patients' responses to such situations, often key to the central dynamics in their particular conflicts, may range from appropriate rage to the more common self-accusatory comments when they are unconsciously furious with their therapists. Such self-deprecation may reflect not only the therapist's inappropriate management of the therapy, but the patient's introjection of those destructive aspects of the therapist, which the patient attempts to work over in order to cure the therapist. It is crucial not to underestimate the intrapsychic disruptions that patients can experience in the face of perceived misinterpretations or technical mismanagement by the therapist. Such temporary misalliances can usually be rectified by either silent recognition and correction of an error when candid acknowledgment of it might be unconsciously experienced as a burdensome therapist confession (Langs, 1975b), or by frank acknowledgment of the therapist's error, along with analysis of the patient's reaction to it, in order to clarify the distinction between transference and nontransference components of the relationship (Greenson, 1971). In addition, this will convey an appreciation of the patient's healthy and correct perceptions, allow the patient to contribute meaningfully to advancing the therapist's work, and promote growth and trust in the therapist.

CONCLUSION

This paper has presented a theoretical and technical examination of the patient's curative capacities with the goal of reconciling feminist values and psychoanalytic therapy. Because of the inherent hierarchical nature of psychoanalytic therapy, many feminists have criticized a traditional therapeutic relationship and sought alternatives to it. It is hoped that this discussion of how it is possible to respect and trust patients for their conscious and unconscious sensitivity and caring has contributed to a fairer conceptualization of psychoanalytic psychotherapy. Recognition of the therapist's humanness, fallibility, and unconscious conflict, as well as the patient's perceptions of countertransference in the therapist and the patient's subsequent restitutive attempts, contributes to a more liberating clarification of analytic practice. An appreciation of how communications reflect the interactive nature of the therapeutic relationship, and of the healthy mutual dependency and reciprocity intrinsically possible in that relationship, advances the responsible exploration of the subtleties and complexities of human feelings and of people in relationships.

REFERENCES

Agel, J. (1971). *The Radical Therapist.* New York: Ballantine Books.
Alexander, F., Eisenstein, S., & Grotjar, M., eds. (1966). *Psychoanalytic Pioneers.* New York: Basic Books.
Balint, M. (1968). *The Basic Fault.* New York: Brunner/Mazel, 1979.
Beauvoir, S. de (1952). *The Second Sex.* New York: Knopf.
Boszormenyi-Nagy, I., & Spark, G. (1973). *Invisible Loyalties.* New York: Harper & Row.
Broverman, I. K., Broverman, D. M., Clarkson, F. E., Rosenkrantz, P. S., & Vogel, S. R. (1970). Sex role stereotypes and clinical judgments of mental health. *J. Consult. Clin. Psychol.* 34(1):1–7.
Chesler, P. (1971a). Marriage and psychotherapy. In *The Radical Therapist,* ed. J. Agel. New York: Ballantine Books.
────── (1971b). Patient and patriarch: Women in the psychotherapeutic relationship. In *Woman in Sexist Society,* ed. V. Gornick & B. K. Moran. New York: Basic Books.
────── (1972). *Women and Madness.* New York: Avon Books.
Chodorow, N. (1978). *The Reproduction of Mothering.* Berkeley: Univ. California Press.
DeRacker, C. T. (1961). On the formulation of the interpretation. *Int. J. Psychoanal.* 42:49–54.
Eichenbaum, L., & Orbach, S. (1982). *Outside In . . . Inside Out.* London: Penguin Books.
Fairbairn, W. R. D. (1940). Schizoid factors in the personality. In *An Object-Relations Theory of Personality.* New York: Basic Books, 1954.
────── (1941). A revised psychopathology of the psychoses and psychoneuroses. In *An Object-Relations Theory of Personality.* New York: Basic Books, 1954.
────── (1944). Endopsychic structure considered in terms of object relations. In *An Object-Relations Theory of Personality.* New York: Basic Books, 1954.
────── (1954). *An Object-Relations Theory of Personality.* New York: Basic Books.
────── (1958). On the nature and aims of psycho-analytical treatment. *Int. J. Psychoanal.* 39:374–385.
Firestone, S. (1970). *The Dialectic of Sex.* New York: Bantam Books.
Foucault, M. (1965). *Madness and Civilization.* New York: Pantheon.
Franks, V. (1979). Gender and psychotherapy. In *Gender and Disordered Behavior,* ed. E. Gomberg & V. Franks. New York: Brunner/Mazel.
Freud, S. (1910). Future prospects of psychoanalytic therapy. In *Therapy and Technique.* New York: Collier Books, 1963.
────── (1912a). The dynamics of the transference. In *Therapy and Technique.* New York: Collier Books, 1963.

────── (1912b). Recommendations for physicians on the psychoanalytic method of treatment. In *Therapy and Technique.* New York: Collier Books, 1963.
────── (1925). Some psychical consequences of the anatomical distinctions between the sexes. In *Women and Analysis,* ed. J. Strouse. New York: Grossman, 1974.
────── (1937). Analysis terminable and interminable. In *Therapy and Technique.* New York: Collier Books, 1963.
Friedan, B. (1965). *The Feminine Mystique.* New York: Penguin Books.
Fromm-Reichmann, F. (1950). *Principles of Intensive Psychotherapy.* Chicago: Univ. Chicago Press.
Gilligan, C. (1982). *In a Different Voice.* Cambridge, Mass.: Harvard Univ. Press.
Gove, W. R. & Tudor, J. F. (1973). Adult sex roles and mental illness. *Amer. J. Sociol.* 78:812–832.
Greenson, R. R. (1965). The working alliance and the transference neurosis. *Psychoanal. Q.* 34:155–181.
────── (1969). The nontransference relationship in the psychoanalytic situation. In *Explorations in Psychoanalysis.* New York: Int. Univ. Press, 1978.
────── (1971). The real relationship between the patient and the psychoanalyst. In *The Unconscious Today,* ed. M. Kanzer. New York: Int. Univ. Press.
Guntrip, H. (1971). *Psychoanalytic Theory, Therapy, and the Self.* New York: Basic Books.
Howell, E. (1981). Women from Freud to the present. In *Women and Mental Health,* ed. E. Howell & M. Bayes. New York: Basic Books.
Kanefield, L. (1983). Women's conflicts about achievement: Reconsiderations of female masochism and penis envy. (Unpublished manuscript, Univ. Massachusetts at Amherst.)
Kaplan, A. (1976). Androgyny as a model of mental health for women: From theory to therapy. In *Beyond Sex Role Stereotypes: Readings Toward a Psychology of Androgyny,* ed. A. Kaplan & J. Bean. Boston: Little, Brown.
Karpel, M. (1976). Intrapsychic and interpersonal processes in the parentification of children. (Ph.D. dissertation, Univ. Massachusetts.)
Klein, M. (1935a). A contribution to the genesis of manic-depressive states. In *Love, Guilt, and Reparation and Other Works.* New York: Delta Books, 1975.
────── (1935b). Mourning and its relation to manic-depressive states. In *Love, Guilt, and Reparation and Other Works.* New York: Delta Books, 1975.
────── (1937). Love, guilt and reparation. In *Love, Guilt and Reparation and Other Works.* New York: Delta Books, 1975.
Langs, R. (1973). *The Technique of Psychoanalytic Psychotherapy.* New York: Aronson.
────── (1975a). The patient's unconscious perception of the therapist's errors. In *Tactics and Techniques in Psychoanalytic Therapy,* Vol. II, ed. P. L. Giovacchini. New York: Aronson.
────── (1975b). Therapeutic misalliances. *Int. J. Psychoanal. Psychother.* 4: 77–105.
────── (1976). *The Bipersonal Field.* New York: Aronson.
────── (1978). *The Listening Process.* New York: Aronson.
────── (1979). *The Supervisory Experience.* New York: Aronson.
────── (1982a). *The Psychotherapeutic Conspiracy.* New York: Aronson.
────── (1982b). *Psychotherapy: A Basic Text.* New York: Aronson.
Little M. (1951). Countertransference and the patient's response to it. *Int. J. Psychoanal.* 32: 32–40.
Miller, J. B. (1973). *Psychoanalysis and Women.* New York: Penguin Books.
Millett, K. (1970). *Sexual Politics.* Garden City, N.Y.: Doubleday.
Mitchell, J. (1974). *Psychoanalysis and Feminism.* New York: Vintage Books.
Rawlings, E. D., & Carter, D. K., eds. (1977). *Psychotherapy for Women.* Springfield, Ill.: Thomas.
Rohrbaugh, J. B. (1979). *Women: Psychology's Puzzle.* New York: Basic Books.

Searles, H. (1973). Concerning therapeutic symbiosis: The patient as symbiotic therapist, the phase of ambivalent symbiosis, and the role of jealousy in the fragmented ego. In *Countertransference and Related Subjects*. New York: Int. Univ. Press, 1979.

―――― (1975). The patient as therapist to his analyst. In *Tactics and Techniques in Psychoanalytic Therapy*, Vol. II, ed. P. L. Giovacchini. New York: Aronson.

―――― (1979). *Countertransference and Related Subjects*. New York: Int. Univ. Press.

Segal, H. (1974). *Introduction to the Work of Melanie Klein*. New York: Basic Books.

Singer, R. (1971). The patient aids the analyst: Some clinical and theoretical observations. In *In the Name of Life—Essays in Honor of Erich Fromm*, ed. B. Landis & E. Tauber. New York: Holt, Rinehart, & Winston.

Steiner, C. (1971). Radical psychiatry: Principles in radical therapy. In *The Radical Therapist*, ed. J. Agel. New York: Ballantine Books.

Strouse, J., ed. (1974). *Women and Analysis*. New York: Grossman.

Sullivan, H. S. (1970). *The Psychiatric Interview*. New York: Norton.

Thomas, S. A. (1977). Theory and practice in feminist therapy. *Soc. Work*, Nov.:447–454.

Whitaker, C. A. & Malone, R. P. (1953). *The Roots of Psychotherapy*. New York: Blakiston.

Winnicott, D. W. (1954). Metaphysical and clinical aspects of regression within the psychoanalytic set-up. In *Collected Papers: Through Pediatrics to Psychoanalysis*. New York: Basic Books, 1958.

―――― (1954–1955). The depressive position in normal emotional development. In *Collected Papers: Through Pediatrics to Psychoanalysis*. New York: Basic Books, 1958.

―――― (1960). The theory of the parent-infant relationship. In *The Maturational Processes and the Facilitating Environment*. New York: Int. Univ. Press, 1965.

―――― (1963). The development of the capacity for concern. In *The Maturational Processes and the Facilitating Environment*. New York: Int. Univ. Press, 1965.

―――― (1965). *The Maturational Processes and the Facilitating Environment*. New York: Int. Univ. Press.

―――― (1967). Mirror-role of the mother and family in child development. In *Playing and Reality*. New York: Basic Books, 1971.

―――― (1969). The use of an object and relating through identification. In *Playing and Reality*. New York: Basic Books, 1971.

Zetzel, E. R. (1956). Current concepts of transference. *Int. J. Psychoanal.* 35:369–376.

2/
Discussion:
Psychotherapy: Egalitarian Values and Transference
Malkah T. Notman, M.D.

In praising Linda Kanefield's attempt to reconcile feminist values and psychoanalysis, this paper points to several issues that need further elaboration. One concern is that a particular set of values, however laudable, may itself acquire an authoritarian twist when presented as *the* goal. In this regard it is important to distinguish between healthy and pathological dependency. Another difficulty arises in relation to the concept of the patient's efforts to "cure" the therapist as a way to preserve egalitarian values. An emphasis on the interactive nature of therapy, it is argued, has more to do with attention to the real and transference relationships, communication, and mutual respect.

Linda Kanefield's paper has an ambitious and important goal: to reconcile feminist values and psychoanalysis. After presenting a thoughtful summary of feminist positions and some aspects of psychoanalytic technique, she introduces object relations and interpersonal formulations about psychopathology, Langs's view of psychotherapy as a bipersonal field, and Fairbairn's, Winnicott's, and others' ideas about the importance to the child of having a mother able to receive the child's love, which is offered as a compensation for depleting and consuming the mother. Kanefield's central argument extends this formulation to emphasize the patient's acting unconsciously as a "therapist or supervisor to the therapist" and thus becoming an active participant in the process of change. According to the concept of therapy as a "bipersonal field," the therapeutic process is conceived as an interactional network in which everything happens as a product of input from both the patient and the therapist. The terms "psychoanalysis" and "psychotherapy" are used interchangeably here—attention to the patient's own recuperative powers and his or her active participation in the process of change is the major focus.

Because the patient in this approach is an active participant, a basis is established for viewing psychoanalysis and psychoanalytic psychotherapy as being founded on a mutual rather than an unequal relationship between patient and therapist. In this way equality, mutuality, and activity are thought to be restored to the woman patient, who has been conventionally stereotyped as passive rather than active, creative, sensitive, and "knowing what is good for herself." The therapists' neutrality, perceived by some feminists as a manifestation of an imbalance of power, is here acknowledged as a potentially useful tool for understanding distortions.

This is a highly abbreviated summary of the many interesting ideas that Kanefield develops in addressing the aspects of the psychoanalytic process important for a fuller understanding of both feminist values and psychotherapy. The background issues are presented in a clear and enlightening way. It is in the application of and conclusions stemming from a consideration of these polarities that some discontinuities emerge. One has at times the sense of a Procrustean attempt to intergrate two sets of concerns and emerge with a theory that will fit a particular value.

Kanefield draws some important distinctions, which have often been overlooked by feminist critics of psychoanalytic psychotherapy. Her comments on the need to differentiate pathological from healthy dependent relationships, as well as conscious from unconscious activity, are crucial and timely. At the same time she fails to acknowledge changes in current thinking—for instance, in her view of "mainstream" psychoanalysis as being instinct-based and limited to "genetic interpretations arising from the distorted transference component of the patient-therapist relationship." The object relations theorists are referred to as representing social determinism in an understanding of the origins of psychopathology rather than consideration of instinctual and intrapsychic factors alone. Later, Kanefield does recognize that the interpersonal, societally influenced emphasis dates back to others as well, such as Sullivan, Fromm and Fromm-Reichmann, Erikson, Horney, and Thompson. Nevertheless, in stating that the contention of Greenson, Erikson, and others that emotional difficulties are both intrapsychic and interpersonal is not accepted by "the mainstream of classical psychoanalysis," she overlooks the influence of these writers on contemporary thinking, the diversity of current psychoanalytic views, and the effects of social change on psychoanalysis.

My own comments will address several points: feminist values and therapy, the patient-therapist relationship, and the concept of the patient curing the therapist.

Feminist values are difficult to define, for, as with psychoanalysis, the core issues can be conceptualized in different ways. One central concept in feminist therapy is an awareness of the effects of social conditions on individuals' behavior and problems, and the repercussions of the patient's behavior on society. In fact, intrapsychic components are sometimes minimized. Gilbert (1980), in her discussion of feminist therapy, cites the difficulty in arriving at a consistent definition. She states that the basic assumption underlying feminist therapy is that "ideology, social structure, and behavior are inextricably interwoven." This feminist alternative to previously existing psychotherapies emerged, according to her, in order to counter the consistently harmful effects on women of the contradiction between ideology and social reality. Feminist therapy incorporates an awareness of the effects of social structure and the prevailing ideology on the behavior of women; it also entails certain principles considered essential for the development of "autonomous and self-actualized" women—values that have been deemed important. Moreover, feminist therapy looks to the eventual establishment of a social structure consistent with these ideas. In its insistence that one must pay attention to social context, feminist therapy can be compared to many movements that have arisen in response to social injustice.

Kanefield addresses well the oversimplifications that have characterized many feminist critics of psychoanalysis as well as the development of some more recent interest in psychoanalytic ideas. In her paper, the emphasis on an interpersonal and object relations understanding of psychopathology and psychotherapy is consistent with feminist values. However, the implications of this point of view are not fully developed; indeed, they are slighted in favor of the emphasis on the activity of the patient.

A further example of this problem can be found in the formulation that the origins of the patient's wish to be helpful to the therapist lie in the child's wish to be useful to the mother. Kanefield's discussion of the child's wish to repair and create the conditions for "good-enough mothering" is sensitive, and it is presented with the understanding that what is meant is the symbolic meaning of these processes. However, to approach this from another point of view and less symbolically: the model of the mother-child relationship, which underlies the formulation of the patient's curative wishes toward the therapist, fails to consider other people in the mother's and the child's world. This focus on the mother has long been criticized as a simplification, for it does not take into account the reality of either the child's development or the woman's life. Social developmental forces, the role of the family, and other influences on patient and therapist do not enter into Kanefield's discussion, other than in relation to therapists' stereotyping their patients according to socialized gender-role expectations.

In another context, in discussing adolescence, Laufer (1982) offers some observations on the emergence in female patients of fantasies of actively caring for or rescuing the mother—or the analyst. She understands these fantasies as evidence of the patient's need for active identification, which serves to defend against passive wishes aroused in the transference. Passive wishes are dangerous here because, as indications of the wish for gratification by the mother, they would interfere with heterosexual attachments. Laufer thus places a defensive interpretation on what might be understood as a similar phenomenon: the wish to care for the mother and rescue her.

Kanefield refers to the values held by therapists that affect therapy; she also notes the stereotyping of women by mental health professionals, who have used different definitions of what is mentally healthy for men and women. It is not clear to what extent this still applies (Franks, 1979). Although women still predominate as patients in mental health settings, the reasons for this are complex. They appear to be connected as much to women's greater readiness to acknowledge problems and communicate their affective states, compared with men, as to submissiveness.

There has been considerable difference of opinion on what a "true" feminist perspective might be. In the process of promoting women's well-being, some feminist therapy has functioned as if there were a latent agenda, in which only a particular outcome is approved. This approach simply substitutes one authority for another. An emphasis on attaining certain goals or developing a particular style may be an authoritarian assertion rather than a universal "good." This may be all too easily overlooked when the goal appears to represent greater freedom, "self-realization," and a reversal of traditional feminine submission. In settings that support women's activity and competence, dependency or helplessness may be frowned upon—sometimes leaving a patient feeling not only dependent and helpless but guilty as well. Moreover the ideology of "strength," "independence," and "autonomy" may be adopted with compliance by a patient whose problems *include* compliance.

It is true that historically feminist values have encouraged assertion and aggression in women. Certainly, it is important to maintain an active stance against social injustice, to recognize it and to be able to act accordingly. Yet current feminist thinking also pays attention to the central role of attachments and relationships for women and supports women's concerns about the potential disruption of relationships. There is a recognition of the importance of healthy dependency. Unfortunately, this aspect is not fully integrated into Kanefield's discussion.

The argument that psychoanalysis is anti-feminist is a longstanding one. Classical psychoanalysis, which originated in the phallocentric culture of Vienna, reflected that culture, which was depreciating and hostile to women. Early theoretical formulations were depreciating of women in several ways. They assumed, for instance, that women felt inferior to men because of "real" anatomical genital inferiority. The female anatomy was seen as deficient rather than different, and has been indicated by the author. Another way in which psychoanalytic formulations were antifeminist was in viewing certain sex roles and behavior as innate rather than the result of socialization. In this psychoanalysts were not unique. To judge what is different from the dominant as inferior is a longstanding historical and sociocultural problem. Nevertheless, the central tenets of psychoanalysis—such as the existence of the unconscious, the role of early experiences in shaping later life, and the importance of conflict and defense—do not in themselves have an anti-feminist orientation.

On the other end, two important principles of feminist therapy are generally cited. The concepts of the "personal" and "political" are considered as broadly overlapping, and the interrelationships beteen psychological and social elements in experience and development are regarded as highly significant. Not only is this true in understanding the patient, but the therapist must also consider the social influences that shape his or her own values.

The second principle of feminist therapy is the one emphasized in Kanefield's paper: that the therapist-patient relationship be regarded as egalitarian. It is here that there appears to be a contradiction. The feminist assertion is that psychoanalytic psychotherapy is based on an unequal relationship, which perpetuates the authoritarian relationships of social interaction. What becomes confused here is an understanding of transference, which may intrude an unequal or authoritarian dimension into the analytic situation because it reflects experiences and relationships in the patient's earlier life, whether or not the therapist wishes to structure it differently. Kanefield recognizes this toward the end of her paper when she states that patients may experience intense mistrust of the therapist because of unconscious factors, regardless of the therapist's caring and skill.

One might ask: What is the effect of deciding that the relationship should be egalitarian and attempting to structure it that way in the face of developmental experiences and transference effects to the contrary? What are the implications of this approach if, on the basis of transference responses, an individual develops expectations, feelings, and perceptions that endow the therapist with omnipotence? Certainly, these must then enter into the therapeutic work, and the implications of the transference must be analyzed. To see the therapeutic relationship as always an interpersonal relationship, open to investigation, and the therapist as contributing significantly to its outcome is consistent with a view of the therapist's behavior as a stimulus for transference development. Nevertheless, this transference overrides egalitarian intentions.

Let us return to the formulation of psychotherapy as an interpersonal experience, which has been seen as a way of resolving the criticism of therapy as an unequal encounter. The concept of psychotherapy as an experience in which everything that happens is the result of an interactive process, with input from both individuals, is not an idea that is unique to Langs (1978). He takes this view further, with his belief that the patient is aware of every negative move on the part of the therapist and that "the patient is unconsciously concerned with and reacting to the therapist all the time without exception." He also develops the concept that patients respond to wrong or "off" behaviors by the therapist as if trying to help or correct or heal them.

In Langs's view, if the therapist maintains appropriate neutrality and is sensitive to the patient and the patient's unconscious content, the patient will respond and indicate the nature of his or her intrapsychic conflicts. If, instead, the therapist acts erroneously and conveys his or her own conflicts or pathology in an inappropriate way, the patient reacts to what is, in fact, an inappropriate and "mistaken" position. The true transference response will be lost. Rather, the response will involve not only productions of unconscious content but some attempt to help or heal the therapist. According to this view, the pathological propensities of both patient and therapist are then passed back and forth. Because pathological or mistaken aspects are assumed to be present in all analyses, this process can be understood as occurring universally. The patient, however, does not always attempt to heal the therapist—only if the therapist's behavior is interfering with a good-enough therapy.

This concept is introduced to "cure" the unequal and thus "unfeminist" nature of the psychotherapeutic interaction. One might ask whether this is the core issue. Kanefield suggests that it is in keeping with the model of feminist goals in prescribing a less passive way for the patient to respond to the therapist. There appears, however, to be some confusion here between a conceptualization of the therapeutic process as a mutually curative or mutually pathological effort and a recommendation for the conduct of therapy.

Furthermore, passivity is primarily dictated by the patient's problems and the way she or he has been socialized. A particular model of therapy does not eliminate these variables. Langs's ideas about the bipersonal field offer a description of his concept of how ordinary therapy proceeds, not a prescription for the solution of inequality. A model that recognizes the importance of patients' activity and therapists' distortions does not in itself resolve the problems of inequality and passivity.

The importance of potential distortions on the therapist's part and the dangers of countertransference interference are amply described by Kanefield. Calling attention to these is very appropriate. It is, however, unclear whether in this view the patient's perception of the therapist is meant to refer to a realistic perception or is conceptualized as referring predominantly to a process of projection or projective identification.

Understanding the patient as someone with integrity and wisdom does not contradict the importance of understanding the transferential distortions that also exist. Kanefield states, "In an atmosphere where the patient is permitted to say whatever comes to mind, where the sessions are allowed to unfold accordingly, and where the therapist maintains the framework of the therapy and patiently provides a safe holding environment for the patient's feelings, the therapist must have the well-placed faith that the patient will unconsciously know what is best." One might argue that more than faith is required. As the patient is expressing fears, distortions, irrational anxieties, anger, phobias, he or she may indeed not automatically know what is best. The point of the therapeutic encounter is that the therapist may aid the patient in discovering the meaning and sources of the symptoms. Faith needs to be supplemented by knowledge, experience, and skill.

One must assume that the therapist is not literally in need of the patient's healing but able to accept the patient's efforts at understanding and his or her own limitations. More broadly defined, countertransference includes not pathological or inappropriate responses to the patient, but also a wide range of unconsciously determined feelings and reactions. It is the responsibility of the therapist to address these. Therapist humanness and fallibility are to be acknowledged, quite apart from the patient's curative attention. The therapist should not be needy to the point of depending on the patient's compassion and helpfulness. The therapeutic situation is one in which the therapist offers the patient the attention and care needed for recapitulation and resolution of conflicts. If the patient really must direct her or his attention to the therapist for fear that the therapy will not be maintained without this, the therapeutic potential for the patient is limited. One must distinguish between the patient's wish to care for or cure the therapist and the patient's capacity to do so. If a patient really could cure the therapist of whatever impediments stand in the way to effective therapy, that patient would hardly need therapy.

It is important for the patient to be recognized as creative and valuable, with nurturant capacities, but the patient is not and should not be primarily there for the therapist's needs. Admittedly, the latter implication is probably not intended by Kanefield. Recognition of the therapist's fallibility and conflicts and appreciation of countertransference, as well as respect for the patient's capacities, sensitivity, caring, and human qualities—all are crucial to the conduct of any helpful therapy. The patients "curative" efforts are not as critical to the concept of the interactive nature of the therapeutic relationship or for redressing inequality as are attention to the real and transference relationships, communication, and mutual respect. Kanefield's discussion has illuminated these complex processes.

REFERENCES

Franks, V. (1979). Gender and psychotherapy. In *Gender and Disordered Behavior*, ed. E. S. Gomberg & V. Franks. New York: Brunner/Mazel, pp. 453–485.
Gilbert, L. A. (1980). Feminist therapy. In *Women and Psychotherapy*, ed. A. M. Brodsky & R. Hare-Mustin. New York: Guilford Press, pp. 245–262.
Langs, R. (1978). *The Listening Process*. New York: Aronson.
Laufer, M. E. (1982). Female masturbation in adolescence and the development of the relationship to the body. *Int. J. Psychoanal.* 63:295–302.

3/
The Effect of the Therapist's Gender on the Transference

Nancy Mann Kulish, Ph.D.

Although many psychoanalysts question whether the gender of the therapist significantly affects the transference, the issue is frequently raised clinically in assigning therapists to certain patients. Gender can also become an important determinant in the patient's choice of a therapist. Psychoanalytic writers agree that for certain patients, gender can contribute to strong resistances, facilitate certain transferences, or affect the order in which given conflicts emerge within the transference. Recently, female analysts have drawn attention to possible differences in how oedipal or sexual issues might be manifested in transferences to male and female therapists. As a basis for discussion, a clinical case is presented of a man with homosexual problems whose choice of a female therapist was important to the transference. Further research on these questions should prove useful clinically and theoretically.

INTRODUCTION

How the gender of the therapist affects the transference in psychoanalytic treatment has received surprisingly little attention in the psychoanalytic literature, although the question has considerable theoretical and clinical importance. Certainly, the question has inherent difficulties, as it focuses on a single aspect of a complex, multidetermined phenomenon. Nevertheless, the issue of the therapist's gender is often raised in several differ-

---

I wish to express my gratitude to Dale Boesky, M.D., and Marvin Margolis, M.D., for their invaluable assistance in the preparation of this paper, and to Nathan Segal, M.D., for his helpful contributions to the understanding of the clinical case.

ent clinical contexts. It is thought, for instance, to contribute to certain strong resistances. It is frequently a major consideration in assignment of cases, with the assumption that gender in some way does affect the course of the treatment. It can also become a central determinant in the patient's choice of analyst or therapist, a choice often inexorably woven into the transference. My purpose here is to explore these issues in terms of their implications for further research and to present an illustrative clinical case, in which gender played a determining role in the choice of the therapist by the patient.

Until recently, whenever the subject has been explicitly addressed in the literature, it has been in the context of classical conceptualizations of the transference, which negate the view that gender may make a difference to its development. Glover (1940), for example, asserts that the sex, personality, or other realistic aspects of the analyst are of little consequence. Indeed, he offers a chiding commentary on the results of a survey in which 50 percent of the analysts responded that the analyst's gender is important to the transference; Glover contends that this response implies a certain skepticism about the validity of the transference phenomenon and its central role as a curative force. Although Greenacre (1959) discusses certain clinical exceptions, she, too, clearly minimizes the effect of gender of the therapist on transference. She describes how there is "a constant, panoramic procession of transference pictures merging into one another," determined historically and genetically.

Freud first introduced the notion of transference in the case of Dora (1905), describing it as new editions, or facsimiles, of infantile impulses and fantasies, revived in the present toward the person of the physician. In "The Dynamics of Transference" (1912), he expanded on these ideas by showing how the individual makes transferences outside as well as inside the analysis to his or her love objects. Freud described the readiness for such transferences in terms of "stereotype plates" which are lodged within the individual. In later writings, Freud (1915, 1920a) showed how transference love in analysis has little regard for the present reality and is a repetition of the past. In all his writings on transference, Freud stressed its inevitability, unreality, and repetitiousness. As depicted by Freud, it is a manifestation of unconscious forces from the past, with little regard for the reality of the person of the analyst. These characteristics of transference give it its power as a therapeutic tool, allowing the analyst access to the patient's infantile conflicts as they are repeated in the treatment.

This conceptualization of transference provides a compelling argument against any major influence of present reality, such as gender, on its development. Transference is a manifestation of unconscious processes and the past, and hence it could be argued that it takes little heed of the gender of the therapist. Experienced clinicians know that the transferences can transform a kindly person into a monster or a narcissistic one into a saint. Maternal and paternal transferences are elicited by analysts of either sex. As demonstrated in dreams, unconscious fantasy displays great elasticity and disregard for the ordinary constraints of reality.

More recent analytic writers have expanded this classical conception of transference in several important ways. Reformulations have been necessitated by Freud's later structural theory and elevation of the aggressive drive to equal importance with the libido. Blum (1971), for example, conceptualizes transference from the vantage point of the structural theory. He sees the transference neurosis as the result of a compromise between the agencies of the mind—ego, id, and superego—between the past infantile neurosis, the present adult neurosis, current external reality, and the analytic situation. Although transference is a regressive repetition, it is influenced by the present analytic situation. Hence, according to Blum, factors such as the age, style, and sex of the therapist can and do influence the transference.

Others have expanded the original definition of transference to include more pathological manifestations. Rather than displacements of neurotic fantasies onto the analyst, Melanie Klein (1952) conceptualizes transference in terms of projections of parts of the self, superego, or internal objects reflecting very primitive experiences. Transferences of severe character disorders, narcissistic, borderline, and psychotic patients have been contrasted by writers such as Heinz Kohut, Otto Kernberg, and Harold Searles with the classical neurotic manifestations (see the review in Langs, 1976). With the related terms of "introjection" or "projective identification," these additions to understanding the more pathological transferences have emphasized interactional issues between patient and therapist.

The recent broadening of the definition of the transference to include interactional issues would allow for a greater role played by the sex of the therapist in actually shaping the course of the emerging transference. Sandler (1976) describes transference in terms of "role responsiveness." Patients, Sandler suggests, try to cast themselves and the analyst into complementary roles, based on their early object relationships. Thus transference is seen as an unconscious attempt to impose an interaction within the patient-therapist relationship. To the extent that role involves generalized patterns and expectations about how a person of a given sex should behave, the gender of the therapist would indeed be relevant to the nature of the transference.

Gill (1982) believes that both participants in the analytic situation come to it with preformed patterns of interaction and expectations of how each other will react. He asserts that the patient's perspective on the reality of the situation may be as plausible as that of the analyst, by whose standards transference is typically measured. Langs (1973, 1976) contends that to understand transference accurately it is necessary to assess the analyst's contributions to the patient's reactions and to separate the patient's distortions from his or her capacity to perceive the analyst realistically. The distortions, according to Langs, make up the basis of the transference.

As Langs (1976) demonstrates in his thorough review of transference, the subject has been marked by considerable conceptual and definitional confusion. Particularly controversial has been this question of the role of reality in the enfolding of transference. Some writers have made no attempt to clarify the relationship and use "transference" loosely to refer to all aspects of the therapeutic relationship. Others distinguish transference from other aspects of the therapeutic relationship on the basis of several criteria: transference has been distinguished from the "real relationship," as well as from the "therapeutic alliance" or "the working alliance"; pathological distortions of the analyst, from relatively nonpathological, veridically based perceptions and reactions to the analyst; reactions stemming the past, from those based on present realities.

While serving a useful—indeed, necessary—purpose, these distinctions nevertheless are not so clear-cut. In outlining therapeutic criteria for differentiating the distorted transferences from the nondistorted "nontransferences," Langs nevertheless stresses that there is a "veridical core to all transferences." Dewald (1976), too, argues that many elements of the real relationship between analyst and patient become woven into the patient's regressive transference experience. Brenner (1980) asserts that there is no justification for a separate term referring to therapeutic or working alliance, which he sees as part and parcel of the transference itself.

Another problem raised by the issue of reality's influence on transference has been its implication for technique. An emphasis on the reality in the relationship has in some instances become a mandate for technical change leading in the direction of providing a corrective emotional experience within the therapy. That aspects of reality influence the transference to varying degrees does not necessarily mean that such realities should be manipulated or exploited to effect therapeutic change. Some of the literature on the impact of gender on the treatment, especially as it relates to choice of therapist, does, however, have such leanings.

Two other dangers lurk in the consideration of the role of reality in the transference. First, in emphasizing realities in the therapeutic relationship, we run the risk of neglecting the unconscious, distorted components so central to the notion of transference. On the other hand, in isolating or designating aspects of the relationship as the "real relationship," we may neglect and ignore the influence of realities on the transference per se.

With these difficulties in mind, for the purposes of this paper I shall define "transference" as the unconscious distortions and fantasies about the analyst that originate in the past. Although genetically and intrapsychically determined, transference is stimulated and influenced by the analytic situation and interaction and the person of the analyst. Even if such influences are kept to an absolute minimum, they can work in silent and subtle ways that are often overlooked. The sex of the therapist is one such influence that may act as an important stimulus to the patient's fantasies in the transference.

CONSIDERATIONS IN ASSIGNING A THERAPIST

Even those analysts who hold to the narrower views of transference do perhaps paradoxically point to instances when the gender of the analyst is important to the the transference. In general, references to the analyst's gender most frequently appear in discussions of (1) initial resistances within the treatment (Bibring, 1936; Greenacre, 1959; Frosch, 1967), (2) homosexual patients (Kubie, 1950; Bieber, 1965), and (3) patients whose histories include the death or loss of a parent (Greenson, 1967).

In 1920 Freud cited the case of a female with strong homosexual tendencies who developed an unrelenting negative transference. Because of her antipathy toward men, he felt she should switch to a female physician or no progress would be made. In his later paper on "Female Sexuality" (1931), Freud confessed that it was hard for him to grasp data about his patients' attachments to the mother as they made paternal transferences to him. Perhaps female analysts could apprehend such facts more easily, he noted, because of the nature of the maternal transferences to them as women. Thus, Freud suggested that (1) certain resistances may become unworkable with certain patients with analysts of a given sex, and (2) certain contents of the mind are made more accessible via transference to one sex or the other—that is, the sex of the therapist facilitates certain transferences.

The first of these observations—that the gender of the therapist contributes to strong resistances, especially in the initial stages of treatment—is a point made repeatedly. Even Kubie (1950), who totally discounts the importance of gender, acknowledges that an analyst of one sex may be preferred over the other in order to facilitate the launching of an analysis. This preference, he feels, may be especially called for in the treatment of certain psychosexual problems, but he does not elaborate.

In an oft-cited paper, Bibring (1936) describes two cases that came to a stalemate in psychoanalysis, necessitating a switch to an analyst of the opposite sex. In both instances the first analyst resembled, in one important aspect, a hated parent of the same sex. The resemblance of the analyst's personality to the original object, combined with the correspondence in gender, did not allow the patients sufficient distance to understand that their fantasies had an origin in the transference, nor did it permit enough confidence in the analyst. Bibring concludes that "a part of reality, represented in the person of the analyst, may exercise a not inconsiderable influence on the course and shape assumed by the transference" (p. 182). Yet as Greenacre (1959), in her discussion of this issue, points out, it was not the reality of the analyst's gender per se that created the difficulty, but that the gender was linked to another, less apparent, but troubling, internal reality for the patients.

Several analytic writers have pointed out that the more disturbed patients—borderline or narcissistic—often explode early in their treatments with strong, primitive feelings which attach to some singular aspect of the therapist such as gender (see Brunswick, 1948; Zetzel, 1970). For example, primitive wishes and fears of merger may be triggered by a female therapist. Another example is how quickly female borderline patients can sexualize their relationships with male therapists. In general, analytic writers, citing clinical experience, suggest that it is better, especially with the more disturbed patients, to choose an analyst of the opposite sex from that of the parent with whom there were the most conflicts in childhood (see Wolberg, 1954; Frosch, 1967). A dissenting voice is that of Ticho (1972), who feels it is preferable that the analyst be of the same sex as the more disturbing parent, although this would hold only for neurotic patients. A major difficulty, in any case, lies in determining initially which parent was the "more difficult." Such a determination would have to rely on the patient's conscious reports and on the clinician's initially incomplete understanding of the case, both of which could be misleading or inaccurate.

Greenson (1967) suggests that for individuals who have lost a parent in childhood, it is desirable to pick a therapist of the same sex as the lost object. Although this choice may seem to be made in order to facilitate or complete identification with the same-sex parent, this is not the reason cited by Greenson. If a person has lost a parent, Greenson argues, the press of transferential feelings for this lost object is so great that unless the analyst is the same sex as the dead parent, the patient will seek individuals of that sex outside of the treatment as objects for these feelings. Thus, the transference becomes more manageable and pointed if the therapist is the same sex as the lost object.

Whereas Freud argued that his being the opposite sex stimulated insurmountable resistance for a homosexual patient, the opposite argument often comes up: namely, that for individuals with homosexual proclivities the transference to the same-sex therapist may become too threatening.

From a different perspective, the choice of therapist of the same sex for adolescent patients is frequently recommended. Here, the same-sex therapist helps to strengthen appropriate sex-linked identifications; moreover, regressive oedipal feelings revived by puberty make a heterosexual transference too dangerously real for the adolescent. Overall, then, for a variety of cases, the therapist's gender is seen as provoking "too strong" a transference, an unmanageable transference, or an unassailable resistance to it. It could be argued that the therapist's gender is no different from other real traits of the analyst, such as race or ethic background, onto which the patient can pin resistances. Such resistances are gambits that can be assailed in the therapeutic work. The nature of the resistances in the cases described here, however, appears to go deeper than that.

In conclusion, the advisability of assigning a patient to a therapist of one sex or the other seems to be a matter of personal experience, rules of thumb, or clinical intuition. No substantial body of research exists to substantiate any of these notions. It has been suggested that the gender of the therapist can create formidable resistances, facilitate certain transferences, or make certain mental material more available in psychoanalytic psychotherapies. However, even in psychotherapies that rely less on the understanding of transference and more on other curative factors, and where perhaps choice of the therapist's gender might be more important, the issues remain unclear. To date, statistical research studies have not yielded convincing or consistent results to demonstrate that the sex of the therapist makes any appreciable or measurable difference to the outcome or process of psychotherapy in general (Seiden, 1976; Goldberg, 1979).

FACTORS IN THE PATIENT'S CHOICE OF A THERAPIST

The choice of a therapist of a given sex by the patient is related to "ready-made" transferences of the patient before entering treatment. Such transferences consist of fantasies—conscious and unconscious—based on a preexisting, intrapsychic "set" the patient has toward the therapist even before the two have met. Fantasies may readily revolve around the therapist's gender since this is often one of the only pieces of information the patient possesses about his or her would-be therapist. If the patient chooses the therapist with gender as an influence, the choice itself is already part of the transference. Clara Thompson, in a clinically rich paper written in 1938, outlines the many possible meanings to such a choice. Some such choices are made for less neurotic reasons than others.

In general, she points to the prejudice at the time in favor of male physicians. Beyond that, patients may choose the sex with whom they feel most capable of intimacy or with whom they believe they have their major problems. At other times the choice may be made to preserve neurotic patterns—for example, females with strong envy toward men who choose a female therapist with the fantasy of having their contempt confirmed. In my own practice of psychotherapy, I have seen many women who fit into this category. Another example might be men who pick a female because they have a strong fear of their position vis-à-vis other men, or a need to feel superior over women. Frequently, the choice of therapist by sex has a defensive character, representing an unconscious protection from a deeper problem. For example, Thompson points to women who fear competition from their own sex and feel it too great a humiliation to be analyzed by a woman. Such a defensive choice may complicate or prolong the treatment, but it can be overcome—unless the analyst in reality fits into the patient's patterns or desires. Difficulties would arise, for instance, if a male patient with a wish for homosexual submission chose a male analyst with a wish for power. Thompson concludes that the most important factor in such circumstances is the therapist's personality, not gender in and of itself.

My own clinical practice consists of a large proportion of patients who have chosen or been sent to me because I am female. The reasons most frequently cited by female patients are their conviction that they would find more empathy from a female therapist and their resentment and hostility toward men. My observations correspond with those of Goz (1973), who suggests that the underlying motives of such patients, often avowed feminists, involve unresolved problems with their mothers. Even with a woman patient who chose me because her previous therapies had ended in actual "seductions" by male therapists, the issues concerned the mother. She quickly attempted to draw me into a sexualized acting out of preoedipal needs for nurturance and conflicts around merger and separation. Frequently male patients, both those who chose and those who are sent to me, have significant problems regarding passivity, so that the choice of a female therapist may have the defensive meaning of drawing back from masculine competition described by Thompson.

I would also agree with Thompson that for the proper unfolding and management of the transference, the therapist's "personality" may be the more important determinant than gender. However, I would not put the question in terms of such a comparison. The question is: What does the therapist's gender *mean* to the patient, as it interacts with the therapist's personality, style, values, and technique? It is conceivable that the therapist's gender, by itself, could have special meaning to the patient, and hence to the transference.

WAYS IN WHICH THE THERAPIST'S GENDER AFFECTS TRANSFERENCE

If the gender of the therapist does affect transference, in what ways does it do so? As Freud suggested in 1931, the analyst's gender may make certain contents of the mind more available. Most obviously, a transference may be maternal or paternal. Analysts will report that patients produce maternal transferences to male and female analysts; paternal transferences, to male and female analysts. Yet paternal transferences seem to be more common with male analysts and maternal transferences with female analysts. Psychoanalytic writers, beginning with Freud, have suggested that this is the case. It seems much more striking that where female analysts are concerned, *sustained* paternal transferences are not reported in the literature (Balint, 1973; Karme, 1979).[1] In my own experience as a psychotherapist, transferences usually take a maternal configuration with brief paternal appearances. In contrast, maternal transferences toward male therapists abound. What accounts for this discrepancy?

One answer may involve the issue of reality and its role in shaping the transference. No matter how neutral and unrevealing the therapist's stance, the patient knows whether the therapist is male or female, and, moreover, may show extraordinary interest in this fact. This piece of reality dictates the shape of the patient's fantasies just as the ink blot dictates the limits of responses on the Rorschach, even for the psychotic. As Stone has stated: "I am prepared, too, to understand that the real personal relationship can slant and at least quantitatively influence the true transference. We do not know all about the dynamic relationship between transference and reality. Resemblances have indubitable importance. To reduce this to an absurdity: . . . One may develop a father transference to a man, perhaps, a woman, but not to a rocking chair" (1954, p. 588).

Note that Stone uses as his metaphor the reduced likelihood of a father transference to a woman. Again, what accounts for this reduced likelihood of a paternal transference toward a female therapist? Some authors have suggested that one possible answer lies with the patient's prevailing level of psychosexual conflicts or level of object relations (Blum, 1971; Karme, 1979). Within the course of a treatment, earlier, more preoedipal constellations become expressed in maternal transferences with male or female therapists. Oedipal conflicts may appear in maternal or paternal

---

[1] In ongoing and as yet unpublished research, I am interviewing seasoned female analysts to gather their impressions and experiences about these issues. Several have reported that paternal transferences to them are not sustained or are subtle and subdued.

transferences, that are more dependent on the gender of the therapist. Zetzel (1970) takes a similar line of argument when she suggests that the specific content of the transference neurosis will be considerably influenced by the respective sexes of patient and therapist for the more mature neurotic patients.

On the other hand, it may be that the preponderance of paternal transferences reported by male therapists and the much greater preponderance of maternal transferences reported by female therapists result from blind spots in the therapists themselves. A therapist of a given sex may be fixed in his or her perceptions and unable to recognize a transference as an opposite-sex one, especially if it is disguised by the patient's own value judgments. Female therapists may have difficulties recognizing themselves as males in the transferences of their patients, perhaps conceptualizing the patients' fantasies as involving the "phallic mother." Moreover, therapists may become caught up in manifest material without carefully considering disguised, unconscious derivatives that would elucidate the transference as an opposite-sex one. In any case, the lack of reported paternal transferences toward female therapists presents an open, and intriguing question.

It is precisely in the central area of oedipal transferences that a void in psychoanalytic research and writing exists. A recent panel highlighted some interesting questions (Szmarag, 1982). Eva Lester pointed out the remarkable absence in the literature of published reports of strong erotic transferences of male patients with female analysts, which contrasts with the frequent, intensely erotic transferences of female patients with male analysts. The panel agreed that both sociocultural and psychological factors within patient and analyst militate against such erotic transferences. Several panelists pointed to how social influences might dictate that a male would relate to a female analyst as a child to an asexual mother. Corresponding pressures on the female analyst could contribute to a countertransference against recognizing or encouraging the expression of erotic feelings in their male analysands. Lester also hypothesized that the spectre of an overwhelming phallic mother interferes with the strongly eroticized transference of a male patient to a female analyst. Another reason for this seeming lack in erotic transferences by male patients to female therapists, in my opinion and that of others (Mogul, 1982), may come from the type of male patient who chooses or is referred to a female therapist. Many of these men may have problems with passivity, which interferes with the expression of strong erotic feelings in the transference.

One of the rare clinical cases in the literature addressed specifically to these issues is presented by Laila Karme (1979). Karme describes a negative oedipal phase spanning 30 sessions in the analysis of a male patient, who throughout this period and the whole analysis maintained a maternal transference. According to Karme, he saw her as "the superior, giving and loving mother" whom he strove to please, and as the castrating mother whom he envied, competed with, and feared (p. 254). Karme raises the question of why the negative oedipal phase was of such short duration, and how it might differ from a similar transference manifested by a male patient toward a male analyst. Although her explanations for the differences are not convincing, the case raises the questions not often enough addressed in my opinion. Namely, how do the oedipal transferences of male and female patients differ with male and female analysts? Are the forms they take different? When are fantasied third parties evoked, for example? What accounts for the seeming lack of eroticized transferences by male patients to female analysts? How are negative oedipal feelings expressed and handled within a relationship with a therapist of the opposite sex? How could these questions be studied?

Finally, several writers have suggested that the gender of the therapist affects the order or timing of the emergence of crucial psychosexual conflicts in the treatment. Glover (1940), who firmly rejected the idea that the gender of the analyst is important, nevertheless could say that "the order of presentation of the psychic material is frequently if not invariably affected by the sex of the analyst, at least in the opening phases of treatment" (p. 326). Blum (1971) states that a maternal transference will appear first with a female analyst. Later, the paternal transference will appear in fantasies about her husband or be displaced onto paternal figures outside the analysis (but note, not directly). The most extensive discussion of this issue is by Phyllis Tyson (1980) in relation to the gender of the analyst in treatment with children. She shows, with many clinical examples, how gender may affect the order in which conflicts are expressed within the transference.

CASE ILLUSTRATION

The type of case most frequently cited in the literature as differentially affected by the gender of the therapist is that involving homosexuality or problems of sexual identity. The following clinical material from a psychoanalytic psychotherapy concerns a man with homosexual problems who specifically chose a female therapist. The material provides some suggestions of what this choice meant for the patient and how the transference may have been shaped by the therapist's being a female.

Presenting Problem

At the time he began treatment, the patient was 44, married with two children, and employed in a prestigious academic position. When he called for his initial appointment, his voice was trembling, almost inaudible, with fear. When he appeared for his appointment, he tried to present a controlled, dignified picture but could not cover his evident terror. Tall and gangly, the patient was dressed in a rather formal, somewhat outmoded fashion; his language was pedantic and highly intellectualized; his manner, pompous and stiff. In a characteristic style, he attempted to control the flow and content of the session—presenting a written vitae of his important life events and setting forth an agenda of philosophical and professional questions for me.

With deep shame, the patient admitted that since adolescence he had struggled with obsessively recurring homosexual fantasies, sometimes acted out in homosexual encounters. He had been in therapy three times in the past for periods of two, one and a half, and one year, at the ages of 21, 27, and 42, all with male therapists. For the duration of each of these contacts, his homosexual preoccupations diminished of their own accord and the patient experienced relief from his persistent anxiety and depression. He felt that being with a kindly male had somehow lulled the impulses into quiescence. Now, however, the patient had decided he had to come to the bottom of his symptoms. Recently moved into the area, he had begun to reexperience the difficulties that had plagued him all his life: the homosexual fantasies and impulses had returned; he was tormented by anxiety and severe headaches; he feared he might lose his new job; his marriage was faltering. In desperation, therefore, he asked a colleague to recommend a female psychoanalytic therapist—a decision that filled him with dread.

The treatment to date has lasted five years, beginning at two times a week and very shortly becoming three times a week. Although it is problematic to present a case not yet terminated, I believe it provides a useful springboard for discussion of the current issues.

History

The patient drew only a relatively sketchy history, as a cloak of repression covers his childhood. Over the years in therapy, a few more memories have helped to fill in the picture. The patient's father was a prominent, respected minister of a Protestant, non-Fundamentalist faith. His mother, very attached to her husband, was active in the parish and social causes. The patient was the youngest of six children, with the eldest a boy, followed by a girl, boy, girl, boy. The patient broke the pattern; he was "supposed to be a girl." His mother kept him in curls and out of school until he was seven and a half, even though he was an intellectually precocious child. She justified her action as a need to teach him herself, but the patient feels she needed to hold onto him. The patient described how his father "saved" him from the clutches of his mother by having him double-promoted in the fifth grade, but became agitated when I questioned him about this obvious discrepancy in timing of the so-called rescue. In general, the family was an intellectually achieving one. Half the siblings have achieved intellectual prominence; the other half, including the patient, have had varying degrees of difficulties in their careers.

The father, a dominant figure in the family, also dominates the patient's affection. He is seen as a kindly man, more loving and able to give physical affection than the mother. His death during the treatment has not helped to change his idealized image. The mother, on the other hand, is pictured as cold, irrational, and difficult. Toward her children, she was possessive and overprotective, not allowing them, even as they got older, to go down the block. Despite her façade of feminine helplessness, she often manages to get her way through hysterical scenes and demandingness. There are hints of her cruelty. The patient recalls, with a feeling of revulsion, once coming upon her naked in the bathtub (probably a screen memory for many such instances). A story recently told to the patient by his siblings is that over the years the father occasionally beat the mother with a strap, but that the older siblings "shielded" the patient from this scene until he left home. Having no conscious memories of such scenes, the patient finds them difficult to fit with his picture of his father; he justifies the notion with remarks of how exasperating his mother could be. (With more than a touch of bitterness, however, the patient summarizes both his parents as imbued with the Christian ethic of nonselfishness and goodness, "living a lie."

Besides his father, the patient's closest ties are to his next oldest brother, Leo. Because they were only two years apart, the two boys slept and played together. In one of the patient's few early memories, the brothers were wrestling and tusseling, which disturbed the parents' weekly Sunday afternoon nap. Angry, the father beat them both. It was Leo who initiated the patient into homosexuality during early adolescence in which the patient performed fellatio on the brother. Leo also pressed his younger brother into anal intercourse, but the patient objected by saying the anus was "dirty." Leo retorted, "What do you think a female's cunt is?" In keeping with this memory, the patient feels Leo was characteristically sarcastic, cruel, yet brilliant. He of all the siblings achieved the most fame, married well, and was clearly the mother's favorite. For the patient, he became a hopelessly difficult object with whom to compete: admired, loved, and hated. He, too, has died during the patient's therapy.

Another early memory is also shrouded in feelings of shame, inferiority, and impotence. Around the age of three, the patient remembers defecating in a back shed. When he proudly brought his achievement to the attention of the family, it was greeted with hoots of derision from his siblings. The patient has also recovered memories of enemas performed by his mother during his early childhood.

Much of the patient's youth was spent in lonely isolation in prep schools, where he had to follow in Leo's footsteps and was left scornfully by Leo to fend for himself. There followed college and graduate school in prestigious institutions. During this time the patient had a homosexual affair with a college roommate, for whom he had genuine fondness and whom he still considers a friend. The patient probably initiated this affair by manipulating the other into making a "first move." He was also inititated into heterosexuality by what he remembers as a frightening seduction by the wife of a college professor for whom he was babysitting.

The patient's steps toward a sustained, successful career have been frustrated by a series of changes in direction, self-destructive behavior, and interpersonal difficulties. He is pained by these unrealized ambitions, as he is undoubtedly talented and exceptionally bright. He approaches each new opportunity with floods of omnipotent fantasies, fears of inadequacy, and dreams of how the new atmosphere at work will provide him a caring, familial environment. Quickly disappointed, he soon gets embroiled in conflict with his superiors and co-workers, especially (before treatment) female ones.

His marriage of 20 years, however, has been stable although problematic. His wife is of a different religion, a professional, described as dependable, down-to-earth, but lacking in the ability to initiate warmth or understand the emotional facets of life. The patient maintains that his sex life with her is is satisfying, speaking of it in vague, flowery terms, although he complains that she is too passive. At times they quarrel and days of silence and estrangement follow. Nevertheless, he values her, wishes to maintain his marriage, and cherishes his children, with whom he tries consciously to model himself after his own father—"dominant, yet benevolent."

Choice of a Female Therapist

Consciously, the patient was clear about his choice of a female therapist: his previous work with the three male therapists had brought symptom relief and comfort, but no real understanding or lasting change. Yet deeper, unconscious motives have emerged during the course of treatment. In order to elucidate these motives, I shall outline the course of treatment, and then present in detail one session in which the patient's associations focused specifically on his choice of therapist.

All three of his previous therapists are described as psychoanalytic; at least one is now a practicing psychoanalyst. From what little I have been able to discover from their reputations, they are all competent and well regarded. The patient has recently, rather reluctantly, acknowledged that all were relatively quiet and "neutral." Although their styles did not differ perceptibly from mine in his mind, he consistently described them and all males as more warm and forthcoming than me, and attributed this difference to my femininity. Of course, other than the patient's sketchy reports, I have no direct knowledge of the nature of the previous therapies. All three were conducted, perhaps intentionally, with a natural end in sight; his first two occurred during college and graduate school, and the last, before he obtained the promising job that brought him to the area. Thus his fear of seeing a female therapist cannot be separated from a possible fear of committing himself to an intensive therapy.

Nevertheless, there is some evidence that his fear specifically concerned therapy with a female. The patient was initially so visibly and vociferously terrified that I speculated that his choice had a forced, perhaps counterphobic, quality. He began treatment by announcing his deep sense of dread and has, until recently, continued to anticipate almost each session with dread. He repeatedly referred to how difficult it was for him that his therapist was female and bemoaned his choice.

For the patient, a "psychoanalytically oriented" female meant a cold, distant one. He lamented the inherent frustrations and coldness of the psychoanalytic therapeutic situation, as he experienced it. From the beginning, the transference took a persistently fixed and extremely negative form. I had determined to proceed cautiously and try to keep quiet. To the patient, I was cold, hostile, withholding, and cruel. He accused me directly of being just like his mother or wife—cold and unaffectionate. Silences were interpreted as a purposeful and cruel withholding of my knowledge which might help him. He charged me with not having "the vestiges of civilized human kindness or empathy." On the other hand, if I did make a supportive empathic statement, he would accuse me of being "mealy-mouthed" or belittling him. He criticized me for not being "active enough," not making enough "interpretations," yet left little room for me to get in a word edgewise as he analyzed his dreams, used his considerable reading to theorize about himself, etc. From a stance of superiority, he critiqued my diction, grammar, choice of words. At one low point, when he was fired from a short-lived position by a female boss, he worked himself up to a paranoid pitch and accused me of conspiring with the females at work against him. While it is an understatement to say his behavior was trying, nevertheless his anguish and conflict were obvious. I believe this behavior reflected a transferential view he did and does hold toward women, but its relentlessness suggested it was a defense against other, more frightening feelings. For months on end the patient did not, indeed could not, let himself string together two consecutive positively toned statements about me.

Early in the treatment, the patient expressed a persistent feeling that I, like his mother and wife, did not appreciate, admire, or delight in him, his masculinity, or his genitals. He felt no support from women in this crucial regard. He wanted, as he put it, to "be stroked" by women, by which at first he meant admired and praised, then literally cuddled and massaged, and ultimately (as disguised in dreams) genitally stroked. As he perceived me as not gratifying, and in fact frustrating, these initially narcissistic wishes, he felt an anger and longing, which he expressed by his disdain and reproachfulness.

The patient took refuge and solace from these feelings in his homosexual fantasies and impulses. He was loath to bring the homosexual fantasies to light, however, as he feared I wanted him to give them up and they seemed the only way he had to cope with his anxieties. Moreover, he feared I would be repulsed by them and disapproving, much as his mother had jealously attacked his friendships with males during adolescence. Because of his own shame, fear of reprisal, and resistance, he found it excruciatingly difficult to describe the details of his homosexual fantasies and behavior. As his projected guilt and the resistance were interpreted, however, he was able to elaborate and explore them further.

In the early months of treatment I repeatedly reminded him that the repulsion and moral indignation he attributed to me were his own feelings and prevented him from exploring the meaning of his fantasies. In a session two years later, he began by announcing that he had been in the grip of obsessive homosexual fantasies. I asked for details—for how long? He answered, "24 hours, no, 48, 58—to be exact, since last session. When it's like this I feel negative toward you. You are remote and cold. You become strangely quiet when I talk of homosexuality." I asked, "Do you mean last time or today? You've hardly given me a chance to get remote today." He laughed, "No, but I feel it today. I preserve the right to experience you that way, even though I know you aren't."

Early on, what the patient revealed were the narcissistic aspects of the homosexuality. Echoing Greek ideals, he fantasied a mutually giving, equal union with a beautiful male, in spirit and in body. The symmetry in the relationship was stressed—the object or selfobject is a mirror of an idealized, loving and beloved self. He and the other lie naked next to each other, caressing each other. Striking is the absence of hostility or competition. All is bathed in a golden, platonic light. This content of the homosexual fantasies corresponded to the stated needs toward me in the transference at that time for admiration and love, and for reassurance about his masculinity.

3. *Therapist's Gender and Transference* /49

It seemed that any perceived narcissistic blow from me or from any significant woman would push the patient into homosexual fantasies and/or behavior. Gradually, however, it became apparent that a breakthrough or increase in positive feeling toward me would provoke a defensive flight into homosexuality, the latter often more symbolic than real (for instance, a visit to a gay bath). The defensive flight is illustrated in the following session.

The patient reported that his wife, after initially refusing, had agreed to accompany him on a business trip. This change of mind had paradoxically made him angry, and he understood he needed to feel cut off from women. He reported a dream in which he went to a "men's only" club at Brandeis University. He was reminded of Judge Brandeis and thought of my husband. (Jewishness was associated with me and his feeling of being excluded.) Not being able to stick with the dream, he anxiously began talking about homosexuality. As I began to see this defensive pattern repeatedly emerge, I wondered if it was a regression from a higher level of psychosexual development, a flight from oedipal conflicts.

A clear indication of the previously mentioned connection between hetero- and homosexuality and its genetic origins came with a trip the patient made across country by car with his recently widowed mother. For days before the trip, the patient became obsessed with the sleeping arrangements in the motels and how he might be able to break away to visit an old homosexual lover, whose home they would pass. To his dismay, during the trip the mother kept suggesting they share a room for economy's sake and put up a screen between the beds. On the way the patient picked up a young male hitchhiker over his mother's protests to ward off the threat to his masculinity and his own sexual feelings. It was not clear whether it was the mother's seductiveness or her treating him as she would a female companion that was the more threatening.

Within the transference, this feared danger was handled repeatedly in the same way, by interposing a male between us. For example, he would come late for sessions after setting up a previous appointment with a male friend or colleague whose kindness and sensitivity he would compare favorably with mine. Clearly, he needed to see me as cold or inhospitable.

His defensive need to distort his perceptions of me was brought home to him in a pivotal session about the buzzer to my office. Unbeknown to me, mixing up the time, he had come very early, only to find his repeated buzzes unanswered. He hypothesized that I set up the situation deliberately to reject, test, or confuse him—"a cruel test," but finally realized he had the time wrong. When he returned for the appointed time, he buzzed insistently and loudly. He then divulged his fantasies about what had happened before the session began. I told the patient that he expected to see me as rejecting, if not cruel, and pointed out that I had on other occasions noticed an insistency in how he rang the buzzer. The patient seemed shaken by the notion that he might need to see me as rejecting.

Thus, behind the image of the cold, rejecting mother is the loathsome female and the seductive, taunting sexual woman. Erotic feelings are turned into feelings of loathing. Two years into treatment, the patient introduced the following dream with the warning I should "steel myself." In the dream he began to approach me in "a sexual way." Then an image of a pig interposed itself between him and me. His associations began with picturing me as the pig but ended on himself. I pointed out that "pig" is what he felt about his own animal impulses, a feeling of revulsion he attributed to me. I added that this switch from himself to the other stemmed from an early time in his life when he was similarly confused. This feeling of loathing and intellectualized discussions of "bestiality" came up repeatedly in subsequent sessions, which were filled with material suggestive of the primal scene.

On another occasion, as the patient was coming up the walk to my office in my home, he spotted an upstairs window of what he surmised to be a bathroom. He was flooded by a memory of coming upon his mother in the bath and being repulsed by the sight. When in the session he began talking vaguely of wanting something from me, and I asked for clarification, he flew into a rage that I was not "earthy" enough and did not understand him. For several sessions thereafter, he was overcome by a sustained feeling of loathing for me.

As the seductive mother, he saw me as taunting him with the sight of my open purse behind the desk—which he fantasied, while knowing better, that I laid out on purpose—or taunting him with my unavailability as he spotted me with my husband at a movie. Thus, the initial view of me as cold and distant protected him from the castration he so desperately feared, but perhaps counterphobicly approached.

His manner of spewing out material in the earlier sessions had a defensive, forced quality. To his expressed horror, frightening and violent dreams and obsessive images, with content of castration or anal sadism, plagued him. He literally filled the sessions with scattered anal, phallic, and aggressive thoughts and references, which did not seem to fall together into an approachable, cohesive meaning. For example, he had the sudden thought of driving a stake into my vagina, to his horror. He poured out recounts of violent dreams that tormented him. I felt he was throwing out material at me, insistent that I respond to it in some way and wounded if I did not. In the initial period, whenever I did address a sexual issue interpretively, by a link to childhood, for example, he did not seem to respond cognitively, but rather felt reassured that I had shown him I neither was appalled by nor shunned his masculine sexuality.

A conscious and ever-present danger experienced by the patient is fear of castration, most frequently at the hands of the woman. His sense of body integrity is fragile, as in dreams in which he is threatened with being crushed in a gorge or hurled off a cliff. Clearly, the phallus is a detachable or detached object, as in his recurrent images or mishaps of lost letters, gloves, briefcases, pieces of things. Like fecal material, the penis will be pinched off or wretched out, as with an enema. Danger looms in the vagina, which already contains the competitor's penis or penises. In his voluminous dreams, trains, rockets, etc., are squeezed into tunnels, or tubelike structures which already contain other vehicles. (In one early dream, he feared his head would be crushed in a "cockpit"-like window of a ticket office, but his brother Leo was able to make the transaction.) As his anxiety about his masculinity, potency, and intactness rises, he seeks relief with homosexual fantasies of fellatio or anal intercourse with intact men; he may masturbate, but then is left feeling totally impotent, with the bodily sense of having no penis at all. Thus, he fluctuates between feeling productive and potent—what he calls "Mode A"—to feeling anxious, useless, and impotent—"Mode B." Mode A must equal masculinity; Mode B, femininity.

His choice of a female therapist may therefore represent the fantasy of stepping into the jaws of a "man-eating" plant. In fact, my own initial stance of caution, silence, and passivity in the therapy complemented these fantasies. Consciously, I had clinical reasons for my attitude. Because of the patient's extreme anxiety, rigid efforts for control, apparently strong aggressive drives, and stilted use of language, he initially presented the possibility of an underlying borderline pathology. Therefore, I determined to proceed cautiously and on a trial basis, at first. However, this attitude was also a response to the image of the cruel, phallic "bitch" relentlessly and eloquently imposed on the therapist by the patient. I believe I defensively recoiled into a softer, more passive pose. A thought that occurred to me after the first interview illustrates this. I wondered if I were "too dumb" to see this apparently brilliant and wordy man. Perhaps the patient had succeeded in making me feel in response to him as he had felt as a child in response to a powerful, controlling mother. At times in the first two years of treatment, I would anticipate the sessions with a vague reluctance, mirroring the dread with which the patient anticipated them himself.

This patient's need to sustain negative images of the female was tied to a possible unconscious motivation underlying his choice of a female therapist: to resolve ambivalence between two unsynthesized sides of himself. The negative view seemed to hold together his masculine identity. Despised, feminine aspects of the self were projected onto the female—the female as "the pig," for example. On the other hand, he seemed to harbor an unconscious wish to have the female, castrated side of himself cured and reconciled within himself. Such a fantasy about cure appeared in a recent dream. In it, he brings both his car, with a gaping black hole, to a mechanic to be fixed and his mother to a benign female therapist for treatment.

Gradually and grudgingly, the patient was able to admit that I was "human after all." With tears in his eyes, he expressed his gratitude for nonjudgmental and empathic listening. With surprise, he perceived that I was able to withstand his attacks. He both feared and wished that I would retaliate in kind or terminate the treatment.

Impulses toward me in the transference, which at first took narcissistic or oral forms, now began to include more phallic expressions, albeit often fleeting. The patient would obsess about whether he had left his fly unzipped before the session; he oscillated on the question of buying a new, spiffier car or a more conservative car like the one his father had had; a move to a more private office brought a disavowed fantasy of his raping me. In the last year, the patient has allowed a more sustained eroticized transference to form in spite of his clear anxiety and defensive efforts to the contrary. For example, he fantasized kissing my breasts and pubic area, or caressing my thigh, or my divorcing my husband to move into an apartment alone. Inevitably, erotic urges toward me are accompanied by homosexual ones, so that this period has been intensely troubling to him. Most recently, homosexual fantasies have given way to manifestly heterosexual ones.

While the current sexual material is very conflicted, his overall stance toward me has softened. He appears more boyish, friendly, even affectionate. He shows a sense of humor, can joke ironically about himself and his defensiveness, and recently admitted that his therapy and I are all-important to him. At the same time he reports a more enjoyable sexual experience with his wife, even as he is more able to talk of his repulsion toward the female body.

In this fashion, oedipal themes have emerged in the context of jealousy of my husband and other patients, dreams of primal scene, and painfully acknowledged feelings of competition with other men. In a striking session after the patient had literally bumped into me and my husband at a concert over the weekend and stood overlooking us for ten minutes, he began by complaining he felt depressed and impotent; he linked these feelings to the content of the musical performance. When I drew his attention to their possible connection with running into me, he was astonished—he had no conscious knowledge of seeing me at the concert. Recent dreams have repeatedly spelled out the patient's traumatic exposure to the primal scene, which may have been played out in his reaction to seeing me and my husband at the concert. Predictably, he has no memory of primal scene and denies such a possibility, just as he cannot remember the beatings of his mother by his father. He does have a vague memory of a "screen" set up in his parents' bedroom.

Inferences about oedipal meanings can be drawn from this material, but they are perhaps overly optimistic. The patient's defensive need to pull away from positive feelings toward me and to deny negative ones toward males can be interpreted as a repressive move from oedipal dangers. The more compelling diagnostic impression, however, is of severe characterological problems involving narcissism and concerns around sexual identity, as well as intense ambivalence. This case resembles the case described by Anna Freud (1952) of the male homosexual who needed other male figures to guard against the loss of his masculinity.

In the second year of life, during the separation-individuation phase, when the sorting out of what is masculine and feminine begins, this man was, according to the history, treated as a girl by his mother in certain ways. This treatment undoubtedly left its mark in the vulnerable and unappreciated masculinity so central to his whole sense of self. His relationship with his mother was overly close, and he fought against her ever-present femininity. Anal fixations and real castration anxiety resulted from forced enemas and a generally over harsh toilet training. The castration anxiety was intensified by the sense of his mother's envy of his masculinity and desire for him to be a girl; by his being exposed, probably repeatedly, to his mother's genitals; and by his visualizing primal scene and the beatings. Early on, he turned from this threat to males; he was thrust into closeness with a brother, close in age. He admired his father and covered over his fear of and deep disappointment in him. Thus, his narcissistic vulnerabilities, precarious masculine identity, anal fixations, and sense of phallic peril left him ill-prepared for the oedipal stage. He was inclined already for a homosexual solution in which castration is undone, narcissism gratified, and idealization toward the father cherished.

The course of my patient's treatment has made abundantly clear the meaning of his homosexuality and homosexual object choice. With another male being, the patient feels intact; there is no threatening, castrated creature. As he has demonstrated through the treatment with me, he projects bad, unwanted aspects of himself onto the female and retains good for the male, himself. Thus, homosexuality preserves his masculine, whole sense of self. The patient's defensive need to pull away from positive feelings toward the female and to deny negative ones toward males can also be interpreted as a repressive move from oedipal dangers. The question arises, then: In view of his professed fears about women and the crucial function a male object choice plays for this man, why should he deliberately have chosen a female therapist with whom to work? In a session that occurred in the beginning of the fifth year of treatment, the patient's associations converged upon his choice of a female therapist and offered some answers to this question.

In the preceding months of the treatment, the patient had been grappling with ambivalence about his growing positive feelings toward me. Pressing needs for more closeness, exemplified by a wish to meet more frequently, were immediately followed by a fantasy of "a cat eating a cat." He spoke of my "loveliness" to him and admired my "beautiful office filled with lovely objects," especially a graceful, feminine-looking plant, whose image merged with that of "a man-eating plant." The patient himself had moved into a new office. His associations to the move suggested an identification with me and brought an acknowledgment of my interpretation that he was curious about what it was like to be female.

The session to be reported was the next to the last before my spring vacation, which I had announced several weeks before. At that time I had arranged to change the last session before vacation from the afternoon to the morning, which meant I would meet the patient at my office in my home. Sessions at my office at home, which occur at earlier morning hours, have brought up sexual material, such as the memory of seeing his mother bathing. In the intervening sessions, forgetting my request for these changes, the patient himself had requested a time change to the morning to accommodate his schedule. We discussed this characteristic need to take control over what makes him anxious.

The Session: After a few minutes of silence, the patient begins, "I didn't forget. Your going away affects me. I don't know if you are actually going away but . . ."

I remark, "As far as you are concerned, I am." We then confirm the exact time and place of the next session, the last before vacation. The patient pauses again and visibly appears uncomfortable. I ask him why he has become uncomfortable.

"You are doing me a favor," he replies. "I feel uncomfortable if I can't reciprocate. I need a desexualized way to do so."

"What do you mean?"

"It goes back to my fear of my passivity we were talking about . . . I had strange dreams last night. We—my family, I think—were sitting around a table. There were different colored shapes of flesh right at the table's edge. Some people were missing some of the things. Not manifestly genital things, but folds of flesh of different colors."

He then associates: "At Passover dinner there was a huge leg of lamb. I carved. I cut into it deeply with one stroke [smiles with satisfaction]. After, I cut smaller pieces. Attached to the side of the bone were protrusions of bloody flesh. Ugh. I officiated. But it saved the children."

"What?" I ask.

"The lamb," he answers. "If you put lamb blood on the doorway, the children would be saved. The death dealers would pass over the house. In the dream, the things were coming up from under the table [makes a gesture near his crotch]. It is important to protect the children. Hmm. Yesterday I was speaking of closeness with Jim [his son]. Have had some homosexual feelings lately. [Pause.] But the Sedar was enjoyable. Lots of laughter. The children were telling me how to proceed. In no uncertain terms I told them I was in charge. With good humor and graciously, mind you! [Pause.] Sunday night I called my sister. We spoke of the need to take care of mother. I have a fantasy—only a fantasy—of bringing her here so she could see me sing in the choir. (Note: an overtly positive feeling for his mother is rare.)

The patient continues with wistful memories of his father and then returns to the lamb, the "virginal lamb" or "vaginal"—like his new office which he enjoys. "Yes, you are right," he comments, "it is like trying out what it's like to be female."

After a pause he exclaims, "I *am* angry you are going (grudgingly)," and elaborates on this.

My intervention here (which unfortunately I do not recall exactly) addresses his feelings toward me. Putting them in perspective, I refer to how, for a long time, he was frightened of his positive feelings toward me, but—the one detail I have in my notes—recently they have been "softening." Hence, I indicate, he is all the more angry at my vacation.

After a pause, he asks (to my surprise), "Then why choose a female therapist?"

"It was an act of venturesomeness," he himself answers, "but at the same time, a resistance, and a craving of some intimacy with a woman. But the truth is that I have gone farther in describing my sexual feelings with you than the other therapists. [Pause.] I think I like a tyrant's power. It's a risk being here naked, as it were—a hell of a risk!"

In my notes I have the following summary of the next session:

Patient is anxious. He allows more positive sexual feelings, then homosexual thoughts intrude. I point out this juxtaposition and remind him of the last time we met at this office, which brought up the memory of his mother, juxtaposed with feelings of loathing. I suggest he experienced the changes in arrangements as seductive on my part. Again he ponders why he chose a female therapist—a brave thing to do, etc. He wonders how I could stand him all this time. Sees I do. Then come fantasies of a stream of feces being propelled all over the room.

Commentary: Clearly, the patient experienced my request for a time change (to avoid missing an additional session) as well as switch in office as sexually seductive. His increased anxiety, defensive efforts to make the request for changes his own, and the appearance of raw anal and sadistic material and threats of castration, all demonstrate his response to this perception. He experienced me as too hospitable—with some basis in fact—which conjured up his seductive mother, from whom he needed to distance himself.

The crux of the difficulty in this session, however, is revealed in the next major intervention, following the dream material. This intervention is consistent with my strategy and reasoning throughout the treatment: to focus on the transference, peeling away negative feelings the patient puts up as blocks against positive feelings toward me. Immediately after my remarks, the patient raises the question of his choice of a female therapist. He draws our attention to his fear of his feelings toward the female, the spectre of the rejecting, seductive, engulfing mother he has painted from the very beginning. In so doing, he has followed my lead. With my intervention, I drew his attention away from the preceding material and to his sexual feelings and fears about me, in this case stimulated by my inadvertent seductiveness and "niceness." But we are both—patient and therapist—too caught up with this fear. This fear of the female has been used like a decoy, a ruckus raised while the real crime is being committed elsewhere. The clues, which I ignored, are in the dream material which has preceded the intervention and his questioning the choice of therapist: the material about the Passover lamb and the "death dealer."

The dream and associations to it suggest that what lies underneath his idealized feelings toward men and his posture as the benevolent father, which he details in this very session, are his identification with the murderous, sadistic father and the butchered sons, the anal-sadistic and masochistic impulses he holds toward the father, and his murderous rivalry toward his brothers. His fear of the female therefore masks a deeper, unconscious fear and hatred of as well as erotic feelings toward, the male: the supposedly benevolent father who stood by as his mother dressed him as a girl and who meted out beatings. While he now can speak of his homosexual feelings toward men, he cannot bear to consider them as directed toward the person of his father.

In bringing up the question of his choice of female therapist, the patient both tries to communicate this insight to me as well as to camouflage it by bringing up his fears about the female. Thus, my intervention missed the mark in two important ways. First, I plainly did not grasp the meaning of the dream and the central conflict about the father it revealed. Second, my use of the word "softening" reveals the nature of the countertransference during the session. This curious choice of wording must represent my shrinking from the vivid and unadulterated sadism in the dream and the Passover scene.

We are now in a position better to understand the patient's choice of a female therapist as a complex, multiply determined act. To follow the patient's own words—first, it was indeed an "act of bravery." His fear of women masks a deeper fear of men, but it is nonetheless genuine and profound. It was its defensive use that gave it the forced quality that I suspected from the beginning.

Second, he does have " a craving for intimacy" with a woman—positive but conflicted yearnings toward a female, which have appeared as preoedipal and oedipal fantasies about me. Because his homosexuality is distasteful and morally objectionable to him, his choice of a female therapist, at some level, represents an attempt to cure himself of his homosexuality.

Yet, on a deeper level, the choice is an unconscious attempt to preserve his position by avoiding exploration of his feelings with and about a male. True, he gained symptomatic relief with male therapists, but only as long as the treatment was neither too intensive and relatively short term. This formulation is supported by that of Bieber (1965), who gives central prominence to the unconscious fear and hatred of the male in the dynamics of male homosexuals.

In this avoidance the patient may have been aided by my own mistakes. In the months preceding this session, his references to wanting to know how it was to be a female and the shifting roles for therapist and patient between torturer and victim pointed to his putting me in a masculine position, as the probing father, not the phallic mother. As has been suggested in the literature, I may have been blocked in seeing myself in the paternal role within the transference and in understanding the material from the masculine vantage point.

Although this patient's choice of therapist made treatment difficult, it has not proved a detriment to the overall treatment. Manifestly, from the intensity of his resistive reactions to a female and the fact that the more hated parent was his mother, this case would seem to fall into the category wherein the selection of a male therapist would be advised. To be sure, such a choice would have made life easier in the treatment, and apparently had proved so in the past. The patient came into treatment with preformed negative transferences toward a woman, a dread apparent even in his initial telephone contact. Toward a man, he had, apparently, a ready positive, receptive transference. A panel of the American Psychoanalytic Association (Payne, 1977) reported that male homosexuals with male analysts develop early, strong, positive and symptomatically stabilizing paternal transferences.

Bieber (1965) describes the transference phenomena of male homosexuals toward him as a male analyst as taking the form of father, older brother, or another influential male. In the early phases, the perception of him usually is that of the good father sought since childhood; this gives way only much later to ambivalence. Hostility commonly is avoided at first. Bieber goes on to point out the unstudied "problem of variance in transference toward male and female analysts." He cites anecdotal data from female analysts indicating that male homosexuals develop transferences that do not appear with male analysts—heterosexual fantasies of romance, for example, and "qualitative" differences in their hostility to men and women.

For the sake of argument, I might hypothesize how the transferences in the present case might have developed differently with a male therapist. There is evidence from what the patient reports of his past contacts with therapists and other men that such transferences would be highly idealized and narcissistic, duplicating his attitude toward his father. Although the transference would essentially be preoedipal, I would speculate that the patient nonetheless would initially appear healthier within this relationship with a male than he did with me. Only after time would the idealization of the male—which crystallized later in childhood—crumble to reveal the disappointments with father and the protective defense against dealing with negative aspects of himself. Moreover, the threat of castration from a female appeared to be closer to the surface and to be more externalized than fears of castration from a male. Thus, the fantasied material and conflicts might indeed emerge in a different order for a male therapist, as suggested by such writers as Tyson (1980). With the female therapist, the maternal preoedipal transferences emerged first with admixtures of anal and phallic conflicts. With a male therapist, I would speculate that the sequence might have shifted.

It is not possible even to speculate on the most interesting question of how an oedipal transference of this male patient to a female therapist might differ from that to a male therapist. To this point, the patient has been dealing primarily with preoedipal issues in spite of evolving erotic transference manifestations. Fleeting oedipal conflicts are emerging in competitive thoughts regarding my husband and, in more derivative form, toward the patient's colleagues. Another question concerns differences in the shape the negative oedipal constellation might take. Karme (1979) reports a shortened, watered-down period during the analysis of a male patient in which negative oedipal feelings were expressed, but not directly toward her person. In the therapeutic session described above and in preceding sessions, feelings toward the erotically loved but hated father seemed to be aimed toward me as a paternal figure, although they were not recognized as such.

Regardless of how specifically the gender of the therapist might have shaped the transference, however, it can be said that it was an overriding, if not organizing, factor in this man's relationship to the therapist. It shaped the content—castration by the female and obsessive speculations and concerns regarding the meaning of my femininity-masculinity as well as his. It proved to be focal point for resistance, a defensive cover gainst deeper conflicts regarding his erotic feelings toward females and ambivalence toward males.

CONCLUSION

It might be argued that because of this particular patient's intense problems with his sexual identity that the therapist's gender took on this strong valence for him. Yet I believe that for other patients with similar problems of homosexuality or sexual identity, the therapist's gender will also prove to be a significant factor in the transference. That the gender of the therapist is so often raised in the assignment of homosexual patients to a therapist has already been mentioned. However, I believe that the issue is not whether or not a therapist of a given gender will be "better," but that the therapist's gender will shape the transferences for such patients in ways that should not be overlooked. I would further speculate that the gender of the therapist would be of central concern or meaning for many patients: patients concerned with issues of sexual identity stemming from the period of separation-individuation and anal ambivalence, and those concerned with phallic-oedipal issues, with the interplay between father and mother. While it can have an organizing influence for the patient, the therapist's gender also organizes his or her way of understanding and decoding the material.

Such speculations about the differences in transferences between female and male therapists are fruitless without the clinical data to back them up. Nevertheless, I believe the questions should be addressed and have attempted to raise some of them in this paper. What is badly needed is the sharing and comparing of clinical experiences between male and female therapists and experienced training analysts who have supervised both sexes extensively. The question of the effect of gender on transference should be an empirical one. The data should shape theories of transference rather than theories blind us to the data. Research on these issues should prove most useful clinically and theoretically.

REFERENCES

Balint, E. (1973). Technical problems found in the analysis of women by a woman analyst: A contribution to the question, "What does a woman want?" *Int. J. Psychoanal.* 54:195–201.

Bibring, G. (1936). A contribution to the subject of transference resistance. *Int. J. Psychoanal.* 17:181–189.

Bieber, I. (1965), Clinical aspects of male homosexuality. In *Sexual Inversion,* ed. J. Marmon. New York: Basic Books, pp. 248–267.
Blum, H. P. (1971). On the conception and development of the transference neurosis. *J. Amer. Psychoanal. Assn.* 19:41–53.
Brenner, C. (1980). Working alliance, therapeutic alliance, and transference. In *Psychoanalytic Explorations of Technique,* ed. H. P. Blum. New York: Int. Univ. Press, pp. 137–157.
Brunswick. R. M. (1948). A supplement to Freud's "History of an infantile neurosis." In *The Psycho-analytic reader,* ed. R. Fliess. New York: Int. Univ. Press, pp. 86–126.
Dewald, P. (1976). Transference regression and real experience in the psychoanalytic process. *Psychoanal. Qu.* 45:213–230.
Freud, A. (1952). Studies in passivity. In *Writings* 4:245–257. New York: Int. Univ. Press.
Freud, S. (1905). Fragment of an analysis of a case of hysteria. *Standard Edition* 7:3–122.
——— (1912). The dynamics of transference. *Standard Edition* 12:97–108.
——— (1915). Observations on transference-love. *Standard Edition* 12:157–171.
——— (1920a). Beyond the pleasure principle. *Standard Edition* 18:3–64.
——— (1920b). The psychogenesis of a case of homosexuality. *Standard Edition* 18:145–172.
——— (1931). Female sexuality. *Standard Edition* 21:219–243.
Frosch, J. (1967). Severe regressive states during analysis. *J. Amer. Psychoanal. Assn.* 15:491–501.
Gill, M. M. (1982). *Analysis of Transference, Vol. I: Theory and Technique [Psychol. Issues,* Monogr. 53]. New York: Int. Univ. Press.
Glover, E. (1940). *The Technique of Psychoanalysis.* Baltimore: Williams & Wilkins.
Goldberg, J. (1979). Aggression and the female therapist. *Modern Psychoanal.,* 4:209–222.
Goz, R. (1973). Women patients and women therapists: Some issues that come up in psychotherapy. *Int. J. Psychoanal. Psychother.* 2:298–319.
Greenacre, P. (1959). Certain technical problems in the transference relationship. *J. Amer. Psychoanal. Assn.* 7:484–502.
Greenson, R. R. (1967). *The Technique and Practice of Psychoanalysis.* New York: Int. Univ. Press.
Karme, L. (1979). The analysis of a male patient by a female analyst: The problem of the negative oedipal transference. *Int. J. Psychoanal.* 60:253–261.
Klein, M. (1952). The origins of transference. *Int. J. Psychoanal.* 33:433–438.
Kubie, L. S. (1950). *Practical and Theoretical Aspects of Psychoanalysis.* New York: Int. Univ. Press.
Langs, R. (1973). The patient's view of the therapist: Reality or fantasy? *Int. J. Psychoanal. Psychother.* 2:411–431.
——— (1976). *The Therapeutic Interaction.* New York: Aronson.
Mogul, K. (1982). Overview: The sex of the therapist. *Amer. J. Psychiat.* 139:1–11.
Payne, E. (1977). Panel report: The psychoanalytic treatment of male homosexuality. *J. Amer. Psychoanal. Assn.* 25:183–199.
Sandler, J. (1976). Countertransference and role responsiveness. *Int. Rev. Psychoanal.* 3:43–48.
Seiden, A. M. (1976). Overview: Research on the psychology of women, II. Women in families, work, and psychotherapy. *Amer. J. Psychiat.* 133:1111–1123.
Stone, L. (1954). The widening scope of indications for psychoanalysis. *J. Amer. Psychoanal. Assn.* 2:567–594.
Szmarag, R. (1982). Panel report: Erotic transference and countertransference between the female therapist and the male patient. *Acad. Forum* 26(3):11–13.

Thompson, C. (1938). Notes on the psychoanalytic significance of the choice of analyst. *Psychiat.* 1:205–216.
Ticho, E. A. (1971). The effects of the analyst's personality on psychoanalytic treatment. *Psychoanal. Forum* 4:137–151.
Tyson, P. (1980). The gender of the analyst. *Psychoanal. Study Child* 35:321–338.
Wolberg, L. R. (1954). *The Techniques of Psychotherapy,* Vol. I. New York: Grune & Stratton.
Zetzel, E. R. (1970). The doctor-patient relationship in psychiatry. In *The Capacity for Emotional Growth.* New York: Int. Univ. Press, pp. 139–155.

4/
Discussion:
Theoretical and Technical Considerations of Cross-Gender Transferences with Male Patients
Phyllis Tyson, Ph.D.

> Contrary to Nancy Mann Kulish's contention that the reality of the therapist's gender influences the transference, this paper looks at the conditions under which reality factors, such as the therapist's gender, recede into the background. The developmental level of the patient's pathology and the therapist's technique are considered to be major factors influencing the probability that crucial infantile object relations and related conflicts will be revived and relived in relation to the person of the therapist—no matter what the gender.

The ways in which the gender of the therapist shapes the transference is an issue, Nancy Mann Kulish suggests, that should not be overlooked. Rather than accepting the traditional view that the therapist's gender is of only minor importance, she asserts that the therapist's gender is often of major importance in the patient's selection of a therapist, in determining the course of treatment, as an organizing influence on the therapist's way of understanding the material, in influencing the therapist's technique, and as a contributor to strong resistances. In support of her previously published conclusion (Kulish, 1984) that the importance of the therapist's gender is an issue that deserves further research, Kulish here presents clinical material that demonstrates how one of her male patients consistently related to her as a woman. The reality of her gender, Kulish felt, was a major factor in determining the man's choice of her as a therapist and in influencing the course of therapy. She cites the observation made by several authors (Stone, 1954; Karme, 1979; Szmarag, 1982), and corroborated by her experience with her patient, that when men are analyzed by women, the father transference is seldom elaborated and there are few reports of strong erotic transferences. This, she emphasizes, is in marked contrast to the reports of the experiences of male analysts with female patients.

From the wealth of theoretical and clinical material Kulish presents, I shall limit my comments to the following: I shall first consider the difference between transference and transference neurosis to point out possible differences between psychotherapy and psychoanalysis. Then I shall discuss the formation of a transference neurosis and suggest two other possible reasons why male patients may not elaborate a father transference or express erotic feelings toward the female therapist; the first reason has to do with the developmental level of psychopathology expressed, and the second, with the attitude and technique of the therapist.

TRANSFERENCE AND TRANSFERENCE NEUROSIS

Discussions and definitions of transference and transference neurosis abound in the literature and I shall not repeat them here. However, an important difference between dynamic psychotherapy and psychoanalysis seems to me to lie in the understanding and use made of transference manifestations. Kulish defines transference as "the unconscious distortions and fantasies about the analyst that originate in the past." As this definition implies, although the therapeutic situation does not create transference, it provides a setting whereby distorting influences from the past can be observed and understood.

However, in the psychoanalytic situation, which usually affords greater continuity and more intense involvement between patient and analyst than in the less frequent psychotherapeutic setting, something additional happens. As the multitude of transference manifestations become activated, the analyst becomes the key object in the repetition and successive unfolding of infantile conflicts, and the transference begins to take a different shape. Rather than a parade of disparate themes, a new organization emerges. The infantile neurosis becomes alive, and although different in form from the original childhood prototype, infantile conflicts become organized, revived and *relived,* through the interaction with the analyst (Blum, 1971). This difference in form has come to be known as the transference neurosis. "In the transference neurosis, the analyst is perceived and reacted to in terms of the crucial infantile object representations, allowing a living redramatization of the distorting influence of the past" (Blum, 1971, p. 43). In the transference neurosis the patient's total personality becomes involved. Eventually all infantile object representations become reactivated as a part of this all-encompassing and continually evolving whole, as the transference leads to the forgotten past (Freud, 1912).

As these comments imply, the transference neurosis, once it emerges, becomes a primary means by which we can begin to understand the patient's past and present psychic reality. If and when a transference neurosis develops (and it by no means develops in the same way or to the same extent in every analysis), it assumes a form whereby conflicts from all developmental levels and affects felt toward all infantile objects eventually find expression. My own experience has been that once a transference neurosis emerges, resistances to the transference can eventually be analyzed so that erotic feelings and the father transference do find expression. This experience leads me to the opinion that if and when a transference neurosis develops, reality factors such as the gender of the analyst recede into the background.

By thus stressing the centrality of the transference neurosis, one should not take the goal of analysis simply as the analysis of the transference neurosis, in this way mistaking the means for the end and disregarding the reality of the patient's past and present. Rangell (1979) points out that although the transference neurosis is the path to the goal, the means by which the origins of the patient's neurosis become manifest, the analysis of the transference can be overdone, obscuring other important and necessary elements of the analytic process. As Rangell puts it, "the analyst roams": "With his free-floating attention, the analyst oversees the patient's associations to past and present, the transference and external figures, the unconscious and reality, dreams, symptoms, memories, and fantasies, the trivial and everyday" (p. 95).

IMPLICATIONS OF DEVELOPMENTAL LEVEL FOR TRANSFERENCE AND TRANSFERENCE NEUROSIS

Important to the consideration of transference and transference neurosis is the developmental level of the patient's psychopathology. A transference neurosis presupposes an infantile neurosis in early childhood. However, there may be, as Blum (1971) points out, internal and external limitations to the extent to which a transference neurosis may develop, or even to its appearance at all. The transformation of a variety of transference phenomena into a transference neurosis depends on whether symptoms, character, and personality structure reflect fixation and regression of arrest and deviation.

Anna Freud (1971) notes that the construction of an infantile neurosis presupposes the successful negotiation of various important developmental steps. Constitutional defects, early deprivations, overstimulation, lack of suitable objects, trauma, all may interfere with the capacity for object relatedness, and hence the achievement of libidinal object constancy (Mahler and McDevitt, 1980) with its integrating and structuralizing effects. The ego may emerge from early experiences as immature, deformed, distorted, lacking integration, and lacking in its capacity to adequately test reality, modulate affects, or instigate defense. Overstimulation or undue frustration may result in a basic amorphous tension associated with a high level of aggressive potential (Weil, 1978), or with premature and excessive genital stimulation (Greenacre, 1952). Affects associated with these states undermine the immature ego's synthesizing capacity. Excessive anger, anxiety, and sexual excitement in turn intensify phase-specific conflicts and predispose the individual to sadomasochistic interactions, sexual perversions, or other deviations which burden later conflicts. Weil (1978) points out that such children develop a projection-expectation mechanism in conjunction with lurid fantasies and fears so that even the adequate mother is experienced as inadequate and bad. Extraordinary ambivalence and narcissistic vulnerability from the preoedipal period then interfere with the Oedipus complex; oedipal wishes and conflicts are inadequately elaborated, and distorted solutions are found. Superego integration and internalization are compromised, and the superego may retain an archaic, sadistic quality which is easily projected (Blum, 1980; Tyson and Tyson, 1984). Anna Freud (1971) notes that such developmental failures result in clinical pictures on the border of much more severe pathology or in disjointed neurotic symptom formation corresponding to preoedipal personality organization.

Optimal early experience, in contrast to the previously discussed picture, contributes to rather than disrupts ego structuralization (cf. Mahler and McDevitt, 1980; Settlage, 1980). Experiences with objects become increasingly complicated and contribute to an increasingly complex and stable internal organization, leading eventually to the infantile neurosis. As Anna Freud (1971) puts it:

> Unlike its forerunners, what is now the infantile neurosis is no longer the ego's answer to the frustration of single trends, but is an elaborate attempt to deal with the whole upheaval caused by the action of conflicting drive derivatives; conflicting, exciting, pleasurable or painful affects; mutually exclusive attitudes toward objects, i.e., with the whole range of the Oedipus complex and castration complex, set against the background of personal qualities and characteristics which have been established from infancy onward, and shaped by the fixation points which have been left behind during development [p. 87].

The reason why analysts place such stress on the transference neurosis is because the transference neurosis transforms varied transference phenomena into an integrated whole, just as the infantile neurosis on which it is based integrates the personality. As Anna Freud goes on to suggest, "Insight into these complex interactions between past and present, background and actuality, ego qualities and instinctual trends, conflicting identifications, opposite id tendencies, etc., are revealed to us in every analysis of an infantile neurosis" (pp. 87–88).

From these comments, it follows that among the several possible reasons that neither the father transference nor erotic feelings are expressed in some analyses or therapies of male patients with female therapists, is that these expressions are derivatives of an Oedipus complex distorted in a particular way. If profound preoedipal pathology interfered with the full flowering of or rapid retreat from the Oedipus complex in early childhood, a fully developed infantile neurosis with its organizing and integrating influences, may not have developed. Although I would agree with Rangell (1979) that every borderline patient has oedipal wishes and conflicts, and every neurotic has preoedipal conflicts and narcissistic issues, in the patients I refer to here, the degree of organization and integration of the ego and the superego that results from an adequately formed infantile neurosis is lacking. A male patient, for example, may be unable to elaborate oedipal wishes with erotic longing toward his mother, either because she was unavailable and seen to be castrating or rejecting, or because the threat of castration from the father was too great; or it may have been that he was unable to view his father as ideal and to wish to be the object of his love. As a result, he may have been unable to experience his positive oedipal wishes in conflict with his negative oedipal wishes, and then unable to resolve these oedipal conflicts by identifying with the moral standards of both parents and thus to internalize a superego. In such instances, which occur often enough, the affects associated with these wishes and conflicts will be experienced as disorganizing until preoedipal psychopathology is dealt with in treatment. As such, these affects will stimulate enormous resistance to the development and elaboration of the transference.

For example, we might expect that a man's expression of erotic wishes toward his female therapist may be extremely threatening. He may fear enactment, suggesting weak ego integration, or he may fear rejection and humiliation, which undermines his sense of masculinity. The lack of gratification of such erotic wishes, once expressed, may stimulate a variety of painful feelings. Furthermore, the emergence of erotic feelings derived from positive oedipal wishes reactivates the infantile mother-child relationship; the patient, without adequate consolidation of ego and superego organization and resultant psychic stability and autonomy, may fear regression to the helpless, impotent, passive-dependent preoedipal position with its attendant fears of loss of love, loss of autonomy, or wishes for and anxieties about merging. Various defenses may be used to ward off the associated anxieties, some of which may lead to heightened resistance to further transference involvement.

Resistance to the father transference with a woman therapist may be equally strong where preoedipal pathology is severe. Prolonged symbiosis or heightened anal-rapprochement aggression may undermine the male sense of body integrity and lead to a feminine identification or heightened fear of castration. Easily projected anger may be displaced from mother to father, interfering with the boy's view of father as ideal, delaying male role identification, undermining the sense of masculinity, and delaying positive oedipal involvement (see Edgcumbe and Burgner, 1975; Tyson, 1982). In addition, the normal identification with the father in attempts to resolve the Oedipus complex, and in further internalization of a superego, remains incomplete (see Tyson and Tyson, 1984).

Ross (1983) points out how a father's envy and hostility to his young son can further complicate the boy's development. Fathers often compete with the mother in mothering the boy, compete with the son for the mother's attention, are particularly aggressive in overstimulating ways, and may be possessive of the young boy in an attempt to relive an idealized relationship with their own fathers. Father's domination "invites" sexualized submission, which excites idealization of the father and denigration of the mother. The resolution of preoedipal ambivalence to the mother is interfered with and the boy is forced to cling to an idealized view of the father, delaying positive oedipal movement. Often exaggerated masculine traits, or caricatures of them, appear, but this exaggerated masculinity does not become fully integrated into the personality and the boy remains fixed at the dyadic, phallic-narcissistic level. The idealized sadomasochistic relationship impedes mature reciprocal relationships with women. Furthermore, the boy's loyalty to his father may be exaggerated by the father's possessiveness and envy of his son's phallic prowess (an envy which may lead the father into unconscious, homosexual seductive interactions with him), and any positive oedipal wishes may lead to feelings of guilt and disloyalty toward father. Again his full engagement with the mother on a positive oedipal level is thwarted. Because this enormous idealization of the father provides some gratification, at least in fantasy, as the boy seeks to maintain the narcissistically gratifying, idealized dyadic relationship with the father, great resistance is encountered when attempts are made to analyze it. When the analyst is a woman, the reality of her gender may then appear to be the primary obstacle.

IMPLICATIONS FOR TECHNIQUE

As my remarks about infantile neurosis and transference neurosis suggest, my clinical experience shows that whether or not a man in therapy with a woman is able to express erotic feelings toward her, or elaborate a father transference, is more dependent on the developmental level of his psychopathology than on the gender of the therapist. Yet determining the highest developmental level achieved is a difficult task and one that may not be readily determined by manifest behavior. What appears to be an arrest may be a regression where preoedipal conflicts defend oedipal themes. On the other hand, what may appear to be resistance to higher-level themes may in fact be the expression of the patient's highest level of functioning.

Frequently, however, the attitude of the therapist and his or her approach to the material determines whether or not unrelated transference themes can be organized into an integrated whole. The analyst must approach the material with free-floating attention, flexibility, and without previously conceived diagnostic notions. The analyst can then see derivatives from all developmental levels and, through interpretation, facilitate their integration.

Here I would disagree with Kulish's approach. She appears at least at times to interpret material according to preconceived attitudes and strategies, a conclusion I have drawn from comments such as: "This intervention is consistent with my strategy and reasoning throughout the treatment: to focus on the transference, peeling away negative feelings the patient puts up as blocks against positive feelings toward me." This position may have made it difficult for Kulish to distinguish between transference, transference resistance, and what may have been reality-based. It may have also interfered with her viewing the material from more than one perspective and dealing with it accordingly. Consequently, the patient's elaboration of a variety of transference themes revealing derivatives of oedipal and preoedipal feelings about father and mother might have been restricted. Her comment, for example, suggests that she views the negative attitude as a resistance to the positive oedipal, but it might equally represent a defense against dependent longings accompanied by regressive fears of merging, a theme frequently seen in patients with homosexual behavior (Socarides, 1978). Her intervention strategy may have also interfered with the expression of negative oedipal themes. That is, if she expects the patient to express (or to resist the expression of) erotic feelings toward her as a woman, she may overlook the possibility that he is defending against erotic feelings expressed toward her as a man. Her preconceived strategy would then interfere with her recognition of the father transference and thus her interpretation forecloses elaboration of the father transference.

Assuming that the possibility of forming a transference neurosis exists, i.e., that the clinical picture represents a regression to an earlier fixation point rather than arrested development, we might further examine the conditions under which transference themes become organized into a transference neurosis. First of all, the treatment situation and the therapist's attitude and approach must facilitate such a development. Except in unusual circumstances, it is generally felt that the intensity and frequency of the psychoanalytic situation is a necessity for the full emergence of a transference neurosis. In psychotherapy, sessions are generally not so frequent and the face-to-face situation tends to play into the reinforcement of reality factors rather than to permit the regressive reactivation of unconscious psychic motifs. Furthermore, the patient's extra-analytic object relations tend to be much more the focus in psychotherapy, and less attention may be directed to the interaction between the therapist and the patient. In these instances I would agree that the reality of the therapist's gender may play a much larger part in determining the kinds of material that emerge and that can be worked through, as contrasted with psychoanalysis, in which the focus is the elaboration and interpretation of the transference neurosis.

Technically, our goal now becomes to replace the patient's "ordinary neurosis by a 'transference neurosis' of which he can be cured by the therapeutic work" (Freud, 1914, p. 154). Recognizing that the transference neurosis is not an entity to be found in the patient but an operational concept, Loewald (1971, p. 61) notes that our task is the "retransformation of a psychic illness which originated in pathogenic interactions with the important persons in the child's environment, into an interactional process with a new person, the analyst, in which the pathological infantile interactions and their intrapsychic consequences may become transparent and accessible to change by virtue of the analyst's objectivity and of the emergence of novel interaction-possibilities." Loewald clarifies that whereas transference manifestations are essentially automatic responses, signs and symptoms, the transference neurosis is a live, responsive process which is changing and changeable.

It follows that preconceived strategies and techniques may interfere with the emergence and full elaboration of a transference neurosis not only in psychoanalysis but also in psychotherapy. Thus, again, I have misgivings when Kulish appears to take a fixed technical stance indicated by her words: "I had determined to proceed cautiously and try to keep quiet." I wondered here whether or not she might be interpreting the "screen" idea to mean that the therapist should be a nonparticipant rather than that the therapist should not contaminate the patient's ideas and associations with his or her own thoughts and feelings. One also wonders why it appeared to be so difficult to keep quiet. Was she struggling with feelings of her own, perhaps a countertransference response not mentioned by her? Furthermore, when she makes comments such as "I repeatedly reminded him that the repulsion and moral indignation he attributed to me were his own feelings and prevented him from exploring the meaning of his fantasies," one wonders if her need to intervene in such a manner may have interfered with her hearing other themes, or interfered with the patient's further elaborating his feelings about her. He may, for example, have understood her repeated interpretation to be a reproach indicating that she was not comfortable with his expression of hostility to her, thus halting further elaboration, exploration, and ultimate resolution of preoedipal aggression. Failure to resolve aggressive impulses would then interfere with full expression of either positive or negative oedipal themes, and neither erotic nor paternal transference themes could be engaged.

Admittedly, the integration of both positive and negative oedipal themes, as manifested by erotic feelings and paternal transference directed toward the female therapist, is a challenge; these are areas of particular resistance, and they may be well disguised. Furthermore, the patient may perceive that his feelings toward his therapist may not be consistent with the reality of her gender, and he may then feel his feelings "don't make sense," or collusively misinterpret paternal transference to be maternal transference.

CLINICAL ILLUSTRATION

I would like to present some clinical material from the analysis of Mr. D. to illustrate the development of a transference neurosis. In this example, preoedipal and oedipal derivatives of the relationship to both father and mother are revived and relived in the transference neurosis, and the reality of the analyst's gender recedes into the background.

Mr. D., a 32-year-old professional, complained that he always felt sexually inadequate and at the mercy of women. He claims that he feels he works hard in the analysis to please me but gets little reward. His thoughts turn to his male supervisor, who keeps asking more and more. He feels that whatever work he accomplished does not count for anything. Often, he feels his supervisor misjudges a situation when giving him an assignment, and often the assignments turn out to be impossible. Yet he never questions his supervisor, just feels that he is doing a bad job. He sighs and says he wishes he could stand up to him. I interject: as he wishes he could stand up to me. He admits he feels angry at me for an earlier comment on his reluctance to express his anger toward me.

The next night Mr. D. has a dream in which he is coming into a classroom and he has not read the assignment. His heart is pounding as he fears he will fail. He awakes very anxious. He comes to his appointment the next day feeling very depressed. He feels I was saying he had to be angry with me or he could not have an analysis, but he couldn't be angry with me, I am his only meaningful relationship. He says he is afraid that he is going to fail at analysis. We reconstruct that he feels with me as he felt as a child with his father—he could never live up to his father's expectations. He then describes the terrible memories of his school days, where his grades were always low and his father berated him, saying there was no excuse for his poor performance. He also remembers repetitive dreams like the one reported, in which he was in class, unprepared, and he would wake up extremely anxious. "I had to be the kind of person my father wanted me to be," he declares. "I couldn't say no. As a kid I was afraid of punishment. Dad had tremendous anger, or he'd give me long, moralistic lectures about what a horrible person I was, but I was afraid of being cut off, having him ignore me; I was afraid of being emotionally abandoned. Then it would have been just me and mother. That was a frightening thought; she was inhuman, she'd attack physically and emotionally, it was just abuse. Dad was like a buffer, he was all I had, but he was so critical."

I ask him if he has ever thought that his father might be wrong. "Well, yes," he answered, "but I used to convince myself that he was right." I say, "Like you felt convinced I was right that you had to express anger toward me." He admits he fears my rejecting criticism, that he is not doing analysis the "right way," and he fears I will quote some moralistic analytic rule that he is breaking. I now understand that the transference reflects the same attitudes toward me as he earlier felt toward his father.

That night Mr. D. dreams that he is coming to his appointment, but instead of my office, the room looks more like an apartment, and instead of my living with my husband, I am living with a woman. In the dream he feels anxious, is afraid that I have had a fight with my husband which has changed my feelings about men, and I will now be hostile toward him. He thinks I may lie on the bed, but I end up sitting on a chair and we have a nice conversation.

Mr. D. finds it difficult to associate to the dream and admits he finds it hard to talk about his feelings about me—he's afraid I will laugh. He comments, "In the dream it was easy to talk, but I was a little apprehensive; I wasn't sure what you were going to say and your husband was not there." Analysis of the dream reveals sexual wishes about me, yet feelings of humiliation at expressing these. He says he feels that his relationship with me is like looking through the window of a candy store; he feels sexually attracted to me and therefore fears that I could easily manipulate him and take advantage of him. He feels I talk to him because of our special relationship, but otherwise he is left out. He claims he feels unmasculine when talking like this. His masculine ideal holds the view that he should be accepted by every woman. To be rejected by me after exposing his feelings not only repeats his oedipal disappointment but also makes him feel he has not lived up to his masculine ideal based on his father's view of masculinity. The presence of my husband in the dream represents his wish to turn from the disappointing, rejecting, and possibly castrating mother to the more loving father. His presence also represents a reassurance that Mr. D. will be safe from acting out his sexual impulses toward me. From his comments about his mother the day before (as well as earlier in the analysis), we come to see that the dream also represents his reassurance that I will not hurt him. By turning me into a homosexual, i.e., living with a woman instead of a man, he ensures that I will not be interested in his penis. Yet his portrayal of me as a homosexual also represents his homosexual wishes in a more disguised way (two women instead of two men). He wishes that I would be the man who protects him from the woman, and who loves him. He confirms this interpretation by describing fears of becoming dependent on me, as on his dad. He is afraid that he will have to give up his autonomy.

Homosexual desires and anxieties as well as many other aspects of this man's relationship with his father were expressed in relationship to me throughout his analysis. Mr. D. expressed not only his fear and longings for passive dependency on me, but also his longings to repeat with me the idealized father-son relationship. He wished I would tell him what to do so that I could be proud and pleased with him. The transference increasingly reflected his wish to view me as a strong, masculine role model. However, such wishes further aroused his fear of homosexuality. He had a dream of being attacked homosexually and felt the attacker in the dream was me. He became extremely anxious and felt I was trying to trap him into homosexuality by "making" him talk about it.

Sexual erotic feelings were also expressed. Mr. D. said he felt that these feelings and fantasies make him feel weak and unmasculine. He knew his fantasies were futile, which made him feel like a small child. His sense of oedipal failure as a source of his passivity and feelings of vulnerability with regard to women then came into the analysis and eventually led to his fears of dependency, loss, and abandonment.

CONCLUSION

Elsewhere (Tyson, 1980) I have suggested that the way in which the patient perceives particular "real" qualities of the analyst, assigns meaning to these qualities, and then utilizes them has relevance to the patient's psychic reality, which in turn influences the evolving transference. I remain of the opinion that it is as a part of this factor that the gender of the analyst finds its place; its importance is not simply as a part of external reality, nor exclusively as part of the so-called real relationship, but as a consequence of the meaning it comes to have for the patient. To say that the reality of the analyst's gender diminishes the male patient's expression of erotic feelings, or decreases feelings derived from the paternal transference, essentially suggests that a man cannot have an analysis with a woman, since vast areas of his unconscious life would not find expression. I feel it to be otherwise. Therefore, Kulish's conclusion may be relevant to psychotherapy in certain cases but, in my opinion, it does not have general applicability. Perhaps the challenge is for the female therapist to devise novel approaches to the male patient's resistances so that we can better facilitate the expression of wider areas of a man's unconscious life.

REFERENCES

Blum, H. P. (1971). On the conception and development of the transference neurosis. *J. Amer. Psychoanal. Assn.* 19:41–53.
—— (1980). Paranoia and beating fantasy: An inquiry into the psychoanalytic theory of paranoia. *J. Amer. Psychoanal. Assn.* 28:331–361.
Edgcumbe, R., & Burgner, M. (1975). The phallic narcissistic phase: A differentiation between preoedipal and oedipal aspects of phallic development. *Psychoanal. Study Child* 30:161–180.
Freud, A. (1971). The infantile neurosis: Genetic and dynamic considerations. *Psychoanal. Study Child* 26:79–90.
Freud, S. (1912). The dynamics of transference. *Standard Edition* 12:99–108.
—— (1914). Remembering, repeating and working-through. *Standard Edition* 12:145–156.
—— (1916–1917). Introductory lectures on psychoanalysis. *Standard Edition*, 15 & 16.
Greenacre, P. (1952). *Trauma, Growth, and Personality.* New York: Norton.
Karme, L. (1979). The analysis of a male patient by a female analyst: The problem of the negative oedipal transference. *Int J. Psychoanal.* 60:253–261.
Kulish, N. M. (1984). The effect of the sex of the analyst on transference: A review of the literature. *Bull. Menninger Clinic* 48:95–110.
Loewald, H. W. (1971). The transference neurosis: Comments on the concept and the phenomenon. *J. Amer. Psychoanal. Assn.* 19:54–66.
Mahler, M. S., & McDevitt, J. B. (1980). The separation-individuation process and identity formation. In *The Course of Life, Vol. I: Infancy and Early Childhood,* ed. S. Greenspan & G. Pollock. Bethesda: National Institute of Mental Health, pp. 395–406.
McDevitt, J. B., & Mahler, M. S. (1980). Object constancy, individuality, and internalization. In *The Course of Life, Vol. I: Infancy and Early Childhood,* ed. S. Greenspan & G. Pollock. Bethesda: National Institute of Mental Health, pp. 407–424.
Rangell, L. (1979). Contemporary issues in the theory of therapy. *J. Amer. Psychoanal. Assn.* 27:81–112.
Ross, J. M. (1983). The darker side of fatherhood: Clinical and developmental ramifications of the "Laius complex." (Unpublished.)
Settlage, C. F. (1980). The psychoanalytic theory and understanding of psychic development during the second and third years of life. In *The Course of Life, Vol. I: Infancy and Early Childhood,* ed. S. Greenspan & G. Pollock. Bethesda: National Institute of Mental Health, pp. 523–540.

Socarides, C. (1978). *Homosexuality*. New York: Aronson.
Stone, L. (1954). The widening scope of indications for psychoanalysis. *J. Amer. Psychoanal. Assn.* 2:567–594.
Szmarag, R. (1982). Panel report: Erotic transference and countertransference between the female therapist and the male patient. *Acad. Forum* 26:11–13.
Tyson, P. (1980). The gender of the analyst: In relation to transference manifestations in prelatency children. *Psychoanal. Study Child* 35:321–338.
——— (1982). A developmental line of gender identity, gender role and choice of love object. *J. Amer. Psychoanal. Assn.* 30:59–84.
——— & Tyson, R. L. (1984). Narcissism and superego development. *J. Amer. Psychoanal. Assn.* 32:63–74.
Weil, A. P. (1978). Maturational variations and genetic-dynamic issues. *J. Amer. Psychoanal. Assn.* 26:461–491.

5/
Early Developmental Processes and Adult Intimate Violence
Linda Jean Strothman, A.M., A.C.S.W.

Although in the past decade domestic violence has been highlighted as a social and political issue, clinical evaluations of this phenomenon have been sparse. This paper views intimate violence as a multidetermined phenomenon, with psychological as well as sociocultural aspects. Specifically, it is proposed that domestic violence entails some failure in the development or maintenance of the capacity for intimacy. From this perspective, selected processes in early development are examined for their bearing on adult participation in violent intimate relationships. Failures in symbiosis, oral-phase precursors of masochistic tendencies, derailments in the development of the self, narcissistic rage, splitting, and projective identification are all discussed with illustrative case material.

Domestic violence occurs in 50 percent of American families (Hilberman, 1980). Each year in the United States, at least six million men, women, and children are the victims of severe physical attacks by their spouses or parents (Gelles, 1979).

In the last ten years, as domestic violence has become highlighted as a social and political issue, a respectable body of literature has focused on the sociological and cultural variables (Pizzey, 1974; Steinmetz and Straus, 1973; 1974; Steinmetz, 1974; Martin, 1975; Roy 1977; Dobash and

---

This paper is part of a more comprehensive work in progress, portions of which have been presented at the Illinois NASW Clinical Lecture Series, January 1982; the first International Pediatric Social Work Conference, Chicago, August 1982; and the NASW Illinois Chapter Second Biennial Symposium, October 1982. The author wishes to thank Ann Schreiner, A.M., A.C.S.W.; Annette Hulefeld, M.S.W.; and Phyllis Spinal, M.S.W., for their assistance in preparing the case material.

Roy, 1977; Dobash, 1979; Fleming, 1979; Gelles, 1979; Walker, 1979; Straus and Hotaling, 1980; Pfouts and Renz, 1981). Descriptions of the feelings and behaviors of men and women involved in intimate violence correspond with reports by clients in therapy; however, explanations of these feelings and behaviors have been mostly in other than clinical terms, with the exception of a handful of articles (Elbow, 1977; Shainess, 1977; Symonds, 1978; Gillman, 1980; Hilberman, 1980).

The feminist movement, in highlighting the social and political aspects of this problem has transformed spouse abuse from a shameful, secret, and individual problem into a social problem of some significance (Pfouts and Renz, 1981). As the stigma has been reduced, countless families who might not otherwise have sought help have made use of a wide range of new services as well as traditional psychotherapy. Highlighting the sociocultural and institutional supports for the continued cultural acceptance of family violence has stimulated change in various institutions that deal with family violence, particularly the legal and law enforcement systems.

An unfortunate byproduct of these efforts has been the trend toward "redefining" the problem of "wife abuse . . . as a *problem not of the individual but of a patriarchial society* in which men held disproportionate power . . . and women were subservient to men" (Pfouts and Renz, 1981; my italics). Clinicians have been repeatedly criticized for "blaming the victim" (Martin, 1975; Fleming, 1979; Hilberman, 1980; Pfouts and Renz, 1981). Psychoanalytically oriented clinicians in particular have been criticized for applying the concept of "female masochism" to abused wives (Martin, 1975; Fleming, 1979; Hilberman, 1980). Although the pejorative use of labels is reprehensible in any context, to attempt to rectify this use of labels by attacking the nosology ultimately solves nothing, since any category can be used in a derogatory manner. To have no categories is to operate on intuition and idiosyncrasy alone, to forever have to reinvent the wheel, and to cut oneself off from accumulated knowledge; to be enslaved to rigidly-construed categories is to mask perception of individual differences, and to abandon creative thinking.

Given the high incidence of domestic violence, most people involved in it will be seen by general practice clinicians rather than by specialists in domestic violence. It is therefore critical that the dynamics of marital violence become integrated into the ongoing theoretical and treatment literature in the major clinical schools of thought and that the theory most relevant to this phenomenon be extracted and systematized.

This paper is part of a more comprehensive work that undertakes the task of placing the phenomenon of domestic violence in the context of developmental and psychodynamic theory. The general perspective of this large work will be summarized before turning to selected aspects of early development that seem to be related to adult participation in violent intimate relationships.

GENERAL PERSPECTIVE

Domestic violence is multidetermined; it is simultaneously an intrapsychic, interpersonal, and social event. A particular incident of intimate violence occurs as a function of the interaction of five variables: (1) the intrapsychic structure, and dynamics of the family members, (2) the structure of the family system, (3) the processes and adaptability of the family system, (4) the amount of acute and chronic stress on the family members, and (5) the influence of cultural norms that encourage (tolerate) or discourage (do not tolerate) violence as a means of expression or conflict resolution. Theoretically, a violent act could occur within any couple. The partners' reactions to this act and the evolution of one incident into a chronic or escalating pattern are influenced most by intrapsychic and interpersonal factors. The cultural milieu and social structure have a profound impact on whether this behavior is seen as a problem by members of the family and whether services are available. Cultural norms interlock with intrapsychic variables so that intimate violence, particularly that directed by men against women, is too often culturally syntonic; it takes place as a function of commonly held internalizations of social roles and infantile reactions to the all-powerful mother (envy, helplessness, and defenses against these). Both men and women then participate in maintaining the devaluation of women and traditional sexual stereotypes (Lederer, 1968; Lerner, 1974; Dowling, 1981).

From a clinical perspective, domestic violence is a symptom not a diagnostic entity, with the violence serving a variety of adaptive and maladaptive functions for the persons involved. Although the function and meaning of violence differ from couple to couple, some patterns of violence seem to vary consistently with personality types. At the same time, even though there is a preponderance of borderline, narcissistic, impulse-disordered, and masochistically-involved personalities in this population, intimate violence does occur across a full diagnostic range. The elaboration of the typology of patterns of violence related to diagnostic types is beyond the scope of the present paper.

Among the universal consequences of living in an ongoing, violent intimate relationship are erosion of self-esteem, disruption of ego functioning, and increased social isolation and feelings of powerlessness in both partners. Over time there is an increasing limitation of perspective, intensified shame, and regression in the personalities of the participants. The reactions of the abused adult are often similar to those of abused children (Martin and Redeheffer, 1980) and, in extreme situations, to those of prisoners of war.

Domestic violence represents one type of distortion in the achievement of intimacy. Intimacy is simultaneously a developmental achievement (Erikson, 1950; Kernberg, 1976), a process (Horney, 1967; Giovacchini, 1976), and a type of ongoing object relationship (Winnicott, 1965; Giovacchini, 1975; Kernberg, 1976; Kohut, 1978). As a *developmental achievement,* it presupposes—indeed requires—(1) a fully developed cohesive self, (2) the capacity to see the other as a separate object with a separate source of initiative (libidinal object constancy), (3) ego development sufficient to allow fusion in self-abandon without fragmentation or panic, (4) superego development sufficient to carry out the need for commitment, and (5) genital supremacy in psychosexual development. Viewed as a *process,* intimacy implies that two people relate on all levels of their personalities. The ability to relate symbiotically without losing the boundaries of the self is essential. The process is dominated by mutuality, reciprocity, orgastic satisfactions, and enhancement of the self. At the same time, as a type of ongoing *object relationship,* intimacy is characterized by commitment and concern for each other, as well as respect for each other's autonomy. The partners function as equilibrating forces for each other due to the presence of ego as well as id involvement. The need for the other is equal even though this may not be obvious; both partners feel on some level that they need each other for survival. Indeed, behavioral roles are often reversed if the relationship is disrupted. Defenses are either similar or complementary (Giovacchini, 1975).

There is some disagreement among theoreticians about the role of aggression in intimacy. Erikson (1950) optimistically describes orgasm in sexual relations as a vehicle for "taking the edge off hostilities," but others see aggression within an intimate relationship as more intractable and inevitable. Kernberg (1980) states: "The couple's emotional relationship permits an intimacy which gratifies many human needs; *but intimacy also threatens the release of aggression.* The danger of uncontrolled intimacy . . . is compensated for by the ongoing re-creation of areas of secrecy and mystery" (pp. 304–305; my italics). Winnicott (1975) presents aggression as "a part of the primitive expression of love." (p. 205) He indicates that "aggression is almost synonymous with activity; it is a matter of part function." (p. 204) Rochlin (1973) views aggression as always a reciprocal part of narcissism, a person's "engine for neutralizing or transcending the constant threats to his vulnerable self." For the domestic violence population, Kernberg's and Rochlin's perspectives seem the most applicable.

If domestic violence is viewed as one type of distortion in the achievement of intimacy, then we may look to the capacities and tasks involved in the development of adult intimacy as a starting point for discovering developmental vulnerabilities related to adult intimate violence. In the first two years of life, for instance, the developmental experiences most pertinent to adult intimate violence seem to be:

1. The quality and intensity of the symbiotic phase, which is drawn on universally in the later process of intimate relations (Giovacchini, 1975, 1976).
2. The adequacy of oral-phase gratifications, since oral fixations predispose toward later masochistic compensations (Berliner, 1947; Panken, 1973; Molinger, 1982).
3. The quality and development of the cohesive core self, which is necessary in order to participate in intimacy without fears of fragmentation of the self (Kohut, 1978).
4. The experiences of narcissistic rage and narcissistic vulnerability in relation to aggression, which establish the prototype for the degree of narcissistic vulnerability throughout life and for the aggressive reactions to cope with it (Rochlin, 1973; Kernberg, 1976; Kohut, 1978).
5. The use of the mechanisms of splitting and projective identification (Ogden, 1979; Grotstein, 1981), which may combine with deficits in the ego, the self, or internalized object relations to facilitate violent intimate relationships. The maintenance of split object relations, in the configuration of differentiated good self and object and nondifferentiated bad selfobject, contributes to a later acting out of the "masochistic triangle" (Horner, 1979).
6. The resolution of the rapprochement subphase of separation-individuation, since failures in this phase are related to continued dependence on the other as an object to be placated or pleased in the preneurotic personality, and may interfere directly with the capacity to protect the self (Horner, 1979), which is directly related to domestic violence.

Difficulties in the oedipal phase often lead to problems in intimacy other than violence (Kernberg, 1980). Nevertheless, unresolved oedipal issues can lead to a condensing of hostility from the oedipal period with pregenital issues, especially rage, leading to an intensified vulnerability for violence. Kernberg (1980) notes: "fear and insecurity vis-à-vis women and reaction formations against such insecurity in the form of reactive and/or projected hostility . . . combines . . . with pregenital hostility and guilt toward the maternal figure. Pregenital conflicts, particularly . . . around aggression . . . [and] the pregenital envy of mother reinforces the oedipally determined insecurity of men regarding idealized women" (p. 301).

Another risk is that such severe problems may occur during the oedipal period that the person regresses in a massive way to an earlier position, thus increasing the risk of later participation in intimate violence. Yet another difficulty that can become manifest during the oedipal period through the interaction of oedipal and preoedipal issues is the acting out of the "masochistic triangle" (Horner, 1979). The preoedipal intrapsychic split of good and bad objects is acted out in the context of a triangle, in which there remains a tenacious attachment to (and lack of differentiation from) the bad object. In this context masochistic behavior then serves as a defense against awareness of early (oral) deprivations from a bad object, and it helps in maintaining the separateness of the good self (Horner, 1979). Here masochistic behavior is seen in the context of object relations rather than drive theory. It is this conceptualization of masochism that is applicable to couples involved in intimate violence.

The most important late adolescent and young adult tasks for the development of later intimacy are: (1) the development of a mature genitality, (2) the development of a mature superego that will allow for making commitments, and (3) the transformation of the self into a firmer and deeper identity. The successful reforging of the self is critical to the avoidance of adult intimate violence. If attempts to re-create the self at this stage fail, then the possibility of narcissistic rage erupting because of the reactivation or repetition of earlier injuries exists. Failures in consolidation of the self can also lead to intensified fears of the opposite sex or of losing the self in intimacy, which leads to the use of violence as a form of distancing and protection.

In adulthood the tasks of coupling and parenting are vulnerable because these tasks require solidity and resilience of the self and adaptive regression, respectively. With coupling, difficulties in establishing power, intimacy, and boundaries can trigger violence (Symonds, 1978). If intimacy has the potential for releasing aggression and primitive introjects (Kernberg, 1976), then if the residual introjects and affects are strong enough, they may be released in a personality that is otherwise fairly healthy. If the adaptive regression required in parenthood becomes too complete and intense, violence may be directed at the wife as a maternal figure or toward the child as a competing sibling, or some other variation.

DERAILMENTS IN THE FIRST YEAR

The first year of life encompasses both the symbiotic phase and the oral phase of psychosexual development. Psychic mechanisms developed during the symbiotic phase are utilized in the process of adult intimacy and therefore affect adult intimate violence. Repeated trauma during the oral phase can lead to the later development of masochistic symptoms, defenses, or character structure, any of which may contribute to intimate violence.

Symbiosis (2–5 Months)

Giovacchini (1976) posits that primitive and higher-level processes occur simultaneously in all adult behavior. Indeed, for certain activities, the activation of particular primitive states is necessary. According to Giovacchini, the crucial primitive process in intimate relations is symbiotic fusion, in which "two people are mutually attuned to each other empathically." He points out that infants who experience a smoothly balanced symbiotic relationship with the mother develop the beginnings of self-confidence with the expectation that their needs can be met and that they are capable of getting them met. He associates rage in adults with failure in the symbiotic phase: "Rage . . . and terror . . . would be a sign of an unsatisfactory symbiotic relationship. Such an infant develops feelings of vulnerability and helplessness and concern about survival instead of healthy self-confidence. He may develop compensatory omnipotence as a defense against vulnerability" (p. 420).

Both men and women in violent relationships commonly display strong feelings of vulnerability and helplessness, which are compensated for by demands to control the partner and by violently expressed rage. In some couples the violence emerges as closeness develops because in their early experiences rage and terror were inextricably tied up with closeness. Rage may erupt over "little things," which on the surface seem inconsequential to the outsider, because the "little thing" represents a failure in the other's "reading." Whether this is an actual or a symbolic failure in symbiotic attunement, it is perceived and responded to as if it had the weight of an early failure, as can be seen in the case of Mr. A. and Miss A.

> Mr. A. and Miss A., both 30 years old, have lived together off and on for three of the five years they have been involved. Mr. A. is a long-distance driver for a petroleum manufacturer, and Miss A. is a medical technologist. Miss A. initiated contact with the domestic violence program following an incident in which "there was lots of pushing and shoving of each other" while they were living together (they separated during the early months of treatment).
>
> A typical sequence of interactions involves one expecting the other to "know" what the other needs. Mr. A. asks Miss A. what she wants for Valentine's Day. Miss A. replies, "If you live with someone you should know." He says he doesn't know and keeps asking. She says if he really loved her, he'd know, and kicks him. He continues to demand that she tell him, saying she is never satisfied. She berates him for not knowing. He can't stand criticism in this area since he sees himself as "generous" (he spends lavishly on gifts for people in his life). At this point he grabs her and puts his hand over her mouth "to shut her up." She struggles and gets away from him, berating him for "suffocating" her and not listening to her. Often he flees or orders her out of the house in order to avoid "really hurting her."

Conversely, Mr. A. expects Miss A. to know when he's in a bad mood and wants to be left alone; he especially wants her to know when he is hurt. Once he and Miss A. had an argument at a party, and he left after calling her names, berating her, and telling her he never wanted to see her again. He walked several miles in pouring rain and was "nearly hit by a truck" before he got home. He was upset that she didn't follow him, look for him, or call him to make sure he got home safely because "she should have know I was hurt when I left and something could have happened to me." When she arrived home, he was furious and the argument began again.

Here violence erupts because one has failed to "read" the unspoken needs or feelings of the other, as the symbiotic mother would appropriately "read" the feelings and needs of her infant. In this couple, one finds an uneasy symbiotic tie because insufficiently attuned responses from one partner threaten the other's inner equilibrium and thus increase that person's sense of vulnerability. In the next exchange with the partner, the vulnerable person is therefore less able to be emphatic, and so the exchanges continue with increasing vulnerability for each. The nature of the symbiotic tie is revealed in another vignette:

Mr. A. frequently goes camping, fishing, or hunting by himself. He describes the outdoors as soothing, as the only place he feels really safe, where nothing can attack him, and where he can sleep peacefully through the night. An important part of his self representation is his conception of his "perfect body." He "doesn't get sick like other people . . . [and] can eat or drink anything without getting polluted." Moreover, he denies needing to dress well for the cold weather because he's invulnerable to such seasonal variables. Mr. A. is invested in not being like his father, who has had many serious, stress-related illnesses.

In the relationship with Miss A., Mr. A. "can't stand" for her to be sick, and she "can't stand" for him "not to take care of himself." In an extreme example, Miss A. has stomach pains over a period of weeks, during which Mr. A. tells her they are nothing and "don't hurt." Finally she gets sicker and is hospitalized. Mr. A. comes to the hospital but is unable to tolerate being there and flees to the mountains. He tells her that she can't get sick or he will leave her.

When Mr. A. tells Miss A. her pains don't hurt, he is talking as if they were in his body and he could both experience them and defend against them with the compensatory grandiosity of his perfect body image. In fact, when she gets sick, he is intensely vulnerable because unconsciously he is part of her—if she is sick, then his body image is threatened. By threatening to leave her if she gets sick, he attempts to control her in response to his own inner vulnerability and sense of helplessness. When he can't make her un-sick with these threats, he flees to the mountains in a rage. This need to maintain the sense of a symbiotic tie in which needs are accurately read and reacted to operates in other relationships, especially the therapeutic relationship, as can be seen with another couple:

> Mr. and Mrs. F. had been separated for some months but were working on their relationship in regular joint sessions with the couple and their individual therapists. Mrs. F. had been angry with her therapist, whom she felt "really understood" her, because the therapist would not speak for her in the joint sessions. One evening the couple left after a particularly difficult session and were later observed by staff members, including the therapists, sitting in a nearby coffee shop. The couple appeared to be sitting and talking. The next day Mrs. F. called her therapist and angrily said, "He was badgering me and you *should have known* that he was badgering me and not let him." Meanwhile Mrs. F.'s mother called the agency demanding to know why someone didn't call the police and protect her daughter when they were sitting in the coffee shop.

In this instance, Mrs. F.'s expectation that her therapist, with whom she had had a symbiotic tie, should read her mind (and act as her mother would have) led to rageful behavior when disappointed.

Oral Phase (0–10 Months)

The development of masochistic formations of varying degrees of intensity in adults has been demonstrated to have some roots in excessive oral-phase deprivations and frustrations (Berliner, 1947; Brenman, 1952; Panken, 1973; Mollinger, 1982). Berliner points out: "Basic emotional disposition is founded on the need for being loved at the level of oral and skin erotism. . . . The child introjects the pain-giving object because of an oral need for its love. . . . The child does not love . . . ill treatment . . . but [does] love the person who gives it. . . . every masochistic patient [had] an unhappy childhood. . . . [that] lives on in the superego" (1947, p. 461).

Symbiosis with and oral dependency on a parent whose treatment fluctuates radically between deprivation, rejection, hostile resentment, or nonaffirmation on the one hand and anxious, oversolicitous, guilty treatment on the other, or whose treatment is consistently negative, lead to oral trauma and create the basic conditions for the development of masochistic adaptations. At this level the child must maintain an attachment and will do so by denying the parent's hostility and nonaffirmation because to recognize this would threaten the relationship. The outcome is that attachment to a hostile object must be both maintained and defended against. Panken (1973) warns: "Retaining the 'good image' of the mother on a pre-ambivalent level, the ego of the child, masochistically and at its own expense, tries to establish and maintain the primitive object relationship . . . [and] remains in a lifelong symbiotic . . . relationship with the undermining parent or later adult partner or parent-surrogate, who for purposes of the individual's own self-preservation, is viewed as benign or 'good' " (pp. 104–105).

Trauma at this level leads to object hunger, a need for tactile contact, exaggerated fears of annihilation, and feelings of helplessness (because the mother-child dyad did not protect the infant from being overwhelmed by such feelings). There are also strong underlying feelings of being rejected and unlovable. The disturbance in mutual regulation (mutual responsiveness) in the mother-child dyad continues into later phases of life. Whether these early traumas lead to the later development of a masochistic character structure or simply to masochistic features in the personality depends on how much these features are reinforced or reworked at later stages of development. However, they are contributory to involvement in violent intimate relationships, as was apparent in the case of Mr. A. and Miss A.:

> Miss A., the oldest of five children, was born when her mother was 33 and her father 45. She describes her father as alcoholic, always working, unavailable, a "good provider" who beat her mother and, to a lesser extent, the children. Mother is described with less definition than father. Miss A. portrays her as a victim who repeatedly suffered serious injuries from father's physical abuse and who failed to protect the children (a task that often fell to Miss A. from a young age). According to Miss A., her relationship with mother was a conflictual one in which there was and continues to be much verbal abuse; yet she claims, "I'm close to my family."
>
> Miss A. has a history of problem drinking. She struggles with maintaining her desired weight, as she uses both food and alcohol to soothe herself when distressed. Miss A. describes herself as "having all my mother's bad characteristics and none of her good ones."
>
> Miss A.'s first romantic involvement occurred at age 23 with a man 12 years older than her and "like my father in temperament, lifestyle." He was extremely jealous and demanded total devotion from her, verbally abusing her when she appeared to be less than totally attentive toward him. The only incident of physical abuse occurred following a party at which she didn't pay sufficient attention to him. He beat her severely, and the injuries required hospitalization. She ended the relationship and took legal action again him. After weeks of his following her and begging her forgiveness, she agreed to resume the relationship, but before this was possible he was killed in an automobile accident.
>
> Miss A. was grief-stricken by the death of her boyfriend and responded with a period of intense self-destructive activity, including drinking contantly for several months, incurring a poor work record, and having an auto accident. She reports praying for someone "with his good qualities and without his bad ones." Mr. A. seemed the "answer to [her] prayers." In describing

her feelings for Mr. A., she stressed that she likes the physical contact of sleeping next to him.

Miss A. was seen twice weekly for individual treatment. In addition, during the initial evaluation period Miss A. and Mr. A. were seen together, and after 18 months of individual treatment, they were also seen jointly by a different therapist, at their request.[1]

In the seventeenth month of treatment, Miss A.'s therapist reported that Miss A. had for some time in the therapeutic relationship shown discomfort with the therapist's lack of hostility toward her. On an intellectual level Miss A. could talk to the therapist about her life and difficulties, but on an affective level she was cautious and distant. Although she could talk about intense feelings outside the sessions, she could not allow herself to experience and share feelings in the sessions. Often she filled up the time with verbalizations as a defense against the uncomfortable quiet of being with another person who was not interacting in an intense and hostile way with her. In the transference she clearly expected such reactions from the therapist. According to the therapist, during this period there had been some pauses in sessions after the therapist had responded empathically; Miss A. seemed "confused on the affective level." At about this time, Miss A. intensified requests for joint sessions with Mr. A. Within the context of her individual treatment, this was seen as a resistance and an attempt to involve the therapist in a situation (a joint session) in which their developing intimacy would be diluted. The therapist would inevitably be easier to cast in a hostile role, since in joint work there would be times when Miss A.'s therapist would seem more allied with Mr. A. or the relationship than with Miss A. To maintain the frame of the individual treatment, Miss A.'s therapist refused to be involved in joint work and began to interpret the resistance on which this was based. Mr. A. and Miss A. were given the option of seeing another therapist in the agency, one who was seeing neither of them individually.

In the first session after Mr. A. and Miss A. had had a session together, Miss A. spent the first 30 minutes describing how well the meeting had gone, commenting on Mr. A.'s reaction, and also complaining about him. Thus, she filled up the session symbolically with other people, which she had been unable to do with the therapist in reality. After this there was a pause during which Miss A. seemed uncomfortable. She then told the therapist that when she was in high school she was able to have "positive relationships," even though she spent a considerable amount of time smoking marijuana or drinking. During this time she kept a journal in which she put down all her negative thoughts and feelings. She indicated she would like to look at it now but

---

[1] In the agency the option of joint sessions is routinely discussed in the assessment period with abusive couples. In some cases individual treatment is recommended, in some cases couples treatment or a combination. Generally there is a period of individual work before any couples work. As we shall see, however, in this case the request for joint sessions had a specific meaning in the context of Miss A.'s individual treatment.

doesn't have it. A previous therapist, seen during the period following the death of her first boyfriend, had asked to see it and never returned it to her. This comment was the most direct communication she had ever made about her fears of the therapeutic relationship. Metaphorically, she was saying, "If I get close, if I share my feelings, you will take them away from me." She then asked the therapist if she [the therapist] "could send for my journal and read it." Metaphorically, she was expressing three things to the therapist. First, she was asking the therapist to intervene on her behalf where she felt powerless to do so. Second, by asking the therapist to "read my feelings in the journal," she expressed a compromise formation—on the one hand, a resistance to the relationship with the therapist because the therapist would know them indirectly, just as when she talks *about* her intense feelings. Finally, she was testing the therapist to see if she would comply and "take away" Miss A.'s feelings.[2] The therapist responded by saying that Miss A. could request the journal herself from the previous therapist, that it was hers and she had a right to it (thus not complying with Miss A.'s conviction that she was powerless to get it and it was lost to her). The therapist added that if Miss A. wanted her to, she would write for the records and request the journal, but that she would return it to Miss A., who could then tell her about it (thus not taking up the offer to "read about my feelings" and not complying with the manifest request but latent test of "taking them away," and placing the sharing of feelings back into the context of the therapeutic relationship).

In this case vignette, we see Miss A. seeking attachment with a hostile object in a repetitive way, as evidenced by her selection and idealization of her first boyfriend; her choosing Mr. A., who interacts with her in painful ways (creating distance, abandoning her when she's sick); and her attempts in the transference to make the therapist into a hostile object and her discomfort with the therapist when she is not. Her oral fixations are apparent in the problems with drinking and eating and the hunger for tactile contact with her partner. Her mother is portrayed as a victim who did not much like her maternal role; she also expressed considerable hostility toward Miss A., both directly in verbal beratings and indirectly in her inaction to protect the children from father's violence. The father is powerful (physically strong), abusive (especially to mother), and remote. These are rather classic characteristics of the families of persons developing masochistic traits (Panken, 1973). Miss A.'s sense of helplessness and fear of annihilation (loss of some part of herself) is expressed in the material about the journals.

---

[2]The concept of "testing" the therapist as it is used here is meant in the contextual framework presented by Harold Sampson and Joseph Weiss from Mt. Zion Hospital, San Francisco. See, for example, their paper "Psychotherapy Research: Theory and Findings" (1982).

Given the importance of symbiosis in intimacy, it seems evident that if the symbiotic phase was overwhelming, dangerous, threatening, or unsatisfying, this emotional climate will be brought to later intimate relationships. Symbiotic attachment to a hostile object leads to later repetitions of this and accompanying masochistic formations to defend against object loss and feelings of helplessness. When two people with feelings of inadequacy begin to reenact experiences in unsatisfactory symbiosis, the synergystic effect is not the "enhancement of two people" that Giovacchini (1976) describes in normal intimacy, but the "de-enhancement" of both, bringing out the worst in each other.

DIFFICULTIES IN THE SECOND YEAR

The second year is also critical to the development of intimate violence because it is simultaneously a period of greater aggression and greater narcissistic vulnerability. If narcissistic aspects are assaulted too often or too severely, narcissistic rage and defects in the development of the self and the ego mechanisms that control aggression may ensue. The cohesive self is developed during this period, and *both* the end product of the self and the process of its development have an impact on later intimate violence. Finally, this is also the period during which the processes of splitting and projective identification develop—processes frequently used in maintaining a violent intimate relationship.

The Self, Aggression, and Narcissistic Rage

According to Kohut (1971), the "archaic grandiose self" and the "omnipotent object" coexist during the symbiotic phase and then gradually separate. Children initially feel omnipotent and enjoy being admired. When they fail to receive the expected admiration or to control the external world, they become aware of their limits and separateness from mother. In order gradually to exchange this grandiosity for healthy self-esteem, children need acceptance of their talents, efforts, and specialness even as they separate. If they do not get it, there is often a wish for mirroring that is split off and continues as a need for reassurance, attention, or applause. This need can create intense vulnerability later in life.

When the child discovers that he or she is not omnipotent and experiences helplessness, one response is to attribute the omnipotence to the parent. By participating vicariously in the perfection attributed to the adult, the child holds onto the omnipotence a little longer and recovers emotional equilibrium. In order gradually to let go of this primitive idealization and internalize the parent's soothing and regulating functions, the child must be able to idealize the parent and the parent must be able to tolerate this idealization and be inherently idealizable to the child. Palombo (1976) makes the case that: "If a boy needs to see his father as a strong powerful protector, one who can reassure him when he feels powerless and helpless, yet . . . his father . . . repeatedly comes home drunk and disheveled, is out of control and abusive, the child will be exposed repeatedly to the trauma of seeing his idol as a god with clay feet" (p. 153). Similarly, a child cannot idealize a mother who is beaten and intimidated and who feels helpless and overwhelmed herself.

Parents who are involved in intimate violence, by that fact alone, may fail to be idealizable, or they may be unable to tolerate the idealizations of their children because these efforts at idealization fall on a depreciated self image. Moreover, since the self is formed through a variety of introjective and projective mechanisms (Socarides, 1968; Kohut, 1971; Ogden, 1979), there is danger that the child will introject the depreciation of one parent by the other. Such depreciation then becomes part of the self (Panken, 1973), and can contribute to the development of masochistic character structure. The availability of only an abused or abusing parent to idealize is thus one link in the intergenerational cycle of abuse. These children are more likely to develop problems in the narcissistic line of development, with or without attendant masochistic features. They grow up to be more prone to narcissistic rage and/or splitting; they also tend to retain in unmodified forms, excessive needs for mirroring, admiration, grandiosity, and perfection. This intergenerational cycle was evident with Mrs. C.:

> Mrs. C., a data-processing clerk, has been married for 15 years to Mr. C., a semiskilled laborer who has been fired from many jobs due to alcoholism. Mr. C. has been hospitalized for alcoholism many times but has never followed through on aftercare. They have one child, a five-year-old son, J. Mrs. C. has been injured seriously enough by her husband to require medical attention several times and hospitalization twice. The violence is increasing in frequency.
>
> Mrs. C. has been in therapy for almost two years. She is seen by her therapist as a severe narcissistic personality who is intensely involved in trying to redo and undo her past in the present relationship, which puts her in increasing danger as Mr. C's capacity for violence increases with alcoholic deterioration and without treatment.
>
> Mrs. C.'s life is filled with deaths and attempts to save others. She is the oldest living sibling in a sibship of six, having one brother who died from SIDS prior to her birth, and two sisters who have died in accidents since becoming adults. She describes both parents as alcoholic and mother as "always in bed" for as long as she can remember. Mother had many ailments,

for which she took many medications, including minor tranquilizers. Father was rarely home; when he was, he beat mother and the children. He was also involved with several other women. Mrs. C. was afraid of her father and remembers being locked in a room by him.

As a child, Mrs. C. said prayers along the lines of "I'll be good if you'll make Mommy well." Mother died in Mrs. C.'s arms at age 15 in spite of her attempts to care for her. Father could not be located for several days, and so the burden of making arrangements fell to Mrs. C. She wondered what she had done wrong and why her bargains with God didn't work. Father immediately remarried, and Mrs. C.'s new stepmother joined the father in being both alcoholic and abusive.

Mrs. C. describes her husband as "the only man ever in my life." Mr. C. frequently accuses her of being crazy or stupid, and she reports that she can't stand it when he says that because she then believes it and has to get him to stop saying it in order to stop believing it. She also indicates, "I married my father . . . sometimes [Mr. C.] is just like a ghost to rise out of the grave and haunt me." Mr. C., however, threatens to kill himself if she leaves him. Mr. C. seems to be both a paternal and maternal figure to Mrs. C., combining the alcoholism and abusiveness with the need to be cared for.

In the twelfth month of her treatment, Mrs. C. was talking about her fear that Mr. C. would hurt her, yet her inability to leave. With much pain, she commented, "I don't know what keeps me from leaving!" The therapist said, "I wonder if it has anything to do with your not wanting to leave your mother." Mrs. C. responded, "I don't know . . . if I'd taken better care of her she would have lived . . . [tears] . . . I used to pray, and make deals with God to let my mother live but she died anyhow . . . My father should have stuck by her and not run around on her, he should have been there [angrily] . . . [pause] . . . If only I stick by him [Mr. C.], he'll get better, he'll change . . . but I can't let him hit me."

Mrs. C. is trying to redo what happened in her childhood with a different outcome. She seeks to stop the violence so as to not be like her mother and to stick by her partner so as to not be like her father; she wants to do a "better" job of caretaking her mother/husband. Her primitive grandiosity is revealed in her conviction that if she just does the right thing she can make another person change (or live). Mrs. C. also has considerable problems in regulating her self-esteem, as evidenced by her reaction to Mr. C.'s calling her stupid or crazy. Mrs. C.'s parents were involved in domestic violence and were not idealizable. Her attempt to identify with her mother has left her with the introject of a drunken, needy, beaten, and unavailable woman, which she has defended herself against by continuing to "try to take care of" her mother/husband. She attempts to make her husband into the object she needs just as she tried to make her mother into the object she needed. Moreover, the pattern of problems in the narcissistic line is now being repeated with her son:

J., age five, a severely borderline child, is being seen in individual therapy, which was begun after Mrs. C. left the shelter and returned to Mr. C. J. has major impairments in ego development, including limited reality testing, poor frustration tolerance, and poor impulse control. In the shelter, in preschool, and in his therapy sessions, he has at times displayed chaotic fragmentation: running wildly, flinging himself on the floor, and saying he'll kill himself. At such time he shows a profound regression in which signal anxiety does not seem to operate. His mental life is flooded with reenactments of the violence and other interactions between his parents. His therapist reports that he has a major arrest at the symbiotic phase, often expressing mother's feelings, fears, and anger. In this context, "there is virtually no self present in his play," which consists of reenactments of intense interactions at home. J. has not had energy available or adequate objects to form an age-appropriate self. His abilities to contain and soothe himself, to engage in purposeful activity, and to enjoy developing capacities are far below age-appropriate levels, although he has developed the concept of "I."

The violence between his parents, his father's alcoholism and chaos, and his mother's utilization of him to express her strong feelings (creating a role reversal in which he is the container rather than she) leave him without idealizable objects, without sufficient encouragement for separation, and without energy available to perform the developmental tasks of creating the self and beginning to separate and individuate. The "self" he has created is preoccupied with violence; it is often chaotic and is something he "wants to kill." The degree to which he is symbiotically tied to his mother and functions as a narcissistic extension or container for her feelings is exemplified by the following vignette:

Six months into treatment, Mrs. C. reported a dream in which her deceased mother-in-law appeared to her in an old frame house and told her that she should stay with Mr. C. (who had resumed drinking heavily after his mother's death) and care for him. The mother-in-law would be watching over them and helping out. Mrs. C. did not tell this dream to her child. Two months later they were driving down a street and passed an old house that was similar to the one in her dream. J. said, "Mommy, see that house? I had a dream last night that Grandma was in that house and she told us to take care of Daddy and that everything would be all right and that you should take care of Daddy and make him better." This was during a period when Mrs. C. was considering more seriously the possibility of leaving.

In general, we can see that as a child, Mrs. C. developed her sense of self amidst chaos, demands for precocious caretaking of others, and unidealizable objects. She is unable to establish a nonviolent adult relationship, in spite of a desire and efforts to do so. Nor can she leave the hateful object, which indicates not only extreme narcissistic vulnerability but some masochistic tendencies as well. She has introjected the depreciation of one parent by the other, as has her son.

With Mrs. C., then, we have seen how not having idealizable objects, and particularly being the child of parents involved in domestic violence, can lead to later problems in narcissism and adult intimate violence. Kohut (1978) stresses the impact that the quality of the experience during the original formation of the self can have later:

> ... the vicissitudes of the early formations of the self determine the form and the course of later psychological events that are *analogous* to the crucial early phase. ... [These experiences] become the *prototype* of specific forms of our later vulnerability and security in the narcissistic realm: of the ups and downs of our self-esteem; of our greater or lesser need for praise, for merger into idealized figures, and for other forms of narcissistic sustenance; and of the greater or lesser cohesion of our self during periods of transition [pp. 623–624; my italics].

He also stresses the vulnerability of the self, which is often overlooked. He explains that "periods of transition which demand from us a reshuffling of the self, its change, and its rebuilding, constitute emotional situations that reactivate the period of the formation of the self. The replacement of one long-term self-representation by another endangers a self whose earlier, nuclear establishment was faulty" (p. 623). In addition, he notes that such external shifts as a move or reversal in a person's social role can "impose on us a drastic change in our self."

The quality of the development of the self and the vulnerability of the self are pertinent to adult intimate violence in a number of ways. First, intimacy requires a secure sense of self, including self-regulating mechanisms so that one can lose oneself in abandon without losing the core self. There must also be a capacity to idealize in a nonprimitive way and to see the other as a whole and separate object that is invested in (i.e., libinal object constancy). Moreover, aggression must be sufficiently sublimated so that it does not erupt violently. If, in particular, the person retains excessive needs for grandiosity, perfection, and mirroring or merging into an idealized other, violent expressions of narcissistic rage may occur when these experiences are unavailable with the partner. If the partner, who has been seen as an omnipotent or mirroring object, fails to be perfect, he or she is attacked with violent rage. The external event may be something small, like dinner not being ready, but the internal, *subjective* psychological event is not small to the abuser. Similarly, when the abuser's self-esteem rests on the ability to maintain an archaic grandiose self, situations that threaten or challenge this may lead to violence. At times the person may even respond with "anticipatory attack" on the partner, taking vengeance for something that has not yet happened. Furthermore, intimate violence often begins or intensifies at transition points such as kohut describes. The case of Mr. A. and Miss A. (described earlier) illustrates some of these points:

> Mr. A. has been in once weekly therapy for a year and a half. He can't manage more frequent sessions because of the intensity of his investment in not needing help from anyone. Mr. A., a severe narcissistic personality, presented with a major depressive episode and has evidence strong fixations in the early oral phase. He is capable of regressing to a position in which he experiences, and defends against, intense annihilation fears.
>
> Mr. A. stated in his first session that "hunting, fishing, and camping are the most important things in my life." He is not able to articulate why this is so, but is adamant about its primacy. Other statements he makes indicates both annihilation anxiety and his use of the woods, mountains, and weapons as a defense against it. In a later session, in describing his lifelong difficulty with sleeping, he states, "I have to stay awake . . . be alert . . . I always wake up every hour at home . . . but I sleep soundly in the woods and mountains." In another session he notes that "the only place I am not lonely is in the forest." Mr. A. owns a large collection of guns for various kinds of hunting and prides himself on being an excellent marksman. When he goes off into the woods and sleeps so soundly, he is usually surrounded by several such weapons. In his words, they're "like a bottle that a mother gives a baby" rather than dangerous.
>
> During a period in which his father was seriously ill in the hospital, Mr. A. said that if his father died, his mother would die in response to that, and he would lose both of them at once and "that would be too much . . . plus I'm next." He has frequently expressed his conviction that he will die young "because men in my family die young." While heredity is the manifest reason, the intensity of his preoccupation and his dread of illness reveal a stark annihilation fear. He defends against this with a compensatory grandiosity manifested in his frequent references to the invulnerability of his body (he doesn't get sick like other people, he can eat or drink anything without repercussions, etc.).
>
> In another session Mr. A. stated that "if anyone attacks me I could kill . . . it would be real easy for me to go to war and fight because of that." He was previously married and was abandoned abruptly by his wife. He likened this event to the great earthquake in San Francisco in 1906 when thousands of people were hurt or killed and there was mass chaos. Again, in his vulnerability to loss, he equates being left with annihilation.
>
> Mr. A. is aware that he experiences Miss A.'s criticisms of him as "attacks" and so spends inordinate amounts of energy "avoiding arguments because I don't want to hurt her." Although he has put much defensive energy into managing his aggression (avoiding arguments, denying anger, channeling aggression into sports, and sometimes drinking to numb feelings), he is still violent in his relationship with Miss A. He also reports flying into

intense verbal rages when someone cuts him off in traffic, and he becomes excessively agitated whenever he has to wait for someone. Given this, aggression can hardly be said to be adequately sublimated.

Certain key elements in Mr. A.'s self representation are: (1) he sees himself as generous and "giving" on a conscious level; (2) he sees his body as highly invulnerable to sickness and stress so that on the most manifest level he is in "good shape"; (3) he sees his father as "rigid, rageful, critical, cold, and stingy," and "always getting an eye for an eye" whereas he himself does *not* have those characteristics and has made efforts to develop opposite traits. These elements interact with aspects of Miss A.'s self-representation. She has a high investment in looking good and not being overweight; and she sees herself as gregarious, fun-loving, outgoing, as well as sensitive, helpful, and sensible.

For this couple, typical fights involve perceived attacks on these sensitive areas of self representation. Mr. A., for instance, will complain about not being able to sleep. Miss A. then tries to get him to take a sleeping pill. This offends his sense of physical invulnerability, and he becomes agitated. She then becomes "rational" and "sensible," urging him to take the pill. When he doesn't, her sense of being helpful is compromised, so she becomes more insistent. He becomes more anxious and puts his hand over her mouth to make her stop talking. She struggles and a fight ensues.

Or, in discussing plans to go out on the weekend, she may suggest that he wear a certain outfit to a certain event. He hears this as a criticism of how he looks, feels attacked, and counterattacks by calling her a "fat slob." Now two parts of her self representation have been "attacked"—her helpfulness and her slim body image. She screams. He calls her another name. At this point he feels "calm" in contrast to her "hysteria," which helps him to regain equilibrium. To defend her own vulnerability, she attacks his calm, hitting him and yelling, "You're just like your father, *cold!*" He hits her back and in the struggle, she is more injured than he. Upset by losing control, he storms out of the house.

In another typical scenario, Mr. A. comes back from a two-week camping trip and Miss A. tells him about going out with her girlfriends to a party, thus asserting her "gregarious, fun-loving self" and saying in effect that she could get along without him. He feels threatened because she was with other people (and this could mean that she could leave him, and to him leaving equates with annihilation). He responds by calling her names. She responds by saying his camping is stupid. This assaults the activity that he has declared most important in his life. He responds by grabbing her and putting his hand over her mouth to "shut her up" and she bites him. He hits her.

With both Mr. A. and Miss A., we see each responding to attacks on his or her self representation with an attack on the other's self representation (either verbal or physical). As this exchange continues, each becomes increasingly narcissistically vulnerable and mobilizes aggression to defend the self. Such a sequence usually ends with her being hit (as he tries to "shut her up"), or one of them making a final verbal assault on the other and fleeing. A similar kind of interaction, in which violence stems from perceived narcissistic injury, can be seen in another couple, Mr. and Mrs. B.:

> Mr. and Mrs. B. are a middle-income couple in their mid-fifties. They have been married for 30 years, although there was a period of separation early in the marriage. Both are of the same ethnic lineage, but Mr. B.'s parents were immigrants and he grew up in a poor ethnic neighborhood, whereas Mrs. B. grew up in a sheltered and privileged environment. Mr. B. makes a good income in the trades. Mrs. B. has a college education and previously held a responsible position in the business world, but has not worked for 20 years. She explains that her husband did not want her to work and also that "I wanted to be taken care of."
>
> Mr. and Mrs. B. have each been in individual psychotherapy once or twice weekly for two years. Both are diagnosed as moderate to severe narcissistic personality disorders who function in the transferences at the mirroring level. Incidents of violence between them have occurred, as far as can be determined from their individual histories, exclusively around incidents in which one of them has experienced a narcissistic injury and become enraged. Although the incidents of physical combat have not been frequent, they have been severe, with the last incident resulting in potentially life-threatening injuries for Mrs. B. Each is capable of murderous rage, but incidents in which Mrs. B. has become enraged and thrown objects at or hit Mr. B. have not resulted in serious injury to him because there is a substantial difference between them in size and strength. Since treatment began, Mr. B. has not assaulted Mrs. B.—a fact in which he takes considerable pride. There have been a few explosive incidents in which threats were made and objects thrown, and Mrs. B. has hit Mr. B.
>
> In the nineteenth month of treatment, Mrs. B.'s therapist went on vacation for two weeks. Shortly before the vacation, Mrs. B. had experienced increased vulnerability following a session in which she realized that she had "never been able to play" and expressed a deep sadness about burying her "real self." In her subsequent interactions with her husband, she was able to share this vulnerability and he was able to hear her and accept it—a new and positive experience for them, but one that also threatened greater intimacy. It should also be noted that this vacation was the anniversary of a two week-vacation during which the therapist became seriously ill and was off for two months instead of the expected two weeks. That occurred at a time that Mrs. B. was experiencing an intense dependency on and demandingness toward the therapist. This time, however, Mrs. B. denied any reactions to the impending vacation. In the session immediately before the vacation she reported how well things were going for her (in effect, saying, "See, I don't need you"). In fact, there had been a substantial improvement during the past year for Mrs. B. emotionally and in her relationship with Mr. B. The therapist accepted the "things are better" report and failed to reflect or comment on

Mrs. B.'s heightened vulnerability or the anniversary aspect of the vacation, thus making the error of responding to the "false self" which was "being good."

The following week, when Mr. B. came for his first appointment that week with his therapist, he indicated that things were continuing smoothly between him and his wife. By his second appointment (the day after Mrs. B.'s weekly appointment would have been), Mr. B. reported that on the previous day Mrs. B. had been very dissatisfied with him and they had argued. She presented him with a list of demands and complaints about his behavior, stating all his deficiencies, all the ways he'd failed her, and all the things he must do to correct these matters. The written communication, which he shared with his therapist, had a tone of absoluteness, entitlement, and self-righteousness, with many statements about how he "ought to hear her better" or "ought to serve her needs better." Mr. B. reported feeling assaulted and provoked by this, sensing that she was intruding on him and demanding that he be perfect. He felt enraged enough to hit her but did not, in part because he has taken much pride in controlling himself and has made gains in therapy. Moreover, he was not as vulnerable as she. He reported that she hit him, knocking him down; he felt insulted and left the house.

In this sequence, Mrs. B. was more vulnerable because of recent gains in therapy and also because her therapist was away and had failed to adequately reflect that vulnerability in the session immediately before the vacation. On the day she would have seen her therapist, she became excessively demanding toward her husband, whom she tried to pull into becoming her mirror. She expressed to him the rage she felt toward the therapist (you didn't hear me; you aren't here to reflect me; you ought to serve my needs better). The quality of demands in her note (the sense of entitlement, contempt, insistence on perfection), as well as their intensity and unequivocalness, reveals the primitive grandiosity from which they emanate, and which has remained split off in the personality. When Mr. B. was not able to meet these demands immediately, or "hear" them properly, Mrs. B. became enraged and hit him, thus abandoning her usual concern for self-protection to the rage within.

A different aspect of the interaction of narcissistic vulnerability and intimate violence emerges in the case of Mr. and Mrs. Z.:

> Mr. and Mrs. Z. are in their forties and have been married 20 years. They came to the domestic violence program following an incident of severe abuse, as a result of which Mrs. Z. was hospitalized for a week. Until the past two years, there had been no abuse, with the exception of one incident, eight years before, when Mr. Z. threw a large vase at Mrs. Z. "out of the blue" from her perspective. There had, however, been "bursts of temper." During the past two years, incidents of abuse occurred six times, the most recent being the most serious.

Both Mr. and Mrs. Z. have been in individual psychotherapy for over two years. Each suffers from severe narcissistic personality disturbance. Mrs. Z. reported that her most recent injuries left her in a semi-invalid condition for several weeks, which evoked intense helplessness, rage, and demandingness from her because "I just got over thinking I was a heart patient." She went on to describe how in the previous 15 years she had had a series of misdiagnoses, leading to the conclusion that she had a weak heart. During all these years Mr. Z. had cared for her and been extremely attentive to her fragile condition. Although she worked early in their marriage, she stopped, both because Mr. Z. wanted her to and because of her medical condition. Two years ago, she learned that she did *not* have a weak heart, and that her pains and other symptoms were explained by a less ominous diagnosis and an easily treatable condition. It took nearly a year to adjust to this new reality, and then there she was, in an invalid status again. She mentioned that Mr. Z. on occasion had told her that if it were not for his good care, she would not be alive. She added that he "would brag to men at work about how he kept me alive . . . he's not God after all." Mr. Z., in his individual work, reported that when he learned of the change in diagnosis he was furious because he felt she had been "putting it on" all those years to be catered to, and he had held his rage at various insults in check "because she was sick." Mr. Z. revealed many areas of unmodified grandiosity in his treatment, including his investment in having many times saved his wife when she took medication improperly.

In this case, it is significant that the violence really began after the couple learned that Mrs. Z. was not an invalid. Both Mr. and Mrs. Z. were narcisstically vulnerable individuals, but Mrs. Z.'s chronic illness had created a certain equilibrium for this couple, which, when removed, left room for much more expression of narcissistic rage. Mr. Z.'s grandiosity at being the excellent caretaker for Mrs. Z. was threatened, as was her availability to him (if she wasn't sick, she could move independently, might develop interests separate from him, and might also make more demands for intimacy). Moreover, a major element that had contained Mr. Z.'s rage when Mrs. Z. insulted him (she's sick and fragile and I have to care for her) was eliminated. Mrs. Z. lost the "right" to care because of her illness, so that now when she ordered Mr. Z. to do something for her with a sense of entitlement, he became enraged and increasingly impatient with her demandingness on her part. Mrs. Z.'s sense of entitlement and lack of empathy for her partner (typical of narcissistic personalities) continued, but without a "legitimate" explanation.

Yet another example of the intertwining of narcissistic needs and intimate violence is found in the case of Mr. and Mrs. C. (discussed earlier):

As was already noted, Mrs. C. had a depressed, alcoholic, and sickly mother who died when Mrs. C. was 15. Her father was abusive to her mother and to the children, ran around with other women, and was not there to care for mother. Mr. C. had an overly close relationship with his mother, who continued to be a nurturing figure in his life until her death three years ago. Mr. C.'s mother, who became a subsitute maternal figure for Mrs. C., asked Mrs. C. to stay with Mr. C. even though he was abusive and alcoholic. In fact, this was a death-bed request to her daughter-in-law.

Mr. C. expects from his wife the type of "constant availability" that a toddler has from the mother, and which Mr. C. inappropriately had with his own mother long into adulthood. He insists that Mrs. C. nurture him in a variety of ways, being particularly exacting about having food prepared *as* he wants it *when* he wants it. The same demands for perfection are made regarding her housekeeping, even though she works full time. He wants an omnipotent object always there with whom he can merge and get his needs gratified. Mrs. C., on the other hand, has retained some primitive grandiosity in her conviction that "if only I am good enough I can make him better," as she tried, and failed, to make her mother better. Her needs for nurturance are as strong as his but have never been met; her unconscious desire is to fix him so that he can care for her. In this couple, he retains excessive needs for perfection in the other, while she retains grandiose expectations of herself.

One evening Mrs. C. was making tacos for dinner. She had all the ingredients (meat, cheese, onions, lettuce) lined up on the counter. She began assembling the tacos into the shells when Mr. C. noticed that she put the cheese on before the meat. He flew into a rage accusing her of being a "fat slob like your mother" and "incapable of caring for me like *my* mother—you don't hold a candle to her!" This incident ended in a severe beating.

On another occasion, they went shopping with their little boy. Mr. C. had been drinking but was still able to walk around and shop. He asked Mrs. C. to buy him a quart of beer and she refused, saying he was already drunk and trying to coax him into the car to go home. He insisted, "I want it now and you're supposed to get what I want." She got into the car with her son. Mr. C. picked up a cement block from the parking lot and without warning hurled it through the front windshield of the car. Miraculously, Mrs. C. and the son were not injured, and they fled on foot to a bus-stop, leaving Mr. C. screaming hysterically in the parking lot. As Mr. C. becomes violent if Mrs. C. threatens to leave, or looks as if she is going to leave, when she left him in the parking lot, his rage increased.

A number of points are illustrated by this case. We see that the retention of an underlying grandiosity combined with magical thinking, keeps Mrs. C. in this relationship: "If only I do things right . . . then everything will be okay." And there is an even deeper hunger for a perfect object to care for her, if only she can "make him right." Mr. C. becomes enraged when his wife fails to be perfectly available, to function as an "environmental mother," or to perform functions that he requires. His alcoholism fits the pattern of "the addictive search . . . that starts in the narcissistic crisis" (Wurmser, 1978). For Mr. C., with his severe narcissistic deficit, the alcohol alternates with his wife as he relates to it or her with "an archaic passive dependency on an all-giving, hugely inflated object" (Wurmser, 1978, p. 160). In the dinner incident, there is virtually no warning that Mr. C. will erupt so violently; it is an example of how an objectively insignificant event can be subjectively highly charged and lead to narcissistic rage. Mrs. C. consistently reports that she often has "no idea when it's coming." Although certain predictable issues are triggers, the thresholds at which Mr. C. will respond with disappintment or violence vary widely.

Earlier it was mentioned that the self is particularly vulnerable during periods of transition. That parenthood may bring out narcissistic vulnerabilities is suggested by the following case:

> Mr. and Mrs. H. have been married for 15 years and are in their mid-thirties. They have an 18-month-old baby whom they frequently refer to as "it," rather than by name. Both Mr. and Mrs. H. have worked in the performing arts in positions that afforded fair amounts of acclaim and narcissistic gratification. Mrs. H. was more prominent professionally than Mr. H. throughout their marriage, and the pregnancy occurred following a setback in her career. There was no violence in this marriage until after the baby was born.
>
> The violence began as an outgrowth of arguments over who was right about how the baby should be cared for, what the baby should eat, and what the baby needed at any given time. Each parent asserts unequivocally that he or she "knows best" about the child. Mrs. H., however, reports feeling inadequate as a parent and feeling ignored by Mr. H., who has become excessively preoccupied with the baby. Mr. H. comments, "I become godlike with this child . . . you pour out love to this child and in so doing you will both be brought to perfection." If the baby falls and hurts his hand, Mr. H. will hold him and say things like: "It won't hurt if you look at Daddy." He behaves as if he could will the hurt away.

Mr. H's direct reports about his feelings about the child and his interactions with the child reveal an "insistence on the perfection of the idealized self object and on the limitlessness of the power and knowledge of a grandiose self" (Kohut, 1978, p. 643). Arguments occur rapidly, sometimes leading to violence, when his wife's responses interfere with this perception. It is significant that violence began for this couple at the point they became parents, a transition that clearly calls for redefining the self representation and for adaptive regression. Grandiosity and aggression that had been channeled into work for both of them suddenly emerged in a more archaic and volatile form as they attempted to make this shift.

Battered women report that violence often begins in the relationship at one of three critical times: (1) shortly after the marriage; (2) during the first pregnancy, especially once the woman begins to show; and (3) after the birth of the first child. Violence commencing with the marriage is reported so regularly that much of the domestic violence literature refers to the marriage license as a "hitting license." This coincidence is interpreted sociologically in terms of the inherent assumptions in a patriarchal family system that the woman is subordinate to the man (Martin, 1975; Straus, 1976; Fleming, 1979). Without minimizing the cultural and structural support for violence, I would reiterate that one of the reasons that violence erupts at these points is because the major modifications in self representation increase narcissistic vulnerability. In addition, the tasks of coupling and parenthood, with their demands for intimacy and adaptive regression respectively, require a solid and resilient core self to begin with. If that is shaky, vulnerable, or prone to fragmentation, the person is undergoing a "double strain"—trying to replace one long-term self representation with another (the adaptive task) *and* undertaking a task that especially demands a cohesive self. There is a high likelihood that violence will erupt under these circumstances. Narcissistic rage may be activated by the recapitulation (real or imagined) of traumas in the original creation of the self (e.g., repetitions of inadequate mirroring). Moreover, in a desperate, primitive attempt to stem the sense of fragmentation, loss of boundaries, or loss of identity that is stirred up, the person uses violent rages to control the partner or the self or evoke rage as a cohesive force in the personality.

An additional factor to consider in domestic violence is masochistic formations, which have been shown to coincide with severe pathology in the narcissistic sector of the personality (Berliner, 1947; Menaker, 1953; Socarides, 1958; Stolorow, 1975; Horner, 1979). Stolorow (1975) points out that the masochistic character needs an audience to whom misery can be dramatized, and that this exhibitionistic behavior serves to shore up a failing self representation through mirroring, as does any type of exhibitionism in a narcissistically vulnerable individual. In particular, masochists seek a response from the audience that (1) forces expression of love, approval, or sympathy; (2) assures them that they have an impact; (3) punishes the audience for previous misbehavior toward them by evoking guilt and remorse; and yet (4) provokes the audience into behaving hostilely toward them, allowing them to reenact the role of the hated child or justifying their own aggression and permitting them to then present with less guilt, a "bill for love" (Socarides, 1958). Several of these demands are evident in the behavior of Mrs. E.:

> Mrs. E. came into a shelter following a severe beating from her husband. She presented herself in such a helpless and fragmented manner on the phone that she had to be virtually coaxed into coming into the shelter. Initially, she evoked much sympathy from workers, who described has as a "walking,

open narcissistic wound." She talked incessantly in a bewildered tone, wondering, "How could he do this to me?" and recounting the details of her pain in an increasingly whining tone. After a couple of days, the reaction of others, both residents and workers, changed from sympathy to saturation, and finally to irritation. Workers began to tell her that she could only discuss "her pains" in individual sessions with her therapist or caseworker, in an effort to contain her. Although initially compliant, Mrs. E. began to break residential house rules, including taking unauthorized overnight absences. Because of the degree of danger involved, staff initially found it difficult to confront her about these infractions. When she was confronted by her caseworker, she behaved like a contrite child, then "behaved" for a period of time, until she experienced the shelter as "too comfortable," after which acting out would resume. It should be noted that when she initially came to the shelter, she was very disorganized, and spent several hours in the parking lot sorting through her belongings trying to decide what to bring with her, particularly having difficulty choosing between clothes that represented different aspects of herself. The constant talking about her pains followed this, and she became more cohesive in the ensuing days.

Mrs. E. thus had a continuous, intense impact on those around her. As she continued to get a response, even if it was negative, she was able to pull her scattered self representation together. The initial sympathy she evoked gave way to irritation and a reenactment of the "chastised child" on at least one occasion with her caseworker. She was able to punish the audience (workers) after they began to cut off her ruminations about pain by acting out and evoking worry about her safety. In addition, she displayed typical masochistic characteristics of an intense, imperative need for love and contact and an equivalent fear of abandonment.

When a masochistic adaptation in a narcissistic personality fails, usually because there is the threat of abandonment or narcissistic mortification from the love object, "masochistic decompensation" (Socarides, 1958) can occur. There may be intense outbursts of fear and rage, urgent demands for love, or self-punishment, including suicide attempts, in an effort to get the object back. At times violence may be directed toward the object in an effort to force love and nonabandonment.

Mr. X., a severely narcissistic man who relied heavily on his "standing in the community" to shore up his fragile narcissism, was humiliated when his wife left him. He sent both pleading and threatening messages through emissaries to her at work and called her constantly at the shelter where she was staying. Finally he demanded that she return before a particular day upon which they were supposed to appear together at an important religious function. He had "told no one she left him" because it was too humiliating. When she did not return, he drank several cans of insecticide, nearly killing himself.

Although Mr. X. was not a masochistic character, he did utilize a masochistic defense at times, including his initial appeals to his wife to return. When this failed, he quickly decompensated to a point of undertaking a dramatic and nearly lethal suicide attempt.

Among the most dangerous forms of hostile expressions are expressions of narcissistic rage in response to perceived attacks on the grandiose self or idealized object. In Kohut's (1971) framework, the archaic grandiose self and archaic omnipotent objects are normal developmental events, which can become arrested in the narcissistic personality. In contrast, Kernberg (1975) views the development of the grandiose self as a pathological structure developed for defensive purposes. Regardless of which view one takes the prominence of grandiose structures in adult psychic life is pathological, and the expression of narcissistic rage may become dangerous. Rochlin (1973) stresses: "Aggression *always* issues—although unconsciously we may distort or symbolize the form it takes—as a reaction to threatened or actually damaged narcissism, whether the loss of our self-esteem is provoked by our own hostility doubts, and demands, or by some sense that others doubt, hate, or otherwise seem to devalue and abuse us" (p. 120). More specifically, Kohut (1978) states: "Human aggression is most dangerous when it is attached to the two great absolutarian psychological constellations: the grandiose self and the archaic grandiose subject" (p. 635).

These comments apply directly to domestic violence. The most dangerous situations are those in which narcissistic rage and/or extreme narcissistic vulnerability operate. There are several reasons for this. Consider, for instance, the cases in which the abused person reports "having no idea that it's coming." Two factors contribute to this. First, given the vicissitudes of narcissistic injury, with its internal thresholds and sensitivities, what may be tolerable one day is not on another—so the abuser may explode unpredictably. We have already seen this unpredictability of violence due to shifting internal sensitivities in the case of Mr. C. On some occasions Mr. C. would fly into a rage because of an imperfection in dinner; at other times, he didn't seem to notice. On the other hand, lack of empathy and underlying grandiosity operative in most narcissistic personalities contribute to the victim's being unusually oblivious to potential warning signs, as can be seen in the case of Mrs. B:

> Mrs. B. came to her first session exuding an air of regalness and formality in spite of her arm being in a sling, her leg bandaged, and her using a cane to walk. She seemed remarkably unconnected from herself except for her experience of fear around the abuse, which she saw as "exaggerated" but the therapist saw as appropriate, given her injuries. The therapist's initial im-

pression was that Mrs. B. was unaccustomed to allowing herself to have unsettling feelings, such as fear. Mrs. B. described the abusive incident that ended with her spending two weeks in the hospital as follows: "We had gone out for dinner . . . I had picked out a lovely place . . . [and] we had a perfectly lovely dinner. . . . He didn't have much to say . . . [Then] we came home and I was walking down the hall, and all of a sudden he hit me and I was on the floor. I hit my head and arm on the way down I guess." She presented herself as calm and charming in interactions with husband, although she conveyed a sense that things should be done the "right way" and that sometimes he didn't behave "properly." In reviewing the evening, Mrs. B. was unable to detect any signs of tension, any signs of danger in this or previous incidents. On the other hand, Mr. B., in relating his side of the story in a separate interview, reported feeling criticized and put down in small ways by Mrs. B. He was aware of his own increasing anger during the evening, and his increasing intolerance of small incidents in which she "treated me like a misbehaving child."

During the first several months of treatment, Mrs. B. became aware of patterns in their interactions that led to tension or arguments, and was thus in a better position to protect herself. However, initially she was highly resistant to becoming aware of the danger to herself, because she was then aware of uncomfortable feelings. Over time she became more comfortable with experiencing her own feelings, and after about a year began to develop occasional empathy for her husband's point of view.

After two years of treatment, Mrs. B. reported an incident in which she was followed home from a shopping center by a man in a car, who by her description to police seemed to be a suspect in several assaults in the area. During this incident there were many points at which she could have gotten help (e.g., driven to the police station rather than to her home), but she did not. She was shaken by her own behavior, seeing the parallel between not protecting herself in this situation and initially not being able to protect herself with husband. Analysis of the incident revealed that although she was aware that the man was following her, she kept telling herself things like, "This is a public highway . . . it's a coincidence," not allowing herself to become aware of the danger. In exploring why this might be so, she ruminated over many possibilities, then paused and blurted out, "Well, nothing like that can happen to *me!*" This was a turning point in her treatment, which led to further understanding of some unmodified grandiosity.

Mrs. B. was less able to protect herself in her marriage because initially she was unable to be empathic to her partner and to tolerate unsettling feelings in herself, which rendered her less observant. Later, in the situation of the man following her, her underlying grandiosity is revealed.

Extreme narcissistic vulnerability in the woman—a compelling need to be admired, mirrored, or pursued—often puts her in jeopardy because this need overrides any concern for safety and perhaps otherwise good judgment. Mrs. K. provides an example:

5. Early Development and Intimate Violence /105

Mrs. K. was an only child whose single, alcoholic mother placed her with relatives and in residential schools from the time she was three years old. A woman with intense abandonment fears, she was first married at age 18 and has not lived without a partner since. Her first two marriages were relatively short-lived but not physically abusive.

During her third and longest marriage, Mrs. K. utilized shelters more than once. Typically abuse would occur when she was hungry for emotional connection with her husband, who was at that time shutting her out. When she would angrily plead for attention, he would hit her. Following an especially severe incident in which she was nearly killed, she described to her therapist that just as Mr. K. "could be abnormally violent, he could also be abnormal in the other direction," giving her an overwhelmingly high feeling of being protected and cared for "like a little girl." Giving up that feeling, which could only be bestowed by a powerful partner, left her feeling empty and alone.

Under other circumstances, Mrs. K. had perceptive judgment about people, was intelligent and sociable. Yet repeatedly she married men with major problems and known histories of those problems "without knowing about it." Over time Mrs. K. was able to see this pattern in her relationships, but seemed in a race with time to change it. When she finally left her husband of many years, she was highly vulnerable. She met an "absolutely wonderful" man but added later, "He reminds me of Mr. K. and I'm worried about getting involved." For the first time she was able to pause before plunging into a relationship with a man who initially praised and idealized her. Nevertheless, she was not able to stop herself, because the need for this reflection and adulation was so great. She married him after a few months (the longest courtship in her life). Within a short time, she died from an incident of abuse.

Mrs. K.'s need for intense connection, reflection, and admiration, combined with her terror of abandonment, interfered with her otherwise reasonable judgment when she was vulnerable. The degree of intensity she needed to feel good and protected could ultimately be provided only by a person with a large amount of primitive grandiosity; it therefore put her in danger. In a sense she was killed by her vulnerabilities.

Mrs. E. (described earlier) also allowed her need for admiration to override everything else:

Mrs. E. described "never being able to please" her abusive mother and "wishing she would have pursued me." As a teenager Mrs. E. once fainted in front of a hospital, hoping that mother would come after her; instead, mother sent someone else and then sent her to live with relatives. Mrs. E.'s desire to be pursued is a main thrust in her psychic life. When she is pursued, she feels good about herself and important.

In the relationship between Mr. and Mrs. E., the regulation of distance is a central problem. Initially when they are together, as in the first weeks of their marriage, "everything is perfect." Then she pulls away because she needs to be pursued. (She may do this physically by leaving or emotionally by withdrawing.) He then feels abandoned and panics, quickly becoming disorganized because her presence is an organizing force for him. Violence often occurs at this point because he needs to hold onto her, to keep her from pulling away, and also because violence is a binding action for him to buttress his cohesion. Mrs. E. has been hospitalized several times as a result.

Given the severity of injuries and the dynamics in the couple, Mrs. E. puts herself in danger of being seriously hurt whenever she runs away so that Mr. E. can pursue her. Yet her need to be pursued in order to feel worthy and cared about outweighs all other concerns.

The tenacious pursuit of revenge, the unforgiving fury and the contemptuous attitude toward the object of wrath so characteristic of narcissistic rage, may lead to an "utter disregard for reasonable limitations." In this fury, the desire to "blot out" the other person may prevail, as in the case of Mr. X.

Mr. X., a severely narcissistic man who relied on his "standing in the community" to shore up his fragile narcissism, was humiliated when his wife left him. On one occasion when his wife was in a shelter, he tracked her down and pleaded with her to come back, promising to do anything she wanted. She insisted on going home, saying, "Look at all the trouble he went to to find me." When she met him and got in the car, he flew into a rage because she had embarrassed him—and stabbed her.

The tasks of becoming a couple and maintaining a relationship require a reordering and maintenance of one's self representations. For persons with significant narcissistic vulnerabilities, these are stressful tasks that can activate narcissistic rage and violence. Persons with intense narcissistic vulnerabilities (whether transient, situationally induced, or characterological) are thus at substantially higher risk for intimate violence than other individuals.

Splitting and Projective Identification

Splitting and projective identification are psychic processes that occur frequently within and between the parties involved in intimate violence. While splitting and projective identification can occur independently, their combination has a synergystic effect that intensifies acting out and perceptive distortions of each other that are typical in an escalating cycle of violence. The use of splitting in abusive relationships is outlined in an excellent article by Irene Gillman (1980), who essentially contends that most battered women and their mates are borderline. Although I do not agree with that conclusion, what Gillman says about splitting in borderline violent couples is accurate and instructive:

The battered woman has two separate and quite distinct dyadic representations: her lovable self in a warm, friendly relation to a good, providing husband-mother and her helpless, worthless self who is in a hateful destructive relation to a persecuting, damaging husband-mother. . . . When splitting is used, quite different opposing descriptions of other people by the battered woman are possible, depending on which self-object representation is activated [p. 349–350].

According to Gillman, the battered woman's spouse has the same contradictory and mutually exclusive sets of internalized images. With borderline abusive couples, one often finds an intense, frequently reversing, roller-coaster relationship, in which the wife describes her husband as "Dr. Jekyll and Mr. Hyde." Ego deficits, high anxiety, and the lack of mastery of ambivalence all contribute to an urgency to act out whichever set of self-object relations happen to be activated at the moment.

In the shelter, this phenomenon was seen in a woman who split staff, other shelter residents, friends, and family, using others' view of her husband as "bad" or "good" to buttress one set of internalized object relations or the other as she vacillated between leaving him and returning to him. There is a risk that once such a woman feels better about herself in a supportive shelter environment, she will have more difficulty staying away from her husband since the more positive regard for herself is associated with the good husband-mother.

Mrs. Y., a 30-year-old woman, has been married for five years and is the mother of an infant. At the time she entered the shelter she reported that abuse was more verbal than physical, but that she was afraid she would be hit because an issue that had led to violence previously was coming up again. She said that she experienced husband as "controlling" in relation to money and activities of hers that were separate from him. Diagnosed as a borderline personality, she began twice weekly treatment.

At the beginning Mrs. Y. stated that she wanted no contact with Mr. Y. and refused the option of outreach contact by an agency therapist. She initiated no direct contact with her husband. She was unable to express directly any positive feelings for him, any sadness or ambivalence. She did, however, frequently drive past his place of employment and other usual haunts of his. Then, when she returned to the shelter, she expressed fear that he might follow her. She also invested considerable energy in plans to attend a friend's wedding at which she expected husband to be present.

In her first session after the wedding, which Mr. Y. did not attend, she talked in metaphorical terms about her anger and sadness at the loss of her husband. She mentioned a friend who was upset because her boyfriend had left her, then referred to her cousin (whom she's close to), who has been married and divorced several times but is now happily married (to a woman Mrs. Y describes as similar to herself). In talking about cousin, she frequently slipped and called him by Mr. Y.'s name. She then complained that the minister at the wedding "didn't tell the truth and made up part of the readings from the scriptures." She ended up saying, "Everyone knows it's Satan who makes people argue."

In previous sessions Mrs. Y. had labeled "bad" those who "don't tell the truth" and "good" those who do. She had stated that her husband didn't tell the truth "because he wasn't baptized in the faith" (therefore it wasn't his fault). She, however, had been baptized and "knew the real truth" about things. In the shelter Mrs. Y. often told other residents "the truth" about their feelings and situations, an intrusive stance that evoked anger in both residents and staff. She did this when she was feeling especially vulnerable.

During the two months Mrs. Y. lived in the shelter prior to the wedding, she increasingly cast her therapist into the role of the "good" object ("you understand me") while posing numerous tests to see if the therapist would tell her what to do (as her mother does). Her shelter caseworker, with whom she had to make a contract regarding her length of stay at the shelter and work with on concrete planning, was cast into the role of "bad" object. She struggled with her caseworker on every issue and delayed making a contract about her length of stay as long as possible by flooding her meetings with complaints about other residents and crises with her family of origin. Shortly before the wedding she finally signed a contract with her caseworker to stay another month. Nevertheless, Mrs. Y. felt "pushed out" of the shelter.

A few days after the wedding, Mrs. Y. went to visit her parents and other relatives, again traveling along routes where she was "afraid" of running into her husband. She arrived back at the shelter and Mr. Y. pulled in behind her, called her, and said he wanted to talk to her. She immediately began screaming when he approached her, striking out first to protect herself from an anticipated attack. A struggle ensued in which she was mildly injured. The next day she pressed charges against husband for battery, with the active support of her family, particularly her mother. Various family members called the shelter threatening to sue the agency because "you didn't protect her from him" and "you're throwing her out in the street." On the same day Mrs. Y. talked to her husband on the phone. She told him she loved him and wanted to return to him but that they would have to have some marital sessions first and he would have to get help, which he readily agreed to.

Within the shelter Mrs. Y. split her self and object representations into a fairly stable pattern in which her bad self was in an antagonistic relationship to her caseworker, who was a displacement for the "bad object" side of husband. (Her husband had "made me sign a contract once" and "threw me out" just as she perceived her caseworker to be doing.) She showed much of her bad self to other residents and staff, evoking anger in others by her demandingness and intrusiveness, which was the very thing she was afraid of having happen to her (having been "controlled" by mother and husband). She showed her good self to her good object, the therapist. She felt her caseworker was punishing her and that her therapist understood her, both things she had felt about husband at different times in the past. Initially she kept husband as the bad object but displaced much of her anger at him onto the shelter milieu and her caseworker. Once she began to feel some loss of husband after the wedding, she made him blameless by saying that Satan is responsible for the arguments. It seems safe to speculate that when she set herself up to be followed by her husband she saw the husband following her as rescuing her from the bad object (the caseworker) who was throwing her out and confirming her bad self, while at the same time the husband hitting her was punishing the bad self. After this incident, the husband was "proved" bad, which she needed to do because she missed him and it allowed her to send a message to her caseworker that she had to stay longer because she was in danger. She was also able to get her family to express her anger at the shelter/caseworker so that she did not have to do it directly.

The process of projective identification is described by Ogden (1979) as having three steps: (1) the fantasy of projecting a part of oneself onto another person and of that part taking over the other person; (2) pressure exerted via interpersonal interaction so that the "recipient" experiences pressure to think, feel, behave in a manner congruent with the projection; and (3) the projected feelings, after being processed by the recipient, being reinternalized by the projector. Grotstein (1981) suggests that "internal objects are *formed* via projective identification of aspects of the infantile self into the images of external [interpersonal] objects." He describes what happens to the infant:

> . . . for projective identification to occur, there must be a conception of a *container* into which the projection can be sent. . . . If the object has transformed the projection and remained unchanged, then the infant feels a greater sense of safety and confidence in the relationship. . . . On the other hand, if the object has been transformed via the identification, either in the infant's mind . . . or in actual interpersonal reality, then the identificatory aspects of projective identification are much more glaringly concrete . . . so that the object is transformed into one's victim [so] that one has created a persecutor [pp. 125–126; my italics].

In intimate relationships, when negative or destructive impulses are projected, violence may erupt at any number of points in the process: if the destructive impulses projected are strong enough, if the "container" is weak enough, if the interpersonal pressure applied by the projector is strong enough, if compatibility of the projection with similar destructive and unmodified fantasies in the recipient close enough, or all of these. Theoretically, if sufficiently intense interpersonal pressure is applied, even a recipient without a pre-existing tendency to comply may be stimulated to act out. Violence may erupt as a result of the recipient acting out a destructive projection; or as a result of the recipient refusing the projection so that the projector becomes enraged; or from the recipient becoming enraged at the interpersonal pressure. We have all heard the exasperated client say, "I don't know what happens to me when I'm with him [or her] . . . I wind up feeling so enraged!" This can be the result of projective identification, whereby one person is more *affected* by the other than he or she *understands*. This does not imply that one person is responsible for the behavior of the other, however.

In a couple, when one partner disengages and doesn't "catch," "contain," or otherwise comply with the projection, the person attempting the projective identification is left with uncomfortable, perhaps overwhelming affects, which can lead to an intensified acting out of these affects. For example, as one partner begins to improve in treatment, the other may escalate provocations to obtain the familiar pathological response, which may lead to violence or impotent rage at not being able to effectively control the other with the projective identification. Violence may also erupt to "break the tension." Such escalations in an abusive couple "bring out the worst in each other."

The vicissitudes of projective identification may also emerge in the therapeutic relationship, as the following case indicates:

> Mrs. G., a 40-year-old woman, has been married for 20 years to an alcoholic husband whose work history is erratic. They have a 12-year-old daughter. Mrs. G. also has an erratic work history, having several times been asked to leave jobs because she can't get along with others. Diagnosed as a severe borderline personality, she has shown psychoticlike fragmentation under stress, frequently uses displacement and isolation of affect as defenses, and evidences some paranoid ideation.
>
> Mrs. G. called the crisis line following an incident in which husband threatened her with a knife. She has been in individual psychotherapy twice weekly for a year and a half. She had previous treatment for several years, ending two years before her contact with the present agency. Mrs. G. reports two significant things about her previous treatment experience: (1) the therapist would tell her at times to leave her husband, point out Mrs. G.'s strengths, and encourage her directly to find employment and otherwise improve herself; (2) the treatment was terminated by the therapist "because she said there was nothing more she could do for me, that I can't change." In the past three years Mrs. G. has lost, through death or relocation, several relatives in the extended family whom she described as "able to keep my husband in line . . . by telling him to treat us better."
>
> In the sixth hour Mrs. G. talked non-stop for nearly the whole hour. She began by talking about feeling depressed after the birth of her child and how she tried to cope with this by going to work. She then went over in detail the jobs she had gotten and lost over the years, the general theme being that she was "edged out by younger women," "let go for no reason," or a victim of office politics. This was followed by a story of conflict with her father-in-

5. Early Development and Intimate Violence /111

law's new, young wife. Mrs. G. reenacted rather than reported the argument, shouting, "You'd better not interfere in my business, B." (using the therapist's first name, apparently unaware that she was doing so). Among the things she "told off his wife about" were: "You shouldn't interfere in children's lives . . . and you shouldn't intrude in people's marriages." This was followed by her revealing her fears that her daughter may have been sexually molested by husband. The therapist, a trainee who the previous day had gone to a workshop on incest, responded to the content of Mrs. G.'s worry in a real-world manner by saying, after empathizing with Mrs. G., that possibly the suspected molestation would have to be reported at some point. Mrs. G. responded with a long list of other people in her life, past and present, who "criticized me . . . thought they were better because they went to college. . . . There was this lady at work once who criticized how I handled my kid and I found out later that she was a bad mother, worse than me!" Although the therapist did not respond to this in the session, she described how she felt "suddenly enraged with Mrs. G. . . . she'd hit my own insecurities about myself as a mother. . . . I felt like the worst mother in the world and had a momentary fantasy of throwing Mrs. G. down the stairs. . . . I wanted in that instance to kill her." This reaction was out of character for the therapist, who commented that "what happened wasn't all me . . . it was more than my countertransference." Mrs. G. had previously reported incidents in which she wanted to kill something (her dog) or someone (her husband or daughter) for misbehaving. The session ended, and Mrs. G. went home and beat her daughter for misbehaving.

From this sequence and what is known about Mrs. G., we can postulate that during this session Mrs. G. projected her "bad mother" image of herself into the therapist, testing to see if the therapist could contain it. The therapist responded to the manifest content and did not act as a container. In other words, the recipient had refused the projection. Mrs. G. became enraged, which she expressed verbally in the session in displaced terms by talking about others. She also attempted a projective identification, in which she tried to put that rage into the therapist, who then felt intense interpersonal pressure to experience this rage herself and had the fantasy of throwing the client down the stairs. The therapist "caught" more of this projection, contained some of it, but was not able to contain it completely; nor was there time, this being the end of the session, for it to be reprocessed and reintrojected by Mrs. G. in less primitive form. Mrs. G. was then left with much of her rage, which she then displaced and acted out on her daughter, thus getting rid of her tension and acting out the "bad mother" in herself.

In the seventh hour, Mrs. G. started the session by talking about various "outside forces" that were against her. She had failed to secure a job this week, and relatives and neighbors had criticized her care of her daughter: "They say I can't see that she's a sexy little girl . . . they say I overprotect her." This material was described by the therapist as a "tirade," from which she sometimes had to tune out for her own protection because of its intensity. Mrs. G. then talked about how she and her husband "don't work together" and "aren't a team." She reported an incident during the week in which Mr. G. came home, didn't like the dinner that she had prepared, and threw the dinner across the room—"like this." At this point Mrs. G. flung a letter opener that was lying on a table next to her across the room, narrowly missing the therapist. She then continued about how her husband and neighbors don't support her. The therapist said, "I wonder if you feel I don't understand the struggle you're in, and that last week when you talked about your worry about your husband and your daughter I really didn't understand." Mrs. G. looked for a split second as if she wanted to attack, but then looked down and said, "Well, maybe. . . . I thought I'd told you too many awful things about myself and my husband and my daughter last week." For the rest of the session Mrs. G. focused on her difficulty in trusting women and her expectations of not being heard.

From this sequence we can postulate that Mrs. G. was still enraged at the therapist's failure to contain her bad self/bad mother the session before, and that she feared and expected retaliation from the therapist—that the therapist might "throw her out" just as her husband had thrown out the dinner. Her inner reality is that "if something's no good, you get rid of it." We can speculate that in addition to acting out the uncontained rage from the sixth hour on her daughter, she probably set up a projective identification with her husband similar to that with her therapist, and that he acted it out, "throwing away" her "bad stuff." Throwing the letter opener was simultaneously a hostile act (because the therapist had not received and held her projection the week before), an attempt to provoke the therapist to throw her out, and another test for the therapist. This time the therapist was able to accept her badness and interpret the interaction between them from the session before.

After 18 months of treatment, a typical set of transactions has developed between the therapist and Mrs. G. Mrs. G. will talk about the losses she has experienced (including the loss of her image of her husband as the "rising young executive" when she acknowledges his alcoholism, the loss of her daughter when she recognizes that her daughter is a separate person who cannot be controlled by Mrs. G.'s fantasies, or the loss of a person through death), or about topics that touch her rage (her husband not hearing her or his violence toward her). After a certain point of intensity, Mrs. G. brings up her previous therapist. At the same time she pulls for her present therapist to berate her husband or tell her to leave by detailing the latest atrocities. The therapist then responds with an interpretation like: "I wonder why you're bringing up Mrs. P. now. I wonder if you're angry because I won't tell you what to do, and if we could talk about your anger at me and your husband."

At this point there are two possible outcomes. Mrs. G. usually sits up straight, in a very proper manner, seeming to contain her body. An expression of panic crosses her face briefly. She moves forward in the chair, her voice becomes more childlike, and she adopts a "sweet smile" while she reports that she has no anger. Meanwhile the therapist feels both emotionally and somatically intense feelings of loss and anger, including at times headaches or gastrointestinal distress that seems directly related to "holding" Mrs. G.'s anger and sadness. If this happens at the end of a session, Mrs. G. may leave and beat up her daughter or become involved in an interaction with her husband in which she gets hurt, in a sequence similar to that reported earlier. If there is time for the therapist to sit with Mrs. G.'s affects and for Mrs. G. to sit with the therapist's refusal to tell her what to do, after some moments of silence, the therapist will say something like: "It sounds like you feel a lot of anger right now and maybe you're not too happy with me today." Mrs. G. is able to chuckle a bit with the therapist in a shared nonverbal communication that acknowledges the correctness of the interpretation. Mrs. G. seems visibly less anxious, the therapist feels her headache dissipate, and Mrs. G. goes home without acting out with her daughter or husband.

This vignette shows both the violent outcome when the client cannot succeed in transacting a projective identification with her therapist as well as the process of reintrojecting the projection in a less primitive form, which Ogden (1979) describes as one of the healing properties of the mechanism of projective identification in the treatment relationship.

This material also demonstrates the use of masochism as a defense in the borderline personality. Horner (1979) describes it: "The tenacity of the bond with the bad object contrasts sharply with the indiscriminate and interchangeable nature of the "designated" good object. The issue of designation versus attachment is highlighted by the easy interchangeability of such people [often sequential therapists]". (pp. 176-177). Horner points to the consequences of the client being successful at the maneuver to get the "designated good other" to be angry at the "bad object" (in our cases, the abusive husband): "This has two important defensive functions: one is to make the anger acceptable to the superego and the other is to avoid the anxiety of intrapsychic conflict . . . Thus, the internal conflict is converted to an external one" (pp. 176-177). The difficulty in these situations is that as long as a preponderance of "designated good objects" is available, the violence is likely to continue.

The case of Mrs. G. illustrates the enactment of projective identification in the therapeutic relationship. Returning to the case of Mr. and Mrs. C., we can see how these processes are enacted within the abusive dyad:

> Mr. C. came home and found the house not tidy enough and the dinner that Mrs. C. was in the process of preparing not to his liking. He began to yell at Mrs. C., calling her a "fat slob." For Mrs. C., this was an assault on her self-

representation because she does not want to be like her mother, whom she described as overweight and not caring for herself or her children. Mr. C. continued to shout, exclaiming, "And you can't ever take as good care of me as my mother did!" This remark hit another vulnerability for Mrs. C., namely her grandiose belief that "if only I can do the right thing I can make him better." Mrs. C.'s self-esteem fluctuates intensely in response to another person's immediate appraisal of her. For instance, if a clerk in the store tells her she looks nice, she feels "wonderful," but if someone else comments negatively on her appearance five minutes later, she feels "awful."

As Mrs. C. described it at this point her "mind snapped" and she felt overwhelmed with her own hurt and Mr. C's anger and depreciation.) Mr. C. then threw all the food she was preparing on the floor and grabbed a knife. He handed it to her and dared her to stab him. Feeling overwhelmed with rage, she went after him with the knife and missed, then began sobbing. Mr. C. left and room and read the newspaper.

In the process of projective identification enacted here, Mrs. C. was the recipient of Mr. C.'s rage, some of which he expressed directly by yelling and throwing things on the floor, and some of which he projected into her. He then exerted interpersonal pressure in the form of a "dare" for her to act on it. He had already hit on vulnerabilities that were highly reactive in her and attached to her own rage, so that she acted out the destructive projection by coming after him with the knife. After this there was no need for him to continue to behave violently, and he went to read the paper.

Another example of the defensive interaction in domestic violence is found in the case of Mr. and Mrs. D.:

Mr. and Mrs. D. had been married 15 years and had three children. Mr. D. owned his own successful business; Mrs. D. worked only occasionally throughout their marriage. Mrs. D. contacted the domestic violence program following an incident in which Mr. D. had hit her during an argument and she had left to stay with her relatives. The incident of violence was a single act of hitting her during an argument rather than a beating. It was not the danger but the humiliation of the incident that brought them both quickly into treatment, where they were each seen individually for a year and then both individually and jointly.

Mr. D. was considered a high-level narcissistic personality. He was notably less grandiose than is typical and seemed to confine his sense of entitlement, deprivation, and demand that his wife be "like me" to particular aspects of the marital relationship rather than extending it throughout his life. Although Mrs. D. had underlying narcissistic vulnerabilities, she was diagnosed as neurotic, with the focus on oedipal issues.

Mrs. D. grew up in a family where "no one touched" and where pleasure, particularly sexual pleasure, was taboo. She has a strong, punitive superego but an underlying desire to be freer, more playful, and more sexually uninhibited. Mr. D. also has some difficulty allowing himself to enjoy things without guilt, particularly independent activities away from the woman he sees himself as destined to "entertain" (as he had to entertain a depressed mother). Nevertheless, he has more access to his capacity for pleasure than does his wife. He considers a good sex life with his wife as very important. Her "not responding" or "not initiating" are the things that most distresses him.

The interaction between them goes something like this: Mr. D. wants to make love, and his wife, after some coaxing, may participate and enjoy it. More often, however, she turns away, or "she'll just be passive and I feel like she's doing it out of obligation." Mr. D. then feels hurt. He may express this hurt immediately or not until the next argument, when he is soon criticizing her for not being more spontaneous, hugging or kissing him when he comes home from work, or initiating sex. She then responds by saying, "I *do* kiss you when you come home from work," whereupon they debate the quality, intensity, or sincerity of the kiss. He may contend, "That's only a peck on the cheek," or comment, "Well, you went right on cooking, and it wasn't until ten minutes later that you kissed me." She complains that "he just wants me to be exactly like him, and I'm different," or "he's too sensitive." In these arguments, he keeps pressuring her to be more affectionate, playful, and physically expressive until she either gives in (which then doesn't satisfy him because he feels it's out of "obligation"), or they both go away angry, or, as in the last argument, he hits her.

In this repetitive pattern Mr. and Mrs. D. served defensive functions for each other. When Mr. D. criticized Mrs. D. for not being more affectionate, it confirmed her sense of inadequacy in this area that was "not allowed" and also punished her for the pleasure she did enjoy. This kept the forbidden feelings inside her in check. Later, when he stopped pressuring her so much as a result of his individual treatment, she became more anxious and uncomfortable and began to deal with her conflicts in this area in her treatment. For Mr. D., Mrs. D.'s distance both served as a repetition of not having his needs met and defended against the possibility of an engulfing closeness such as he had experienced with his mother. After Mrs. D. began to change, becoming slightly more spontaneous, so that the possibility of getting what he had been asking for increased, Mr. D. sought a divorce. Manifestly, it was because he didn't have the patience to wait, but unconsciously he was frightened. In terms of projective identification, we can see that Mr. D. kept projecting his idealized image of a romantic relationship onto Mrs. D., pressuring her to live up to his fantasy of "the loving partner." When she resisted the interpersonal pressure and didn't comply, he eventually hit her. The violence came when the recipient refused the pressure and the projector became enraged.

As we saw with Mrs. G., projective identification can be a tool for change in treatment (see Ogden, 1979). The therapist, who is the recipient of the projective identification, tries to process the feelings and fantasies of the client on a higher level before they are reinternalized by the client. What happens in dysfunctional violent couples, however, is that the feelings and fantasies that go back and forth in projective and introjective identification exchanges tend to have a synergistic effect because both partners have similar underlying vulnerabilities. With participants in intimate violence, then, these mechanisms often escalate the brutal war between them. Because of the underlying similarity of character structure (Giovacchini, 1975), we see mutual acting out rather than psychological change. On the other hand, if one partner begins to change the mechanisms of projective identification, he or she may indirectly assist the other in growing also.

CONCLUSION

As we have seen, domestic violence is a multidetermined symptom rather than a diagnostic entity, with the violence serving a variety of adaptive and maladaptive functions for the couple. Problems in development that relate to the establishment of the capacities necessary for participating in adult intimacy are relevant to understanding domestic violence. In particular, an exploration of some aspects of development during the first two years of life sheds light on cases of intimate violence. Difficulties in the symbiotic phase, for instance, may be reactivated in adult relationships, leading to expressions of rage for symbiotic failures. Problems in the oral phase can invoke masochistic compensations which may contribute to domestic violence. In general, there are problems in the development of the self, with residues of narcissistic vulnerability and narcissistic rage. Indeed, cases in which narcissistic rage and vulnerability predominate are viewed as the most dangerous. The use of such primitive mechanisms as splitting and projective identification may further escalate the pattern of violence in intimate relationships.

REFERENCES

Berliner, B. (1947). On some psychodynamics of masochism. *Psychoanal. Q.* 16:459–471.
Brenman, M. (1952). On teasing and being teased: The problem of moral masochism. *Psychoanal. Study Child* 7:264–685.
Chodorow, N. (1978). *The Reproduction of Mothering: Psychoanalysis and the Sociology of Gender.* Berkeley: Univ. California Press.
Dobash, R. E., & Dobash, R. (1979). *Violence Against Wives.* New York: The Free Press.
Dowling, C. (1981). *The Cinderella Complex.* New York: Summit Books.

Elbow, M. (1977). Theoretical considerations of violent marriages. *Soc. Casework* 58:515–526.
Erikson, E. H. (1950). *Childhood and Society.* New York: Norton.
Fleming, J. (1979). *Stopping Wife Abuse.* Garden City, N.Y.: Anchor Books.
Freud, S. (1919). A child is being beaten: A contribution to the study of the origin of sexual perversions. In *Sexuality and the Psychology of Love.* New York: Collier Books, 1953.
Geller, J. (1978). Reaching the battering husband. *Soc. Work with Groups,* 1(1):27–37.
Gelles, R. J. (1979). *Family Violence.* London: Sage Library of Social Research.
Gillman, I. S. (1980). An object relations approach to the phenomenon and treatment of battered women. *Psychiat.,* 43:356–358.
Giovacchini, P. L. (1975). *Psychoanalysis of Character Disorders.* New York: Aronson.
——— (1976). Symbiosis and intimacy. *Int. J. Psychoanal. Psychother.* 5:413–436.
Grotstein, J. (1981). *Splitting and Projective Identification.* New York: Aronson.
Hilberman, E. (1980). Overview: The wife beater's wife reconsidered. *Amer. J. Psychiat.* 138:11.
Horner, A. (1979). *Object Relations and the Developing Ego in Therapy.* New York: Aronson.
Horney, K. (1967). *Feminine Psychology.* New York: Norton.
Kernberg, O. F. (1975). *Borderline Conditions and Pathological Narcissism.* New York: Aronson.
——— (1976). *Object Relations Theory and Clinical Psychoanalysis.* New York: Aronson.
——— (1980). *Internal World and External Reality.* New York: Aronson.
Kohut, H. (1971). *The Analysis of the Self.* New York: Int. Univ. Press.
——— (1978). *The Search for the Self,* Vol. 2, ed. P. H. Ornstern. New York: Int. Univ. Press.
Lederer, W. (1968). *The Fear of Women.* New York: Harcourt Brace Jovanovich.
Lerner, H. E. (1974). Early origins of envy and devaluation in women. *Bull. Menninger Clinic* 38(6):538–553.
Mahler, M., Pine, F., & Bergman, A. (1975). *The Psychological Birth of the Human Infant.* New York: Basic Books.
Martin, D. (1975). *Battered Wives.* San Francisco: Glide.
Martin, H., & Redeheffer, M. A. (1980). The psychological impact of abuse on children. In *Traumatic Abuse and Neglect of Children at Home,* ed. J. Williams & J. Money. Baltimore: Johns Hopkins Univ. Press.
Menaker, E. (1953). Masochism—a defense reaction of the ego. *Psychoanal. Q.* 22:205–220.
Miller, A. (1981). *Prisoners of Childhood.* New York: Basic Books.
Mollinger, R. N. (1982). Sadomasochism and developmental stages. *Psychoanal. Rev.* 69:379–389.
Ogden, T. (1979). On projective identification. *Int. J. Psychoanal.* 60:357–373.
Palombo, J. (1976). Theories of narcissism and the practice of clinical social work. *J. Clin. Soc. Work* 4(3):153.
Panken, S. (1973). *The Joy of Suffering: Psychoanalytic Theory and Therapy of Masochism.* New York: Aronson.
Pfouts, J. H., & Renz, C. (1981). The future of wife abuse programs. *Soc. Work* 26(6):451–455.
Pizzey, E. (1974). *Scream Quietly or the Neighbors Will Hear.* New Jersey: Ridley Enslow.
Rochlin, G. (1973). *Man's Aggression: The Defense of the Self.* Boston: Gambit.
Roy, M., ed. (1977). *Battered Women.* New York: Van Nostrand Reinhold.
Sampson, H., & Weiss, J. (1982). Psychotherapy research: Theory and findings (Mini-series of Postgraduate Education Committee, San Francisco Psychoanalytic Institute.)
Settlage, C. (1977). The psychoanalytic understanding of narcissistic and borderline charac-

ter disorders: Advances in developmental theory. *J. Amer. Psychoanal. Assn.* 25:805–834.
Shainess, N. (1977). Psychological aspects of wife battering. In *Battered Women,* ed. M. Roy. New York: Van Nostrand Reinhold.
Socarides, C. W. (1958). The function of moral masochism: With special reference to the defense processes. *Int. J. Psychoanal.* 39:587–597.
Steinmetz, S., & Straus, M. (1973). The family as a cradle of violence. *Society* 10:50–58.
———, eds. (1974). *Violence in the Family.* New York: Harper & Row.
Stolorow, R. D. (1975). The narcissistic function of masochism (and sadism). *Int. J. Psychoanal.* 56:441–448.
Straus, M. (1976). Sexual inequality, cultural norms, and wife beating. *Victimol.* 1:54–76.
——— & Hotaling, G., eds. (1980). *The Social Causes of Husband-Wife Violence.* Minneapolis: Univ. Minnesota Press.
Symonds, M. (1978). Psychodynamics of violence-prone marriages. *Amer. J. Psychoanal.* 38:213–222.
Walker, L. E. (1979). *The Battered Woman.* New York: Harper & Row.
Winnicott, D. W. (1965). *The Maturational Processes and the Facilitating Environment.* New York: Int. Univ. Press.
——— (1975). *Collected Papers: Through Pediatrics to Psychoanalysis.* New York: Basic Books.
Wurmser, L. (1978). *The Hidden Dimension: Psychodynamics in Drug Use.* New York: Aronson.

6/
Discussion: Culture and Development in Adult Family Violence
Shirley Cooper, M.S.

Early developmental difficulties, family dynamics, and sociocultural factors, particularly as these relate to the role of women, may combine to lead to violence between family members. Linda Jean Strothman has ably distilled and identified developmental deficits that can lead to disruptive violence in adult intimacy. This paper urges further, similar investigations, which may facilitate preventive intervention.

Linda Jean Strothman asserts the valid view that psychological as well as sociocultural forces play a decisive role in family violence. Although her emphasis rests on disruptions in early development, replayed by both partners in the marital relationship, she notes that domestic violence is "simultaneously an intrapsychic, interpersonal, and social event." Delineating five interrelated variables that characterize domestic violence, Strothman stresses the complexity of such incidents, while taking as her field of study the intrapsychic and interpersonal factors she has witnessed in her work with battering families.

Drawing on her experience with such families, Strothman comments that, although cultural factors play a significant role in intimate violence, "the evolution of one incident into a chronic or escalating pattern [is] influenced most by intrapsychic and interpersonal factors." She asserts that those who commit family violence tend to fall predominately within "borderline, narcissistic, impulse-disordered, and masochistically involved personalities." Yet she indicates that family violence occurs across a full diagnostic range, testifying to the significance of sociocultural factors in this complex process.

The astonishing fact that in each year at least six million men, women, and children are the victims of severe physical attacks by their spouses or parents suggests that our culture at least tolerates, if not encourages, violent behavior. And the problem does not stop there. Hilberman and Munson (1978) report that one-third of a sample of over 200 children who witnessed violence had somatic, psychological, or behavior disturbances. In addition, Hughes and Barad (1983) observe: "Studies of spouses involved in abusive relationships have reported that many batterers and victims were raised in violent homes. Thus, children of violent marriages may also be viewed as at risk for adult involvement, as perpetrators or as victims, in domestic violence" (p. 526).

From another direction—the study of divorce—Judith Wallerstein (1983) gives testimony that marital disharmony can have profound effects on the lives and development of children. Defining the experiences of a divorcing family as both a crisis and a developmental challenge, which begins "with the critical events of parental separation and culminates at late adolescence and young adulthood" (p. 231), she notes that the reduction or continuation of conflict between the divorcing parents can be an important influence on whether the family and children will pass through hierarchical adaptational tasks or remain fixated at an acute conflict-ridden phase. It seems reasonable to extrapolate from these observations that children who witness repeated violent episodes will experience even more difficulties in successfully negotiating developmental tasks and processes than those affected by divorce.

Common myth has it that women invoke—and perhaps deserve—violence by excessively dependent behaviors. Lerner (1983), however, reports that in fact "research in marital systems has indicated that both partners tend to be at the same level of psychological differentiation or independence" (p. 699), despite wide agreement that women *show* more dependent behaviors openly. According to Lerner, the culture expressed in traditional family systems often requires women to sacrifice personal competence and autonomy in the process of providing for the dependency needs of their husbands and children. She comments, "this sacrifice of competence, clarity and growth cannot be understood in terms of its 'secondary gains' or 'masochistic gratifications' (although these may be present), nor can it be analyzed successfully solely in light of the patient's projections, infantile wishes, irrational anxieties, early deprivation and distorted internalized object representations" (p. 704). A more systemic view of the family's needs in promoting the woman's dependency must be considered.

Such views credit culture as an important shaping influence on female development. Gilligan's (1982) work further emphasizes the interrelationship between cultural and psychological forces in shaping morality, calling into question "current maps of development." She notes:

> . . . we are attuned to a hierarchical ordering that represents development as a progress of separation, a chronicle of individual success. In contrast, the understanding of development as a progress of human relationships, a narrative of expanding connection, is an unimagined representation. . . . In this light, the observation that women's embeddedness in lines of relationship, their orientation to interdependence, their subordination of achievement to care, and their conflicts over competitive success leave them personally at risk in mid-life, though generally construed as a problem in women's development, seems more a commentary on our society and on the representation of development itself [p. 209].

Strothman takes her place, then, with such thinkers as Gilligan and Lerner, who recognize the importance of culture in shaping development.

Yet the fact that all marital relationships are not characterized by periodic eruptions of violence requires that factors other than sociocultural ones be considered to explain domestic violence. This leads naturally to the search for interpersonal, intrapsychic, and family system variables for a fuller explanation of violent dysfunction in marital relationships. It is here that Strothman's material makes its most useful contribution to this thorny social problem—a problem that may well recapitulate itself in generation after generation.

Utilizing theoretical considerations from the works of Erikson, Kernberg, Giovacchini, Horney, Kohut, Mahler, Rochlin, Winnicott, and others, Strothman cites incidents of marital violence to illustrate dysfunctional partnerships. Failures to negotiate significant developmental phases and tasks, particularly as these distort the capacity to achieve effective intimacy, are implicated in triggering and maintaining violence between mates. In addition, Strothman understands violence as a process and as a form of impaired object relations. In its earliest phases, the object tie is characterized by intense symbiosis, often accompanied by severe masochism, brittle vulnerability, rage, terror, and annihilation anxiety. The case illustrations often and vividly testify to the permeability of boundaries between mates and the rage that ensues when vital psychological needs are unmet by one of the partners. Case after case vignette portrays how dangerous closeness can become, with the eruption of violence serving, at times, to disrupt that closeness and providing a maladaptive, modulating vehicle for the temporary recovery of a separate, but still vulnerable self.

Moving on to the tasks of the second year of life, Strothman utilizes the works of Kohut, Kernberg, Palombo, Rochlin, and Ogden to point to deficits derived from this developmental phase that can lead to violent intimacies: extreme narcissistic rage and vulnerabilities, splitting, entrenched masochism, and a variety of introjective and projective defense mechanisms. The constant and urgent need for validation, idealization, retention of grandiosity, along with the never-ending search for mirrored perfection, are illustrated graphically by Strothman's case accounts.

Strothman comments that domestic battery often begins at the point of marriage, a first pregnancy (particularly when the woman begins to show), or after the birth of a child, and she suggests how these events lead to psychological disequilibrium, threatening the self representation of each partner. The identification of specific stressful periods is particularly useful for the development of preventive strategies for intervening with at-risk populations. Battered shelters can and do serve multiple purposes: they are refuges, respites, shelters and opportune settings for remedial services. These aids, however, are typically brought into play after the fact. To intervene before violence erupts, we must come to know which life circumstances pose hazards for people. As a society, we must then be willing to apportion resources to create essential preventive strategies and services.

Laced throughout her culling of theoretical conceptions that contribute to a deepening understanding of this significant problem, Strothman's case illustrations document the difficult—but not impossible—work of treating and helping battered victims. Although there is much yet to be learned, Strothman's excellent rendition of what is now known points us in the right direction. To acknowledge that domestic violence may occur in 50 percent of today's families without a concomitant commitment to alter that situation leaves us all victims of brutality.

REFERENCES

Gilligan, C. (1982). New maps of development: New visions of maturity. *Amer. J. Orthopsychiat.* 52:199–212.

Hilberman, E., & Munson, K. (1978). Sixty battered women. *Victimol.* 2:460–471.

Hughes, H. M., & Barad, S. J. (1983). Psychological functioning of children in a battered women's shelter: A preliminary investigation. *Amer. J. Orthopsychiat.* 53:525–531.

Lerner, H., (1983). Female dependency in context: Some theoretical and technical considerations. *Amer. J. Orthopsychiat.* 53:697–705.

Wallerstein, J. (1983). Children of divorce: The psychological tasks of the child. *Amer. J. Orthopsychiat.* 53:230–243.

II
THE CLINICAL SITUATION

7/
The First Session
Robert Langs, M.D.

The communicative approach to the first session stresses both manifest and latent messages. Patients express themselves on two levels: directly, in respect to the history and nature of their madness, and in an encoded fashion, with regard to the unconscious interaction with the therapist. Here the often-unrecognized stimuli from the therapist for these unconscious expressions are discussed. Prominent among these is the unfolding of a secure or deviant frame. Interpretation of initial resistances, both gross behavioral and communicative ones, is necessary in most first sessions, as is management of the ground rules. In this regard, the patient's fear of secure-frame therapy is explored.

Traditionally, the first session has been viewed as one of history-taking, assessment, and relative activity for the psychoanalyst (see Gill et al., 1954; Langs, 1973). Even those analysts who advocate relative silence and tend to follow the leads of the patient reveal considerable active exploration in their work in the first hour. For many, then, the interventions of the therapist during the first session are considered to be somewhat different from those offered in subsequent hours.

In previous writings (Langs, 1973, 1979, 1982), I have delineated the basic goals and techniques of the first session as viewed from the communicative approach. Now I wish to extend those writings by looking in more detail at the techniques used in the first hour. In particular, how does the nature of the therapist's interventions differ under what I call basically deviant and secure-frame conditions? This consideration leads to a discussion of the type of diagnostic profile generated through a communicative approach to the first hour and to reflections on patients who abandon treatment after the consultation session.

AN OVERVIEW

Not surprisingly, communicative studies have shown that the spiraling conscious and unconscious communicative interaction between patient and therapist begins as soon as the patient obtains the name of the treating person. All the interactional forces mobilized in both participants to treatment exist from the outset. As a result, the communicative principles of validation (Langs, 1982)—encoded confirmation on the interpersonal and cognitive levels—apply to the first session as well as to all subsequent hours. Moreover, it has been shown that the manner in which a therapist works in the first hour conveys important aspects of both the implicit and explicit ground rules of psychotherapy; it thus indicates to the patient the mode of cure that will prevail in the treatment experience.

Based on clinically validated investigations and on the considerations outlined above, it has been advocated that the psychotherapist and/or psychoanalyst[1] adopt a basic listening stance in the first session, listening in the same manner as he or she attends to the patient's material in subsequent hours (Langs, 1978). Furthermore, with certain exceptions (noted later), the therapist's interventions should adhere to the communicative principles that govern the general treatment experience (Langs, 1982). In addition to the adoption of a basic listening stance, this implies the use of interventions (when called for by the patient's material) that are in the main interpretive or directed toward the establishment and rectification of the psychotherapy (the framework). In principle, the approach eschews questions, confrontations, clarifications, and noninterpretive interventions such as directives, self-revelations, and the like, since interventions of this kind do not obtain derivative validation from the patient (Langs, 1978, 1982).

The first session, then, entails listening, permitting the patient to freeassociate, and responding primarily in terms of interpretations or framework rectification and establishment efforts. It is not a directed hour because the very attempt by the therapist to query the patient and to direct his or her free associations may be unconsciously perceived by the patient as destructive and as reflecting needs to control and manipulate. Such efforts also tend unconsciously to direct the patient toward the production of manifest content material without encoded messages (i.e., nonderivative expressions), and they lead to a mode of cure that emphasizes action discharge rather than genuine insight (Langs, 1982).

It should be pointed out that virtually every first session requires a measure of interpretive intervention because of the emergence of early

---

[1] The two modalities require comparable principles in the area under discussion and will not be further distinguished.

resistances within the patient. This principle is in keeping with the position of Gill and Muslin (1976), who advocate the early interpretation of transference and resistances in the psychoanalytic experience. They base their proposal on the recognition that a patient may be quite resistant even though he or she is free-associating—a finding confirmed in communicative studies that have identified *communicative* resistances in the presence of manifestly flowing free associations and surface cooperation. These resistances are evident when a patient fails to manifestly represent an intervention of the therapist (an *adaptive context*) or to accompany a disguised representation with a general bridge to the therapy. (These representations faciliate the interpretive process, which is constituted by a statement that begins with a represented intervention of the therapist and then proposes an explanation of the patient's encoded perceptions of the therapist in light of the intervention at hand.) Communicative resistances can also be seen when the patient fails to provide the therapist with meaningful encoded or derivative perceptions (which may be latent in manifest associations), thereby precluding the identification of pertinent unconscious perceptions as well as meaningful reactions to these perceptions.

In principle, the expansion of our understanding of the nature of early resistances—which are expressed on both the communicative and gross behavioral levels (e.g., lateness, absence, silence)—has produced an understanding of major reasons for intervening early in the treatment experience. These signs of therapeutic need in the patient and of danger to the treatment experience have been termed "indicators"—they are indications of pathology or madness in the patient, or signs of a need for intervention. There are two classes of indicators—gross resistances and symptoms or interpersonal difficulties—and either form may emerge in a first hour. In general, the appearance of resistance indicators on any level is a significant reason for the therapist to consider intervening if the communicative material permits—that is, if the patient has represented a critical intervention of the therapist (an adaptive context) and provided the therapist with a meaningful, coalescing series of selected perceptions of the therapist in light of the intervention at hand.

In this regard, it should be understood that the therapist's interventions include silence, all types of active comment, and every dimension of the therapeutic setting. The derivative material involves camouflaged or disguised messages contained in the patient's manifest associations, which take on definitive latent meaning in light of the implications of an adaptive context. Furthermore, each patient will *select* from among the many universal meanings of an adaptive context *those implications that are most pertinent to his or her own madness*. Once perceptions have been registered unconsciously and communicated in encoded fashion, the patient will respond to these perceptions with behaviors and fantasies, as well as with corrective efforts when the therapist has been in error—with *models of rectification*.

In substance, then, it is proposed that the first hour is a highly meaningful session in which the patient communicates both manifest and latent meanings. The therapist should respond to such material in a manner designed to obtain derivative validation from the patient, and consequently, the development within the patient of positive introjective identifications, a sense of sound holding and containing, and specific cognitive insight. In this way, even though the first session involves a consultation with and evaluation of the patient, it is simultaneously a means by which the therapist directly and indirectly proposes a model of treatment and cure. Indeed, quite often, the therapist provides the patient with a necessary initial demonstration of just how this process will take place. All departures from this validating model are unconsciously perceived by the patient as basically in error, as reflections of the madness or countertransference of the therapist, as a departure from the ideal frame and conditions of treatment, and as fraught with inappropriate defenses and gratifications.

THE EARLY ADAPTIVE CONTEXTS

Without concentrated thought, it is relatively easy for a psychotherapist to overlook the many interventions made to patients before the actual initiation of the first session. These adaptive contexts serve unconsciously to organize patients' material, producing one of the two threads contained in their associations. Thus, while patients enter treatment with the manifest intention of telling the psychotherapist the nature and history of their madness, they will simultaneously (and again, quite unconsciously) reveal the story of the therapeutic interaction and transactions up to the very moment at which they speak.

Manifestly, then, the therapist (as a rule) hears of the patient's illness, while latently, the therapist hears of the patient's unconscious perceptions of the therapist's efforts to this point and of the patient's reactions to these perceptions. Patients unconsciously select in exquisite fashion those aspects of the history of their emotional dysfunctions that simultaneously convey in disguised or camouflaged form pertinent selected perceptions of the therapist in light of the initial stimuli the latter generates.

Among these early adaptive contexts, there is, first, the person from whom the patient obtains the name of the therapist and the information that this individual passes on to the patient. (Ideally, this information is confined to a statement that the therapist is an effective clinician who can be of help, a telephone number and the location of the therapist's office, and little or nothing more.) There is also the therapist's response to the first telephone call, whether initially through an answering service, an answering device (this is ideal because of the total privacy it offers), or a direct telephone response by the therapist. Everything that the therapist does or does not say is of importance in the course of that telephone conversation; these become important intervention contexts for the first hour.

Ideally, the therapist will listen briefly as the patient presents his or her need for a consultation and then propose an hour for their meeting that will be available for future sessions (so that the fixed time of the therapy can be established without initial deviation). The therapist should also provide the patient with his or her office address (if this information is needed) and obtain the patient's telephone number in case there is need for an emergency contact. Furthermore, with patients who are depressed or suicidal (or homocidal), there should be a brief investigation of the patient's ability to manage such self-destructive impulses until the consultation hour (for details, see Langs, 1982). In all, during the first telephone contact, the therapist should be professional, brief, convey a sense of therapeutic concern, and not engage in an extended dialogue.

If the therapist adheres to these basic principles and does not engage in an extended conversation, or become involved in noninterpretive interventions and self-revelations, the telephone contact initiates the offer of a *secure-frame psychotherapy*. This type of treatment modality (Langs, 1982) is one in which all of the basic, ideal ground rules of psychotherapy are in effect—a set fee, length of sessions, frequency, and time; the patient on the couch and the therapist in a chair, out of sight behind the patient; the patient's use of the fundamental rule of free association and the therapist's use of evenly hovering attention; the patient's full responsibility for all sessions for which the therapist is available; the therapist's neutrality (the use of appropriate silence, interpretations, and managements of the framework directed toward its establishment) and his or her relative anonymity; and the existence of complete privacy and total confidentiality.

On the other hand, if the therapist deviates in some fashion during the first telephone call, the patient will experience the promise of a *deviant-frame psychotherapy* and respond accordingly. This second basic treatment modality involves the alteration of one or more of the fundamental ground rules of psychotherapy—e.g., not holding the patient responsible for all sessions for which the therapist is available, not maintaining total privacy or confidentiality, not providing the patient with a fixed hour or length of session, or engaging in alterations in anonymity (though much of this is unlikely to occur during the first telephone contact).

A second set of adaptive contexts unfolds when the patient comes to the therapist's office. The ideal setting for the psychotherapist is that of a solo, private office with its own bathroom and separate office entrance and exit for the patient. The suite should be fully soundproofed. Any departure from this ideal, such as a shared waiting room or the use of a public lavatory, becomes a deviant-frame adaptive context, which at times can be of considerable importance. In addition, the very manner in which a therapist furnishes the office—ideally, in good taste but not lavish—creates adaptive contexts for the patient. In general, a well-constructed setting contributes to the holding relationship between the therapist and the patient, while notable deviations impair these holding qualities. As a rule, patients will find these adaptive contexts of significance only when they are perceptively deviant. (This principle applies to the transactions of the first telephone call as well.)

Next, of course, there is the manner in which the therapist greets the patient and begins the consultation hour. Again, the ideal is for the therapist to address the patient by name and to do so with the formal use of Mrs., Ms., Mr., Dr., or whatever. Both first and last names should be utilized. The therapist should also introduce him- or herself as either Dr., Ms., Mrs., or Mr., using his or her first and last name. The isolated use of first names should be avoided, but the greeting should be accompanied by a handshake. The patient is then directed toward the consultation room, allowed to proceed first, and the therapist closes the door(s) behind the twosome. Next, the patient is allowed to find his or her own way to the chair in which the consultation will be held. There should be a single, and clear-cut choice of the chair (e.g., the patient's chair should be without an ottoman while the therapist's chair should have an ottoman). If necessary, the patient can simply be directed to the appropriate sitting place. The consultation session should not occur with the patient on the analytic couch, but should be conducted on a face-to-face basis.

To this point it is distinctive and a departure from all subsequent hours for the therapist to greet the patient by name, introduce him- or herself, shake hands with the patient, and direct the patient, if necessary, to the appropriate chair. In all future sessions, the therapist merely greets the patient with a "hello," without making use of the patient's name or engaging in a handshake. Similarly, it is only in the first hour that the therapist begins the session. In all other sessions, this prerogative is left to the patient, even when the therapist has an important or emergency announcement. In the first session, however, it is critical that the therapist establish the nature of his or her contact with the patient and indicate therapeutic concern. Thus, perhaps the most apt beginning to the consultation hour is: "With what can I be of help?" In this way the therapist begins to make clear the therapeutic nature of the relationship and his or her intention to assist the patient in seeking insightful cure.

All departures from this type of opening scenario may be considered deviant interventions; they become important traumatic adaptive contexts for the patient in the initial session. Adherence to these basic principles contributes to the development of a secure-frame psychotherapy and is then unconsciously perceived as such by the patient. In either case, once the session has begun, the therapist adopts a basic listening stance. Again, departures from the basic approach outlined here will be experienced unconsciously by the patient as deviation from the ideal therapeutic position.

Following the therapist's initial query, the patient is permitted to free-associate. With patients who do so largely without interruption, the therapist simply listens and begins to formulate the material, generating silent hypotheses, broad and specific impressions, and definitively formulating the material in the form of tentative or potential interventions—doing so in terms of the prevailing adaptive contexts and the patient's responsive, selected encoded perceptions, as well as secondary reactions. Although the listening process in the first hour does resemble attending to the patient's material in subsequent sessions, it is complex. On the one hand, it is somewhat skewed toward the surface and an evaluation of the patient's psychopathology, assets, acute problems, and other basic clinical considerations. At the same time, however, the therapist must engage in the basic communicative listening and formulating process directed toward the understanding of unconscious elements. This is done by identifying the prevailing indicators (symptoms and resistances), the most critical adaptive contexts, the most pertinent encoded perceptions, and the main reactions in the patient to these perceptions.

In time, the therapist will indicate to the patient that psychotherapy can be helpful, and will also structure the ground rules of the psychotherapy. However, the listening process must also prepare the therapist for the necessary interpretive and framework management interventions called for by the patient's material.

In this regard, it may be noted that the final exceptions to the rule that the first hour is handled in a manner comparable to all other sessions are: (1) the therapist will invoke the fundamental rule of free association one or more times in the first session depending on the continuity of the flow of the patient's associations (the invocation of this rule is quite rare in subsequent hours); (2) the therapist will structure the ground rules of the psychotherapy with little or no derivative material from the patient, doing so because of the necessity of defining the initial conditions of the treatment and the treatment relationship (in all other the sessions, the management of the ground rules will be carried out *at the best behest of the patient's derivative expressions);* and (3) at the end of the hour, where appropriate, the therapist will again shake hands with the patient (in subsequent sessions, there will be no handshake between patient and therapist until termination).

As the first hour unfolds, the ways in which the therapist maintains his or her silence and/or intervenes become additional adaptive contexts to which the patient responds consciously and unconsciously. Those interventions that pertain to the framework of treatment are especially critical—whether the therapist secures the frame or deviates. In this regard, there are several unusual, *anticipatory* adaptive contexts that may arise in this particular hour. Involved here is an expectation by the patient that the therapist will deviate in a particular fashion, as illustrated by the anticipation that the therapist will complete an insurance form. This type of expectation leads the patient, on an encoded level, to characterize the implications of the proposed deviation and the selected perceptions of the therapist which would emerge if he or she were to act accordingly. Often, a patient will introduce this type of intervention context toward the end of the first hour, and it behooves the therapist to manage the relevant ground rules and to interpret the patient's material as it pertains to such a context. As a rule, the patient's earlier associations contain *derivative directives* that point to the need to maintain the ideal frame; in addition, they provide the therapist with selected encoded perceptions that point to the detrimental consequences of the proposed deviation.

Through the accumulation of the therapist's interventions, especially those which impinge on the ground rules of the psychotherapy, the patient begins to sense the development of either a secure-frame or a deviant-frame psychotherapy. On this basis, a particular constellation of anxieties and danger situations is mobilized, and these account for the patient's subsequent encoded perceptions and reactions to these perceptions. Because of this, each of these treatment modalities must be considered separately in terms of the patient's conscious and unconscious experience, as well as the type of intervention that will be called for from the psychotherapist.

THE SECURE AND DEVIANT FRAMES

As noted, the interactional influences on the patient are considerable. They include the implications of each intervention made by the therapist, including periods of silence, active comments, behaviors, and the setting. There is, in addition, an extremely important broad adaptive context to which each patient reacts depending on its nature: the presence of either a fundamentally secure or a basically deviant set of conditions (frame) to the treatment experience and relationship.

In the course of the first hour, patients quickly, though unconsciously, recognize that they are being offered a set of treatment conditions that are fundamentally ideal and frame-securing, or, in the presence of one or more fundamental alterations in the ideal set of ground rules, that they are faced with a basically deviant treatment paradigm. In the latter case, they will respond to the sense of deviation as well as to the specific meanings of the alteration in the framework that has been invoked. Overall, the inherent holding, support, and ego strength offered to patients is quite different in the two situations, as is the nature of the anxiety and danger situation created by the conditions of treatment.[2]

A therapist's ability to create the ideal, secure-frame conditions of treatment constitutes a very powerful mixture of inputs into the patient's treatment experience. Using the seven dimensions of the therapeutic interaction (Langs, 1982, in press b), we may recognize that the *secure frame* inherently speaks toward basic trust, clear interpersonal boundaries, and a strong sense of reality, which supports the patient's capacity for reality testing (through the secure frame, the therapist behaves in a manner clearly consonant with the role of psychotherapist). The *mode of relatedness* offered to the patient is potentially that of a healthy, therapeutic symbiosis, while the *mode of cure* is potentially that of true insight. *Communicatively,* the patient is in a situation where it is safe to speak openly on both the conscious and unconscious levels, and there is no basic need for communicative defense. The main pathological *dynamic* inputs arise from within the patient, rather than from the therapist (though always in response to the secure-frame stimuli), and the *genetic* factor tends to be organized in terms of fantasy and transference—mainly, as distorted views of the therapist in light of secure-frame intervention contexts. The therapist's *identity and narcissistic balances* are viewed to be intact so that the constructive aspects of the patient's identity, narcissistic balances, and self concept are inherently supported. Finally, the secure frame expresses the *sanity* of the therapist.

In all, then, the secure frame offers much that is constructive, holding, and containing for the patient. It is a frame that is inherently ego-enhancing; it lends support to the healthy defenses of the patient, as well as healthy expressions of instinctual drives and superego functions. Indeed, in almost all cases, the patient will, on a derivative level, direct the therapist toward the development of this type of treatment condition; in essence, the patient unconsciously requests secure-frame psychotherapy.

---

[2] Both support and danger apply to both patient and therapist, though the focus here will be mainly on the patient (see Langs, in press a).

And yet, despite this rather universal appeal for secure-frame treatment, all patients (and therapists) experience this type of frame as anxiety-provoking and as a danger situation. Indeed, for some patients, the danger is so great that it appears to preclude secure-frame psychotherapy. In essence, the secure frame not only offers the best hold to the patient, but also restricts and limits the patient, thereby rendering the psychotherapeutic situation a claustrum which the patient greatly fears. Through such ground rules as responsibility for all sessions and lying on the couch, the patient will feel constrained and entrapped and will become fearful of an outbreak of impulsive fantasies and behaviors of a sexual and/or aggressive nature—on his or her own part or from the therapist. Furthermore, the therapist capable of securing the frame is seen as powerful and competent, and is therefore viewed as potentially dangerous because he or she is stronger than the patient. In addition, notable reactions of envy are mobilized, as are major forms of death anxiety.

The secure frame creates various forms of separation between patient and therapist (e.g., the patient does not look at the therapist, does not obtain direct reactions to his or her material, and must often experiences the therapist's appropriate silences). In this way it tends to engender a significant measure of separation anxiety in the patient. Moreover, because of the restrictive and seemingly dangerous qualities involved, persecutory and paranoid anxieties are not uncommon.

However, it must be stressed that the secure frame is inherently constructive and supportive, designed for the patient's therapeutic needs. The patient's fantasies of danger, loss of control, vulnerability, persecution, and the like are mainly transference-based and distorted rather than founded on entirely accurate unconscious perceptions. Indeed, the patient does veridically (mainly unconsciously) perceive the true qualities of the secure frame, but then tends to exaggerate and elaborate on these attributes to the point of distortion. (There are as well some patients who are strongly and sometimes totally convinced of the dangerous qualities of the secure-frame relationship and treatment situation, and who respond with intense defensiveness, mainly in the form of endeavoring to have the therapist alter one or more of the basic ground rules of treatment.)

In sum, then, the ideal therapeutic frame—which a patient requests unconsciously in virtually all instances—is also unconsciously perceived as perhaps the most dangerous therapeutic possibility. Mobilized in the patient are fundamental paranoid-schizoid and depressive anxieties, as well as a powerful sense of deprivation of pathological modes of relatedness and gratification—a situation that is anxiety-provoking in almost all instances. The dilemma experienced by patients in this regard creates many significant problems for the psychotherapist as well (discussed later).

As for the *deviant frame,* any alteration in the basic ground rules creates a sense of basic mistrust in the patient toward the therapist and a blurring of interpersonal boundaries (a deviation is usually overgratifying for the patient and creates an overly close or sometimes excessively distant relationship). An alteration also tends to impair the patient's reality testing (the therapist's behavior in regard to the ground rules is dissonant with his or her fundamental role as a psychotherapist). As for the *mode of relatedness,* the framework deviation promises some form of pathological autism, symbiosis, or parasiticism—depending on the specific nature of the alteration in the frame. In addition, there is a shift toward action-discharge and merger forms of *cure,* largely because every alteration in the ground rule is a form of uninsightful action on the therapist's part—a maladaptation that promotes similar efforts by the patient. *Communication* is restricted because of the appropriately dangerous image of the therapist, and on an unconscious level, the patient's derivatives become concentrated on the deviant conditions if there is any measure of encoded meaning in the patient's associations. Because alterations in the frame express the psychopathology or countertransferences of the therapist, it is the therapist's *dynamics* and *genetics* that are selectively worked over by the patient in terms of his or her own madness. On the whole, nontransference reactions from the patient predominate, so that the genetic components of the patient's material are constituted in terms of selective, but valid, unconscious perceptions of ways in which the therapist is in actuality, on some level, repeating a past pathogenic interaction. In addition, patients correctly but unconsciously perceive a deviation by the therapist from the ideal frame as a perverse act, which is pathologically gratifying both sexually and aggressively for the therapist.

In terms of *narcissism and identity,* a deviation is consistently experienced as an expression of narcissistic pathology in the therapist and as reflecting the pathological use of the patient as a selfobject; it also conveys impairments in the therapist's identity. Finally, the invocation of a deviation is viewed as an act of therapist-*madness.* In general, as the expressions of therapist madness intensify, those of patient madness tend to diminish—though only up to a point, since extremes of therapist madness tend to intensify patient madness as well.

Given that all these traumatic and pathological consequences are sources of danger and anxiety, we must also consider what the deviant frame offers to the patient. In this regard, each alteration in the frame interactionally provides the patient with a measure of pathological, megalomaniacal, and omnipotent fantasy typical of those who violate a ground rule or boundary. Each deviation also provides the patient with a pathological mode of relatedness and with pathological satisfactions and defenses. There is inappropriate sanction of superego disturbances and the offer of specific counterphobic defenses (escape from the claustrum) as well as manic ones (escape from separation anxieties). Furthermore, the patient is greatly relieved when the work of the psychotherapy unfolds around the primary input of some form of therapist madness. The patient's madness then recedes into the background, and the patient mainly reacts selectively to the actual implications of the therapist's deviant interventions. There is something far less potentially overwhelming and less personal in unconsciously carrying out the work of therapy around the therapist's pathological inputs instead of the patient's own madness. Even though the patient's pathology is involved in both instances, the patient finds reassurance in unconsciously realizing that the therapist in some measure shares the patient's illness—or at times, has an even greater share than the patient. In all, deviant-frame interventions offer the patient a variety of pathological modes of relatedness, satisfactions, and defenses. It is for this reason that the deviant frame is so often sought consciously, though on an unconscious level there is always a significant measure of protest.

INTERVENTIONS IN EACH FRAME

The secure-frame therapist holds the patient well but creates an inevitable danger situation in the form of a claustrum and depriving relationship that generates phobic-paranoid and separation anxieties. Because this danger situation and the attendant anxieties are experienced in the first session, it follows that the therapist must be prepared to interpret the patient's material in this light. Even more, because these anxieties—ultimately forms of death anxiety—may lead to the failure of the patient to return for ongoing treatment, the relevant interpretations are often imperative.

In most instances, the patient will represent the secure-frame adaptive context, usually by mentioning one of the ground rules or through a close, derivative representation (e.g., the responsibility for all sessions may be alluded to indirectly when a patient mentions the pressure to be on the job each day and the penalties for absence). In addition, there will usually be a meaningful derivative complex, which portrays the patient's unconscious perceptions of the constructive aspects of the secure frame and reactive fantasies of endangerment and specific threatening consequences. The ideal intervention, then, entails an interpretation of the patient's anxieties regarding the secure frame as reflected in these associations. Instinctual drive and genetic elements must be included if available. The main indicator subjected to interpretation is, as a rule, a sign of early resistance such as silence or an indication of the patient's reservations about entering ongoing psychotherapy.

Overall, in most secure-frame first sessions, there are signs of gross behavioral resistances, a well-represented frame-securing adaptive context, and a meaningful derivative complex, which reveals the patient's unconscious perceptions of the secure-frame claustrum and his or her distorted, transference-based responses. Interpretation of the attendant anxieties, unconscious perceptions, and reactive unconscious fantasies, carried out as specifically as possible, will often enable a patient to enter and remain in secure-frame psychotherapy. Failure to make such interventions typically leads to premature termination, often after the first hour.

In a deviant-frame situation, the patient consciously usually accepts the altered conditions of treatment, but unconsciously attempts to have the therapist modify the deviation and resolve the countertransferences on which it is based. Shored up by pathological defenses and gratifications, the patient's anxieties begin to develop around the pathological and disturbing aspects of the frame alteration. For example, the consistent offer of make-up sessions tends to evoke unconscious perceptions of the therapist as seductive, self-sacrificing, infantilizing the patient, easily manipulated, defending against aggressive impulses, and the like. It is these encoded perceptions that are experienced as danger situations and which create the anxiety leading to resistances in the deviant-frame patient.

Under these conditions, interpretation of the patient's selected encoded perceptions of the implications of the deviant intervention context, and rectification of the frame alteration to the greatest extent feasible, will tend to enable the patient to continue in treatment. Even in those situations where the frame deviation cannot be rectified, as in a clinic setting, the therapist's capacity to show the patient the meaning of his or her material in light of the deviation is inherently reassuring and insight-producing for the patient. An intervention of this kind by the therapist helps to neutralize the negative images and introjects that have been generated by the deviant situation. Failure to interpret such material—and usually, it is clearly conveyed in the first hour—may also lead to premature termination.

In summary, an understanding of the nature of secure- and deviant-frame psychotherapy, including the anxieties and danger situations each mobilizes in the first hour, enables us to recognize that patients communicate meaningfully in the first session and do indeed produce material that meets the criteria for intervening (Langs, 1981, 1982, in press c). Indeed, the frequent expression of early resistances in the first session conveys the patient's need for intervention. In other words, it is possible to maintain a basically frame-securing and interpretive approach in the first session and to intervene in a fashion consistent with all other hours.

CLINICAL ILLUSTRATIONS

Case Example 1

Mrs. A. is seen by a woman therapist, Dr. B., to whom she was referred by her obstetrician. Mrs. A. herself makes the telephone call to the therapist. The conversation is brief: there is a request for a consultation, an hour is arranged, and the therapist's office address provided. The patient arrives on time and is seen in the therapist's consultation room, face to face. The therapist's office is entirely private and in a professional building.

The therapist begins by asking how she can be of help. Mrs. A. replies that her obstetrician sent her to the therapist because of a postpartum depression. She wants to know why she is suffering. It was her third pregnancy, and she wonders if the anxiety was caused by the medication she took, because she is allergic to painkillers. She had a panic attack four days after going home from the hospital and thought she was going to die. Her obstetrician gave her sleep medication and suggested that she see Dr. B. She is not sure that the therapist can help and asks directly about the causes of such things as anxiety attacks and postpartum depressions. She then falls silent.

The therapist intervenes to suggest that instead of her answering, Mrs. A. continue to see what comes to mind. The patient then describes her tubal ligation—which she requested—and mentions that when she felt anxious, her husband gave her a body massage, which helped. A friend thought that the depression might be related to an earlier stillbirth due to congenital defects. With her second pregnancy, she had had an amniocentesis, but she decided not to do so with the last pregnancy because she did not want to have an abortion. The pregnancy was difficult and the patient just wanted it to be over. During the time, she went to a mental health clinic with her daughters, whom she was unable to manage, and established that she was the mother and they her children. She had been able to put her foot down ever since and could sleep better, but the anxiety would not go away.

The patient's mother helped out after the baby came home, but her husband had to be away briefly. Mrs. A. was frightened of being alone. She is also afraid that her daughters will be kidnapped. At this point Mrs. A. again asks the therapist if she isn't going to say anything and again expresses her thought that maybe her problems come from the medication. The therapist responds that it is still too early to say anything and suggests that the patient continue to speak awhile longer.

Mrs. A. continues. She knows she has to stop worrying. She had a bad hospital experience. If it had been her first, she never would have gotten pregnant again. There was an attempt at natural childbirth and it failed; moreover, it took four attempts at spinal anesthesia before it was effective. Some of the drug moved upward, and Mrs. A. had difficulty breathing; at the same time she felt considerable pain in her genital area. She then had difficulty sleeping and felt agitated.

Driving to her first session, Mrs. A. was extremely fearful of having a panic attack. One of her brothers was killed the previous winter in a car accident while going to a dinner with other members of the family. One of the patient's daughters asked to visit the family just before the accident, and the patient refused—she could have been killed.

The patient also expresses concern about needing surgery and her allergies to pain medication. She doesn't like using pills and wants the therapist to be helpful.

The therapist intervenes, pointing out that Mrs. A. is speaking of occasions when she has been helpless to prevent something bad from happening—in the hospital, losing a child, her brother's death. She was frightened in the car coming to her session, and there must be some connection between these thoughts and her symptoms. There is a sense of the patient's not knowing what's inside of her and trying to get some help through different methods, which don't work. Some relief came when psychotherapy was recommended; the patient seemed prepared to tolerate learning what is inside of her. Even though the panic reaction is recent, these kinds of worries have been going on a long time—the patient should thus expect that it will take some time to resolve them in therapy.

The patient responds by saying that the therapist is right, this is not the first panic attack she has experienced. There was an earlier episode while driving a car during a move from an apartment to a new house she and her husband had bought. Her neck muscles became tense. She woke up her husband, who took her to an emergency room, where she received a tranquilizer. The patient is frightened that the panic attack will return and feels that it is good that she try to carry out therapy.

At this point the therapist arranges once weekly treatment with the patient, who accepts full responsibility for a regular fee. No bill will be given to the patient, and the patient will be seen on the couch, with responsibility for all of her hours. Once Mrs. A. agrees to the structure of treatment, the therapist obtains her name and address.

The patient then remarks that her mother did not want her to come to a therapist; her mother feels that Mrs. A. can solve her problems herself. Mrs. A., however, feels she cannot do so alone. She wonders why the therapist wants her on the couch and asks what it is for. The therapist again asks the patient to say what comes to mind. Mrs. A. imagines being relaxed, but perhaps she will fall asleep on the couch. It seems nice not to have to face the therapist, yet it feels strange. The couch looks ominous,

Freudian. It is anxiety-provoking to talk to a stranger. Yet Mrs. A. usually talks a lot; she is afraid of being boring. This consultation is different from the counseling she had at the clinic. She is used to more of a give-and-take, even though she expected some of this. It will be good to get therapy started.

At this juncture the therapist points out that time is up. The patient and therapist shake hands, and the patient leaves. The following day the patient cancels the therapy by telephone without stating a specific reason.

Commentary: This session illustrates the unconscious perceptions of a highly frame-sensitive patient to a therapist's capacity to develop and secure the ideal conditions for the psychotherapeutic experience. It also demonstrates one possible consequence of a therapist's failure to interpret the patient's material in light of the secure-frame adaptive context—the premature termination of the treatment.

In brief, the main *indicators* in this hour are the patient's anxiety, her panic attacks, and her postpartum depression. There are also signs of a fear of being alone and concerns about the safety of her children. Initially, the patient seems quite interested in treatment and only toward the end of the session, in the comment about her mother not wanting her to come to a therapist, are there latent signs of reluctance to be in therapy and of possible resistance. As will be formulated, this may have emerged because of the therapist's failure to intervene correctly in a form that would have obtained validation.

The main *adaptive contexts* for this hour are the therapist's relative silence, the unfolding secure-frame treatment situation, the therapist's specific effort at intervention, her structuring of a secure-frame treatment, and her other, more minor, comments. Early in the session, the secure frame seems to be represented in derivative form by the patient's allusion to her own pregnancies (and to her womb); later in the hour, it emerges in the references to the car in which her brother was killed. Still later, the secure frame is represented by one of its manifestations—the analytic couch. Overall, then, there are sufficiently close (relatively undisguised) derivative portrayals of the secure-frame adaptive context to foster interpretive intervention.

Turning to the main elements of the *derivative complex*—the patient's unconscious perceptions, and her reactions to these perceptions in terms of fantasy and models of rectification—it is possible to cite both positive and threatening images in response to the prospect of a secure-frame psychotherapy. On the positive side, there is the patient's comment that medication makes her sick—implying that therapy without medication (i.e., with a secure frame) would be most constructive. In addition, the allusion to the patient's ability to put her foot down with her children suggests that a secure-frame therapeutic paradigm would be strong and helpful. In all, however, these images are relatively well disguised and not especially powerful—particularly when they are compared to the patient's unconscious perceptions of the more threatening aspects of the secure-frame treatment situation.

On this negative side, the patient's comment that she lost a child in a stillbirth speaks immediately to the danger of annihilation within a claustrum. Fears of penetration and harm within that claustrum are also expressed in the patient's refusal to have an amniocentesis. In addition, the patient's fear of being alone speaks for secure-frame anxiety.

That the secure frame is seen as unsafe and as not offering sufficient protection is touched on in the patient's fear that her daughters will be kidnapped. Even the reference to the ineffective spinal anesthetic points to the patient's mounting anxieties regarding the therapist's relative silence, her asking the patient to free-associate, and the patient's fears of the medical procedure—here, the psychotherapy—being offered to her. These anxieties are touched on when the patient alludes to not being able to breathe or to sleep well and calm down.

Another very strong indication of the patient's claustrophobic secure-frame anxiety is expressed in derivative form when Mrs. A. alludes to the death of her brother in a car accident—while within a claustrum. The patient's fear that her daughter, had she gone to visit Mrs. A.'s relatives, would have been killed in the same accident speaks strongly to the patient's own anxieties about entering a claustrum where she, as her brother and her own fetus, might be destroyed. Similar, but less powerful implications are contained in the patient's response, after the therapist's intervention, that her anxiety attacks began when she bought a new house—creating what should have been a more secure holding environment. Finally, the patient's dread of the couch and its Freudian qualities speak to deep anxieties regarding the unconscious perceptions, fantasies, and memories that would emerge within a secure-frame treatment experience.

It would seem, then, that when the therapist failed to interpret these representations of the secure-frame space, including the patient's encoded perceptions of the fantasied but terrifying consequences of entering its confines, the patient discontinued her treatment. It seems likely that Mrs. A. was suffering from some form of phobic-paranoid separation syndrome, and that she was highly sensitive to the claustrum—especially to the potential for the loss of control of hostile, murderous, highly destructive impulses. In light of the therapist's constructive efforts to secure the frame and to interpret some of the patient's anxieties, Mrs. A.'s images and evident beliefs of the consequences of entering a secure-frame therapy appear to be anxiety-laden and representative of a major fantasied or transference reaction. As noted by Gill (1982), this type of response is built from a kernel of truth and has a measure of plausibility, though it is indeed greatly exaggerated and even distorted. It seems likely as well that an analysis of the secure-frame anxieties in this patient would have been tantamount to the analysis and resolution of her particular form of psychopathology or madness.

In principle, then, the therapist should have identified the representations of the secure frame—the womb, the automobile, and finally the couch—and utilized them as a basis for pointing out the patient's expectations of secure-frame therapy—annihilation or death, penetration and a toxic form of harm, and finally the emergence of terrifying images. This constellation could have been used as the basis for helping Mrs. A. to understand her concerns about entering psychotherapy, and her reluctance to do so (as expressed through her mother's comments). Conscious insight into the nature of this patient's unconscious perceptions of the secure-frame situation as highly dangerous, of the sources of her mounting anxieties and emergent resistances, as well as her unconscious, positive introjective identification with the therapist as someone who was capable of managing, coping with, and understanding these issues—all might have provided Mrs. A. with the understanding and ego strength to remain in treatment and explore further. Clearly, without such efforts by the therapist, the patient took flight from the therapy—most likely, in the belief that she was truly endangered.

Case Example 2

Mr. D. calls Dr. E.—a woman therapist—stating that he has gotten her name from a therapist who did not have time to see him. He also mentions Dr. E.'s husband, himself a practicing therapist, only to state that the referring therapist told the patient that while Dr. E. is quite competent, her husband never refers patients to his wife. No discussion ensues, and an appointment is arranged.

The patient arrives 10 minutes late, stating that he went to the wrong office—he went to the office of the therapist's husband, found the door locked, and finally realized his error. When the therapist then asks what she can be of help with, the patient say he's been having some problems with his wife and was away, spending some time with his parents in Atlanta. He is trying to straighten out his life and his marriage of 15 years. (They have three children.) The patient saw a rabbi who recommended a marriage counselor, but he has little faith in that approach—two people sitting around in front of an objective third person, who listens and says what is good and bad, just won't work.

Mr. D. wants to move to Atlanta, where there are better opportunities. But his wife is opposed to it; she is tied to her family. He resents her attitude; moreover, he feels pressured by *his* parents to move to Atlanta. His wife refused to go with him during his recent visit there and things have been tense since his return; they are not talking to each other. There was an earlier period of discord. At that time the patient got involved with a woman who lives in their apartment house, and his wife became involved with her husband. Mr. D.'s wife would go to bed early and it interfered with their sex life. He would go upstairs to talk to this woman. Initially, there was no sex. Earlier today he and his wife argued about the neighbors. They had decided not to get involved again—but his wife saw Mr. D. looking at the woman. Mrs. D. is going to tell the woman's husband if need be.

Mr. D. says he calmed down in Atlanta, even though he has been laid off his job. He nearly canceled the session today because of a new job interview, but a group was involved and they couldn't get them all together. In Atlanta he saw a therapist who was helpful and showed him something about himself each session. Mr. D. wonders if this is what Dr. E. will do—give insight into people's problems. He'd be glad to share what the previous therapist told him. He wonders what Dr. E. thinks of marriage counseling. He thinks that it is really individual therapy that helps. With a woman therapist, he should get a different perspective. He then asks the therapist if it is all right to continue; she seems distracted or worried.

Mr. D. shifts to some comments about his mother, whom he sees as very strong on one level, and without self-confidence on the other. His brother developed colitis trying to get along with her and attempted suicide. Things got better when he moved out, but then his wife was killed in an accident. Mr. D. can't tolerate his mother for too long without getting depressed. His father is rigid and somehow endures. Mother has mood swings and is provocative, interfering. When his brother was getting married, mother invited people his brother didn't want to the wedding, so he simply eloped and canceled all the plans. A woman neighbor called Mr. D. in Atlanta, but his mother objected to any third parties staying with them. Mother wrote to Mr. D.'s children defending his absence. She came into Mr. D.'s bedroom and told him everything would be all right. Later on, after being provocative, she wanted Mr. D. to come into her bedroom to apologize.

Mother is a great obstacle. Mr. D. wonders if this is stuff the therapist can get into. Aren't marital problems caused when people can't communicate?

At this point the therapist intervenes. She says that before the patient came to his session, he went to her husband's office. The patient mentioned that in marriage counseling there were too many people involved in the therapy, which led him to wonder if it could help. With his upstairs neighbors there had been sexual contact with outside people, and a lack of trust, with people talking about each other. Mr. D. also mentioned his brother's sense of outrage about uninvited guests, and there were other themes of large groups of people, including the interview which he was glad the company had canceled. In all, Mr. D. seems to see therapy with her as involving too many people and is telling her that it should be canceled—that it should not be carried out this way.

In response, Mr. D. says his previous therapist built up a lot of momentum and he simply has to continue with treatment. Despite his problems with his wife, they are continuing in the marriage. For now, they both take sleeping pills and sleep in separate bedrooms; however, he's starting to feel more positive—they seem to be moving together even though they are not talking much. His wife sees that he is not involved with other women. Mr. D. needs someone to talk to.

At this point the therapist structures a secure-frame psychotherapy for Mr. D. He does indeed continue his sessions subsequently.

Commentary: In this situation, the referring therapist modifies the therapist's relative anonymity by revealing the personal fact that her husband is a psychotherapist. Although this deviation cannot be rectified, it lends itself to analytic exploration and might lead the therapist to secure the frame by providing the patient with assurances that his treatment will be totally confidential (i.e., that her husband will be entirely uninvolved). In any case, as if to accentuate the importance of this deviation, the patient goes first to the husband's office. The consequent lateness is an important gross behavioral indicator, since often such behaviors speak for major resistances to entering treatment.

The therapist's silence facilitates the patient's working over of this initial framework-deviation adaptive context. In displaced fashion, through encoded derivatives, Mr. D. reveals that his selected unconscious perceptions of the therapist in light of the deviation center on a menage-à-quatre (the patient, the present therapist, the therapist's husband, and the referring therapist). The patient thereby characterizes the unconsciously perverse, boundary-breaking sexual qualities to this deviation, which he also represents as being brought into the parental bedroom. Indeed, on another level, the therapist's husband is unconsciously viewed as the patient's intrusive mother, who needs to be excluded from his bedroom and, by implication, from the treatment experience. In similar fashion, the patient offers a strong model of rectification in proposing that the involvement with the other couple must end if his marriage is to continue—i.e., both the referring therapist and the therapist's husband must be excluded from the treatment situation if the psychotherapy is to unfold meaningfully and safely.

It is evident, then, that on an unconscious, derivative-camouflaged level of communication, this patient intensely works over, in both behavior and language, the deviation in the frame that initiated this treatment experience. On the other hand, as the patient becomes aware of the privacy of the therapist's office and of her use of secure-frame-oriented silence, there is evidence that he envisions the treatment setting as a safe harbor similar to his parent's home, where he was able to reconstitute his resources. Nevertheless, there then follows the image of the death of his brother's wife in a car accident—a sign of secure-frame claustrum anxieties with attendant fears of annihilation. It seems likely that as the therapist moves further toward securing the frame, these anxieties and issues will become central to the patient's communicative expressions and working through.

The patient's representation of the deviant adaptive context of the break in anonymity at the very beginning of the hour facilitates interpretive intervention. The main indicator is the patient's lateness, which must be taken as a sign of initial resistance. There are also latent concerns regarding the confidentiality of the treatment and a fear that in some way the therapist will repeat aspects of the patient's traumatic relationship with his parents, especially his mother (here, the genetic formulation is primarily in nontransference rather than transference terms). There follows as well a strong, coalescing derivative complex, which includes the patient's selected encoded perceptions of the therapist in light of the deviation (viewed primarily in terms of the patient's own sexual psychopathology and his problems in his relationship with his mother) and important models of rectification—the intruder should be excluded. Because of the richness of this communicative network, interpretive intervention can readily be made.

In the actual session, the therapist does indeed intervene around the deviant adaptive context in a manner that suggests her intention to secure the frame as tightly as possible. Perhaps the major failing in the therapist's effort is the omission of the genetic figure—the patient's mother—in the intervention. It is critical in all such interpretations to include instinctual drive and genetic material whenever present. Nevertheless, the therapist does provide the patient with a strong sense of insight into his perceptions of her in light of the deviant adaptive context, and she includes allusions to the critical model of rectification.

The patient's response to the intervention reveals a significant measure of interpersonal and cognitive, derivative validation—the hallmark of a correct interventional effort. There are positive images of the other therapist and of the efforts that both the patient and his wife are making to maintain their marriage—the interpersonal level of validation. There is also cognitive derivative validation in the patient's statement that his wife sees that he is not involved with other women and that on this basis their marriage can be sustained. Here, in encoded fashion, the patient conveys his fresh, unconscious perception of the therapist's ability to exclude third parties to the treatment experience. On this basis, the patient decides to continue the psychotherapy.

It might have been possible for the therapist to include some allusion to the patient's secure-frame anxieties in her interpretation. In addition, it should be noted that the therapist seems to have inappropriately delayed both her interpretation and the structuring of the psychotherapy. The latter should take place no later than 30 minutes into a 45- or 50-minute session. As for the former omission, there was a juncture midway into the hour when the patient thought the therapist was distracted, at which point the therapist might well have intervened. By then she had a strong indicator in the patient's lateness, a represented deviant adaptive context, and a clear derivative complex, with strong, selected encoded perceptions and a significant model of rectification. Nonetheless, even though the therapist bypassed this particular moment for intervention, the patient continued to express himself with additional compelling derivatives that enabled the therapist to intervene quite well toward the end of the hour.

In principle, a failure on the therapist's part to interpret the material related to the deviant adaptive context might have led to the premature termination of this treatment experience. It seems clear that the patient was quite anxious about the break in relative anonymity and the presence of third and fourth parties to the treatment experience, despite the fact that he accepted a referral of this kind. (That he did reflects the patient's split feelings and attitudes toward the deviation: wishing for it on one level, and opposing it on another.) The patient's own communication of powerful models of rectification speaks clearly to his need to have the therapist secure as much of the frame as possible. Had the therapist failed to do so, and had she shown herself unable to understand the patient's material, disillusionment might have set in, the patient's anxieties might well have mounted, and the therapist might have been experienced as someone who sanctions maladaptation through action discharge such as affairs and other modifications in appropriate interpersonal boundaries. It seems evident that the therapist's validated interpretation contributed greatly to the continuation of this treatment experience.

CONCLUDING COMMENTS

My own extended clinical investigations of secure- and deviant-frame first hours, and of these treatment paradigms in general, have pointed to a number of vital issues requiring further investigation. Among these, perhaps the most critical is the realization that some percentage of patients will not tolerate secure-frame psychotherapy at all—even in the face of validated interpretations of the attendant anxieties, perceptions, and fantasies. It is equally true that there are patients who will not accept deviant-frame psychotherapy, though initial impressions suggest that these may be somewhat fewer in number than the first group. Given that the communicative therapist is committed to an understanding of the patient's derivative or unconscious communications and their use as a guide to intervening, and given that these camouflaged or disguised expressions consistently point to the patient's need for a secure-frame therapy, the issue of the intolerance of some patients for this treatment modality is of considerable significance.

Initial observations indicate that it is extremely difficult to identify in advance those patients who find sufficient safety in the secure-frame treatment modality to remain and carry out the work of psychotherapy, compared with those who find such a frame persecutory to the point where they either force the therapist to engage in basic deviations or leave the treatment experience. Attempts to define the critical factors distinguishing these two groups of patients have yielded only preliminary impressions. Several identifiable groups of patients seem consistently to take flight almost immediately from the secure-frame paradigm—but even these show occasional exceptions. In the main, these are patients who appear to dread the experience of subjective madness and the communication of derivative or encoded expressions that give access to this madness. Indeed, these patients tend to some extent to prefer nonderivative (flat and empty) to derivative communication. They evidence a recognition that encoded expressions will reveal the sources and meanings of their underlying madness, and that these revelations will be quite unbearable. They are, then, patients who wish to carry out psychotherapy with the primary input of madness coming from the therapist (expressed through basic deviations from the ideal frame), and they will not accept a sane, frame-securing therapist for any extended period of time.

Many of these patients appear to be functioning quite well in their careers, though there are almost always signs of marital or social stress. Much of this functioning is founded on action discharge, as can be seen in reports of business manipulations, multiple affairs, flight from those with whom the patient is close, and other evidently pathological forms of behavior. The impression is that such patients have managed through rather desperate, action-supported, intrapsychic and interpersonal defenses, to seal off an agitated and primitive psychotic core. Furthermore, they dread the modifications of these defenses and the emergence of their madness on a subjective level—a dread accompanied by the anticipation of virtual psychic disintegration. These patients often present themselves with little motivation for therapy. Sometimes they enter treatment only at the insistence of others; sometimes there has been an outbreak of unaccustomed anxiety, which they wish desperately to seal off. Another group presents mainly physical symptoms, utilizing the somatic channels of expression as a means of conveying their madness without meaningful derivative content.

There are patients who dread the exploration of an acute recent or past trauma, which is in some overwhelming fashion connected to the madness they are attempting to seal over. Especially terrified of secure-frame treatment are patients with a history of a recent major accident or injury, the death of someone regarding whom there was considerable conflict, an earlier life experience with the traumatic loss of parents, siblings, or especially with the suicide of a family member. In addition, patients who have experienced some type of birth trauma, either themselves or in the case of a family member, are also fearful of the secure-frame situation since it is seen as creating a claustrum in which utter disaster once occurred—and will occur again.

In all these cases, the patient unconsciously supports secure-frame therapy even though he or she is consciously terrified and opposed to its creation. There is indeed a split between the conscious and unconscious wishes and mental constellations, as well as an unconscious split through which the secure frame is seen as safe and necessary in one sector, and as a place of mental and physical violation in another. Clinical experience indicates that interpretation of these anxieties and fantasies based on the available material in the first hour enables some of these patients to continue in treatment; however, some do not do so despite derivative validation of the therapist's efforts.

The patient who is terrified of a secure-frame treatment experience will insist on one or another basic deviations from the ideal psychotherapeutic frame. Most often, this entails insisting that the therapist agree in advance to complete insurance forms and a total refusal to explore the issue involved before reaching a decision. The message from these patients is quite clear: Either the therapist agrees to include the third-party payer or the patient will leave. More rarely, the patient will insist on a reduced fee or on not being held responsible for missed sessions because of business commitments. Here, too, it is characteristic that the patient adamantly refuses to continue treatment unless the deviation is agreed upon in advance; analytic exploration is entirely eschewed even in those situations where the material in the first hour has permitted the therapist to offer a validated interpretation of some of the unconscious factors involved (i.e., there is strong derivative support for maintaining a secure frame).

How then is the therapist to respond to these patients? Clearly, in selected cases interpretation does not enable the patient to remain in treatment, while deviation creates a deviant-frame paradigm for which the patient then unconsciously attacks the therapist. Furthermore, whenever a therapist combines a deviant condition to treatment with efforts at interpretation, he or she is seen as quite split and as quite mad. In most instances, the patient then will leave treatment prematurely or create side issues with the therapist through which the underlying rage and disappointment are expressed.

It can be seen then that the seemingly self-evident solution to this dilemma does not, in the actual clinical situation, tend to produce a successful treatment outcome. Those communicative therapists who have attempted to agree initially to the patient's proposed deviant conditions to treatment, in the hope that later rectification can be accomplished, have repeatedly found that the result is often an extremely chaotic treatment experience with premature termination. As a consequence, the therapist is damned if he or she adheres to the secure frame and damned if he or she does not—and the patient is damned as well. Continuation of a deviant-frame paradigm also proves difficult or impossible in that the patient's derivative material consistently points to the need for rectification—a measure the patient consciously opposes.

For now, the solution to this imposing problem awaits our further understanding. Some therapists have indeed found it feasible to deviate initially and to eventually rectify the frame, though as noted, this has not been the typical experience. Some other approach through which these patients could be maintained in treatment, and yet the treatment experience not destroyed, is required. For the moment, communicative psychotherapists can gain hope in the realization that this paradigm is one of the first to begin to investigate why patients leave treatment, and that it has already discovered some critical factors.

In summary, this paper has attempted to demonstrate the need for interpretive interventions in most first sessions, whether secure or deviant frame in nature. It has stressed the two levels of communication in the first hour, the manifest story of the patient's madness and the latent story of the ongoing and prior therapeutic interactions. Communicative listening has led to new ways of evaluating a patient's capacity for psychotherapy and the nature of the patient's psychopathology. It has also been discovered that patients of all diagnoses, psychotic to neurotic, will at times remain in secure-frame psychotherapy, while certain selected patients from both categories will fail to do so. This finding has led to new ways of considering the nature of the patient's and the therapist's madness, as well as the factors in continuation of treatment and cure. Major dilemmas remain; it is hoped that the present contribution has pointed to some of the factors involved and possibly to avenues of resolution.

REFERENCES

Gill, M. M. (1982). *Analysis of Transference, Vol. I: Theory and Technique* [Psychol. Issues, Monogr. 53]. New York: Int. Univ. Press.

———, & Muslin, H. (1976). Early interpretation of transference. *J. Amer. Psychoanal. Assn.* 24:779–794.

———, Newman, R., Redlich, F., & Sommers, M. (1954). *The Initial Interview in Psychiatric Practice.* New York: Int. Univ. Press.

Langs, R. (1973). *The Technique of Psychoanalytic Psychotherapy,* Vol. I. New York: Aronson.

——— (1978). *The Listening Process.* New York: Aronson.

——— (1979). *The Therapeutic Environment.* New York: Aronson.

——— (1981). *Resistances and Interventions: The Nature of Psychotherapeutic Work.* New York: Aronson.

——— (1982). *Psychotherapy: A Basic Text.* New York: Aronson.

——— (in press a). Danger situations for psychotherapists: making interpretations and securing the frame. *Int. J. Psychoanal. Psychother.*

——— (in press b). *A Workbook for Psychotherapists: Vol. 2: Listening and Formulating.* Emerson, N.J.: Newconcept Press.

——— (in press c). *A Workbook for Psychotherapists: Vol. 3: Intervening and Validating.* Emerson, N.J.: Newconcept Press.

8/
Latent and Manifest Effects of Audiorecording in Psychoanalytic Psychotherapy
Elizabeth Murray Frick, Psy.D.

Although audiorecording of psychotherapy is common practice in clinical training and research, its use raises the question: Does it distort the treatment process? Three types of conclusions in the literature about the effects of audiorecording are examined. Various investigations suggest the unreliability of patients' manifest consent to taping as an index of its actual impact and point to its adverse effects. In this light, segments of a patient's and therapist's verbatim commentaries in a taped hour are analyzed. A listening-validating process, which evaluates all the patient's associations, is used to show the potential exploitative and seductive meanings and implications of the audiorecording. It is concluded that although audiorecording does distort the therapeutic interaction, the treatment process remains available for investigation and therapeutic intervention.

The use of audiorecording plays an important role in both the training and personal treatment of many analysts and psychotherapists. Verbatim recording of therapy sessions has been increasingly proposed in the literature as a significant methodological advance, upon which research into the psychoanalytic process may rest. However, such gathering of empirical data for the benefit of supervision and research raises a highly controversial question. In what way does the audiorecording of psychoanalytically oriented psychotherapy affect the ongoing treatment process? If investigation into the therapeutic process is to be pursued in ways which are both clinically and scientifically relevant, all aspects of the therapeutic setting must be carefully scrutinized for their potentially distorting effects.

THREE EVALUATIVE PERSPECTIVES

A review of the literature can be organized in terms of three types of conclusions reached about the effects of audiorecording and their associated methods of evaluating these effects: (1) investigations concluding that audiorecording has little or no effect on the ongoing therapeutic interaction; (2) investigations concluding that audiorecording is subject solely to a personalized interpretation, which is for the most part disproportionate to the reality stimulus and more in keeping with past relationships, thoughts, and fantasies; and (3) investigations concluding that audiorecording carries a universally disturbing communication to the patient, which is predominantly realistic and in keeping with the stimulus.

Each set of conclusions outlined has been derived from discrepant modes of investigating and evaluating the phenomena under question. The first category of investigations relies primarily on the patient's direct verbal elaboration about taping for validation of its effects. Implications of the taping situation are not viewed as "grist for the mill," but rather taping is thought to exert little or no influence on the therapeutic process.

The second category of investigations relies for the most part on a type of listening that explores primarily the manifest content of the patient's associations and therapist's interventions for their potential meaning and for validation. Analysis of the neurotic aspects of the patient's reactions is considered to be of primary importance. The patient's manifest and latent material is continuously scrutinized for its allusions to the therapist, with primary emphasis given to its distorted, inappropriate, and neurotic qualities.

The third category is based on a type of listening and evaluating that takes into account both the obvious implications and the latent meanings of the patient's associations and behaviors. It is founded on the premise that the language of unconscious expression is based on and conveyed through image derivatives—that patients often do not directly reveal their disturbed reactions to events within the therapeutic setting. Thus, the patient's material must be decoded and viewed within the context of the ongoing therapeutic interaction. Input from the therapist is considered to maintain a high degree of importance, and what the patient says and does is monitored in an attempt to locate critical contexts for patient disturbance. In addition, there is a view of patient reactions which takes into account the possibility that certain aspects of responses to taping may not be neurotically based, but rather represent valid, non-neurotic perceptions.

Audiorecording Viewed as Having Little or No Effect on the Ongoing Therapeutic Interaction

The following investigations rely on a manifest level of listening or a similarly direct method of data collection that depends exclusively on concrete surface commentaries as evidence in determining the effects of audiorecording on the therapeutic process. Manifest agreement to taping is taken at face value and derivative communication is not related to the conditions of treatment or to the ongoing relationship with the therapist. The implications of taping are not viewed as open for interpretation in treatment, but rather are considered to have no observable influence. No effort is made to validate clinical hypotheses.

Qualitative Investigations: These clinical studies either (1) rely on clinical impressions about the effects of audiorecording in psychotherapy, or (2) never consider its effects. The work of Carl Rogers is an excellent example of the second position. In 1942 he discussed the advantages of electronically recording interviews for supervision and raised no significant concerns about the effects of recording on the therapeutic interaction. In a similar vein, Holahan and Slaikeu (1977) studied the effects of contrasting degrees of privacy on client disclosure and found that reduced privacy decreased self-disclosure. The most striking aspect of this study was that although all interviews were tape-recorded, the authors never considered this a variable of clients' experience of privacy. Others have advocated the use of audiorecording and have never paused to seriously question its effects (Symonds, 1939; Covner, 1942a, 1942b; Bergman, 1948; Bierer and Strom-Olsen, 1948; Blackey, 1950; Shakow, 1960; Harmatz, 1975; Korchin, 1976).

In a clinical paper investigating therapeutic playback, Stern (1970) remarks that audiorecording did not interfere with the analytic process and that confidentiality remained unimpaired. Stern presents sections of a verbatim transcript of what he describes as a model taped session. In this brief clinical vignette, the patient's productions centered on feelings of anxiety, losing control, passive seduction, homosexual submission, shame about exhibitionism, feeling used, and wanting to withdraw from the entire situation. The patient was clearly sexually aroused, with fantasies of intercourse with the therapist. He stated: "I have this basic distrust of you. . . . I always have to keep up my guard . . . you're the dangerous mother . . . she played me . . . used me like an instrument . . . she amplified her own feelings against me somehow . . . I was not allowed to have any free choice . . . she played me like a toy" (pp. 568–569). Yet Stern does not see any of his patient's associations as latent derivative perceptions of his experience of being taped. Instead, he concludes,

"Relevant for our presentation is that in this average example, the analytic process is unfolding unimpeded by simultaneous recording" (p. 569).

Quantitative Investigations: Lamb and Mahl (1956) studied the manifest reactions of patients during psychiatric interviews to sound recording and found that most of the patients went on to give productive interviews. Patients who gave consent to recording and made no further comments about it were considered to have had no reaction. In a study of the effects of audiorecording in 75 social casework interviews, Kogan (1950) concluded that tensions present during the first several recording sessions tended to disappear and thus did not interfere with the interviewing process. Kogan took patients' manifest consent to taping as evidence that it had no effect. No effort was made to evaluate latent resistance. It is noteworthy that only 10 percent of the clients returned for further recorded interviews. Other studies have reported similar findings (Friedman et al., 1978).

Audiorecording Viewed as "Grist for the Mill"

The following clinical and quantitative investigations rely primarily on a manifest level of listening and data collection that takes into account the patient's surface commentaries as evidence of the implications of taping. Encoded, disguised associations by the patient are sometimes linked to the use of the tape recorder, but are primarily interpreted as personalized responses, which are for the most part seen as disproportionate to the reality stimulus and more in keeping with the patient's past relationships, thoughts, and fantasies. Little effort is made to validate interventions. Deviations in the ground rules of privacy and confidentiality are not thought universally to impair the therapeutic hold. Rather, as in the case of audiorecording, they are considered to be available for interpretation and working through. In fact, a number of these investigations consider the stimulus of the tape recorder to function as a catalyst in treatment, further enhancing and quickening the development of the transference.

Qualitative Investigations: Gill and his colleagues were perhaps the first to vigorously question the effects of audiorecording in psychotherapy and to show keen sensitivity to its potential influence. As early as 1948, Gill and Brenman raised the following highly substantive questions:

> How does the fact that a patient is treated in a research program influence his relationship with the therapist? What, accordingly, is the nature of the patient's productions? . . . Would he feel that the therapist was "using him" to

learn something and not basically interested in helping him? . . . What would it mean if he enthusiastically accepted being part of such a program and said he would be delighted to contribute something to scientific progress? Might it conceal resentment at being a guinea pig? . . . How would knowledge of the recording effect [sic] the therapist? . . . Would his feeling about his patient be altered by possible guilt for "using" him for research purposes? . . . Or do all of these problems speedily become of no real significance once treatment is under way? [pp. 105–106].

After acknowledging these potential complex issues, the authors commented that they had sufficient experience with taping to show tentatively that possible negative influences were largely unwarranted. They stated, "When patients are told in a matter-of-fact way that the sessions will be recorded for further study by the therapist, they can accept this and for all practical purposes 'forget it' " (p. 106). On the other hand, Gill and Brenman pointed to the "deep reluctance" on the part of therapists to taping. No clinical data were presented to support their hypothesis that taping had little or no effect on the ongoing therapeutic process.

In sharp contrast to this earlier paper, in which taping was considered to have little or no influence on the patient, Gill in a later investigation acknowledges that patients do have concerns about confidentiality and many times do not speak openly and freely when the tape recorder is present. He implies, however, that the influence of recording is open for interpretation in the therapeutic interaction and may indeed function as a catalyst in treatment. "Recording points up and makes available for scrutiny and recognition factors that operate and influence the behavior of the two parties in every interview" (Gill et al., 1954, p. 120). Searles also argues that the negative effects of taping can be interpreted successfully and suggests that the tape recorder may serve as a transitional object for the patient and the therapist (see Langs and Searles, 1980).

Nearly two decades later, Gill and his colleagues put to rest earlier questions about the potential negative effects of taping on patients and became much more preoccupied with the use of audiorecording in the development of objective and exact methods of data collection, as evidenced in their statement, "In some form recording is the *sin qua non* of all scientific research" (1968, p. 233). For Gill, it is the therapist's concerns about the recording situation that have the potential to exert negative, unanalyzable influences on treatment. He points out that if the analyst has conscious or unconscious reservations about taping, he or she will be unable to help the patient work through any resistances to it. Others have also concluded that analysts resist recording primarily for defensive reasons (Redlich, Dollard, and Newman, 1950; Harper and

Hudson, 1952; Lamb and Mahl, 1956; Beiser, 1966; Carmichael, 1966; Friedman et al., 1978).

Quantitative Investigations: Sternberg, Chapman, and Shakow (1958) have investigated the problem of intrusion on privacy in psychotherapy research. They present a clinical vignette in support of their conclusion that the use of recording devices in treatment has little significant effect on the therapeutic process. The authors cite a patient whose 130th session was videorecorded. Several sessions later, this patient reported a dream she had had the night before the taped session, which revealed exhibitionistic wishes and fears of sexual assault by her analyst. The authors concluded that the filming heightened the patient's transference and produced minimal lasting effects.

On the other hand, the results of a semiprojective cartoon series, designed to indirectly tap feelings about being overheard or overseen, suggest considerable negative reactions to intrusion of privacy. Also noted is an "unspoken" resentment, in which subjects felt that they were being exploited for the benefit of others. Sternberg et al. conclude, "This might serve as a caution to the psychotherapy project not to take at face value the initial positive response of persons asked to participate" (p. 202).

Haggard, Hiken, and Isaacs (1965) have studied the effects of audiorecording and filming on the psychotherapeutic process by using several observational situations. In a "control case," the therapist took extensive notes during the session. Effects of the various recording situations were then determined by comparing the responses of the research patients to those of the control patient. The results of this investigation showed that the frequency and quality of the concerns of the control patient were virtually indistinguishable from those of the three research patients. These findings, however, must be viewed with great caution as note-taking is in itself a mode of observation. In other words, it is not surprising that the concerns expressed by the control patient were indistinguishable from those expressed by the three research patients.

Audiorecording Viewed as Having Latent Influences

The following clinical and quantitative investigations raise serious questions about the potential interactive effects of taping on the psychoanalytic process. They go beyond the patients' surface commentaries in response to taping and attempt to tap more latent and disguised implications. Also implicit in these studies is some conviction of the patient's inherent therapeutic need for a confidential and private treatment. Most important, these investigators question whether or not taping carries a universally valid, disturbing communication to the patient, which is primarily non-neurotic in its perception.

Qualitative Investigations: Freud (1916–1917) directly addressed the effects of breaches of confidentiality and privacy on the therapeutic process and can be quoted in implicit support of the position that the verbatim recording of psychoanalytic sessions carries a universally disturbing communication that cannot be merely analyzed away. He contended that when third parties are introduced, patients do not communicate meaningfully about their pathology but rather give manifest accounts of complaints and symptoms. Perhaps more important, Freud (1912b) was convinced that the technique required for research directly opposes that necessary for a therapeutic psychoanalysis.

Langs, drawing on extensive clinical observations, notes that the therapist is in a continuous unconscious communicative interaction with the patient, who is—without exception—at all times consciously and unconsciously concerned with and reacting to the set of conditions within which treatment evolves (see Langs, 1973, 1974, 1975, 1976a, 1978a, 1979, 1981, 1982; Langs and Searles, 1980). He offers a listening-validating process, which provides principles and guidelines for organizing the patient's material in an effort to evaluate the manifest and latent implications of audiorecording. Critical to this process is the exploration of the patient's associations for the key reality stimulus that precipitates the patient's responses and attempts at adaptation. A therapeutic intervention such as taping is considered to be a primary organizer of the patient's material. Primary emphasis is placed on evaluating the patient's associations in order to differentiate those perceptions and introjects which are, for the most part, valid and non-neurotic, from those which are primarily distorted and thus function as clearer expressions of the patient's neuroses. Detection, rectification, and interpretation of these valid and non-neurotic perceptions and introjects of the therapist and the therapeutic setting are essential to insight-oriented treatment.

Langs holds the firm conviction that taping is a deviation in the therapeutic framework that carries universal, unconscious sexual implications, including exposure and exploitation of both the patient and the therapist; it thus significantly alters the therapeutic process. Others have addressed the inherent therapeutic qualities of the holding environment and its implications for treatment (Milner, 1952; Winnicott, 1954, 1956, 1958, 1963a, 1963b, 1965; Bleger, 1967; Viderman, 1974; Modell, 1976).

Langs (1981, 1982; Langs and Searles, 1980) points out that patients with low self-esteem will often permit themselves to be used and exploited, which only serves to repeat past negative experiences and further confirm and reinforce their pathology. Greenacre (1959) notes that an increase in fixation of the patient's pathology is even greater when the therapist repeats past hurts and traumas. Others have commented on the patient's unconscious motivation for remaining in pathological relationships (Strachey, 1934; Racker, 1957; Stone, 1967; Balint, 1968; Strupp, 1978).

Roose (1960) audiorecorded two years of an analysis with an asthmatic patient in a research project investigating this syndrome. He concluded that although his patient raised no direct objections or comments about the tape recorder at the time of the initial session, the taping situation significantly interfered with and altered the psychoanalytic process. Specific manifest references to the tape recorder by the patient did not appear until the eleventh taped hour. At this time the patient complained directly that "his life was no longer his personal property and he regretted his agreement to the recording" (p. 321). Other associations during this session coalesced around fears of sexual exposure and concerns about confidentiality. When recording ceased in the third year of the analysis (due to lack of funding), the patient remarked on the absence of the tape recorder and reported a recent dream in which boxes of garbage were being thrown out. Roose concluded, "An effort to use recording as a validating technique was unable to surmount the restriction imposed on the experiment by the objective conditions of the research project itself" (p. 333). Others have questioned the potential seductive implications of taping (Cooper, 1975).

Quantitative Investigations: The following studies do not accept patients' manifest consent to taping at face value; instead, they attempt to investigate its effects through a combination of direct and indirect methods of data collection. All rely on quantifiable criteria measures. Three of these studies (Roberts and Renzaglia, 1965; Gelso and Tanney, 1972; Gelso, 1973) qualify as true experiments in concurrence with the standard criteria of Campbell and Stanley (1963; see also Gelso, 1974). Each of these empirical studies strongly suggests the potential adverse effects of audiorecording on the therapeutic process.

Roberts and Renzaglia (1965) studied the influence of tape recording on counseling and concluded that taping adversely affected certain aspects of the counseling process. Their results showed that with the tape recorder in full view, clients made significantly more favorable comments about themselves than when they thought that their sessions were not being recorded. Interestingly, the results also showed that therapists made more appropriate interventions when they believed that no recording was being made. In addition, it was found that therapists estimated their performances consistently and candidly whether or not they felt that their reports could be verified.

The findings of Gelso and Tanney (1972; Gelso, 1973, 1974) support those of Roberts and Renzaglia. These later investigations indicated that clients whose sessions were audiorecorded were much more likely to feel inhibited and blocked than those whose sessions were not. Manifest consent to taping was considered a poor indication of its potential effects. Others have reported a positive correlation between audiorecording inhibition and high anxiety (Sauer and Marcuse, 1957; Van Atta, 1969).

Summary of Literature Review

The results of the clinical and quantitative investigations just mentioned indicate that when the introduction of audiorecording is evaluated using a level of listening that takes into account both the patient's manifest and latent references to the taping situation, the audiorecording is seen as significantly distorting the therapeutic process. In contrast, studies that evaluated patients' material for its manifest content only conclude that taping has little or no effect on the therapeutic process. The following findings support these conclusions:

1. Those empirical studies which qualified as experiments and investigated the implications of audiorecording through indirect methods of data collection (methods that did not rely solely on patients' manifest commentaries) found that taping imposed numerous adverse effects on the treatment process. Specifically, audiorecording was found to heighten inhibition (Roberts and Renzaglia, 1965; Gelso and Tanney, 1972; Gelso, 1973). Most important, these studies concluded that the patient's manifest consent to taping was a highly unreliable index of its actual potential effects.

2. Those investigations which did not rely on a clinical validating methodology, quantifiable criterion measures, or adequate control groups concluded that either audiorecording was "grist for the mill" in treatment or that it had no effect whatsoever. These findings were primarily based on broad clinical impressions, which were not grounded in the systematic analysis of clinical material. For the most part, patients' manifest consent to taping and verbal elaborations were taken as evidence that it had no effect. It must be stressed, that patients' manifest commentaries about taping were examined primarily from initial or early treatment sessions. The quality of these commentaries may have proved different as treatment progressed.

3. Finally, in those investigations which concluded that taping had no effect, all clinical data presented, almost without exception, if carefully

searched for both manifest and latent associations to taping, indicated the highly seductive, depressive and exploitative meanings that taping carried to the patient (Sternberg, et al., 1958; Stern, 1970).

CLINICAL VIGNETTE

The Patient and Conditions of Treatment

Mr. B. is a single, black professional in his late forties who sought treatment at a small outpatient clinic as the result of an acute depressive episode. The onset of his depression was directly precipitated by attendance at an important social gathering of professionals, where he made inappropriate, "off-color" remarks and subsequently felt tremendous remorse. He became so severely depressed that he was unable to return to work for nearly one month.

The therapeutic setting within which Mr. B. began treatment contained multiple deviations of confidentiality, privacy, and anonymity. Upon arrival at the clinic, he was first interviewed by a psychiatric resident and assigned to a therapist. At this time he was also evaluated for medication and given a prescription for sleeping pills. Although Mr. B. had the financial means to pay for therapy, no fees were charged for treatment. Before each therapy session he was required to report to a receptionist, who kept a record of his visits. One month into treatment, Mr. B.'s first therapist announced that she would be leaving the clinic shortly for full-time private practice. He was offered private treatment with her at a reasonable fee; however, he chose to remain at the clinic and requested an immediate transfer to a new therapist.

For the following nine months, Mr. B. was seen in twice weekly psychotherapy by a white, female therapist at a regularly scheduled time and place. Because the therapist was an intern in training at the clinic, there was an impending forced termination and implicit breach of the therapist's anonymity, from the time of the first session. Although the therapist did not inform the patient that she was discussing his case with third parties, supervision was implied due to her student status. With the exception of the initial session, the first four months of treatment were audiorecorded.

The Initial Session

Mr. B. began the initial hour stating that he felt depressed, unsure of his perceptions of others, and debilitated in attempting to relate to family and friends. He described himself as having become increasingly less tolerant and more suspicious of colleagues at work; he also found himself withdrawing from family and friends, frequently not answering his telephone for long periods of time. He commented, "Life for me is fighting everyone. I only feel safe in my apartment alone where no one can get me." Mr. B. blamed himself for being paranoid and sick. He reported a longstanding history of highly disturbed object relationships and a childhood in which the needs of his mother were the primary focus of their relationship. With considerable depressive affect, he described how, when he was a little boy and hungry, his mother made him wait while she ate first. Thus, Mr. B. represented as his first mode of relatedness, one in which interpersonal relationships were highly exploitative, parasitic, and persecutory.

Mr. B.'s presenting symptoms of depression, anxiety, and suspicion, as well as his recollections of a maternal figure who was greedy, exploitative, and preoccupied with her own needs, must first be considered as potentially valid and non-neurotic, selected encoded derivative perceptions and introjects of the therapist and therapeutic setting. The conditions of Mr. B.'s treatment thus far provided a background that contained a valid basis for deep-seated mistrust. Like the mother who ate before her child, the patient's first therapist had left the clinic, placing her own needs first. Similarly, the second therapist, a student, was treating the patient out of her need for clinical training. Once her training requirements were met at the end of the year, she would also leave him. On the other hand, one must consider the extent to which these conditions and mode of relatedness also met the pathological needs of this patient, as it was clearly within his means to seek a more private, confidential treatment.

Three-quarters of the way through this initial session, the therapist intervened to state the basic ground rules of treatment, which included the time and place of sessions, frequency of sessions, length of sessions, fundamental rule of free association, and date of termination. At this time she asked Mr. B. for permission to audiorecord all future therapy hours. Without requesting further explanation, Mr. B. responded that it made him feel "very special" that the therapist wished to tape his sessions. He told her that she should feel lucky to have him as a training case because he was "bright, articulate, willing to talk, and more like a private-practice patient." He considered it a good idea for her to review all of his sessions and "pick them apart in detail." He revealed that he made a practice of taping most of his personal telephone conversations in an effort to protect himself and ensure that he was not "liable for anything." Furthermore, he elaborated that if a "copulation" [sic] was made of all of his taped sessions, the therapist might discover something "classical in his case," which could then prove useful in the treatment of future patients with similar disturbances. Mr. B. recommended that the therapist keep records of his sessions in her "archives" for future reference. Other associations at the end of the hour coalesced around Mr. B.'s general feelings of distrust and difficulties in accurately interpreting the motives of specific fellow employees at work.

Examination of Mr. B.'s direct and indirect associations to the therapist's request to audiorecord reveals multiple levels of meaning. Manifestly, Mr. B. felt quite gratified, as evidenced in his statement that he felt "very special." However, he also used the phrase "pick them apart," which implied judgment and criticism, and he referred to himself as a "case," which is highly intellectualized and impersonal, and likely a valid introject of the therapist's unconscious perceptions of him at that time. His suggestion that the therapist review his tapes and keep them in her "archives" implied a perception that the therapist would take a part of him away from the hour with her. Highly narcissistic patients who have experienced an early traumatic defect in the mother-child relationship many times anticipate that the therapist will idealize them and participate in merging, mirrorlike fantasies. With the audiorecorded sessions, the therapist has the patient's thoughts captured on tape to take away from the hour with her, and this implies a lack of separation and appropriate boundaries.

Mr. B. pointed out that the taping of his sessions might prove beneficial and useful to the therapist and future patients, not to himself. Also noteworthy was his apparent unconscious substitution of the word "copulation" for "compilation," which again implies a coupling, joining, or merging of boundaries with sexual undertones. Mr. B.'s subsequent associations in this hour to feelings of mistrust toward peers at work must be viewed in the context of the ongoing therapeutic relationship. Through a process of unconscious selectivity he was enable to convey to the therapist the latent meanings of his immediate relationship with her. It may be recalled that exposure of his verbal comments in a public setting was reported by the patient to have precipitated the intense depressive episode for which he sought treatment.

Overview of First Four Months of Treatment

Over the subsequent four months of treatment, the patient made few direct references to the tape recorder. During this period he experienced considerable relief from his depressive symptoms; however, he continued to be highly mistrustful and suspicious. Frequent references to his mother appeared in his commentaries. She was described as "reaching, grabbing, and sucking him dry." There were also numerous associations to "white people," who were described as nice on the surface but basically not respectful of blacks and not to be trusted. In addition, Mr. B. made numerous attempts to disturb the treatment framework in other significant ways. He asked the therapist to explain his problems and behaviors to his superiors at work. Other proposed treatment deviations included requests for extra sessions, changes in appointments, advice and guidance, and medication.

With all the deviations of privacy and confidentiality inherent in this therapeutic setting, it would be difficult to prove definitively that these associations and behaviors were all related directly to the taping. Nevertheless, they appear to contain encoded commentaries on the implications of this deviation. During this four-month period, efforts were made by the therapist to interpret to the patient some of his valid, unconscious perceptions of feeling exploited and used as a result of the taping and other breaches of confidentiality and privacy. However, in light of the continued taping, they had no significant observable effect on alleviating his paranoid symptoms. The patient's material following such interpretations frequently included associations to people who say one thing but do something quite different. These commentaries conveyed a split image of the therapist, who, on the one hand, understood what was going on while, on the other hand, did nothing to rectify the situation.

The session selected for presentation represents a turning point in the therapist's ambivalence about the destructive implications of taping. In it, the patient clearly and directly represents the tape recorder as the primary stimulus that is evoking his disturbance.

The Previous Session

The patient began the previous hour very upset, complaining about the clinic receptionist: "They should treat me better at this clinic." He further noted, "The people out there [in the reception area] treat you like steer." It reminded him of how he had kept an incompetent employee on his payroll when he was the director of a company because he had some "redeeming value." He then began talking intently about black politicians who do not have the strength to stand up firmly for issues that he knew they believed were right. He told the therapist that he had no power at work; he was "like a capon in a chicken yard." The therapist intervened in this session in an attempt to link herself with the incompetent employee because she did not stand up in the face of clinic policies which disturbed him immensely. Subsequent associations were made by the patient to people who are insecure and shaky about their positions.

It is noteworthy that Mr. B.'s associations are colored with some positive images of a person who has some redeeming value. The fact that in the past the therapist had attempted to interpret some of the valid and disturbing implications of the treatment setting may account for these positive introjects. On the other hand, her failure to rectify these conditions explains his unconscious perception of her as weak, insecure, and unable to stand up for issues she knows are right.

The Session

Mr. B. was on time for the session. The hour began:

> Mr. B.: I was sitting out there and I was feeling pretty good, not too apprehensive; things have been looking up. And then I heard you put that thing in there [the tape in the tape recorder] and start that thing, and it sort of bothered me and I don't know why, and I was thinking about how I was feeling pretty good and that thing just bothered me. Do you do anything with those things? Do you?
>
> Therapist: Something has brought that up. Let's see what comes to mind.
>
> Mr. B.: I don't know why. I felt apprehensive, twinges of anxiety, fearful of coming in. I don't know why. I was sitting out there reading a magazine. I didn't know if you were in here or not. I was wondering, then I heard the thing click and I said, "Oh, my God." Then the door opened. Prior to that I hadn't given it too much thought. I was sitting out there with a relatively open mind. Then I heard that and it just sort of took the edge off, left me cold. I don't know why. Do you—Does it really do you any good? Do you really get anything out of it? It bothers me. I used to keep notes and wasn't encouraged to do that. I just wondered. Today it sort of bothered me. I don't know if there is anything to be read into it. I was relaxed until I heard that. [Silence.] Like now, it's like feeling you have to perform. I still can't get a handle on that. It's like being aware that the thing is there and trying not to pay any attention to it. But this time, it just sort of broke through. It just sort of broke through.

Commentary: Mr. B. begins the hour directly telling the therapist that her use of the tape recorder is causing him to feel disturbed, apprehensive, anxious; that he was fearful of entering the consulting room. Mr. B. is indicating that the taping has functioned as a barrier in treatment, impeding him from entering the session with an open mind necessary to comply with the fundamental ground rule of free association. He copes with this highly anxiety-provoking situation by exerting intense interactional pressure on the therapist to respond to his question. In this way he attempts to gain relief and rid himself of inner tension by putting it back into the therapist. Mr. B. further offers the therapist a model of rectification through indirect supervision, as evidenced in his encoded comment that he used to keep notes but was advised by his supervisor not to. There is evidence that he has been defending against anxiety about the taping in the past when he comments, "But this time, it just sort of broke through."

> Mr. B.: I was feeling pretty good . . . [Laughing loudly:] I've been tearing my neighbor up. I've been wearing her out and I'm not one to embark on these relationships because of, number one, fear of rejection and, num-

ber two, they involve a certain amount of closeness and responsibility and all of that . . . But, she has nerve enough to be slick. S-L-I-C-K. She approached me about assuming some obligations . . . It was odd, because situations like that in the past I have not been able to handle too well, but with this there was no problem. She comes up to the apartment and she doesn't look like she needs any extra meals, but she [laughs] orders some Chinese food . . . She's big on somebody spending money on her . . . She was using, reaching, but I didn't respond like I ordinarily would have, where I felt anxious, apprehensive, and cut off cold. When you're in a compromising situation, like having intercourse, you're supposed to acquiesce, but it didn't work like that.

Commentary: Mr. B. has shifted from directly referencing the taping situation to a rich variety of derivative commentaries, which begin to organize and coalesce meaningfully around this deviation and shed further light on its specific meanings and implications for him. This new material begins to provide derivative validation for the initial silent hypothesis that taping is the key reality stimulus disturbing him. Exhibiting a low level of communicative resistance, he associates to a relationship with his neighbor that is highly parasitic, seductive, and overtly exploitative. He represents a mode of relatedness in which someone is out to harm and manipulate him, in which his needs are not considered. Like the therapist who is using him to meet her training needs, his neighbor is using him for sex and money, expecting him to be responsible and assume obligations he experiences as disturbing and inappropriate. Furthermore, Mr. B. is saying that this is something that she doesn't need to do. His associations also represent an unconscious perception of the therapist's relationship with her supervisor. He may be accurately perceiving and introjecting her anxiety about performing and acquiescing in supervision. There may also be a similar representation of the supervisor, who is making unreasonable demands on the therapist and intruding into the therapeutic relationship. Furthermore, Mr. B. may be unconsciously perceiving the therapist as gratifying her narcissistic and sadistic needs by performing for a third party and requiring him to submit to her. Mr. B.'s sadistic sexual behavior represents not only an allusion to what he perceives is being done to him, but also what he would like to do to the therapist in retaliation. Like his neighbor, Mr. B. perceives the therapist as insecure, unsure of her position, dangerous and seductive. In this contaminated field, he recognizes a great deal of shared pathology.

It must be emphasized that Mr. B.'s pathology is contributing significantly to his selective responses to taping. There is certainly evidence that he has exaggerated, distorted, and instinctualized its meanings and implications. Nevertheless, the therapist, while not overtly seductive, has exploited and exposed him. On one level, the taping is highly narcissistically gratifying. The therapist is perceived as using the patient because he is so impressive and fascinating. Under such conditions, patients often experience further pressure to act out their impulses and actually seek out similar modes of relatedness with outside figures, thus reinforcing their pathological equilibrium. Because Mr. B. is working over essentially valid unconscious perceptions of the therapist, the extent of disturbance he brings to this situation remains secondary.

Mr. B.: We lay up there, me inside of her, for at least an hour. Something I read a long time ago about how Indians can do this. This is one of their— whatever . . . Even with her talking about money, I didn't lose my erection . . . Basically, I'm a cut above, sexually, and so far things seem to validate this. It's like the fact that she thinks I can elicit a climax from her. No. No. It's making her think she wants to. She has to call it before she'll come . . . But all of these things do seem to hold a tremendous amount of fascination for her. And she just couldn't understand how I could stand in the face of such duress, talking about money, me inside of her [laughing]. She remarked that it was fun, strange, and odd at the same time, because this was something that she had never done. We enjoyed ourselves immensely.

Therapist: It bothered you that she was being slick, using you, expecting you to perform and, uh, assume obligations, be responsible, and you saw this as her insecurity, but her tremendous fascination with you was also somehow very enjoyable.

Mr. B.: [Laughing loudly:] She brought these little suppositories with her. She asked me to get her one out of her coat. So I went to the other room and found the thing wrapped in Kleenex. I found this little round piece of candy and put it in the Kleenex and dropped the suppository on the nightstand. I gave her the Kleenex and she said, "What is this?" [Laughing:] She said, "Oh, my God, I must have left it at home." I said, "No problem, I probably have an extra one here on my stand." It was only after I had told her that I had taken hers and put it there that she believed me. She has this attitude that I'm a player, that I have women running in and out. But this time, I thought I'd milk it for all it's worth. [Laughing:] It's just a play on words. She has a nice chest, too, If I turn red. It's not too easy for me to turn red. If you're black and turn red it must really have struck you. [Laughing:] She called me the next day and asked if I planned to call her. I looked at the clock and told her, "Yeah, I was going to call you at 9:30." It was 9:15. I said, "Let me call you back." So I waited until about 10 to call her back and didn't talk too long. She kept me up until 4 that morning. It's lucky she doesn't live on the north side. It would have been a long way to go. It really made me come alive, but I don't want to get involved in any entangling relationships. There's nothing about her that is particularly outstanding. She has big eyes. It's been very discreet. No need. She's divorced. The mystique is gone. You've got it and you don't want it anymore. There is only one thing bad about it: she can look out her window and see when my light is on. I know what you're thinking. Most people think that you give somebody something and that's all they want and then they go and leave you.

Commentary: Mr. B. continues to communicate derivative associations that further organize meaningfully around the taping, as well as the other multiple deviations of confidentiality and privacy inherent in his treatment. Listening to this material in the context of these deviations, it is clear that he continues to feel exploited and used by the therapist. He vividly describes his girlfriend's use of him and in return, his use of her. He copes with the highly depressive implications of the reality of this relationship through reaction formation and action discharge, employing manic defenses in an attempt to repair narcissistic injuries. As with his neighbor, he flaunts his sexual prowess with the therapist in an effort to impress, fascinate, and gain her admiration. At the same time, however, he is communicating to her through disguised messages—"I can't be responsible for meeting your needs. I can't take care of you. I need for you to take care of yourself." Mr. B.'s association, "Even with her talking about money, I didn't lose my erection," and his comment that he could maintain his erection for at least an hour are indirectly representative of his ability to communicate so well in the treatment hour and work so hard therapeutically in the face of so much duress in the treatment situation. Also contained in these associations is his wish to seduce the therapist and his perception of the taping as narcissistically exciting and evidence of the therapist's sexual fascination with him.

It must be emphasized that there is a great deal of interactional pressure present during this hour. The patient laughs loudly, at times uncontrollably, and gesturing continuously to the therapist. It is as if he were holding the therapist captive, in the face of highly charged, grandiose expressions of his intense aggressive and sexual needs, in retaliation for her requiring that he submit and be held captive by the taping. His latent message to the therapist is: "If you are going to force me to perform, I'll show you how well I can do, but I'll also show you how it feels." Mr. B. also notes his negative feelings when his privacy is threatened, as evidenced in his comment that he feels "bad" that his neighbor can look out of her window and see when his light is on.

The therapist intervenes with a direct playback of derivatives, an intervention critically lacking in reference to the patient's sexual and aggressive material. This intervention is clearly in error, as the patient has provided the therapist with ingredients of a full communicative network, including the adaptive context of taping, the indicators of disturbance, and the coalescing derivative network and bridge to treatment (all of which necessitate an interpretation linking the specific meanings and implications of the taping directly to the therapeutic interaction). This omission represents an instance of counterresistance on the part of the therapist. The high degree of interactional pressure, the primitive sexual idiopathic meaning that the deviation carried for the patient, and the fact that this was a vested-interest deviation for the therapist, reinforced by her supervision, probably account for her failure to make an appropriate intervention at this time.

Mr. B.'s commentaries following the therapist's intervention further serve to aggrandize himself and repair his self image. Associations to hostile manipulation and trickery appear in his material. His association to hiding his neighbor's prophylactic contains multiple meanings, around which some conjectures can be made. Because the therapist was unable to hold and contain him and avoided his highly sexually charged material, this may represent an allusion to inserting or dumping back into the therapist, forcing her to contain the unadulterated, raw contents of his pathology without protection. Mr. B.'s comment that he will "milk it for all it's worth" is an indirect allusion to the therapist's use of him and his use of her in return; it represents the highly aggressive and sexualized meanings and implications that this relationship holds for him.

Mr. B.: You know I just don't go around having sex with people . . . Maybe I did it this time because I thought I was in complete control of things. When she talked about my doing my part, I asked her what it would consist of. She said, "Well, about 25 dollars a week . . ." Well, that was just a feeler. Do you really think that I need to pay somebody to be my friend? . . . I'm special . . . She's no "10." I just have problems with people who are beggars . . . But this didn't bother me, and I'm very pleased about it. Another time I would have been completely defensive, trying to explain my budget and my commitment. When she approaches it again, I'll make her feel a little ludicrous and tell her that seemingly she gets just as much, if not more, out of it than me. Maybe she should give me some money [laughs] . . . It bothers me, but it's a matter of being in control of a situation, and it's something that I have lacked for a very long time.

Therapist: You're saying that she's getting more out of the relationship than you reminds me of your comments about the tape recorder. You started out telling me that you felt anxious, apprehensive about coming in, and cut off after hearing me put the tape in, feeling like you had to perform and wondering what I was doing with the tapes and getting out of it because it bothered you. And now, you're telling me about a situation where someone is using you and getting more out of the relationship than you are, and I think there is a parallel here and that you are telling me that my taping your sessions is disturbing you and making you feel used here, that I'm getting more out of it than you. But, like in other situations you've described, you feel compelled to acquiesce and out of control of the situation, where you feel you need to be in control.

Commentary: Mr. B. continues to represent a highly parasitic mode of relatedness. Contained within his associations to money are embedded derivative references to free treatment. Mr. B. is telling the therapist indirectly that she is "no 10." His treatment is flawed and not worthy of a fee. He represents an image of how exploitative it is to charge no fee and to pretend to give treatment while taping. Even though he pays no fee for therapy, there is a veiled message that the therapist is getting more out of the relationship than he is, and therefore should pay him for the tapes of his performance. He is providing her with the training she needs and getting little in return.

The therapist's intervention following this material directly identifies the taping situation as the key reality stimulus that is disturbing the patient. It represents an effort to interpret the unconscious meanings of this deviation to the patient, as expressed in his derivative associations, and to link these meanings and implications directly to the therapeutic relationship. Although this intervention accepts the valid core of perceptiveness in the patient's associations, the therapist again avoids the specific, highly seductive and aggressive idiopathic meaning that this deviation carries for the patient. Counterresistance continues to be evident in the therapist in light of the patient's highly primitive sexual material, which she has difficulty containing. Mr. B.'s further associations must be searched for unconscious meanings and implications of the therapist's intervention. In light of the therapist's effort to understand and interpret the patient's unconscious communications, partial validation is likely in his further derivative responses; however, some disturbance associated with her failure to address the highly specific meanings and implications of this deviation for him is probable.

Mr. B.: It's very mechanical and impersonal. I don't know quite why it's so upsetting. I just couldn't block it out of my mind. Maybe you need to do it. Yeah [laughing], last week was really something. You know, it's odd, you just don't seem to find relationships now where somebody isn't looking for something other than what's tangible. I told my neighbor, "You're just used to people gouging you all of the time. There are other facets of life that you should look into and, if you'll allow me, I'll open your eyes because you are partially blind right now, and I want you to see things that you don't see too well." The point was very well taken by her and we enjoyed ourselves tremendously. I took stock and said, "Hey, you're really in control here, not trying to be what others want you to be." I told her, "Look at all the time they took to negotiate Iran, maybe we can negotiate things on down the line on this. I don't want to be in a relationship that adds to responsibility and expectations. That's why I don't initiate things. I think what's best is that we become neighbors again like it was. But I'll always leave my door open, just in case."

I stay to myself, mostly. Nobody knows too much what I do. I'm assuming she thought I was some kind of fruit. People have a tendency to think that if you're not questing after women. I have a neighbor downstairs who's involved in the church and real down on gays. Maybe she thought I was gay because I didn't hit on her. She was very attractive, but it just didn't materialize. I do have one close friend in the building who is very up on everything that's going on, and he really keeps me informed.

Therapist: I see that our time is up.

Commentary: Mr. B.'s associations following the therapist's intervention provide striking partial validation and an unconscious model of rectification and effort to supervise the therapist, who has been only partially correct. Mr. B. first responds manifestly that the taping is mechanical and impersonal. This commentary must also be viewed as an unconscious perception of the therapist's intervention, which left out the highly specific personalized meanings and implications of the patient's material. Mr. B. further associates to exploitative and destructive relationships, and offers the therapist unconscious supervision, implicitly telling her that she is partially blind and that if she will only listen and allow him, he will open her eyes to things that she doesn't see too well. Mr. B. perceives the therapist as partially blind as the result of her inability to offer him a complete interpretation as well as her continued use of the tape recorder, in view of its highly destructive and disturbing implications.

There is, however, evidence of some positive introjection of the therapist's healthy functioning (in her attempt to understand the truth in the patient's unconscious communications to her) when Mr. B. comments, "The point was very well taken by her." Mr. B. offers the therapist a model of healthier functioning in his statement, "I think what's best is that we become neighbors again." Noteworthy of his tremendous ambivalence and deep reluctance to give up this highly gratifying pathological mode of relatedness is his comment that he will leave his door open, just in case. Following the therapist's intervention, Mr. B. felt more in control and showed hope that perhaps, as in Iran, where people were held captive against their will for a very long time, he and the therapist can negotiate about the tape recording on down the line. It must be stressed, however, that Mr. B.'s further associations hint at the more negative implications of the therapist's inability to contain him and rectify the recording situation;

they may represent his unconscious perceptions of her inability to do so as being related to some difficulties she may be having with her own sexual identity (as evidenced in his statement about others' concerns about his sexual identity). Mr. B. ends the hour with an association to a positive figure, a friend who keeps him informed.

Overview of the Succeeding Five Months

Shortly after the session presented, taping was stopped by the therapist at the behest of the patient. In the final taped hour, Mr. B. began the session anxious and depressed, telling the therapist that the previous week had been "rough." He was scheduled at work to give an oral presentation to a large group of professionals on a topic he was quite familiar with; nevertheless, he felt that he "just couldn't handle it." He had canceled a similar oral presentation the previous year out of similar fears of self-exposure even though it put his job in some jeopardy. He stated:

> I just don't want to do it . . . It's a hassle and chore just getting started. I don't want to interact with other people . . . You know, I used to think I was an asset and now I'm just barely toddling along.

Approximately halfway through the session, Mr. B. mentioned the tape recorder. He said:

> At first it didn't really make any difference, but now it seems to pose some threat. I guess it's just that I don't want anybody going over, you know, my thoughts or ideas once I say them. It doesn't matter. It just might fall into somebody else's hands inadvertently. I don't mean that you'd give it to somebody. People steal. I'm just out of joint.

Mr. B. further associated to feelings of uneasiness and wishes to remain "sitting at home," where he felt safe. At this point in the hour the therapist turned the tape recorder off. She then linked Mr. B.'s associations, as well as his anxious and depressed feelings around his upcoming oral presentation at work, to his similar feelings about her taping his therapy sessions. She stated that under these conditions he was telling her both directly and indirectly that the taping needed to stop in order for him to get well.

Although detailed process notes were not available on the remaining half of this session, it is noteworthy that Mr. B.'s depression lifted significantly after the cessation of all recording and that two weeks after the taping stopped he gave his scheduled oral presentation at work with a great deal of success. Subsequent sessions contained positive associations to his good functioning and feelings of unconditional acceptance by others at work for what he had to offer.

Through the use of a level of listening that searched all of Mr. B.'s associations for the possible manifest and latent meanings and implications of the recording situation, it became apparent that no interpretation, no matter how timely, complete, and accurate, could detoxify the negative and destructive implications of taping for this patient, as long as this deviation was left unrectified. Mr. B. came to treatment feeling depressed, paranoid, and exploited. The therapist continued to repeat these past hurts and traumas, which only reinforced his sickness and made its resolution impossible. Mr. B. knew unconsciously what he needed to heal in treatment and was able to communicate this eloquently to the therapist.

Following cessation of all recording, Mr. B. made further efforts to correct other disturbances and alterations in his treatment. He discontinued taking medication to sleep at night and terminated his relationship with the prescribing physician. He made no further requests of the therapist to communicate with his supervisor at work; in fact, he told the therapist quite directly that he wished to "keep work and therapy separate." In addition, Mr. B. discontinued asking for time off work for treatment and instead came on his personal time. He no longer "used" the clinic by requesting carfare for travel to and from his sessions, and he reported drinking significantly less.

Furthermore, Mr. B. discontinued his relationship with his neighbor and became involved in a hobby that necessitated joining a group of other interested professionals, who met weekly and attended activities together over the weekend. Mr. B. commented that even though most of the people in his group knew more about this activity than he did, he still felt comfortable with them. Although these gains appear quite striking, many of Mr. B.'s earlier depressive and paranoid preoccupations surfaced around the meanings and implications of the impending forced termination, which once again represented the use of the patient by the therapist and the disregard of his therapeutic needs.

DISCUSSION

In an independent attempt to validate the hypothesis that taping distorts the therapeutic process, a clinical case study was presented. Although manifest consent to taping was initially given with a high degree of enthusiasm, when the latent meanings of the patient's associations were evaluated, the exploitative and seductive implications of taping for this patient became apparent. (It must be noted, however, that the treatment process remained available for investigation and therapeutic intervention.)

These findings appear to confirm that the patients' manifest consent to taping and initial direct commentaries about the taping situation do not function as valid and reliable indicators of its actual potential effects. In the session presented, the patient was able to state directly to the therapist that the taping situation was troubling him. Although he was unable to manifestly allude to the rich and multidetermined meanings that the taping held for him, his manifest commentaries did correlate with his derivative expressions. Thus, one must be cautioned not to discount patients' manifest associations.

The hypothesis that audiorecording affected the therapeutic process was consistently validated in the patient's derivative communications to the therapist over a four-month period. Validation of this hypothesis was further evident in the patient's symptomatic relief following the therapist's interpretation of the meanings and implications of the taping situation and the cessation of all recording.

The above findings may be relevant not only specifically to the use of audiorecording but also to all purported deviations in treatment. Many such deviations occur in clinic settings and training institutions, which comprise a necessary part of our health care delivery system. The goal here is not to critique such institutions as having no therapeutic value, but rather to understand the implications of such settings so that patients can be offered the very best treatment possible under a set of conditions that are admittedly less than ideal. It is hoped that future investigations will test out clinical hypotheses utilizing a comprehensive validating methodology in an attempt to understand the implications that deviations from the ideal therapeutic framework hold. Such efforts are critical to the advancement of the science of psychotherapy and are no less vital to the individual psychotherapist in the developing the strength and conviction needed to maintain sound therapeutic effort. Although the exact reporting of data will perhaps never be completely resolved while preserving the sanctity of the treatment relationship, results of this investigation suggest the need for consideration of alternative means of data collection.

REFERENCES

Balint, M. (1968). *The Basic Fault.* London: Tavistock.
Beiser, H. R. (1966). Self-listening during supervision of psychotherapy. *Arch. Gen. Psychiat.* 15:135–139.
Bergman, P. (1948). Round table: The objective evaluation of psychiatry. *Amer. J. Orthopsychiat.* 19:463–491.
Bierer, J., & Strom-Olsen, R. (1948). The recording of psychotherapeutic sessions: Its value in teaching, research and treatment. *Lancet,* 254:957–958.
Blackey, E. (1950). The use of audio-visual aids in training. *Soc. Casework* 31:366–371.
Bleger, J. (1967). Psycho-analysis of the psycho-analytic frame. *Int. J. Psychoanal.* 48:511–519.

Campbell, D. T., & Stanley, J. C. (1963). *Experimental and Quasi-experimental Designs for Research.* Chicago: Rand McNally.
Carmichael, H. T. (1966). Sound-film recording of psychoanalytic therapy: A therapist's experience and reactions. In *Methods of Research in Psychotherapy*, ed. L. A. Gottschalk & H. A. Auerback. New York: Appleton-Century-Crofts.
Cooper, S. (1975). Hold the hardware: The use and abuse of tapes in clinical teaching and learning. *Amer. J. Orthopsychiat.* 45:573–579.
Covner, B. (1942a). Studies in phonographic recordings of verbal material, I: The use of phonographic recordings in counseling practice and research. *J. Consult. Psychol.* 6:105–113.
────── (1942b). Studies in phonographic recordings of verbal material, II: A device for transcribing phonographic recordings of verbal material. *J. Consult. Psychol.* 6:149–153.
Freud, S. (1912a). The dynamics of transference. *Standard Edition* 12:99–108.
────── (1912b). Recommendations to physicians practicing psycho-analysis *Standard Edition* 12:101–120.
────── (1916–1917). Introductory lectures on psycho-analysis. *Standard Edition* 15 & 16.
Friedman, C. T., Yamamoto, J., Wolkon, G. R., & Davis, L. (1978). Videotape recording of dynamic psychotherapy: Supervisory tool or hindrance. *Amer. J. Psychiat.* 135:1388–1391.
Gelso, C. J. (1972). Inhibition due to recording and clients' evaluation of counseling. *Psychol. Reports* 31:675–677.
────── (1973). Effect of audiorecording and videorecording on client satisfaction and self-expression. *J. Consult. Clin. Psychol.* 40:455–461.
────── (1974). Effects of recording on counselors and clients. *Counselor Ed. Supervision* 14:5–12.
────── & Tanney, M. F. (1972). Personality as a mediator of the effects of recording. *Counselor Ed. Supervision* 12:109–115.
Gill, M. M. (1979). The analysis of the transference. *J. Amer. Psychoanal. Assn.* 27:263–288.
────── & Brenman, M. (1948). Round table: Research in psychotherapy. *Amer. J. Orthopsychiat.* 18:100–110.
────── & Muslin, H. L. (1976). Early interpretation of transference. *J. Amer. Psychoanal. Assn.* 24:779–794.
────── Newman, R., Redlich, F. C., & Sommers, M. (1954). *The Initial Interview in Psychiatric Practice.* New York: Int. Univ. Press.
────── Simon, T., Fink, G., Endicott, N. A., & Paul, I. H. (1968). Studies in audio-recorded psychoanalysis, I: General considerations. *J. Amer. Psychoanal. Assn.* 16:230–244.
Greenacre, P. (1959). Certain technical problems in the transference relationship. *J. Amer. Psychoanal. Assn.* 7:484–502.
Haggard, E., Hiken, J., & Isaacs, K. (1965). Some effects of recording and filming on the psychotherapeutic process. *Psychiat.* 28:169–191.
Harmatz, M. G. (1975). Two channel recording in the supervision of psychotherapy. *Prof. Psychol.* 6:478–480.
Harper, R., & Hudson, J. (1952). The use of recordings in marriage counseling: A preliminary empirical investigation. *Marr. Family Living* 14:332–334.
Holahan, C. J., & Slaikeu, K. A. (1977). Effects of contrasting degrees of privacy on client self-disclosure in a counseling setting. *J. Counsel. Psychol.* 24:55–59.
Kogan, L. S. (1950). The electrical recording of social casework interviews. *Soc. Casework* 31:371–378.
Korchin, S. J. (1976). *Modern Clinical Psychology.* New York: Basic Books.
Lamb, R., & Mahl, G. (1956). Manifest reactions of patients and interviewers to the use of sound recording in the psychiatriac interview. *Amer. J. Psychiat.* 112:731–737.

Langs, R. (1973). *The Technique of Psychoanalytic Psychotherapy*, Vol. 1. New York: Aronson.
────── (1974). *The Technique of Psychoanalytic Psychotherapy*, Vol. 2. New York: Aronson.
────── (1975). The patient's unconscious perception of the therapist's errors. In *Tactics and Techniques in Psychoanalytic Therapy, Vol. II: Countertransference*, ed. P. L. Giovacchini. New York: Aronson.
────── (1976a). *The Bipersonal Field*. New York: Aronson.
────── (1976b). *The Therapeutic Interaction*, Vols. 1 & 2. New York: Aronson.
────── (1978a). *The Listening Process*. New York: Aronson.
────── (1978b). A model of supervision: The patient as unconscious supervisor. In *Technique in Transition*. New York: Aronson.
────── (1978c). *Technique in Transition*. New York: Aronson.
────── (1978d). Validation and the framework of the therapeutic situation: Thoughts promoted by Hans H. Strupp's "Suffering in psychotherapy." *Contemp. Psychoanal.* 14:98–124.
────── (1979). *The Therapeutic Environment*. New York: Aronson.
────── (1981). *Resistance and Interventions: The Nature of Therapeutic Work*. New York: Aronson.
────── (1982). *Psychotherapy: A Basic Text*. New York: Aronson.
────── & Searles, H. F. (1980). *Intrapsychic and Interpersonal Dimensions of Treatment: A Clinical Dialogue*. New York: Aronson.
Milner, M. (1952). Aspects of symbolism and comprehension of the not-self. *Int. J. Psychoanal.* 33:181–185.
Modell, A. H. (1976). The holding environment and the therapeutic action of psychoanalysis. *J. Amer. Psychoanal. Assn.* 24:285–308.
Racker, H. (1957). The meaning and uses of countertransference. *Psychoanal. Q.* 26:303–357.
Redlich, F. C., Dollard, J., & Newman, R. (1950). High fidelity recording of psychotherapeutic interviews. *Amer. J. Psychiat.* 107: 42–48.
Roberts, R., & Renzaglia, G. (1965). The influence of tape recording in counseling. *J. Counsel. Psychol.* 12:10–16.
Rogers, C. R. (1942). The use of electrically recorded interviews in improving psychotherapeutic techniques. *J. Orthopsychiat.* 12:429–434.
Roose, L. J. (1960). The influence of psychosomatic research on the psychoanalytic process. *J. Amer. Psychoanal. Assn.* 8:317–334.
Sauer, R. C., & Marcuse, F. L. (1957). Overt and covert recording. *J. Project. Tech.* 21:391–395.
Searles, H. F. (1965). *Collected Papers on Schizophrenia and Related Subjects*. New York: Int. Univ. Press.
────── (1975). The patient as therapist to his analyst. In *Tactics and Techniques in Psychoanalytic Therapy, Vol. II: Countertransference*, ed. P. L. Giovacchini. New York: Aronson.
────── (1976). Transitional phenomena and therapeutic symbiosis. *Int. J. Psychoanal. Psychother.* 15:145–204.
Shakow, D. (1960). The recorded psychoanalytic interview as an objective approach to research in psychoanalysis. *Psychoanal. Q.* 29:82–97.
Strachey, J. (1934). The nature of the therapeutic action of psychoanalysis. *Int. J. Psychoanal.* 15:127–159.
Stern, M. M. (1970). Therapeutic playback, self-objectification and the analytic process. *J. Amer. Psychoanal. Assn.* 18:562–598.

Sternberg, R. S., Chapman, J., & Shakow, D. (1958). Psychotherapy research and the problem of intrusions on privacy. *Psychiat.* 21:195–203.
Stone, L. (1967). The psychoanalytic situation and transference. *J. Amer. Psychoanal. Assn.* 15:3–58.
Strupp, H. (1978). Suffering and psychotherapy. *Contemp. Psychoanal.* 14:73–97.
Symonds, P. M. (1939). Research on the interviewing process. *J. Ed. Psychol.*, pp. 346–353.
Van Atta, R. (1969). Excitatory and inhibitory effect of various methods of observation in counseling. *J. Counsel. Psychol.* 16:433–439.
Viderman, S. (1974). Interpretation in the analytic space. *Int. Rev. Psychoanal.* 1:467–480.
Winnicott, D. W. (1954). Metaphysical and clinical aspects of regression within the psychoanalytic set-up. In *Collected Papers.* London: Tavistock, 1958.
——— (1956). Symposium on transference. *Int. J. Psychoanal.* 37:386–388.
——— (1963a). Countertransference, the theory of parent-infant relationships. In *The Maturational Processes and the Facilitating Environment.* New York: Int. Univ. Press, 1965.
——— (1963b). Psychiatriac disorders in terms of infantile maturational process. In *The Maturational Processes and the Facilitating Environment.* New York: Int. Univ. Press, 1965.
——— (1958). *Collected Papers.* London: Tavistock.
——— (1965). *The Maturational Processes and the Facilitating Environment.* New York: Int. Univ. Press.

9/
Discussion:
A Critique of Robert Langs's Conceptions of Transference, Evidence by Indirection, and the Role of the Frame

Merton M. Gill, M.D.

Although in agreement with conceptualizing the therapy situation as a bipersonal field and with the importance of exploring indirect communication, this paper criticizes those by Robert Langs and Elizabeth Frick on three counts. It disagrees with their belittling of conscious data with a concomitant, unacceptable reliance on inference as validation; their attribution of universal meanings to external stimuli; and their displacement of emphasis from essentials to details. It is argued that Langs's insistence on the rapid establishment of what he considers a secure frame in his conduct of an initial interview puts too heavy a burden on the patient, and that Frick's conclusions about recording are circularly influenced by her prior convictions.

The papers by Robert Langs and Elizabeth Frick are discussed together because they are both based on Langs's now well-known theory of technique. I shall first deal with general principles and then take up the cases. Elsewhere I have expressed my agreements and disagreements with Langs's principles (Gill, 1984). I welcome this opportunity to specify both agreements and disagreements in terms of the clinical data the two papers afford.

My general *agreements* with Langs relate to the important insights into the therapeutic situation that he has demonstrated and widely taught—namely, that the therapy situation is bipersonal (that is, that the patient's experience of the relationship is always contributed to by both participants), that the analysis of the relationship has priority, that within this priority the patient's view of the therapist's contribution should be the first to be made explicit, and that the patient's experience of the relationship must often initially be inferred from its disguised representation in the patient's associations. In regard to the first session, I, too, believe that it should be governed by the same principles as apply to the continuing therapy; that the same principles apply in a broad range of the extrinsic factors of frequency, couch or chair, nature of pathology, and experience of therapist; that interpretation of the patient's experience of the relationship should be as early as possible; and that the circumstances of the referral are likely to play an important role in the patient's initial response.

Despite these major agreements, I also have important *disagreements* with Langs: (1) my greater emphasis on the significance of conscious data versus Langs's primary emphasis on encoded derivatives, and (2) my rejection of Langs's contention that certain stimuli have a universal meaning in favor of a perspectival view, which holds that the meaning of an external stimulus can be determined only by its particular meaning to any particular person. This difference of opinion finds its sharpest expression in our differing views of what Langs calls the "frame." Langs argues that what he defines as the secure frame is the correct and indeed only way to organize the setting of the therapy so that it is mutative in the best sense, while an insecure frame can only result in palliation (lie therapy) at best. Frick's view is the same in that because recording violates the allegedly optimal frame, it is universally experienced as exploitative and damaging to a therapy. This premise of universality of meaning is linked directly, as Hoffman (1983) has argued, to Langs's essentially noninteractional or "asocial" conception of transference proper, since in Langs's conception transference in its purest form includes no significant contribution from an objectively definable, current external stimulus.

Langs further argues that patients universally experience the external setting he describes as the secure frame in two ways: they want it and they fear it. They want it because they know it provides a secure "hold." They fear it because it means a claustrum to them, where there will be no escape from their terrifying wishes. If they are to remain in therapy their wish for the hold has to be stronger than their fear. A powerful aid to their wish is an appropriate interpretation of their fear, although the fear may be so great that not even an appropriate interpretation can overcome it. At the outset let me note the danger of circular reasoning this formulation entails: If the patient discontinues despite an appropriate interpretation, it means the fear was too great; the possibility that the interpretation was inappropriate is excluded.

My two primary disagreements with Langs and Frick lead me to a basic disagreement with their way of evaluating clinical material. They find the proof for their view that there are universal meanings to the frame in derivative encoded meanings, that is, in what is finally inference. Two facets of our differing views on conscious material must be distinguished.

One is how much light such material sheds on the patient's psychopathology. The other is how much attention should be paid to conscious data in validating conclusions reached by the therapist and in the plausibility to patients of such conclusions offered to them by the therapist. It is the latter facet that is my primary concern in this critique.

I believe the conclusions Langs and Frick have drawn are by no means necessarily demonstrated by the material; indeed, that the conclusions are often tendentious, selective, and sometimes even far-fetched. They are tendentious because of the fixed expectations. They are selective in that attention is paid to whatever is consistent with their conclusions but whatever is equally plausible but inconsistent with their conclusions is ignored. For instance, Frick interprets that in the therapeutic situation Mr. B. feels compelled to acquiesce as in other situations he has described. In fact his description of his situation with his neighbor was one in which he did not acquiesce. Indeed not only was he very much in control, but he even sadistically toyed with her. Frick does, it is true, plausibly suggest that he might like to do to the therapist what he did to his neighbor. But if a wish is inferred from behavior that is inferred to be a disguised reference to the relationship, inference becomes piled on inference. The possibility of plausible, even if invalid, conclusions grows great indeed.

As an illustration of a far-fetched interpretation: Langs considers that a manifest reference to an accident in an automobile is necessarily an implied reference to the feared claustrum of the allegedly optimal frame. I realize that Langs provides safeguards for the validity of his interpretations, and I value his delineation of such phenomena as the adaptive context and a bridge to the therapeutic situation. Nevertheless, I believe he vastly underrates the ingenuity with which an agile mind can construct an even complex network of inference which is not necessarily correct.

Paradoxically, Langs argues that the very fact that the conclusions are inferential and based on derivatives makes them all the more secure. What is so problematic about this reasoning is that it confirms his view that he is irresistibly drawn by the evidence rather than by any preconceived expectations. Indeed, he insists on how unusual his kind of validation is in our field. Langs insists that his technique in fact follows the patient's directives. Frick follows this reasoning in her depiction of her middle category in which "the patient's manifest and latent material is continuously scrutinized for its allusions to the therapist, with primary emphasis given to its distorted, inappropriate, and neurotic qualities." Neither Langs nor Frick leaves room for such continuous scrutiny that reaches conclusions *other* than theirs and does not *a priori* give primary emphasis to distorted, inappropriate, and neurotic qualities. In other words, a theory like mine, which emphasizes attention to conscious data in addition to encoded derivatives, is not closed to the possibility that the patient's experience is primarily a correct assessment of the here-and-now reality of the analytic situation.

Lubin (1984) believes the difference between Langs's search for allusions and mine is that Langs looks for specific stimuli and I look for general ones. I believe Lubin may be mistaking my view that frame stimuli are not always the most significant specific stimuli, for a failure to look for specific stimuli. Langs and I agree that the therapist's interventions are crucial stimuli, but he gives priority to frame issues, while I believe they need not be the important ones in a particular situation. Langs's view that frame meanings are primary and universal parallels his dichotomy between veridical and distorted. Whereas the classical analyst belittles reality in favor of subjective experience, Langs in effect belittles idiosyncratic subjective experience in favor of a fixed meaning of external reality. I argue that both must be equally taken into account in assessing any individual experience.

One problem Langs's view leads to is that, despite its vaunted dismissal of the significance of manifest associations, it accepts these when they are consistent with its predetermined beliefs. If the patient agrees with the therapist's interpretation of how he or she experiences the recording, for example, that is taken at face value. Important possible meanings of such interactions may therefore be ignored. This denial of possible different meanings of a particular interaction, somewhat paradoxical in the light of the importance interaction is given in theory, is accompanied by an overvaluation of the power of interpretation. I mean the implication that almost any patient will accept the frame imposed by Langs if only the correct interpretation is made.

Lubin (1984) has suggested that my overestimation of both the value of conscious data and the power of interpretation to reduce the effect of interaction accounts for the greater activity of my technique in contrast to Langs's waiting for derivatives to appear. I will not deny a personal tendency to overactivity in the therapeutic situation, although I do not consider it to be a necessary concomitant of the principles of psychotherapy I espouse. I agree that some actions for some patients are not resolvable by interpretation and even a mere quantity of activity can become irresolvable by its sheer amount. I am aware of the fact that Langs does consider silence to be an intervention, that an important reason for silence is to encourage the presentation of derivatives, and that he emphasizes missed interventions too. Our differing views on silence and activity stem, then, from our differing views of the role of conscious data. He discourages exploration of such data; I believe he thereby loses an essential bridge to validation and to making interpretation meaningful to the patient.

Despite the fact that Langs suggests that his technique wipes out the usual distinction between psychoanalysis and psychotherapy, I believe he follows the same dichotomy of analyzability or nonanalyzability that is usually held. In effect, he sets up the claustrum and patients can or cannot accept it. He underestimates the importance of the patient's conscious experience. He offers a procrustean bed instead of tailoring his expectations and demands to what a particular patient is likely to be able to accept. I find especially unreasonable and overwhelming the demands he seems to lay down from the very beginning. Nor does he seem to take adequate account of the possibility that a patient who does accept the allegedly optimal frame at once may be doing so out of pathological motives—masochistic submission, for example. I realize that Langs's emphasis on the frame is to provide the patient with a desirable hold, but he does not seem to realize that a patient can only gradually come to understand and appreciate his intent. The precise detail in which Langs constructs the proper frame provides a clue to its rigidity and demandingness. He tells us that the time of the first consultation should be the same as the subsequent therapy, when one should or should not shake hands, when one may use the patient's name, that the couch must always be used, and so on.

THE CASE ILLUSTRATIONS

Langs's First Patient

The first patient Langs describes seems much less ready to accept treatment than does the second, despite the help she received from previous counseling. Indeed, the very fact that she did get help from a treatment that was probably very different from the present one may have worked against her accepting this treatment.

Langs says that initially the patient seemed quite interested in treatment and that signs of possible resistance appeared only toward the end of the session. I suggest, on the contrary, that signs of resistance appeared early. The patient directly asked for help three times. The first time she said she wasn't sure the therapist could help and she asked specifically about such things as anxiety attacks and postpartum depressions. The therapist asked her to continue. The second time the patient asked the therapist if she wasn't going to say anything, and the therapist replied it was too early. The third time the patient said she would like the therapist to be helpful. Now the therapist intervened with a somewhat indirect reference to the claustrum. She also said that the patient seemed prepared to tolerate learning what is inside her. Not only do I find this unduly optimistic (of course I have the benefit of hindsight), but it seems to me it might be experienced by the patient as implying that she had frightening things inside her. Then the therapist commented that these worries had been going on for a long time and therefore the patient should expect it would take some time to resolve them in therapy. I would speculate that the patient experienced this remark as a discouraging warning, that it would be some time before she could expect any relief.

The patient did agree that she had had trouble before and felt it was good that she try to carry out therapy. But no sooner did the therapist "arrange" the conditions of the treatment than the patient began to express her doubts again.

I suggest that rather than the "deeper" issues of the claustrum, it was the more "superficial" issues of the patient's feeling that the therapist would continue to respond as indirectly to her appeals for help as she was now doing, would banish her to the couch, and that help would be a long time coming that frightened the patient away. Her tentative agreement that it was good that she try to carry out therapy was met by what, I suggest, she experienced as a barrage of demands.

I am not suggesting that one should have been simply supportive and reassuring to this frightened woman. Like Langs, I believe that an interpretation of the bipersonal field was in order. But I believe that that interpretation should have been directed not to a fixed formulation about the frame, but to the clear indications of concern about what the patient experienced as the therapist's distance and unhelpful attitude. Nor am I suggesting that the therapist interpret at once the genetic reasons that the patient experienced her in this way, although I do argue that the therapist should make explicit what there is in the interaction that is leading the patient to experience her in that way. I would hope that such an intervention would mean to the patient that the therapist understands how she feels, finds it plausible, and is not offended by it. The patient might have elected to continue despite what, I suspect, would be misgivings that would not dissipate for some time.

Langs implies that had a frame interpretation been made properly the patient would have continued. I doubt it. He also says that "analysis of the secure-frame anxieties in this patient would have been tantamount to the analysis and resolution of her particular form of psychopathology or madness." Not an implausible formulation, despite my misgivings about putting it in terms of "secure-frame anxieties." But is it not asking far too much of any patient—and surely of this one—to expect an interpretation in those terms to be helpful in the first session?

Langs's Second Case

Langs's reconstruction of the implications of the first session show how the therapist was biased by the expectation that resistance would be attributable to a frame problem. What the patient said about the referral included a remark, ignored by Langs, around which one could make quite a different reconstruction of the session. I mean that the referring therapist said that the husband of the woman to whom he referred the patient never refers patients to his wife. Assuming that confidentiality is indeed the central issue, why could the patient not have assumed from this remark that the husband and wife therapists were indeed very conscious of confidentiality and thus provided safeguards to preserve it?

As an alternative possibility, how do we know that the patient did not construe this as reflecting the husband's doubts about his wife's competence? Maybe that is why the patient went to the husband's office first. The talk about interfering and difficult people relates primarily to the patient's mother and wife. Perhaps these are disguised references to the possibility that the therapist—a woman—is also a troublemaker. What are we to make of the patient's asking whether it was all right to continue and that the therapist seemed distracted and worried? Another allusion to her possible incompetence? Is this why the patient wonders "if this is stuff the therapist can get into"?

The patient responded to the therapist's intervention about the frame by saying that the previous therapist had built up a lot of momentum and he simply had to continue with treatment. This is not necessarily a validation of the interpretation. True, he wishes to continue, but there is no specific reference to the content of the interpretation. This is an example of how dubious an indirect validation by an alleged derivative can be. Again, if the patient is so concerned about confining the relationship to one therapist, why does he say he would be glad to share with this therapist what the previous therapist had told him? Does he think she needs help?

Langs makes a good deal of the alleged model of rectification, although again I am not persuaded that the material his conclusion is based on could have only the meaning he infers. Would I not be equally entitled to infer that the patient's statement that despite his problems with his wife, they are continuing in the marriage—a statement made apparently in response to the therapist's interpretation, be it noted—means that he will continue with the therapist despite his misgivings about her competence?

Langs is reasonably sure that the way the therapist handled the frame issue was what enabled the patient to continue. At one point he declares that "on this basis the patient decides to continue the therapy." I doubt that very much; in any case, it cannot be more than a speculation. I find the fact that the previous therapist had been helpful a more likely explanation for the patient's decision to continue. If one therapist could help, maybe another one can too.

But my point is not to show that my construction is right and Langs's is wrong. It is rather to show that I can arrive at a different construction, which is at least as plausible as his. And here, I believe, I can illustrate the value of questions for information about the patient's mental content—questions Langs considers hinder the development of the derivative communications that reveal the patient's deeper feelings. I would have asked what significance the patient attributed to the referring therapist's telling him that the husband of the woman to whom he was being referred never referred patients to her. There must be a reason the patient elected to tell this to the new therapist. I don't know what the patient would have answered, but it might have pointed in a direction neither Langs nor I suspect.

Frick's Case

Frick certainly builds a plausible case about how the patient was affected by the recording. She fails, however, to take into account a major factor in her construction—namely, how the therapist communicated her own feelings about the taping to the patient. The therapist made clear that she regarded it as an exploitation and invited him to ask her to stop it. How else could he understand her interpretation that he linked her with an incompetent employee because she did not stand up in the face of clinic policies that disturbed him immensely?

The therapist does not confine herself to interpreting that he *experiences* her this way—thus closing the possibility that his experience, however plausible to him, is not an unequivocally valid assessment of the situation. She makes clear that she considers it valid. She tells us how exploitative it is to charge no fee and to pretend to give treatment while taping. At other times the therapist does tell us the patient is experiencing her in certain ways, but without implying that he is necessarily correct. Frick comments, for example: "The therapist is perceived as using the patient because he is so impressive and fascinating."

The therapist, consistent with Langs's teaching, dichotomizes the patient's productions into valid and neurotic. She thus loses the opportunity to help him see how he experiences a situation as exploitative when this is only one possible understanding of it, however plausible it may appear to be. I believe the patient is therefore deprived of an opportunity to experience the rigidity of his construction in the most affectively meaningful context—namely, his relationship with her.

Lubin (1984) has argued that Langs is more egalitarian than I am because he is willing to consider that the patient's criticisms of the therapist are correct, while I usually stop with saying how the patient experiences the therapist. Hoffman (1983) has pointed out that a therapist's conclusion that the patient is correct can have the effect of protecting the *therapist* against further painful exploration. In Frick's example, had the therapist in effect not agreed with the patient that she was unable to stand up to allegedly exploitative clinic practices, but instead encouraged his further elucidation of how he justified this view, she might have learned more about his experience of her work.

There are several possible examples I can cite of interpretations of the material different from Frick's, but I emphasize that these are only *possible,* since I don't have the data to back them up. This may in part be because we are, after all, given only a small portion of the actual verbatim exchange. But it may also be because the material is heavily influenced by the therapist's convictions of what is most relevant. One example is the issue of how a black man is treated in the clinic and by a white therapist. Another is the issue of exhibitionism. In the initial manifest complaint about the taping the patient describes the feeling that he has to *perform.* I suggest that this issue could as well serve to organize the material as the taping. The therapist comes close to doing so in her interpretation that the neighbor woman was expecting the patient to perform and that he enjoyed her fascination with him. Frick correctly recognizes that the therapist may have had a countertransference inhibition to translating the vivid sexual and aggressive material into the therapeutic situation. But had she done so, would the accent not have fallen on the performance rather than on the taping as such?

I suggest that a good deal may have been lost by failing to maintain the taping while continuing to explore its meaning. It may be that the patient's improvement after the taping was stopped owes much to this unanalyzed interaction. I find it striking that we are not told anything about how the patient experienced the interruption of the taping. I agree that the meaning of the taping needs to be explored, but is the meaning of stopping it any less significant?

I also recognize how difficult it is for a therapist to continue taping in the face of the conviction that it is gravely damaging to a therapy.

CONCLUSION

I suggest that in addition to an undervaluation of conscious data and a mistaken attribution of universal meanings to external stimuli, both papers illustrate a displacement of emphasis from essentials to details. Frick herself points out that the taping is only one facet of the general problem of what she considers "the patient's inherent need for a confidential and private treatment." I believe that what a patient needs is a treatment that is genuinely empathic with his or her subjective experience and that such a treatment is not necessarily totally private and confidential in the sense in which Langs and Frick demand that it must be.

It is trustworthiness a patient needs. That attribute may or may not accompany confidentiality, but confidentiality is not a sine qua non for it. It is true that Langs's bête noire is the therapist who fails to provide the patient with a secure frame as a hold, while mine is the distant, depriving analyst. Insofar as we both attribute universal meanings, even if in opposite directions, we are both wrong. What matters is how each individual patient experiences how the therapist behaves. I agree that patients need to feel securely held to be treated successfully, but I argue that what constitutes a secure hold is individually rather than universally determined. One must surely not overestimate the importance of a word, but words do provide clues to overall atmosphere. That is why I was so struck by Frick's reference to the *sanctity* of the treatment relationship. I suggest that by "sanctity" she means the secure frame as defined by Langs.

Frick fails to distinguish adequately whether recording *affects* a therapy or whether recording *distorts* a therapy. Of course it affects a therapy. Any condition of the therapy affects it, including the conditions demanded by Langs's conception of the necessary frame. But some conditions affect a therapy more than others. Patients are differentially affected by various conditions. And indeed, consistent with Langs's own principles, how a condition affects a therapy is determined by the therapist as well as the patient. The effect of recording on a therapy may be very different for a therapist who starts out with the conviction that recording is invariably harmful from the effect if the therapist is convinced that it is not necessarily so. The most difficult position to maintain is an open-minded assessment of each instance.

I admit that I am a partisan of recording. I consider it essential for research. I am therefore biased to overlook its possible harmful effects. My experience persuades me that recording can often—not necessarily always—be done with no deleterious effect on the therapy, if its effect is looked for and dealt with. I do not see how we can resolve this issue until partisans of opposing views are willing to submit their recordings to each other for study. I cannot agree that Langs has demonstrated his view, or at least that he has demonstrated its inevitability for a therapist who does not share his convictions. In short, I cannot agree that attention to hidden meanings of the patient's experience of the relationship will inevitably lead to Langs's conclusions.

Again, I believe there is a circularity in Langs's reasoning. It is that only if one conducts a therapy as he believes it should be done will one find the data that validate his views (Lubin, 1984). What is not taken into account in this reasoning is the therapist's self-fulfilling prophecy in conducting a therapy the way Langs believes it should be. It is the same assumption that engenders the dichotomy between distortion and veridicality. It leads to what I believe is the erroneous conclusion that the patient can accurately read the therapist's *unconscious* ("probably a valid introject of the therapist's perceptions of him at that time," notes Frick).

We must be grateful to Frick for providing us with verbatim material, however partial, and however skewed by the cessation of the recording when an exploration of its meaning to the patient had scarcely begun. I am glad that despite her views on recording, she sees its importance for research and is willing to say that "although audiorecording does distort the therapeutic interaction, the treatment process remains available for investigation and therapeutic intervention."

We need not only more comprehensive data of the kind Frick has given us, but also data by therapists who are persuaded that taping is not necessarily exploitative. We have only begun to explore its many possible and differing meanings for different patients and therapists. I find it striking that despite my very major agreements with Langs and my appreciation of his contributions, my disagreements lead to such different conclusions about how to conduct therapy; I am amazed at how differently we evaluate the same data. Again, I suggest that only more detailed data collected from our different points of view and submitted to each other for study will enable us to begin to resolve our differences.

REFERENCES

Gill, M. M. (1984). Robert Langs on technique: A critique. In *Listening and Interpreting: The Challenge of the Work of Robert Langs*, ed. J. Raney. New York: Aronson, pp. 395–414.

Hoffman, I. Z. (1983). The patient as interpreter of the analyst's experience. *Contemp. Psychoanal.*, 19:389–422.

Lubin, M. (1984). Views on neurosis, listening, and cure: A discussion of Gill's comment on Langs. In *Listening and Interpreting: The Challenge of the Work of Robert Langs*, ed. J. Raney. New York: Aronson, pp. 415–430.

10/
Frame Deviations and Dreams in Psychoanalytic Psychotherapy
Frank P. Troise, A.C.S.W.

> It is not without good reason, however, that I have maintained that every man possesses in his unconscious an instrument by which he can interpret expressions of the unconscious of another.
>
> —Sigmund Freud (1913b)

Since Freud's (1900) original understanding of the psychology of dreaming, the dream has been studied extensively for its transference and unconscious fantasy implications. Little has been written, however, about the use of dreams to study the realities of the therapeutic relationship. This paper examines the dreams of patients in which there is a manifest representation of the therapist and a "therapeutic frame deviation" (Langs, 1976a). Clinical evidence is reported that strongly suggests that such dreams are an attempt to cope with the therapist's failure in managing the therapeutic framework.

Between 1912 and 1915 Freud articulated the basic ground rules and setting for psychoanalysis in his five fundamental papers on technique (1912a, 1912b, 1913a, 1914, 1915). Since that time much has been written about the need for flexibility in the use of the basic ground rules and posture of the analyst/therapist,[1] particularly in psychoanalytic psychotherapy. According to the literature, modifications are necessary at times, lest the therapist appear inhuman (Freud, 1912a). They may be

---

The author would like to thank Robert Langs, M.D., for his help in revising this paper.

[1] Because the principles in this paper apply to both psychoanalysis and psychoanalytic psychotherapy the terms "analyst" and "therapist" will be used interchangeably.

needed for certain preoedipal conditions such as narcissistic disorders (Kohut, 1970), useful as "parameters" (Eissler, 1953) in removing obstacles caused by ego defects, and helpful in providing a "corrective emotional experience" (Alexander et al., 1946) to mend developmental lesions. At the same time many point to the need for consistency in the management of the therapeutic framework and underline the curative capacity of the secure "holding environment" (Winnicott, 1965) or "psychoanalytic frame" (Bleger, 1967). With the exception of extensive empirical research by Langs (1976a, 1976b, 1977, 1978a, 1978b, 1979), however, the literature is silent with regard to the disturbing effects of alterations in the therapeutic framework in psychoanalytic psychotherapy.

The therapeutic framework (Langs, 1982) can be defined as follows. It includes a secure, private and professional office setting; a fixed fee; a regular hour and set time for each session; and a totally private and confidential dyadic relationship between patient and therapist, with an absence of physical contact as well as both prior and present social involvement. The patient has full responsibility for all scheduled sessions and follows the rule of free association, while the therapist maintains relative anonymity, uses exclusively interpretive interventions, and upholds the rule of abstinence. Langs's (1982) research reveals that the development and maintenance of the therapeutic framework is the single most important factor in the unfolding of the psychotherapeutic process. A secure framework will provide the arena for both the expression and cure of psychopathology and give rise to primary transference expressions. Through these conditions, the therapist offers a secure hold that affords both patient and therapist a healthy mode of relatedness based on a maximal degree of nonpathological gratification. Langs further states that deviations from the basic ground rules set up a pathological mode of relatedness, which basically fortifies pathological defenses and, in some cases, increases symptomatology.

Because dreams provide revelations of unconscious processes, I shall use them to further demonstrate how the patient is particularly sensitive to alterations in the ideal therapeutic setting and framework of treatment. As we shall see, a frame deviation may provide the stimulus for a patient's dream. The manifest and latent content of the dream may then reflect a pathological interactional syndrome between patient and therapist rather than "transference distortions."

The dreams studied here have a manifest representation of the therapist and of the actual frame deviation or "adaptive context" (Langs, 1978a), i.e., the therapist's interventions that stimulated the patient's conscious and unconscious responses. We shall therefore be considering a class of dreams that has had considerable prior attention—undisguised dreams of the therapist.

Several authors have suggested factors in the manifest representation of the therapist in the patient's dreams. M. Gitelson (1952) points to the possibility of countertransference, which prompts transference in the patient. He further states that the analyst may have introduced something into the treatment that is a re-creation of an early interpersonal situation for the patient. At one point Gitelson cites a case in which the analyst offered an inappropriate reassuring intervention and the patient produced an undisguised dream of the analyst. I. Harris (1962) believes that the formation of such dreams is prompted by the patient's transference. On the other hand, M. Rosenbaum's (1965) cautious conclusion is that these manifest dreams of the analyst may be concerned with an aspect of the patient's "real relationship" to the analyst. In his study Rosenbaum notes two personal communications from M. Grotjahn and G. Seitz. Grotjahn suggests that reality has entered the analytic situation, while Seitz remarks that when the analyst deviates from a neutral posture, the patient is likely to produce a dream in which the analyst is undisguised.

R. Gillman (1980) has found that this type of dream material can point to a breakdown or rupture in the therapy. He notes that five patients in his practice produced dreams in which he appeared undisguised as a response to breaks in the "analytic barrier," where "reality" intruded upon the analytic situation. These deviations involved moving from a professional private office to a home office, the signing of an insurance form, a patient's driving past the therapist's house, the loss of a patient's check, and a patient's meeting with the therapist's office partner at a social affair. Gillman also suggests that "undisguised transference dreams" may reflect a specific character defense or appear as a defense against an emerging transference neurosis.

Langs (1980) states that when the therapist's inappropriate needs are directly gratified, undisguised dreams of the therapist may follow. He also postulates that if the patient is experiencing a need for direct, noninterpretive gratifications, these dreams may reflect an eroticized misalliance and pathological interactional syndrome, with contributions from both patient and therapist.

This study will provide clinical evidence that the manifest representation of the therapist and frame deviation in patients' dreams signifies the presence of a mutually pathologically gratifying therapeutic interaction centered on a frame deviation. Although in the dreams studied here both therapist and deviation are manifestly represented, the findings imply that the same principles may apply to those dreams in which only the therapist is undisguised. Such a dream should be analyzed in light of a possible frame deviation. Also, in the dreams presented here the current therapeutic interaction resembles, to some degree, a past pathogenic relationship for the patient. In sum, one previously unrecognized factor in the report of manifest dreams of the therapist is the impingement on the patient of an inappropriate alteration in the ground rules of therapy or analysis. Such dreams are therefore an aspect of the patient's attempt to cope with such stimuli. Furthermore, in vulnerable patients they reflect a responsive failure of communicative, intrapsychic and interpersonal defense. The patient's presentation of the dream to the therapist is then a form of conveying the destructive properties of the frame deviation. Often it signals the patient's wish to rectify the pathological situation and restore a healthier mode of relatedness in the treatment.

CLINICAL ILLUSTRATIONS

Dream Example 1

Mr. A., a 24-year-old man, entered twice weekly psychotherapy with a male therapist after abruptly terminating a previous treatment with a female therapist. He was over indulged and infantilized in his symbiotic relationship to his parents. The patient was having difficulty functioning autonomously and was also abusing marijuana.

In the initial consultation Mr. A. asked the therapist to make appointments from week to week rather than adopting a regular appointment time. The patient was unsure about how he would be spending his days during the summer months and did not want to be restricted to regular appointment times. The therapist explained that the ground rules of treatment included the necessity for consistent appointments. Two regular hours per week were scheduled.

In the fourth session the therapist changed an appointment time to accommodate the patient. In the following hour the patient presented a dream:

> I am in what appears to be both you and Dr. R.'s [the former therapist] waiting room. I wasn't sure if I had the right appointment time. I look into your office and you are forcing a long marijuana pipe down a teenage patient's throat.

The associations following the dream revolved around the patient's confusion about why the therapist in the dream would force drugs on someone, particularly since drug abuse was a problem for the patient. Mr. A. was puzzled about why the therapist would be harmful in the dream. He further mentioned that although he appreciated the therapist's thoughtfulness in changing the appointment time, he did wonder if the therapist would eventually give up on him as his parent had. The patient then spoke of how his mother, through nonverbal facial cues, would coach him at the dinner table on how to respond to his father. Mr. A. often felt confused and unsure about whether he should attend to his mother's facial cues or to his father's long lectures. He felt that his parents undermined each other and this always left him confused.

In this material there is a manifest representation of the changed appointment in the dream—"I wasn't sure if I had the right appointment time." The remainder of the dream can then be organized as encoded messages or derivatives given unconscious meaning in light of the implications of this adaptive context—i.e., deviant intervention. The manifest dream contains latent (encoded) perceptions of the therapist as someone who gives conflicting messages, like the patient's parents, creating confusion similar to that experienced by the patient in the past. It seems likely that the change was experienced as a homosexual penetration, as evidenced by the phallic quality of the pipe being forced down the teenager's throat in the dream. Furthermore, the therapist is viewed as destructive and unethical since he is forcing illegal drugs on a patient in the dream. The open door in the therapist's office and the intrusive behavior of the therapist with the teenage patient in the dream further suggest the loosening of appropriate boundaries. Despite Mr. A.'s conscious appreciation of the therapist's accommodation, his unconscious perception reveals a more harmful view of the experience.

In this vignette the therapist had re-created a past pathological interaction similar to the symbiotic relationship between Mr. A. and his parents. He did this by inappropriately gratifying the patient's wish to be indulged in a special way through an uncalled-for appointment change. In light of the therapist's statement regarding the necessity for regular appointment times, he had clearly conveyed a double message to the patient. The therapist's changing the appointment time therefore created a "therapeutic misalliance" (Langs, 1982)—i.e., a conscious or unconscious collusion between patient and therapist that bypassed adaptive insight in favor of some maladaptive form of symptom alleviation. The patient's encoded perception of the implication of the frame deviation was valid and nondistorted.

The frame break is, of course, processed unconsciously through the patient's own psychopathology and genetic experience. It is this link between the deviant frame condition and a past pathogenic relationship that poses a threat to the patient's basic security in the treatment. The patient unconsciously perceives the real threat of being in treatment with a therapist who is acting similarly to his parents. It is likely that this threat causes a weakening of the ego's disguising function during the dream. The reality stimulus (frame deviation) adds strength to the unconscious wish—thus, a manifest representation of the therapist and the toxic stimulus. Although the patient unconsciously perceives the destructiveness of the therapist's behavior, there is some measure of pathological gratification involved in being indulged by the therapist. The patient can continue to exploit these negative introjects of the therapist to maintain his psychopathology and resistance. On the other hand, the reporting of the dream to the therapist reflects the patient's wish to rectify this pathological interaction.

Dream Example 2

A male patient, Mr. B., in twice weekly psychotherapy at a clinic, often suggested to the therapist that he should "get his pen and pad" when the patient reported a dream. (The therapist's practice was to take notes only when the patient reported a dream.) The patient had the following dream:

> I dreamt that we were in this office and you were taking notes. Your pen had a tape recorder in it.

Mr. B. found the dream quite amusing and associated to his grandfather, who had collected Parker pens. He remembered his affection for his grandfather, but also how his grandfather embarrassed him at family gatherings by telling "family secrets" about the patient. The patient continued by saying that his grandfather's last years were characterized by senility and how he could "not be left alone" lest he leave the stove on or be absent-minded in some way that could cause an accident. Before the grandfather's death, Mr. B. became increasingly frightened as he watched his elder "slip in and out of reality." He wondered if this would happen to his own parents.

There is a manifest representation of the frame deviation in the dream—the therapist's note-taking. The dream and the patient's associations contain derivatives pertinent to the latent content of the dream, which can be organized around the undisguised frame deviation. Consequently, we can propose that the therapist's note-taking has stimulated concerns in the patient about the therapist's reliability, competence, and "containing" functions (Bion, 1977). In the associations these concerns are unconsciously displaced onto the grandfather, for fear of exposing to both patient and therapist the highly threatening yet gratifying aspects of this deviant condition. At the same time this material also suggests that the patient's unconscious response to the therapist's note-taking evokes unconscious perceptions of the therapist's unreliability, absent-mindedness, and forgetfulness as it relates to those images of the senile grandfather.

In reality the note-taking does imply that the therapist is having some measure of difficulty functioning appropriately within the actual therapeutic hour. Indeed, the therapist needed to share the material with a supervisor and study it after the session because of his problem in organizing and interpreting the patient's material during the actual session. This would account for the images of the grandfather who "can't be left alone" lest he be destructive in some way. In addition, the therapist had a high regard for dream material, and the image of the grandfather who "collects Parker pens" may be seen as pointing to the therapist's wish to hold onto or collect something belonging to the patient. This measure coincides with the patient's wish to be pathologically gratified in some special way by the therapist, whom he asks "to get his pad and pen" as he reports his dreams.

The dream image of the therapist's pen containing a tape recorder also suggests the patient's concerns about the confidentiality of the treatment. This relates to his associations about the grandfather who would embarrass the patient by exposing "family secrets" to other family members. The treatment took place in a mental health clinic where patients' charts were reviewed by clinical, clerical, and administrative staff. In fact, on one occasion Mr. B. was required to meet with the administrative director of the clinic because his income had increased and this warranted a fee adjustment. The increased income was reported to the therapist by the patient, and the therapist, bound by clinic policy, scheduled a meeting between the patient and the director to discuss a fee increase. Consequently, the sharing of the patient's material, as it relates to the exposure of "family secrets," was a realistic concern.

The patient's unconscious wish to be gratified by the therapist in some special way (i.e., note-taking) is aligned with the therapist's inappropriate gratification through the frame deviation. This reality stimulus adds strength to the patient's unconscious wish and impairs the ego's disguising function during the dream work. However, once the patient is awake and reporting the dream to the therapist, the ego's disguising function is restored and the latent content of the dream, pertaining to the frame deviation, is displaced onto a genetic figure.

Dream Example 3

Sloane reports the following vignette in his *Psychoanalytic Understanding of the Dream* (1979, pp. 243–260). He describes a young woman who entered analysis because of marital discord. The patient was having an extramarital affair during this first treatment period. The patient eventually left the analysis with the male therapist, only to return again for a six-month period. During this second treatment the patient presented four dreams that were thinly disguised sexual dreams. The therapist recognized that these dreams were a response to the therapeutic relationship.

Before presenting the dream material, it is important to note some of the conditions of treatment and the frame deviations. The patient was regularly seen in the study of the therapist's home and on one occasion in the living room. In the first treatment period the couch was utilized, but when the patient returned the second time, this formality was dispensed with and the patient sat up. At another time the therapist lent the patient a magazine article, which the therapist thought might interest her. In one analytic hour the therapist remarked that the patient was not wearing stockings despite the fact that it was a cold day and noted that the patient was also wearing a miniskirt that exposed her thighs in a suggestive way. He commented that this was unusual for her in an attempt to bring her seductiveness to her attention. On another occasion, the patient came to her hour early and the therapist took her by the arm and led her into another room to avoid encountering the previous patient. It is important to note that most of the forementioned deviations were followed by the patient presenting dreams of a sexual nature. The therapist recognized that these dreams were concerned with the therapeutic relationship and also noted the possibility of countertransference.

Here we shall look at the one dream that alluded to both the impingement and some of the frame deviations. It is the second of the four dreams presented by the patient.

> I'm coming into your office. My friend N. is also there, as if she were visiting. As I'm coming in the door you are going out through the same door and we try to avoid bumping into each other. But as often happens we manage to get into each other's way. We move together in the same direction until we finally manage it correctly and each goes his way [Sloane, 1979, p. 247].

The dream suggests an additional adaptive context—the patient's statement that oftentimes the patient and therapist "manage to get into each other's way."

The patient's associations to the dream involved the therapist's remarks concerning her exposed thighs and miniskirt. She stated, "We seem to be going over the same ground repeatedly. I know I am reacting to you the way I reacted to my father, with Bob and Jim and now with you. I seem to pick out men who I should know are going to reject me, but even so, when the situation actually arises I think it's real. I can't believe it's all fantasy. When you had me sitting in your living room I really believed you were doing it deliberately in order to show me my place even though my better sense told me otherwise" (p. 248).

The therapist was impressed by the patient's statement that "we try to avoid bumping into each other. But . . . we manage to get in each other's way. We move together in the same direction." The therapist thought that the patient felt that they were both having the same fantasies and this was a manifestation of countertransference. The therapist posed this as a question to the patient, and the patient recalled the incident where the therapist led her by the arm into another room. She continued, commenting on how it was the first time she had ever been touched by the therapist and how she felt it was an intimate thing and represented a secret between her and the therapist. The patient also mentioned the magazine article lent to her by the therapist. It, too, seemed a gesture of intimacy.

Following the presentation of the dream, then, the patient readily associated to a number of frame deviations that were stimuli for the dream. The therapist asked the patient if she felt that the therapist was also having similar sexual fantasies and the patient mentioned a specific frame deviation—the physical contact with the therapist (which was represented in the dream). The patient associated to both genetic and extra-analytic experiences but spoke freely about her sexually tinged, intimate feelings toward the therapist. On a manifest level she began to tell the therapist about her confusion whether these feelings were fantasy or reality. However, she stated that "it's a repetition of what you call the infantile trauma" and that this "pattern has been repeated over and over again." It appears that these are disguised derivatives pertaining to the repetitious pattern of frame deviations introduced by the therapist. Obviously these deviations have sexual meaning for the patient. The patient's remark about "infantile trauma" and her statement about how she feels both patient and therapist continue to go over the same ground appear to be additional encoded perceptions of the repeated traumas impinging on her through the repetition of sexually tinged frame deviations (i.e., the home office, a session in the therapist's living room, the physical contact with the therapist, the therapist's lending the patient a magazine article, and the therapist's remark concerning the patient's exposed thighs).

Here we see how the persistence of these frame deviations led to the manifest representation of the therapeutic misalliance both in the dream and in the associations following the reporting of the dream. The frame deviations blur reality for the patient and threaten her basic security in treatment. Again, both communicative and intrapsychic defenses are incapable of contending with this overstimulation through repeated frame breaks. The reality of these frame deviations gratifies the unconscious wish for sexual intimacy with the therapist.

DISCUSSION

The clinical evidence in this study suggests that deviating from the basic ground rules or secure frame of treatment may prompt undisguised dreams of the therapist. Such dreams are an attempt to cope with the trauma that impinges on the patient because the frame deviation threatens the patient's basic security or hold in treatment. Langs (1982) has noted that the patient's response to frame deviations is typically split. The patient will derivatively communicate the destructive properties of the deviation based on the wish for a healthier mode of relatedness. On the other hand, he or she may also attempt to exploit the frame deviation for its pathological gratification. The dreams presented here support this theory.

Second, the fact that these dreams are undisguised representations of the therapist and frame deviation points to failures in communicative and intrapsychic defenses in certain vulnerable patients. It appears that for this group of patients the current frame deviation repeats a past trauma or a previous pathogenic relationship. Because the past trauma or pathogenic relationship has already weakened the patient's defenses, he or she is susceptible to both the repetition of the trauma and a pathological response to a current reality situation that resembles this damaging genetic experience. Arlow (1963) has noted that reality situations that resemble past traumas will evoke pathological responses. In these dreams the patients associated to the genetic link in an unconscious attempt to alert the therapist to the destructive properties of the current frame deviation.

As mentioned earlier, Gitelson (1952), Harris (1962), Rosenbaum (1965), Gillman (1980), and Langs (1980) have presented a variety of reasons for the manifest representation of the analyst in patients' dreams. They have pointed to the possibilty of countertransference, breaks in the analytic barrier in which "reality" intrudes on the analytic situation, and the analyst's loss of a neutral posture. The present study sheds some light on a previously unrecognized possibility—that inappropriate alterations in the ground rules of treatment can prompt undisguised representations of the therapist, which point to a real, pathological interactional syndrome between patient and therapist. The patient's response to the frame deviation may be pathological, based on his or her psychodynamics, but the unconscious perceptions of the therapist and the misalliance are predominantly valid and nondistorted (Langs, 1978a). The dreams in this paper illustrate how the therapist had, in reality, acted inappropriately by deviating from the basic therapeutic framework.

In the first vignette the patient unconsciously experienced the changed appointment as a homosexual intrusion; in the third clinical illustration the deviations were also eroticized. These examples suggest that some frame deviations are experienced by patients as being sexually tinged since they alter the necessary boundaries between patient and therapist. Langs (1980) has postulated that undisguised dreams of the therapist may occur in the presence of an eroticized misalliance and interactional syndrome.

In all three vignettes the frame deviation evoked conscious and unconscious images of the therapist as harmful, exploitative, and inconsistent. These dreams and the patients' associations further reflect a sense of a poor hold and a lack of containment on the part of the therapist. In all the vignettes the alteration of the boundary between patient and therapist evoked some imagery that pointed to some blurring of reality. It also appears that the deviations caused some basic threat to the patients' security in treatment, despite the inappropriately gratifying nature of the frame deviation.

There is one last implication of this study. As illustrated, the manifest representation of the therapist, in some patients' dreams, reflects the presence of a pathological interactional syndrome centered on a deviation in the therapeutic framework. It is perhaps possible, then, that when the patient manifestly mentions the frame deviation and its negative impact, along with negative perceptions of the therapist, a similar phenomenon may exist. This direct reference during the therapeutic hour may signal the presence of a highly disturbing interactional syndrome that has caused the breakdown of communicative defenses, prompting the patient's conscious realization of the destructive properties of the frame deviation. My experience has been that when this occurs, the frame deviation is often a re-creation of past trauma for the patient. Further research in this area is needed.

REFERENCES

Alexander, F., French, T., et al. (1946). *Psychoanalytic Therapy: Principles and Applications.* New York: Ronald Press.
Arlow, J. (1963). Conflict, regression and symptom formation. *Int. J. Psychoanal.* 44:12–22.
Bion, W. R. (1977). *Seven Servants: Attention and Interpretation.* New York: Aronson.
Bleger, J. (1967). Psychoanalysis of the psychoanalytic frame. *Int. J. Psychoanal.* 48:510–511.
Eissler, K. R. (1953). The effect of the structure of the ego on psychoanalytic technique. *J. Amer. Psychoanal. Assn.* 1:104–143.
Freud, S. (1900). The interpretation of dreams. *Standard Edition* 4 & 5.
——— (1912a). The dynamics of transference. *Standard Edition* 12:97–108.
——— (1912b). Recommendations to physicians practising psycho-analysis. *Standard Edition* 12:111–120.
——— (1913a). On beginning the treatment. *Standard Edition* 12:121–144.
——— (1913b). The disposition to obsessional neurosis. *Standard Edition* 12:311–326.

——— (1914). Remembering, repeating and working-through. *Standard Edition* 12:145–156.
——— (1915). Observations on transference-love. *Standard Edition* 12:157–171.
Gillman, R. D. (1980). Dreams in which the analyst appears as himself. In *The Dream in Clinical Practice,* ed. J. M. Natterson. New York: Aronson, pp. 29–44.
Gitelson, M. (1952). The emotional position of the analyst in the psychoanalytic situation. *Int. J. Psychoanal.* 33:1–10.
Harris, I. D. (1962). Dreams about the analyst. *Int. J. Psychoanal.* 43:151–158.
Kohut, H. (1970). The analysis of the self. *Psychoanal. Q.* 42:441–451.
Langs, R. (1976a). *The Bipersonal Field.* New York: Aronson.
——— (1976b). *The Therapeutic Interaction,* Vols. 1 & 2. New York: Aronson.
——— (1977). *The Therapeutic Interaction: A Synthesis.* New York: Aronson.
——— (1978a). *The Listening Process.* New York: Aronson.
——— (1978b). *Technique in Transition.* New York: Aronson.
——— (1979). *The Therapeutic Environment.* New York: Aronson.
——— (1980). The dream in psychotherapy. In *The Dream in Clinical Practice,* ed. J. M. Natterson. New York: Aronson.
——— (1982). *Psychotherapy: A Basic Text.* New York: Aronson.
Rosenbaum, M. (1965). Dreams in which the analyst appears undisguised: A clinical and statistical study. *Int. J. Psychoanal.* 46:429–437.
Sloane, P. (1979). *Psychoanalytic Understanding of the Dream.* New York: Aronson.
Winnicott, D. (1965). *The Maturational Processes and the Facilitating Environment.* New York: Int. Univ. Press.

11/
Discussion:
The Therapist Undisguised in Dreams and Reduction of Resistance
Joseph M. Natterson, M.D.

Dream material is presented that contrasts with Frank Troise's clinical findings and challenges his theoretical explanation. In this case, the therapist appears undisguised in dreams at precisely the time when the therapeutic process markedly accelerates and deepens. Such findings clearly suggest that the regular attribution of such dreams to some technical or attitudinal disturbance in the therapist's approach is incorrect. In other words, the factors described by Troise operate in some situations, but not in all.

In his paper, Frank Troise presents clinical material to demonstrate that erroneous attitudes and behavior by the therapist can lead to dreams in which the therapist is manifestly portrayed. From his clinical presentation, which I find clear and convincing, Troise makes an inference of a general nature, with which I disagree. Troise asserts that the therapist's manifest portrayal is regularly a function of therapist error, and he believes this can be explained by the concept of "frame deviation" (Langs, 1975). He especially emphasizes therapist error that provides pathological gratification for the patient.

I am, of course, aware of the literature on the undisguised representation of the therapist in dreams. Most of these articles rest heavily on the traditional assumption of a sharp distinction between the manifest and latent content in dreams, and the sense, if not the explicit conviction, that if a representation is manifest, it is somehow wrong, inauthentic, or otherwise unreliable or misleading. I am most familiar with Gillman's (1980) paper on this subject, which Troise also discusses. Gillman offers an empirical study, and his findings are informative and stimulating. His results indicate that manifest dreams of the therapist have three discern-ible sources. First, they emanate from a break in the analytic barrier—inadvertent in Gillman's cases, but which could include the kind of neurotic acting out by the therapist described by Troise. The second cause is a resistance to a deepening of transference—which bears some similarity to Gitelson's (1952) original paper warning of the therapeutically ominous implications of an early undisguised dream appearance of the analyst. Third, patients of a certain type, perhaps becaus of specific childhood traumas, may tend to dream more frequently than other patients of the undisguised analyst.

Papers such as those by Troise and Gillman have two distinct effects, one laudable and the other regrettable. They provide valuable clinical examples which persuasively inform the reader of specific conditions in which the therapist tends to appear undisguised in dreams. Such instances do frequently occur, and therapists need to be alert to such circumstances. In this way a useful function is served. However, insofar as the papers attempt to explain most dreams of this type on the basis of the author's particular clinical observations, misleading causal assumptions may occur.

It seems quite clear from Troise's paper that he believes the undisguised representation of the therapist usually, if not invariably, indicates therapeutically erroneous behavior by the therapist—in Langs's terms, some "frame deviation." According to this point of view, a therapist is not expected to appear undisguised in dreams, except for these interesting pathological circumstances. My extensive clinical experience with dreams simply does not support this position. I reiterate here that I am not questioning Troise's clinical findings and explanations of his own case material; however, I do not find his generalizations acceptable.

Now, I will present several dreams from a very crucial period in the psychoanalytic therapy of a young woman. These dreams illustrate conditions other than those postulated by Troise in which the therapist appears unmodified in dreams.

CLINICAL ILLUSTRATION

Ms. S., a 28-year-old woman, came to therapy because of chronic discontent in her marriage. She had been married for about eight years to a Jew, whom she had married against the wishes of her Protestant establishment parents. As her parents seemed to become more accepting of her husband, she began to lose interest in the marriage. She had no children. When she first came to see me, she was becoming an extremely successful, creative executive for a firm in a field related to entertainment.

Initially, she saw me on referral by a young woman friend, who had recently completed successful psychotherapy with me. Ms. S. was obviously quite ambivalent about her marriage; from one weekly session to the next she stated that she had to leave her husband or that she really loved and needed him. She was also involved in a very exciting love affair with a married man, who was the chief executive of her firm. Ms. S. was highly intelligent and verbal, but she displayed a remarkable inability to take any stable position of attitude or action regarding the significant people in her present or her past. She had a somewhat wistful feeling about her friend who had achieved a successful psychotherapeutic relationship with me and who had enormously improved the quality of her intimate relationships.

Ms. S. did reveal that she was disappointed in her father for being out of touch with his feelings, with her brother for wasting his youth and talents, and with her mother for having been so neurotic and ambivalent, especially during the patient's adolescence. With her charm, beauty, and talent, Ms. S. had always been the "star" in her family. But it was obvious when she came for therapy that her narcissistic resources were no longer sufficient to control anxiety and depression.

It was no great surprise to me that Ms. S. discontinued psychotherapy after about three months. During this brief period of therapy she had no dreams. She had decided that she should remain married, hence the need for therapy no longer existed—or so she rationalized.

Several months later Ms. S. called me, wishing to resume therapy, confidently and correctly expecting that I would find time for her. She informed me that she had fled therapy before, that she had now made the irreversible decision to get a divorce. And she was now ready to remain in therapy in order to discover and resolve her major conflicts.

In the early months she talked a great deal about her parents, indicating a considerable restoration of faith in her father as an effective, caring parent, while she continued to be considerably more cautious about her mother. When I made occasional gentle efforts to bring these parental attitudes into her relationship with me, she regularly provided an interesting response. She assured me that she was familiar with transference and that no doubt she had transference reactions since all patients do. Nevertheless, she could only let herself be aware of me as a wise, avuncular figure to whom she could reveal all her confusions, uncertainties, and inconstancies. It would be impossible to experience transferential turbulence in her relatedness to me.

She reported fairly frequent dreams and worked on them with increasing fluency. Ms. S. was seeing me once per week during this period. Although she dated and was attracted to numerous men, only one man became of sustained importance to her. He, however, had been living with another woman for several years, and this relationship gradually became the focus of Ms. S.'s anxiety, as she was becoming stabilized in the rest of her life.

Then Ms. S. made a visit to her parents' home in another part of the country. She had the startling and heartening experience of having her mother affirm Ms. S.'s current romantic and career interests instead of assuming a negative and discouraging attitude. Immediately after the visit, Ms. S. experienced a surge of self-confidence; she increased her therapy to twice weekly; and she told her lover that he must choose between her and the other woman.

During the three-week period in which the above events unfolded after her visit to the parents, she reported several dreams, of particular interest to the subject of this paper. I was portrayed undisguised several times. Never before had I been manifestly present in Ms. S.'s dreams.

A few days after the visit to her parents, she reported the following dream:

> I am in a country house—it's like our home in New Hampshire when I was a child. I am in the bedroom talking with my father. Jack [a friend] is there. A blonde woman in a black bathing suit is there. Jack seems to be in the shadows, making it safe for me. I am very sad; my mother is dead. I ask my father if he intends to marry the woman in the black bathing suit. He replies, "Yes." Jack is like a safe harbor.

And then a second dream:

> I am at my parents' home; it is partly like the house I grew up in. Jim [her lover] is there. I see dishes in front of me. Mother brings in an egg soufflé, but it has dirty dishwater in it, as do the plates—it's unpleasant, inedible. I wonder if my mother likes Jim. I touch Jim; he irritably tells me not to touch him. Then it's like a short story, and he is gone, but he will return, as in the story. Then I go to a movie matinee; a man is on a podium. I think how nice it would be to live in a small town like this [affluent New England resort village]. A man approaches me, and we begin to make out. I wish the man were Jim. I undress, but I become bored, I want to cross the aisle to retrieve my clothing, but it's embarrassing. I feel anxious and depressed, and I awaken.

Ms. S. began this session with unusual enthusiasm. She announced that her dreams constituted an "epiphany." She associated abundantly and made the crucial interpretations herself. She had discovered for the first time that *she* had entertained hostile, destructive, eliminative attitudes to her mother due to her wish for her father. Consequently, she now realized that she could no longer dump all the blame for the chronic tension in the family on her mother. In effect, she had now reversed the formula of "Mother tried to get rid of me to monopolize father."

Many other interrelated issues arose in connection with these dreams, but time, space, and purpose do not permit further elaboration here. I thought that the comforting and shadowy Jack character in the first dream might be a fairly direct reference to me, but I said nothing about this.

Ms. S. arrived for her next session with her usual breezy manner, but she was visibly annoyed with me. She felt that I had not appreciated the importance of her "epiphany" in the preceding session. She was hurt and felt undermined. She spontaneously noted that these were the same emotions which had so disturbed her relationship to her mother. And she furthermore recognized that she could permit the emergence of negative transference feelings to me as she was becoming more able to acknowledge her destructive oedipal urges toward her mother. She said, "Now, I am more able to let you become a real person. It is no longer necessary for me to protect your image in the therapy."

So Ms. S. was no longer totally disavowing transference reactions to me. In her next session she reported the following dream:

> I am back in high school. You had arranged for us to talk with another dream expert about my "dirty dishwater dream." The other expert is Dave [a moderately high executive in a firm with which Ms. S. does business and a man she doesn't respect]. I don't want to have the consultation, but I'm not really bothered until we get to his firm. Then I strenuously protest to you about his instability, his possible indiscretion. You go to lunch, and you are in the cafeteria line of the firm, in the back, still waiting for Dave. Then I am at my high school cafeteria with my close friend Judy. Dave is at her table. I try to find you. I feel guilty that you gave up your lunch for me. Also, you are having a love affair, and I am advising you about it.

Many associative elements arose in connection with this dream, but of primary interest here is the first undisguised appearance of the therapist in a recalled dream of this patient. One could employ Troise's criterion and assume that I had deviated in some significant way from the frame. If Ms. S.'s charge against me had been correct and I had indeed behaved like her mother, then it would support such a view. However, my impression then and now is quite the opposite. I was relating to Ms. S. in an optimal therapeutic mode throughout this period of therapy. Perhaps Gillman's (1980) notion of a reaction to the deepening of the transference would be more apposite. Yet this assumption should be held cautiously, inasmuch as S. had concomitantly informed me that she was now *able* to perceive me as a *real person* who may make mistakes and onto whom she can project transference reactions. Such a meaning would render less plausible the notion that she dreamed of me undisguised as a defensive move against transference. In *this* instance, it seems to me that the deepening of the transference and the dreams of me without disguise were congruent rather than conflicting phenomena. It seems that each reinforced rather than opposed the other.

The fact that the patient was referred by a former patient, a "frame deviation" according to Langs (1975), does not seem to have demonstrable relation to the timing of my manifest appearance in the patient's dreams. The increased frequency of therapy may well have contributed in some unspecified way to my undisguised dream apperance, but obviously this has nothing in common with the acting out by the therapist described in Troise's cases.

Unconsciously, she was still seeing me as the incapable mother who could not provide adequate nourishing for Ms. S., because of my own needs for nutrition. She was continuing the family drama in her dream.

In the following session, she reported two brief dreams in which I did not explicitly appear. In one, Jim calls Ms. S. He is at his home, and his girlfriend walks in. So he pretends he is talking with a business associate. Then Ms. S. hears him tell his girlfriend that they will go for a walk with the dog. The second dream was a recurrent dream of many years duration. In it she is at her boarding school; she is lost and is trying to find rooms.

The therapist is no longer visible in her dreams. The oedipal wishes, guilt, and punishment are evident to Ms. S., but the transference aspect is less evident. The sessions in this period were replete with therapeutic commitment. Ms. S. was reporting a drastic reduction in anxiety in her life, a gratifying increase in her ability to relate honestly and effectively to other people in her life. She attributed this to the important unconscious discoveries she was making.

Two more dreams were then reported:

You come to my family home for a therapy session. So my parents will meet you, and I don't like that.

I am going to a business awards dinner, but I'm going to have a session with you first. The session is to be in your office, but it is somewhere else. I feel a time pressure, but you insist that I relax, that there is no pressure. I am on the phone to Jim. I'm worried about what to wear to the dinner. The important thing was the pressure of time, but you were minimizing the importance of the time factor and the therapy session. Then something like I am swimming, and I discover I'm pregnant. But I don't want to tell the guy because I don't want a baby or marriage. I realize I'm still not divorced, and the divorce would be final in time for everything connected with the pregnancy. Then I am in the auxiliary pool of my boss's mansion. It has dirty water and is cluttered with kids' toys. His wife is there.

Among Ms. S.'s associations was her report that she felt distinctly angry with me in the dream for being cavalier in my attitude to her. She was not conscious of hostility to me, and we related the anger to guilt feelings connected to the intense sexual rivalry with mother while she simultaneously continued to feel closer and warmer to her mother (and to me).

These dreams and their meanings are obviously rich, complex, and polyvalent. My discussion of them has not attempted to be comprehensive. Rather, I have scrutinized the appearance of the undisguised therapist.

CONCLUSION

By coincidence, I was studying Troise's paper when these events in Ms. S.'s therapy occurred. I have not ventured a systematic study of my dream records, but I suspect that my findings in the dreams of Ms. S. are typical. That is, the appearance of the therapist in the manifest dream content may often occur when therapy is proceeding well—perhaps even especially well.

I assume that Troise's understanding of the overt presence of the therapist in his cases is as valid as my different understanding of my case material. Overgeneralizing about clinical experiences may not only be misleading, but may also diminish therapist's sensitivity to unique meanings of clinical phenomena.

Premature closure limits creative, imaginative activity. Generalizations about the undisguised therapist in dreams are premature. Such generalizations should be avoided by authors and doubted by readers.

REFERENCES

Gillman, R. D. (1980). Dreams in which the analyst appears as himself. In *The Dream in Clinical Practice,* ed. J. M. Natterson. New York: Aronson, pp. 29–44.

Gitelson, M. (1952). The emotional position of the analyst in the psychoanalytic situation. *Int. J. Psychoanal.* 33:1–10.

Langs, R. (1975). The therapeutic relationship and deviations in technique. *Int. J. Psychoanal. Psychother.* 4:77–105.

12/
The Onset of Unconscious Perception
Roy M. Mendelsohn, M.D.

The earliest phases of development are explored with an eye on the structural foundations of unconscious perceptions. The self is defined from a perceptual point of view, and the role of body ego experiences in the formation of representational structures is portrayed. The early part self representations appear to center on definable aspects of body ego experience, which are represented separately and consolidate into a whole. Speculations are presented about the original body ego experiences underlying psychological symbiosis and the inclusion of a stimulus outside the self through representation within the self. The role of perception in the mechanism of splitting, as well as its relationship to the functioning of unconscious perceptions, is elaborated. Finally, the differing effects of the therapist's interventions are discussed in terms of empathic responses to unconscious communications and empathic failures.

INTRODUCTION

Some years ago, when I was a beginning therapist, I saw a young boy who did nothing in his life or with me but sit and rock and moan loudly. I saw him daily, but his behavior never varied. I spoke with him about many things. At first I put into words the theories I was learning about the causes of his "illness." As time went on, these words felt empty and hollow to me. My words slowly reflected my growing frustration and anguish. I spoke with a wise supervisor about my reactions and wondered how long I should keep working with him. The supervisor's response was that I should continue as long as I continued to feel that anguish and despair, and so I did. One day, after eight months, this young boy spoke to me for the first time. I was startled as he told me of the little man on his shoulder shouting obscenities in his ears. That morning the little man had spoken in a different voice and so he could now talk. The man's words were reflections of my words, especially the ones I uttered in my anguish and despair. In the years that followed, it became quite a revelation to me as this exquisitively sensitive child reacted to any defensive or pathological reaction on my part with the active return of this destructive man on his shoulder.

Since that time, I have had the opportunity to work with a small number of children regarded as "autistic." These children sought forms of interaction with me that clearly reflected their need for growth-producing experiences. Whenever I was able to provide such an experience, they proceeded to attack it and attempted to engage me in varied forms of pathological interaction. They sought out any weaknesses and vulnerabilities in me that would reinforce their efforts. Whenever they succeeded in doing so, all communication ceased. They gradually taught me what determined a healthy interaction and what defined a pathological interaction. As I learned, they became more articulate about themselves. It became possible for me to observe how their development proceeded and how different aspects of the self representation system coalesced from part self representations into a whole unit. My experience seemed to shed some light on something I had not seen described in a cohesive and continuous fashion. It occurred to me that I might be observing processes that reflected the earliest steps in human psychological development. I found that my understanding of other individuals was enhanced and broadened by what I was learning from this group of children.

PERCEPTIONS OF THE SELF AND THE OBJECT WORLD

Jacobson, in her important work *The Self and the Object World* (1964), provided a conceptual framework for a deeper understanding of early development. It is well recognized that to fully comprehend mental events, it is essential to have a grasp of developmental lines and sequences. Yet an understanding of psychological content depends greatly on validation from the individual who has expressed that content. The nature of what is considered to be validating varies according to the area of mental activity involved. Manifest content is significant and reveals the functioning of the ego and the conscious to preconscious realm of mental activity. However, for a fuller understanding of a given event it is essential to see its connection to latent content. Hypothesizing the line of development of a given psychic event adds a further dimension. This has been the most difficult area, since in the domain of early development there is considerable uncertainty about what is validating. Jacobson (1964), along with Hartmann (1939) and others, went far in defining the differences between ego, self, and self representations.

In this presentation, the self is defined exclusively from a perceptual point of view. An effort is made to develop a concept of the self that includes the varied aspects of perceptual experience that go into its overall makeup. The role of the perceptual processes in forming the self is delineated. Representations of body ego experience make up the self system and, along with the concurrent object impressions, are included within expanding perceptual boundaries to comprise the totality of the self. Many authors, beginning with Freud (1940), have emphasized the importance of body ego experience as the foundation for all mental events. Although this concept has been generally well accepted, there has been some difficulty in appreciating its significance. It has also been difficult to determine the specific body ego experiences that underlie the varied structures and functions observed in later development. Consider, for example, the experience of identity and autonomy. This later development implies that at the outset of development there exists a core body ego experience of separateness, which is at the foundation of the sense of autonomy and identity. The primitively organized children I have seen all initially displayed a body ego experience of objectlessness. In the course of their progressive development, this core of objectlessness evolved into an inner sense of identity and autonomy. Only during the time that self (and object) representations began to form, however, did a lack of differentiation emerge. In other words, the lack of differentiation was an intermediary step from objectlessness to autonomy. The experience of lack of differentiation appeared to be essential for the processes of introjection and internalization to occur. This developmental progression was immediately evocative of Mahler's descriptions of the symbiotic process (Mahler, Pine, and Bergman, 1975).

In considering Jacobson's work, one must recognize limitations in ego psychological theory available to her at the time. She tended to make giant leaps in formulating sequences of developmental processes, without giving sufficient definition to each step. My experience has indicated that the self representations seem to center on clearly definable aspects of body ego experience. These body ego experiences are represented separately and ultimately consolidate to form a whole self representation. Those body experiences that can be represented without the necessity of a defensive response consolidate into a whole, good self representation. There are three facets: (1) the instinctual body ego experiences of optimal gratification, (2) the body ego experiences evoked by the use of autonomous ego functions, and (3) the body ego experience that results from the original intrauterine connection to the maternal environment. This latter aspect has been beautifully portrayed by Grotstein (1981) as the background object of primary identification. Those body ego experiences that include a defensive response are represented and consolidated into a whole, bad self representation. Again, there are three facets: (1) the instinctual body ego experiences of overstimulation, (2) the body ego experiences of reactions to impingement, and (3) the body ego experiences of sensory deprivation.

The object relations theorists have advanced our understanding of the significance of interactions with the external world. The effects of these interactions on intrapsychic structuralization during early development, however, have been a matter of controversy. The insights gained have had fragmentary value, for they suffer from the lack of a metapsychology that encompasses instinct theory, ego psychology and a psychology of the self. Some of the difficulty stems from the concept of libido as discharge-seeking rather than object-seeking. Libido theory was formulated before structural theory and has been never fully revised. In recent years it has become evident that revision is necessary. The idea of libido as discharge-seeking can be maintained in explicating the complex structures observed in the later phases of psychosexual development. Yet when an attempt is made to trace the developmental line of a given more advanced structure, it becomes apparent that libido is involved with an object at each step. Kohut (1971) attempted to deal with this observation by postulating two separate lines of narcissistic development. Even earlier, Fairbairn (1954) responded to this dilemma by developing a theory of object relations that eliminated instinct theory. His rationale evolved from his observation that libido was object-seeking from the outset of development. This was a serious deficiency, since libido theory has shed so much light on the human psychosexual experience throughout life. Certainly it is essential to include in our formulations the nature of the processes and mechanisms involved in interactions with the external world, as well as the manner in which those interactions are represented in the internal world. At the same time, however, we need to conceptualize the intrapsychic events and interactional processes that further the expansion of the totality of the self.

Jacobson (1964) hypothesized a brief state of primary narcissism at the outset of development, before the formation of a representational world. The initial representations of the self, then, are poorly differentiated and reflective of a symbiotic interaction. Jacobson pointed out that once a representation has formed, the state of primary narcissism no longer exists. Implicit in this formulation is that the lack of differentiation is a developmental advance. It also implies the presence of a body ego experience of an interaction with an object that is both inside and outside the self. In addition, Jacobson postulated an original undifferentiated energy state, which is only identified as libidinal or aggressive when the structures are available to represent it. That is, a mental structure is necessary to represent instinct as libido or aggression.

My observations have been that, from the outset of development, there is a primitive capacity for the perceptual body ego experience of differentiation. This is the core of the nuclear self that is objectless. In addition, there is much evidence to indicate that perceptual processes function *in utero*, suggesting the presence of a primitive interaction with the intrauterine environment. This intrauterine experience is the foundation for the formation of the background object of primary identification. In my opinion, the concept of primary narcissism is not only unnecessary for an understanding of psychic events, but it is inaccurate and confusing.

Kernberg (1980), Jacobson (1964), Mahler et al. (1975), and others have hypothesized an initial phase in which self and objects cannot yet be differentiated. Object relations theorists, particularly Melanie Klein (1955), Fairbairn (1954), and Bion (1968), have indicated that at the outset there is a phase of primitive objectless differentiation. It requires developmental progression, through interaction with an object in the external world, for a lack of differentiation to evolve. This lack of differentiation fosters the experience of fusion and merger that is essential for the self (and object) representations to form. This concept underscores Freud's (1940) description of the original ego as a body ego under the dominance of a reality principle. Only with advances in development and the formation of self and object representations does the pleasure principle begin to assert itself. Later, with sufficient structuralization, there is a return to the dominance of the reality principle in a new way.

We need to be able to conceptualize a body ego experience for the foundation of the perception that the object in the external world is separate and independent of the self, and yet can be included within the self. In this regard, I shall indicate the significance of what I call "the self with object qualities." My conception refers to a body ego experience, at the border of biophysiology in the interior of the organism, which encompasses the effects of bodily processes and the manner in which they are perceived. This continuum of biophysiological demand is represented according to its effects on perceptual processes. One aspect is represented as instinctual activity that is optimally gratified. Another aspect is represented as potentially traumatic and overstimulating. Yet another aspect has the perceptual impact of an impingement and is represented as an object impression. Finally, there is the aspect of the continuum that is unperceivable. Throughout the course of development, the capacity to represent this continuum increases. It is this perceptual activity at the interior that establishes the body ego experience necessary as a foundation for the internalization of the perceptions of the object in the external world. Ultimately, the ability to perceive and represent the unseen aspects on the continuum of "the Self with object qualities" is the body ego experience at the foundation of the perception that the object in the external world has unseen objects of its own.

Advances in development are dependent on processes of internalization. It is thus essential to have a theoretical construct elucidating a body ego experience of activity that is simultaneously inside and outside the self. The site at which the body makes a demand for mental representation is on a continuum with a dimension that is outside the perceptual boundaries of the self. It evokes a body ego experience of the perception of activity outside the self, yet inside the organism. In the intrauterine environment the developing embryo has an interaction with stimuli originating outside the self. In this primitive embryonic state there is a stimulus from outside the self that is simultaneously inside the self. These interactions provide the body ego experiences that underlie the formation of the self (and object) representations. These are the body ego experiences at the foundation of the fusion-merger experiences of post-uterine life. This conceptual framework allows libido to be formulated as object-seeking. It eliminates the idea of an early phase of primary narcissism and expands Jacobson's hypothesis of an initial, undifferentiated energy state. In this framework there must be an available structure for instinctual demand to be represented as libido. The earliest structures available for representation are the self representations formed from the body ego experience of engagement with an object. This concept is vital to ground the clinical observation that progress in psychotherapy is determined by the nature of the interaction.

A major fault in Jacobson's *The Self and the Object World* (1964) is the confusion in her use of the concepts of the early infantile defenses of denial and splitting. Kernberg (1980), in defining the self-object-affect units that comprise mental structures, has detailed the mechanism of splitting in early development. His descriptions, however, tend to be static and mechanical; they do not portray the processes involved in these splitting mechanisms. In describing the dynamic processes involved in the formation of splits, I shall define splitting as a translocation of perception. This means that a given stimulus is represented away from the source of the stimulation. I shall explicate the reasons for this perceptual translocation.

My focus is on perceptual processes as the regulators of self experience. Perceptual processes are a function of the ego. Some authors have conceived of the ego as embedded within the self; others have presented the self as embedded within the ego. My presentation is devoted to a description of the experiences resulting from the activity of the perceptual processes. The boundaries of the totality of the self are formed by the functioning of the perceptual processes, and it is within these boundaries that representations are formed and consolidate. The self as presented here is a supraordinate concept. The mode of operation of the perceptual processes determines the composition of the body ego experiences and object impressions that are represented to comprise the totality of the self. The role of body ego experiences in the formation of mental structures places emphasis on the effects of perceptual processes.

Hoffer (1952) and Spitz (1955) stressed the idea that the perceptual processes function as psychic organizers. These authors developed a theoretical framework for tracing the effects of early developmental processes on later development. Both focused on the role of perceptual processes, but their speculations appear to be contradictory. This may in part be due to the adultomorphic effect of any attempt to describe the early events of infantile life. The contradictory ideas concern the high priority given to the representational capacity of visual experience during the earliest stages of the formation of mental structures. The optic tracts are the last to attain myelinization and functional capacity. Temporally, the capacity for visual representation coincides with the establishment of consensual validation. I shall attempt to clarify the manner in which perceptual processes participate in the formation of psychic structure. The establishment of consensual validation and the consolidation of part self representations into a whole occur concurrently. It is at this point in development that the visual perceptual processes can exert their organizing influence.

Mental events are multidetermined and exposed to numerous influences. Ultimately, it is the manner in which they are perceived that reveals the forces that led to their formation and that affect them. Visual perceptual processes are the last, in the maturational sequence of perception, to exert their representational influence. The visual processes possess a more advanced organizational capacity. The perceptual processes that are closer to body ego experience, such as touch, smell, and taste, have a higher representational capacity. Consensual validation means that the various perceptual modalities are integrated as a functioning unit. The manner in which consensual validation is established and the interrelationship to the developing representational world will be described.

A number of authors have called attention to the almost universal existence of a level of regressive functioning that, under certain conditions, can reach psychotic proportions. This phenomenon has been described by Michael Balint (1968) as the "basic fault" and by Bion (1968) as the psychotic sector of the personality. Although it is a common clinical observation, there has not been a clear exposition of its place in the sequential scheme of development. The plethora and intensity of instinctual demands that the primitive perceptual processes are confronted with at the interior of the organism reach traumatic proportions. The traumatic effects of these biophysiological demands can only be integrated at a later point in development. I shall present the idea that instinctual demand can be present within the organism and yet remain outside the self.

In the history of psychoanalysis, it took a long time to appreciate the profound impact on human experience of interactional processes. In recent years there has been a clearer delineation of the role of introjective and projective processes in early structure formation. The increasing understanding of the mechanism of projective identification has broadened an understanding of the effects of the therapeutic interaction. Analysts have always known of the important effects of countertransference responses. Nevertheless, there has been much disagreement about the exact nature of those effects. The patient's perceptions of the analyst tend to be attributed almost entirely to transference distortions. Moreover, the importance of the patient's unconscious perceptions of the analyst is not fully appreciated. In part, the confusion in this area is a result of the absence of a theoretical substrate on which to base a distinction between transference distortions (based on fantasy) and unconscious perceptions (based on body ego experience). In practice, every analyst knows of the importance of the patient's unconscious perceptions, although they might not be identified as such. Verification of interpretive communications depends on a patient's derivative reactions and responses. Much effort has been exerted to explain the processes that operate in these interactions.

Earlier I referred to my therapeutic experiences with a number of children described as autistic. These were children who were viewed as divorced from the external world of reality, as having shut out all human relationships from the realm of their experience. In my therapeutic work with them it appeared quite different. They taught me, in some painful ways, that at times I unwittingly offered them a pathological relationship. On each occasion that I did so, they did in fact close me out. It was specifically at these moments that they were divorced from a human relationship. When I displayed any willingness or capacity to examine the part I played in the interaction, they began to communicate with me. At the time this was a startling revelation to me, and it had a profound effect. It confronted me with the task of exploring my own motivations whenever these children ceased communication. Each time I did, I was immensely rewarded with human communication from children who otherwise would not communicate at all. It alerted me to how I had simply explained the differences in these children and other patients, as the difference between individuals who were analyzable and those who possessed "ego deficits" or "developmental arrests." Gradually I became aware of the powerful influence my own pathological or defensive responses had on the therapeutic process with all my patients. With the children I described, the effect was immediate, concrete, and impossible to deny. With others, it was more subtle, elusive, and easy to rationalize.

For the past 10 years, Langs (1977) has been writing about the significance of the therapeutic interaction. He has stressed the idea that the management of the framework and ground rules of psychotherapy reflects the therapist's healthy or pathological functioning. He has also emphasized the role of patients' encoded derivatives and unconscious perceptions. The intellectual framework he develops establishes a listening process that can distinguish between expressions of transference distortions and unconscious perceptions. The unconscious perceptions of a patient can serve as a guide and supervisor for the therapist. Langs's work, however, has not been well grounded in developmental theory. He has not provided a foundation for the observations he so accurately defines.

In this article I intend to address the processes, mechanisms, and sequences of the earliest phases of structure formation at the foundation of unconscious perceptions. An explication of the original body ego experiences by which a stimulus outside the self is included, through representation, within the self gives a developmental foundation for the role of unconscious perceptions in interactional experiences. The differing effects of the therapist's interpretive activities when they are based on empathic responses to unconscious communications and when they are based on empathic failures will be explored. These effects are illustrative of the manner in which unconscious perceptions are manifested in a therapeutic interaction.

CLINICAL ILLUSTRATIONS

Case Example 1

Adam was a wizened-looking, four-year-old boy with no identifiable communicative speech and only occasional sing-song vocalizations. He wandered endlessly from place to place and submissively complied to external physical directions. After being diagnosed on several occasions as autistic, brain-damaged, or retarded, Adam was referred for a series of diagnostic sessions to determine whether psychotherapeutic intervention was feasible and to aid his family in making decisions concerning his future. The family had been advised that institutionalization was necessary and the only question was when.

In the first two sessions, which occurred on consecutive days, Adam stood silently and then awkwardly moved from place to place, gesturing with his fingers wiggling in front of his poorly focused eyes. He seemingly paid no attention to the therapist, who sat silently and attempted to grasp any possible meaning from his behavior. By the third session, the therapist began to sense that the empty outer shell of Adam's mannerisms, behavior, and minimal sing-song vocalizations surrounded an inner perceptual experience that he was either unwilling or unable to communicate. The therapist stated that, for himself, fingers were a vehicle for reaching and touching the outer world and in watching Adam he sensed that Adam was admonishing his fingers to prevent them from being drawn into exploring that world. Adam was seemingly unaffected by this communication from the therapist; he continued what appeared to be aimless wandering and gesturing with his fingers. The therapist became aware that he had become internally disengaged from Adam and was thinking about his next appointment. At precisely this point, Adam turned to the therapist and asked, "Are you listening?" How amazing to hear these words spoken, and what an amazing coincidence that this occurred at exactly the moment that the therapist was not listening.

Webster's defines "coincidence" as events that occur simultaneously, take up the same place and space, and are exactly alike in shape, position, and area. Here was a therapist whose attention had strayed away from a child, who immediately addressed a question in response to that occurrence. The child, amazingly, communicated verbally when he had previously been portrayed as being without communicative language. Where did these words come from? How had he developed the capacity to form them and direct them? What was the significance of this striking event?

It was on the basis of these three words that the therapist embarked on a psychological journey with this four-year-old patient in a long-term intensive therapeutic interaction. He was seen four to five times per week for six years, three times per week for three years, and weekly until he finished his therapy at age 17.

The therapist's immediate response to Adam's question was to state that, in fact, he had not been listening, his attention had strayed; that he had been affected by a feeling of rejection by Adam of his efforts and had responded by turning away. Adam became somber and tentatively began to explore the therapist's chair with his fingers. (Much later, he spoke of this moment. He recalled the therapist's voice echoing inside him and evoking an inner feeling of containment and safety.)

Following this initial communicative sentence, for a long period of time Adam spent his sessions silently exploring other objects in the room and the therapist's body with his fingers. Periodically he retreated into seemingly aimless gesturing and posturing, alternating between exploring and retreating. Then Adam brought two toy soldiers to a session. One was wounded and bandaged, the other intact and upright. Nonverbally he portrayed their interaction. The therapist responded by reflecting upon his reaction to Adam's play. The therapist spoke of the hurt and damage inflicted upon the soldier, and the stiff and ineffective efforts of the erect soldier in addressing these wounds. The therapist verbalized his own inner feeling of being ineffective and stiff as he experienced a gap between Adam and himself.

There was no immediate response, but the following morning Adam awoke very early and spoke his first communicative sentence to his parents. "Take me to ferapy." On that day he arrived looking entirely different. His face was worn and haggard. He looked terrified. He was restless, agitated, and irritable. Periodically he made sounds that were alternately whining and anguished. The picture was of a child being viciously bombarded by some internal process and helpless in managing the onslaught. The therapist spoke to what he sensed was occurring inside Adam, and as he did felt his own inner sense of stiffness dissolving. At this moment Adam approached the therapist, at first stiffly and tentatively. He gradually molded himself into the therapist's lap. This continued for several sessions.

Adam indicated, at first behaviorally and slowly with monosyllabic verbalizations, that the therapist's voice was too loud, or the lights were too bright, or the surrounding noises of the street too intense. Everything hurt. The therapist found a way to gently hold Adam, turned out the lights, and drew the shades to diminish the noise level. During this period of time, Adam was sleepless, and appeared to be in a constant state of terror. He spent many sessions in the arms of the therapist, with the therapist either silent or softly talking. The therapist remembered the earlier play with the two soldiers. He spoke of Adam's need for buffering and containment, and of the impact of stimuli from the outside and from the inside. There were several sessions where Adam simply slept the entire time.

Slowly, Adam began to talk, first from the position of being cradled by the therapist. He gradually shifted from that position to physically moving around the room. At times he was contained; at times he was agitated. He talked about the internal creatures that assaulted him and the occasional figures that comforted him. When he spoke of the assaulting figures, his agitation mounted. When he spoke of the comforting figures, he appeared contained. He also spoke of mischievous and fun-loving creatures, and he smiled. Although he had exhibited a variety of facial expressions, this was the first time he had smiled. His communicative speech was soft, with many words difficult for the therapist to understand. The names he assigned to the mental objects that populated his mind, however, were spoken very clearly. His descriptions were accentuated by his whole manner and captured the particular function and effect that these objects had on him.

The "Make-a-Dos" were the most variable. They changed from mischievous, fun-loving, impish characters, to angry, hostile, troublesome creatures, to very frightening, provocative, seductive figures who escalated in size. They were associated with an inner feeling of overexcitement and irritability. The name of these figures shed some light on his lifelong episodes of severe constipation. There had been two occasions earlier in his life that required hospitalization, when he had not had a bowel movement for as long as a month. The "Make-a-Dos" emerged as creatures with instinctual qualities ranging from goodness to badness to an ominous quality.

The "Big Black Pops," on the other hand, were dark, partly hidden, sticklike figures. They were extremely explosive, prohibitive, and frightening. His whole being was immobilized when he felt their inner presence. The prohibitive qualities were unmistakable. In contrast, "The Big Pain" was a maternal figure who suffered intensely at the expression of any suffering. Everything that involved conflict or psychic pain in turn hurt the "Big Pain." This figure was constantly whining and commiserating. "Pa-Ba" was an undernourished, undeveloped, undefined, deprived, and helpless infant. Interspersed with Adam's description of these inner objects was the gradual emergence of the soldier. This figure varied from being firm, steadfast, reality-bound, and insisting on performance to being soft, understanding, and warmly responsive. In the presence of the soldier, there was always an aura of containment.

Case Example 2

Ben was a small, frail, 11-year-old child. His frailty was accentuated by his stiff-legged manner of walking and stilted, carefully controlled speech. He chose his words carefully and deliberately, with pauses between each word. His voice quality was soft, abrupt, and robotlike. Throughout his childhood he had been fearful, easily intimidated, and unable to function in school settings. He was brought to the therapist after a period of six months during which he had become profoundly withdrawn and retreated into his own room. Ben resisted coming to the first session, but quickly agreed with the therapist that he appeared to have many inner obstacles that were affecting him and that it would require a lot of work to undo them. Sessions were arranged three times per week in response to Ben's association to how he learned about computers. He would seek help, and then need a day or two by himself to try it out. Then he was ready for more.

This derivative association to the question of meeting was the only communication of this nature during the early sessions. Ben submissively came to his appointments and spoke only in monotonous clichés, which took the form of reporting a daily activity or event. The sessions were experienced by the therapist as lifeless and devoid of direction, and the therapist felt an increasing sense of frustration.

Ben then began to talk about the computers he was interested in. They could be developed to such a degree that they could eventually control the people who made them. The people who programmed them would go on thinking they were in charge, but the computer would use all the programmed information to control the programmer. This reminded him of R_2D_2, the robot in *Star Wars*. He appeared friendly and helpful, but Ben thought he was putting everyone on. He was really teasing them. That was his way of being in charge. The therapist then stated, "I have felt controlled and trapped by what has been occurring between us. I have contributed to it by continuing to try to gain some superficial understanding of your words and actions rather than sharing with you my inner sense of being teased, put on, and being controlled." The entire quality of the interaction changed. Ben's immediate response was to appear stunned and to draw back with a look of hurt and confusion. He quietly spoke of how frightened he was and how much he was trying to communicate with the therapist. He felt very hurt that the therapist saw his efforts as being controlling and teasing. His voice was no longer hesitant, and he spoke with feeling for the first time.

Ben arrived at the following session with a determined look on his face, and proceeded in what at first seemed to be an effort to move and rearrange the furniture in the room. The therapist silently moved to the side as he felt an important communication was occurring. The therapist implicitly encouraged the patient to continue. Ben turned all of the furniture in the room upside down and placed himself in a chair so that he was covered completely. The therapist stated that he thought Ben was showing him in actions his response to what had been said the previous session. After a short silence Ben began to talk from beneath the chair. He had suddenly remembered an incident when he was four years old and hiding under a table in exactly the position he was in now. His mother had been walking by and he had reached out and tripped her. At the time he felt anger, mischievousness, and a sense of mastery. His mother fell, hurt herself, got up in a rage, and attacked him for his actions. The patient felt completely crushed and shattered. It felt to Ben as if this event had been a crucial turning point in his life. From that point on he had lost all feeling of fun and spontaneity. He became contained and fearful and constantly carried a mental image of an attacking voice that made any spontaneous feeling a source of danger. He also spoke of the despair he lived with that any expression of emotion would drive others away leaving him totally abandoned.

The therapist stated that he had attacked Ben with his voice, and it must have reminded him of that inner attack. Ben was silent and remembered how he often retreated to his room silently hoping someone would enter. One day his father burst into his room, which frightened him at first, since he was startled and feared some attack. Ben was surprised that his father had entered in order to talk with him. He then thought of the many times in school when he had been bored, how much he wished he could be mischievous and play tricks on his teachers. He had always been too afraid. Ben then began animatedly to fantasy the many ways he could make fun of and tease people by caricaturing their mannerisms. He then made a comment on how warm and sunny the day was.

Case Example 3

Charlie began psychotherapy at the age of seven, when his surrounding environment felt totally inadequate to deal with his inability or refusal to complete any task. Charlie's wild clowning and disruptive behavior alternated with periods of profound depression and explosive temper tantrums, usually in response to a demand or frustrating task. The overall picture was of a controlling, greedy, highly manipulative child who managed to engage one adult after another in feeling sorry for him and taking care of him.

Initially Charlie was seen one time per week. The idea of meeting more frequently provoked an intense negative reaction. The first two years were occupied with teasing and spinning fantasies of his life, wishes, and hopes. Many of the fantasies were explosively aggressive and some were highly eroticized. There were repeated efforts to engage the therapist into joining him in his manipulative, conniving plots, or in the acting out of his fantasies. Charlie would tease the therapist about his interpretive responses. The depreciatory teasing always had an element of relief.

Slowly, Charlie made both himself and the therapist aware of his deep inner sense of inadequacy covered by his provocations and manipulations. A serious separation anxiety, addressed by the therapist, led to Charlie's establishing his sessions three times per week. A concern with inner fragmentation was manifested in frequent nightmares and in the threat of separation from familiar objects. The sessions most difficult for Charlie were those in which he felt empty, wordless, blocked, and restless. At these times it seemed as if he could hardly tolerate keeping himself within the confines of the office. In his effort to deal with this anxiety Charlie found a plastic, egg-shaped puzzle, which broke down into many pieces and could be reassembled. He wanted to use it to help him be able to talk and not run from the office. The following session occurred at this point in the therapy.

Charlie entered the office, took out the puzzle, disassembled it, and began to put it back together. As he did so, he spoke of his difficulty when something didn't immediately fit. He wanted to discipline himself to be able to search for and find just the right piece. The therapist responded by metaphorically relating the pieces of the puzzle to the pieces of himself. At first Charlie reacted with delight and elaborated the metaphor. However, as the session was ending, Charlie stated, partly with the teasing, depreciatory qualities that characterized his reaction to interpretive efforts, but also with a note of sadness and despair, "What good does it do to talk about pieces of a puzzle? What does that have to do with me?" The therapist stated that he thought it had everything to do with Charlie, including his attempt to deal with the separation at the end of the hour by making the therapist see and feel his despair and feel the anxiety that Charlie experienced as his inner contents came closer to him. Charlie remained silent for the remainder of the session and left appearing somewhat dejected.

Charlie entered the next session, following a weekend, extremely excited and eager to talk. He had been invited to someone's house over the weekend. This was an activity he had always previously avoided. On this occasion he decided to go. When it came time to go to sleep, he was filled with a state of panic. He felt the temptation to return to his home, but decided to stay in his bed for a while. He began to think about the puzzle he had been working on in the therapist's office and of the therapist's words. He thought to himself, "What are these pieces of myself? They must be the things I feel and think about." He began to allow himself to be filled with and observe what entered his mind.

Charlie thought of his interest in *Playboy* magazine and his sexual excitement. This immediately led to a recollection of his masturbatory experiences. A tremendous feeling of shame and embarrassment filled him as he thought of it. The associative chain was interrupted by a feeling of anxiety and uncomfortable excitement. His thoughts shifted to what he was capable of and what he was incapable of. He recalled the sports in which he was an effective participant. He also thought of his schoolwork and how overwhelming and frustrating it was. He could feel the potential inside of him that was not being realized, and the frustration associated with it. As his inner feeling of inadequacy mounted, his thoughts shifted again to a favored place in the country. Here he could be with himself and feel free, contained, and soothed. This inner calmness was immediately interrupted by memories of his rage in response to the intimidating attacks of demanding teachers. These memories were alternatingly of his being totally intimidated, reacting in a rage, and being humiliated as a result; or of his total submissive retreat.

Charlie's memories then moved to his family. He recalled his mother's efforts to empathize with his suffering. At times this was quite helpful, but it was so easy for him to manipulate her by his suffering. He could make her feel guilty and get his way. He thought of his father's contempt for Charlie's greedy behavior or inadequacies in performance; yet how much he looked for his father's curtailment. This quickly shifted to a feeling of being impinged upon by the frightening aspects of his father's anger at him. He thought of his dog, whom he loved dearly, and of his overattachment to material objects. He began to realize that when he was confronted with a separation, he attached comforting qualities to some material object that would be envied by others. As his thoughts roamed to the things he was most interested in, such as fireworks and guns, and how alone he felt with those interests, he began to have an inner sensation of coming together. It reminded him of the sensation of completing a puzzle, finding the right piece and having it click into place. The panic had dissolved. He spent the remainder of the weekend feeling himself a whole and separate person.

THE EFFECT OF EMPATHIC RESPONSIVENESS AND EMPATHIC FAILURES ON UNCONSCIOUS PERCEPTIONS

In these clinical examples, the therapist's acknowledgment of the patient's unconscious perceptions evoked an inner sense of containment. Empathic responsiveness in a therapeutic interaction requires validation by the patient's unconscious perceptions. A lapse or failure in the therapist's empathy is unconsciously perceived by the patient, and the resulting interaction demands a defensive adaptation. Until the therapist can identify the source of that failure and rectify it, the interaction remains a stimulus to be defended against. It is only when the patient's unconscious perceptions are validated by the therapist that a process of inner exploration and inner integration can take place.

In the initial period with Adam it was difficult to determine the presence or absence of emphatic responsiveness. Adam reacted in a way that offered the therapist little evidence of how he was being perceived. The therapist's attention was focused on Adam and his thoughts occupied with the interaction. The therapist's unconscious perception was of a child wanting to reach out and fighting against that wish. When the therapist communicated his perception to Adam, it seemingly was ignored, and the therapist reacted by withdrawing his attention. An empathic failure ensued that immediately prompted Adam's question, "Are you listening?" The therapist became aware of his lapse and the reasons for it, acknowledged Adam's unconscious perception, and Adam responded by communicating more freely in his exploratory behavior. Much later he described this moment as one in which he felt safe and contained. Also later, Adam was able to communicate his unconscious perception of the therapist as stiff and uneffective. The therapist's validation of this perception was followed by Adam's relinquishing his autistic defenses. As the therapist, with Adam's participation, lost his stiffness and was capable of once again establishing an empathically responsive interaction, a communicative process of inner exploration emerged.

With Ben, a background of empathic responsiveness was initiated with the establishment of the frequency of sessions. The therapist was unconsciously perceiving Ben's efforts to control the relationship, but was reacting defensively to his perception. For the therapist, the consequence was a mounting sense of frustration and blindness to the underlying significance of this quality in the interaction. Ben derivatively communicated his unconscious perception of the controlled therapist. The therapist validated Ben's perception, but his frustration and blindness led to an empathic failure, which was manifested in an attack on Ben's attitude. This elicited in Ben the memory of an attack that was a parallel of the therapeutic interaction. The therapist's validation of Ben's unconscious perception reminded Ben of his wish to be reached and was associated with an inner sense of the return of his spontaneity in a background of containment. This was expressed in his delight in the idea of mimicking authorities and sudden awareness of the warmth and brightness of the day.

The manner in which the interaction was perceived was largely determined by the development of the individual, the background relationship already established, and the therapist's intervention. The empathic responsiveness of the therapist to what was reactively available and unconsciously determined evoked a feeling of safety that began with the therapist recognizing the value of Adam's unconscious perceptions. It was shown in Ben with the feeling of warmth associated with the therapist's acknowledgment of Ben's unconscious perception of being attacked.

In an effort to understand such phenomena it is important to develop metapsychological constructs that can portray the role of perception in development and the role of unconscious perceptions in adaptive interactions. The pathway by which a stimulus that is outside the self can be included within the self needs to be delineated. The therapeutic interaction involves an experience outside the self that is enhancing or hurtful to and included in the processes and functions operating within the self. It is thereby essential to have a definition of the self that can be traced to its very beginnings.

THE NUCLEAR SELF—A DEFINITION

Any definition of the early processes at the foundation of self experience is, of necessity, highly speculative. A conceptual framework that is useful must broaden our view of what is observable, though it is drawn from abstractions of experience that is not observable. As noted earlier, body ego experiences are at the base of all mental productions. The most advanced experiences of identity, autonomy, and separateness thus have a body ego experience at their foundation.

If we define the self as determined by the activity of the perceptual processes, then the nuclear self is manifested with the dawning of the functions of perception. This first occurs during intrauterine life and is profoundly influenced by the surrounding maternal environment. Winnicott (1958), with the concept of holding, and Enid Balint (1963), with the concept of primary love, allude to this intrauterine model as a reflection of the maternal figure's influence on the earliest experiences that provide definition to the nuclear self. Bion's (1968) metaphor of the container and the contained makes direct reference to this model.

Influenced by the stimuli of the surrounding maternal environment and biophysiology, then, these anlage of autonomous perception begin to delineate a boundary for the nuclear self. This boundary, however, is limited by the nature of these anlage and by the ego's capacity to represent the perceptions. Initially, the ego is a body ego. Each perceptual activity has a dual function: to represent a stimulus as a mental impression and to organize these mental impressions into an identifiable unit. Distant receptors have a low representational and a high organizational capacity. Close receptors have a high capacity to represent stimuli and a low capacity to organize these stimuli as emanating from a given source. In early development, touch, temperature, smell, and taste will be most represented (and in those body geographic zones most highly innervated). Distant receptors of hearing and sight will be least represented, and their organizational influence will be very limited.

The representations of the activity of these primitive perceptual processes will gradually coalesce according to the nature of the stimuli and capacities of the child. These are the beginnings of psychic structuralization, of what will become a self representation system. The self representations form within the boundaries of the nuclear self and reflect differing responses to varied stimuli. Advances in development, together with the maturation of the autonomous ego functions, consolidate these part self representations into a totality. This process is accelerated as the distant perceptual processes exert their organizing influence (see Hoffer, 1952; Spitz, 1955).

How a given body ego experience is represented varies according to the particular locale at which the activity of perception takes place. This is important in understanding those body experiences at the foundation of unconscious perceptions. Unconscious perceptions are manifested either by derivatives that express their activity or by the internal state reactively evoked by a stimulus. The unconscious perception of an interaction is initiated by a stimulus at the periphery (the point of contact with the external world). This has a different effect than a stimulus at the interior (the point of contact with the impact of biophysiology). This difference could be seen in Adam's representations of the "Make-a-Dos" and the "Big Black Pops." The "Make-a-Dos" were instinctual in nature and reflected the effects of contact with the demands of biophysiology. In contrast, the "Big Black Pops" were prohibitive in nature and reflected the effects of contact with the impinging stimuli of the external world. Whereas the impinging qualities of the "Make-a-Dos" were overstimulating, the impinging qualities of the "Big Black Pops" were attacking, patterned after an object in the external world.

Unconscious perceptions of an interaction, then, register the effects of a stimulus at the periphery. But representation also depends on the nature of the stimulus and the state of the mental mechanisms available for its registration. Voluntary bodily processes are more perceptible to the early body ego. Involuntary bodily processes are registered with diminished intensity, or not registered at all. The consolidation of the part self representations into an entity is accompanied by the concurrent integration of these perceptions. Indeed, unconscious perceptions, to be functional, depend on some degree of integration. Consensual validation refers to the integration of the perceptual processes; it results in the dual functions of representation and organization being available in all perceptual modalities. Visual and auditory stimuli can thus affect other sensory modalities and vice versa.

The capacity to register and express the effects of unconscious perceptions, then, is dependent on the developmental step of establishing consensual validation. Perceptual contact with the external world will be of greater or lesser intensity depending on the nature and impact of the contact. Contacts of diminished intensity, or with little evocative connection to the representations of bodily processes, have little effect. Contacts of great intensity, or with a high degree of evocative connection to the representations of bodily processes, will have a great impact. Thus, with Adam, the therapist's lapse of attention was immediately unconsciously perceived as a potential threat. There was an evocative connection to the experience of abandonment and its profound effect on bodily processes.

This quality of a lapse in attention would have affected Ben with little impact, since it did not establish such an evocative connection. For Ben, however, the therapist's intervention tinged with frustration had a powerful impact on his unconscious perceptions. There was an evocative link to the screen memory of trauma that made him exquisitely unconsciously perceptive of these interactional qualities.

THE BACKGROUND OBJECT OF PRIMARY IDENTIFICATION AND ITS SIGNIFICANCE FOR THE NUCLEAR SELF

The first perceptual contact with the external world is intrauterine. The primordial nuclear self registers the containing, regulating aspect of a primary identification with the buffering, physiological, and metabolizing function of the intrauterine maternal environment. This forms a representation in the nuclear self, which is excellently named "the background object of primary identification" by Grotstein (1981). The background object of primary identification is expanded through the containing, regulating interactions with the mothering external object in postuterine life.

The background object of primary identification, then, is the representation of a body ego experience of contact with the intrauterine environment. It is present at birth and establishes a foundation for the introjection and representation of the activities of perception in interaction with the external world. It is this representation that allows a psychological symbiosis. Indeed, the mothering figure's psychological containment and regulation of the infant's emotional interchanges depend on the presence of this body ego experience. There is already a mental vehicle by which a stimulus emanating from outside the self, through its evocative connection to a structure inside the self, can be included and contribute to its expansion.

When Adam was verbally uncommunicative, much of the therapist's understanding of the interaction depended on inferences. Adam's play with two soldiers appeared to the therapist to exactly parallel how the therapist was experiencing the interaction. He saw Adam as being wounded and damaged, and himself as being stiff and ineffective in helping him. The therapist's realization of his stiffness had implicit in it the potential for undoing it. The therapist was offering his help to Adam and also indicating his openness to be helped. This quality parallels the mutuality that is involved in symbiotic interactions.

The therapist's communication had a profound effect on Adam, who became impinged on by stimuli that previously he had seemed oblivious to. Adam molded himself to the therapist; the therapist felt his stiffness dissolve and was able to buffer Adam from the traumatic impact of stimuli. Gradually, as the therapist continued to contain and hold him, Adam appeared to enter a state of fusion with the therapist. He seemed to shift from a position of warding off the stimuli of the external world to one of fusing himself with the stimuli of the extenal world. Although the stimuli were at first powerful and impinging, in the arms of the therapist Adam was soothed and comforted. The interaction was reminiscent of Mahler et al.'s (1975) description of the psychological symbiosis of early development.

For Adam, this state of lack of differentiation could only evolve when the therapist was emphatically responsive with consistency over time. This is consonant with the idea that psychological symbiosis can only evolve when an interaction is empathic to and resonant with inner need. In other words, the state of lack of differentiation that characterizes symbiosis evolves out of an empathic interaction. It does not appear to be present from the outset.

In addition, it seems that the psychological symbiosis has to have a body ego experience at its foundation in order to transpire. I am postulating that this body ego experience is represented as the background object of primary identification. With Adam, the degree of fragmentation in his mental representations appeared to reflect a faulty representation of the background object of primary identification. One consequence of the symbiotic interaction with Adam was the representation of the soldier as a containing figure. This new representation was consistent with my formulation here of the process by which new self and object representations are formed. That is, the background object of primary identification is the body ego experience underlying symbiotic interactions, and these symbiotic interactions are necessary for the building of new self and object representations.

QUALITIES OF GOODNESS AND BADNESS: THEIR REPRESENTATION IN THE NUCLEAR SELF

Goodness refers to the representation of experiences that have no necessity for defense, whereas badness refers to the representations of experiences that require defense. The clinical vignettes of Adam and Charlie serve as a sample of interactions with a number of patients in whom self fragmentation was a factor. It appeared to me that the representations of the varied aspects of experience tended to cluster into definable facets of the self, which were indicative of the manner in which they had formed. The varied part self representations are united into a whole, according to their qualities of goodness and badness. These differing facets of goodness and badness create lines of cleavage, which are later identifiable when the self representations are under stress.

The Part Self Representations of Goodness

An all-good self representation is formed from the body ego experience of three facets of goodness. As one facet, the primordial nuclear self registers the *containing, regulating, metabolizing effects of the intrauterine environment* as the background object of primary identification.

Second, an *instinctual facet of goodness* is represented in the self. This is instinctual activity that is perceived and represented without the need for defense. The object in the external world provides empathic contact, which results in a multiplicity of body ego experiences. Those aspects of the interaction that are optimally gratifying to an instinctual demand are represented as the good instinctual aspect of the self. At this early stage of development, the instinctual activity is mainly oral.

The third representation is of the *activity of the autonomous ego functions*. The infant, in this nuclear condition, has the seeds of what will become a conflict-free sphere of the ego. Although the autonomous ego functions are not yet structuralized, effective, or readily accessible, they are present in a state of readiness to be evoked and amplified in response to appropriate stimuli. The optimally frustrating element of empathic responsiveness is necessary to both evoke and support these functions.

The empathic object in the external world is thus not only empathic with the instinctual demands of the infant, but with the anlage of the infant's autonomous functioning. An empathic mother responds to the beginnings of function barely visible within the infant. These functions are amplified by her empathic activity. The body ego experience within the infant is one of resonance and connection. An object outside the self amplifies a function within the self. This quality of interaction has awakened the activity of the ego. Optimal gratification in an interaction depends on qualities of optimal frustration. It is essential for the empathically responding object in the external world to be sensitive to when the developing infant can wait for the gratification of instinctual demands. The period of waiting is occupied with the exercise of the autonomous ego functions. These functions are exercised and utilized to participate in the building of psychic structure, and to engage in defensive and integrative activities. Hartmann (1939), in calling attention to this crucial aspect of early development, expanded psychoanalytic metapsychology to include the psychology of the ego.

My contention is that psychic representation is initiated with the dawning of perceptual activity *in utero* and manifested by the background object of primary identification. This view also suggests the existence of primitive defensive activity. Perception, being a function of the ego, would of necessity have at least some reactive discriminatory capacity. Adam's representations of the instinctual "Make-a-Dos" gives some credence to this conception. Although Adam had withdrawn from the stimuli of the external world very early in his development, he continued to represent the stimuli of the internal world of biophysiological demand. His withdrawal was not complete, in that he was extremely reactive to the stimuli of interactions with objects in the external world. These interactions influenced the part self and part object representations that had formed. Ego functions, engaged in defense, were seemingly present from the outset. Yet the absence of optimally gratifying and optimally frustrating interactions had not provided sufficient representation and consolidation of the qualities of goodness for these ego functions to participate in the building of psychic structure. In Adam, the qualities of goodness were only mobilized in the presence of a background of lapsed empathy. His original question, "Are you listening?", indicated the existence of a capacity momentarily to organize the qualities of goodness into a whole—specifically, in response to an empathic failure. These organized qualities of goodness, however, were not consistently present at the point of contact with the external world. Instead, these qualities of goodness seemed to be organized around and responsive to the need for defense.

At the onset of development, the facets of goodness have to be represented at the interior to allow the processes of internalization and structure building to take place. The foundation of unconscious perceptions lies in these body ego experiences. The qualities of a therapeutic interaction will resonate with these developmental structures. Thus, the interventions of the therapist, when empathic to a patient's unconscious communications, will be validated by derivative expressions of these qualities of goodness. This is particularly true of the manner in which the therapist manages the framework of the therapy. The qualities of containment, regulation, optimal gratification, and optimal frustration are most powerfully communicated in this dimension. Langs (1977) has consistently drawn attention to this frequently overlooked aspect of the therapeutic interaction.

The Part Self Representations of Badness

An all-bad self representation is formed from the body ego experience of three facets of badness. One facet represented as part of the bad self is *instinctual*. This representation is of the primitive state of the union of the libidinal drives that are beyond the bounds of phase specificity, as well as the aggressive drives requiring defense. Libidinal activity is on a continuum of intensity. The overstimulating dimension of that continuum mobilizes a defensive response and is represented as a part of the bad self. During early development, the focus is on the erotogenic zones of orality. The overstimulating aspect will be represented as greed in the bad self.

The aggressive qualities of instinctual demand, when contained and regulated, are differentiating in their effects. Those that are not regulated, however, require defense and are represented within the bad self.

The second facet represented as a part of the bad self encompasses the body ego experiences of reacting to impingement. Included are stimuli whose effect is to encroach on or strike the perceptual processes with great force or intensity. The reactions to this impingement—fight, flight, and/or withdrawal—embody the defensive capacities of the ego.

Finally, the third facet represented as a part of the bad self involves the body ego experiences of sensory deprivations. Because it is virtually impossible to provide a totally empathic environment, there is always a sector of sensory deprivation.

Initially, these qualities of badness are represented at the periphery (the point of perceptual contact with the external world). They serve a protective function and will facilitate differentiation. These bad qualities all involve responses that are modeled after the reactions to impingement. That is, there is a fight against, a flight from, or a withdrawal from the source of stimulation.

Optimally gratifying libidinal activity has a binding function. That is, there is a movement toward and inclusion of the source of stimulation. The good self representations, forming at the interior, modulate the potential traumatic effect of biophysiological demands and the effects of bodily processes. A state of lack of differentiation, as we have seen, is a prerequisite for the psychological symbiotic interaction necessary for structure building to occur. Yet the bad self representations, forming at the periphery, offer some balance to that lack of differentiation. When the stimuli of interactions with the external world possess overstimulating, impinging, or depriving qualities, they are immediately evocative of the defensive responsiveness of these represented qualities of badness. Although the all-bad self representation and the all-good self representation are consolidating as separate entities, there is a line of connection between them. The representation of instinctual activity in the good self shades into the representation of instinctual activity in the bad self, maintaining a line of continuity.

THE CONSOLIDATION OF THE REPRESENTATIONS OF THE SELF

Initially, the three facets of the all-good self are represented separately as their sources are different. There is some overlap, but there is sufficient difference to form lines of cleavage. The three facets of the all-bad self are also represented separately. Again, their sources are sufficiently different to form lines of cleavage. The integration and maturation of all perceptual processes occurs concurrently with the consolidation of the part self representations into a whole.

As was pointed out, the earliest boundaries of the self are body ego experiences represented primarily as a result of the activity of the near receptors of touch, taste, and smell, and only minimally through the distant receptors of hearing and sight. The maturation of the perceptual functions and the interrelated formation of self and object representations increase the availability of the organizing function of the far receptors. The various perceptual modalities then function in unison. The manner in which unconscious perceptions are activated and manifest their functioning is directly proportional to the degree of integration of the organizing and representational functions of perceptual processes. In this fashion, emotional nuances in an interaction can be perceived through one perceptual modality and evoke a total response. The boundaries of the self gradually become more delineated and organized as the representational and organizational functions achieve continuity with all perceptual processes. Consensual validation is thus possible. Consensual validation means that both functions of representation and organization become available to all perceptual modalities.

Adam, even with the state of fragmentation that dominated his psychic functioning, was capable of a transient experience of inner consolidation of the all-good self. It was evoked by the unconscious perception of a lapse in the therapist's attention. Consensual validation had to be functional, at least momentarily, to accomplish this perceptual act. Qualities of goodness were so insufficiently represented in Adam, however, that this degree of consolidation could not be maintained.

Splitting as a Translocation of Perception

Unconscious perceptions are a reflection of the effects of a stimulus occurring at one locale and having continuity with its representation in another sector of the personality. What are the original developmental processes that embody this quality of perception? Kernberg (1980) has described splitting as self-object-affect units organized and split off from each other according to their good and bad qualities. But he does not give any indication of how this evolves. With a small group of children, such as Adam, I have had the experience of participating in interactions that eventuated in the formation of new representational structures. From the manner in which this transpired, I have attempted to abstract a concept that may illuminate these early processes.

The mechanism of splitting can be described as a translocation of perception. That is, it is a process in which the representation of a stimulus occurs away from its source. This conception provides for an underlying body ego experience, at the foundation of unconscious perceptions. (A similar view can be taken of repression proper. Primal repression refers to the interface of the realm of biology, making demands, with the mental realm of representation. Repression proper is an active mental process in which perceptual attention is directed away from a sequence of psychic events and attracted to another.)

Stimulation is continuously present at the interior from the effects of our biophysiological makeup. In addition, stimulation is present at the periphery from the effects of interactions with the external world. The impact of biophysiology is variable, depending on the manner in which its demands can be represented. The perceptual processes register a certain amount as phase-specific instinctual gratification. These perceptions are enhanced by the containing, ministrating interactions with the external world, which provide a body ego experience of stability evocative of the background object of primary identification. On the other hand, the optimally frustrating qualities of an empathic interaction amplify the autonomous ego functions. These good part self representations consolidate into a whole at the interior. The point of perceptual contact, however, is at the periphery.

The intensity of the biophysiological demands is such that a certain amount is overstimulating and potentially traumatic. The impact is that of an impingement. As we have seen, this aspect is represented as the instinctual aspect of the bad self. The body ego experiences that result from impinging, nonemphatic interactions with the object in the external world are represented at the periphery. These stimulate reactions to impingement and are represented as a facet of the bad self. The impinging qualities of the interactions with the object in the external world evoke the impinging quality of the biophysiological demands. These bad part self representations along with the representations of sensory deprivation organize into a whole at the periphery. Thus, the developing all-bad self representations are forming at the periphery, though the instinctual stimulus is at the interior.

It is this translocation of perception, in which the representation of a stimulus occurs away from its source, that I am postulating as the basis for the mechanism of splitting. It has formed to further the developmental process, to serve a protective function, and evolves as the major defensive activity of the primitively organized ego.

"The Self with Object Qualities" and "The Object with Self Qualities"

There is a continuum from those body ego experiences which are represented as phase-specific instinctual gratifications in the good self; to those body ego experiences of overstimulation with qualities of impingement which are represented as the instinctual aspect of the bad self. This continuum extends to body ego experiences of biophysiological demands that are of such an intensity that they cannot be represented as aspects of the self. They do, however, leave mental impressions of an impact that is impinging and instinctual. These impressions, in not being included within the self representations, have the independent qualities of an object. They are forming as bad instinctual object impressions, which will ultimately become more organized and represented as the bad instinctual aspect of the object. The continuum also extends to the dimension of biophysiological demands that cannot be perceived and represented. It is this aspect of the continuum that is present within the organism, but is independent of the self. As the capacity for instinctual representation increases, the continuum shifts, and more is included within the self.

This formulation accounts for the original body ego experience by which stimuli originating outside of the self (yet within the organism) are included within the self. I have named this continuum "the self with object qualities." The manner in which the "Make-a-Dos" were represented in Adam captured the qualities of this continuum. These instinctual representations were on a continuum from being fun-loving (represented as an aspect of the good self), to being irritable and impinging (represented as an aspect of the bad self), to being ominous and frightening (represented with the qualities of a bad instinctual object). It is the latter end of the continuum that is the portal of entry of instinctual demand. An interaction that provides empathic responsiveness and its associated containment should have the effect of including more of this continuum within the realm of self representation. Conversely, an interaction that is nonempathic will intensify the threat of this continuum.

When Melanie Klein (1955) described the oedipal conflict as originating very early in development, her concept emerged from observations of object impressions with instinctual qualities that were intense and potentially disruptive. Balint (1968), in his concept of the basic fault, also revealed the influence of this continuum. Bion (1968) described it as the psychotic sector of the personality. It is the body ego experience that ultimately forms the basis for object-related perceptions. And this capacity for perceiving the object as having independent objects of its own is a necessary component of the oedipal conflict. In that sense it can be seen as a precursor of the oedipal conflict.

As we have seen, the mental representations of the good self grow and consolidate as a result of the activities of the empathically responding external object. The interactions with the object in the external world are also on a continuum. Those aspects that are optimally gratifying have self qualities, those aspects that are optimally frustrating have qualities of prohibition, and the prohibitive aspects shade into the area of being unempathic and impinging, as well as sensorily depriving. I have named this continuum "the object with self qualities." The ongoing interactions with the object with self qualities are represented and advance the expanding structuralization of the representations of the good and bad self. Through these interactions, mental impressions of a poorly differentiated quality begin to form what will evolve into an object representation system. Together, the self with object qualities and the object with self qualities provide the necessary body ego experiences by which stimuli originating outside the self can be included through representations within the self.

DISCUSSION

Adam's psychic functioning manifested the effects of severe pathological distortions in his development. The therapist attempted to establish a surrounding external environment that would evoke good self representations. For the therapist, the task was one of offering optimal gratification (in the form of empathic responsiveness to expressions of unconscious communication), optimal frustration (in the form of abstaining from participation in the reinforcement of pathological defenses), and the qualities of a transitional object (in the form of implicitly encouraging Adam to utilize the relationship in whatever way was dictated by his development). The therapist was offering an interaction that was nonimpinging but responsive to the unconscious communications expressed in Adam's behavior. Initially, Adam did not seem to respond. Then a lapse in the therapist's empathic responsiveness instigated a momentary level of organization in Adam, which permitted an integrated, interactively communicative expression. Adam had been unconsciously perceptive of the therapist's lapse in attention. It required the presence of consensual validation for this perceptual act to have taken place, implying a consolidation of the part self representations into a unity.

Adam's unconscious perception of the therapist's defensiveness was again manifested in his play with the soldiers, which seemed to mirror the therapist's stiffness. When the therapist validated Adam's unconscious perceptions, it resulted in a dramatic shift in Adam's communicative behavior. The organizing influence of the representation of the background object of primary identification became manifest. In the first instance, when the therapist acknowledged his own disengagement, Adam felt contained and openly engaged in an exploration of the therapist. In the second instance, with the therapist's acknowledgment of his stiffness, Adam relinquished his autistic posture, molded to the therapist, and began verbally to communicate his inner experiences. In both instances, the acknowledgment was accompanied by a change in the therapist's attitude.

Adam had made the therapist aware of the lapse in empathy, but it was essential that the therapist see the source of it in himself and effect a change.

Ben, on the other hand, displayed manifestations of pathology with a higher level of organization of the self representations. Initially, Ben was fearful of the new relationship and resisted coming, but he felt unconsciously understood by the therapist when the frequency of sessions was determined by his derivative association. In this way he was programming the therapist. Yet Ben, in his submissive attitude, then communicated his experience of being controlled. The therapist, who unconsciously perceived this quality in the interaction, defended himself against the experience of being a controlling figure and thus no longer offered empathic responsiveness. When the therapist then communicated his feeling of being controlled, he was unaware of its source and so implied that the motive was within Ben. The background of empathy that had been established was traumatically ruptured and mobilized Ben's resources. He responded by revealing how the therapist's intervention was experienced as a parallel repetition of his developmental trauma. The therapist finally grasped the part he had played in creating the rupture and was able to validate Ben's unconscious perception. The result was the emergence of self representations of mischievousness and self-assertiveness. His derivative association to his fear of his father bursting into his room and surprise that he had wanted to talk with him reflected upon his unconscious perception of the change in the therapist's attitude.

In approaching Charlie therapeutically, the therapist was able to maintain a consistent, nonimpinging and empathically responsive interaction. Charlie exerted intense interactional pressure on the therapist to elicit responses that would reinforce his defensive postures. The therapist, however, provided qualities in the interaction that were unconsciously perceived as containing to Charlie. Charlie expressed this in his feeling of relief, his deprecatory teasing, and in his gradually revealing the extent of his inner disturbance. It is vital to move from the external, through the interaction, to address conflict and distortion in the interior. The qualities of containment in the interaction made it possible for pathological distortions to become accessible for alteration, integration, and change.

With both Adam and Charlie, when the therapeutic interaction provided containment, a clearer picture of the composition of the self representation system emerged. With Adam, we have already seen how the concept of the self with object qualities sheds light on the variable characteristics of his "Make-a-dos." They seemed to represent the effects of biophysiological demands and gave some definition to the original body ego experience by which a stimulus outside of the self could be included within the self. The "Big Black Pops" were highly threatening and portrayed the manner in which prohibitions were experienced, whereas the "Big Pain" depicted an object impression that was painful to be connected to. The soldier reflected the representation of the therapeutic interaction.

It appeared that Adam experienced a lack of differentiation when the therapist's empathic responsiveness was consistent and uninterrupted. It also appeared that during this period a stimulus outside the self (the interaction with the empathically responding therapist) had been included within the self (a firmer, good self representation and a representation of the new figure of the soldier). The effect was to amplify and expand the containing function of the background object of primary identification, in line with the concepts of the object with self qualities and the self with object qualities.

Adam's ability to maintain a good self representation was tenuous, dependent on the unconsciously empathic qualities of the therapeutic interaction. The bad self representations were most clearly represented by the figure of "Pa-Ba," in which the aspects of deprivation and impingement predominated. "Pa-Ba" was not defined; it was a fragmented self representation. The dangerous instinctual qualities of the "Make-a-Dos" were also fragmenting in their effects.

In the case of Charlie, the lines of continuity in the self representation system are clearer than in Adam. With Charlie, we see the aspects of body ego experience in a process of organization rather than a state of fragmentation (as in Adam). Thus, when Charlie experienced the fragmenting panic of his separation anxiety, he invoked within himself the listening, integrating (containing) attitude of the therapist. The associative chain of thoughts and imagery reflected the varying representations of the self and object, and their lines of continuity. The fragmented part self and part object representations were consolidating into a whole under the organizing influence of the background object of primary identification.

The instinctual aspect of the good self was represented in Charlie's thoughts of *Playboy* magazine and the associated sexual excitement. The line of continuity of instinctual experience could be traced as the bad self representations emerged with memories of masturbatory activity, accompanied by shame and embarrassment. This progressed with building intensity to the poorly represented inner experience of danger with the qualities of a bad instinctual object. The autonomous ego functions represented in the good self were expressed in the thoughts of activities in which he effectively used his skills. Sensory deprivation represented in the bad self was portrayed in the recollections of unrealized potentials. The representations of the country, with its associated sense of containment, manifested the qualities of the background object of primary identification. The reactions to impingements represented in the bad self were pictured in the memories of rage and retreat in response to intimidating figures.

In sum, during the earliest phases in development, instinctual demands are registered in an ongoing interrelationship with the physiologically buffering contact with the external intrauterine environment. Stimuli that are independent of the perceptual processes are occurring both inside and outside the organism. The interrelationship of inner demand and outer metabolic response establishes a body ego experience by which a stimulus outside the self (defined by the activity of perceptual processes) is included within the self. Ths is the original body ego experience at the foundation of the psychological symbiosis in postuterine life. Ultimately, it develops into more differentiated forms of identification, which foster the expansion of mental representations and structures within the self. It is by this pathway that empathic responses in an interaction are unconsciously perceived. When the containing, metabolizing presence of the background object of primary identification is actively functional, the therapist's interpretive activity can be included within the self. When the therapist's activities responded to the patient's unconscious experiences this representation is evoked, and the adaptive reactions to impingement no longer need to be mobilized.

REFERENCES

Balint, E. (1963). On being empty of oneself. *Int. J. Psychoanal.* 44:37–56.
Balint, M. (1968). *The Basic Fault.* New York: Brunner/Mazel.
Bion, W. R. (1968). *Second Thoughts: Selected Papers on Psychoanalysis.* New York: Basic Books.
Fairbairn, W. R. D. (1954). *An Object-Relations Theory of Personality.* New York: Basic Books.
Freud, S. (1940). An outline of psycho-analysis. *Standard Edition* 23:144–207.
Grotstein, J. A. (1981). *Splitting and Projective Identification.* New York: Aronson.
Hartmann, H. (1939). *Ego Psychology and the Problem of Adaptation.* New York: Int. Univ. Press, 1958.
——— & Loewenstein, R. M. (1962). Notes on the superego. *Psychoanal. Study Child* 17:42–81.
Hoffer, W. (1952). The mutual influences in the development of ego and id. *Psychoanal. Study Child* 7:31–41.
Jacobson, E. (1964). *The Self and the Object World.* New York: Int. Univ. Press.
Kernberg, O. (1980). *Internal World and External Reality* New York: Aronson.
Klein, M. (1955). *New Directions in Psychoanalysis.* New York: Basic Books.
Kohut, H. (1971). *The Analysis of the Self.* New York: Int. Univ. Press.
Langs, R. (1977). *The Therapeutic Interaction: A Synthesis.* New York: Aronson.
Mahler, M. S., Pine F., & Bergman, A. (1975). *The Psychological Birth of the Human Infant.* New York: Basic Books.
Spitz, R. (1955). The primal cavity: A contribution to the genesis of perception and its role for psychoanalytic theory. *Psychoanay. Study Child* 10:215–240.
Winnicott, D. W. (1958). *Collected Papers: Through Pediatrics to Psychoanalysis.* New York: Basic Books.

13/
Discussion:
On a Scientific Method for Psychoanalysis
J. Alexis Burland, M.D.

In its efforts to propose an addition to perinatal ego developmental psychology, Roy Mendelsohn's paper raises the question of a scientific method for psychoanalytic research. It is suggested that the model used in the physical sciences—in contemporary Western culture the standard for the establishment of "truth"—can be adapted to the unique characteristics of the carefully controlled clinical psychoanalytic laboratory and the adequately developed and standardized "analyzing instrument."

Roy Mendelsohn's most interesting paper raises a question that has increasingly concerned the behavioral sciences, and psychoanalysis in particular: How do we define a "scientific method" that takes into account the vast differences between clinical and laboratory research, but also recognizes the need for verification and validation both in the interests of expanding our own knowledge and in answering our critics, for whom only laboratory research has a format in which "truth" can be proved? Mendelsohn prudently characterizes his proposals as "speculative," but as with many another psychoanalytic author who has characterized his proposals similarly—including Freud in *Beyond the Pleasure Principle* (1920, p. 24)—a tone of apology is conveyed. That ought not have to be the case. That it is reflects, perhaps, our training in chemistry, physics, zoology, and physiology, which, coupled with our Western cultural faith in "science," has created within us a definition of "truth" related only to the material sciences. We accept this version of truth as absolute, even though it is but a declaration of faith not that different from any other. After all, not all cultural systems agree with it, and in the time span of human civilization, it is a late arrival. Other value systems have existed longer and with greater numbers of adherents.

Mendelsohn offers a hypothesis concerning very early—even perinatal—ego functioning. His speculations are metapsychological and consist, in a sense, of the further elaboration of what are metaphorical statements designed to convey (in an admittedly concrete manner) abstract, dynamic mental developmental processes. How is the reader critically to assess and respond to such speculations? On what basis is the reader "convinced" or "unconvinced"? How can one "test" the author's hypotheses to verify—or discredit—them?

Ricoeur (1977) discusses this question at length in his article on the question of "proof" in Freud's psychoanalytic writings. His "thesis is that psychoanalytic theory . . . is the codification of what takes place in the analytic situation and, more precisely, in the analytic relationship" (p. 836). From the analytic experience, he limits the data he would utilize to what is verbalized by the analysand in the context of the analysand's communicating it to another (i.e., the analyst/transference object). What is said of significance will thus primarily reflect psychic (as opposed to material) reality, and it will enable one to enter into a story—the narrative of the analysand's life. The concluding psychoanalytic explanation of the analysand's problems must then meet four criteria: it must conform to an established system of theory (i.e., "Freudian psychoanalysis"); it must be in keeping with the universalizable "rules" established for the decoding of the text of the unconscious; it must be capable of being incorporated into the working-through process with resultant symptom amelioration; and it must raise the case history to the "sort of intelligibility we ordinarily expect in a story" (pp. 836–844).

Ricoeur's schema is a functional, pragmatic one, which starts with a fairly stringent definition of the limits of the acceptable data base, or the characteristics and dimensions of the "laboratory." I recently reviewed a book on psychoanalytic theory by a research psychologist (Lewis, 1983), one "trained in psychoanalysis" (not further defined) and clearly sympathetic to it. What brings it to mind is how clearly different the data from laboratory research is from that obtained in the clinical psychoanalytic "laboratory," even when addressing similar issues and from a similar theoretical perspective. In fact, the differences in the conclusions reached can be explained better by the differences in research format than by their "truth" or "falseness." Clearly, the definition of the laboratory and what is and what isn't acceptable as data are important if understandable exchanges between researchers are to be possible.

One can separate out as two factors the nature of the data and its source, on the one hand, and what is done with that data on the other. With regard to the former, Ricoeur's schema presents some difficulties for me, and surely for Mendelsohn. Here I refer to Ricoeur's limiting his acceptable data to *verbalizations* by the patient. Perhaps he means this term in the broadest sense, including the "music" that accompanies the words—i.e., the affects, the gestures, the tones of voice, etc., upon which all analysts rely for guidance in how to "hear" the words themselves. But the problem is further compounded when one is dealing with the analysis of a child—let alone a largely nonverbal and autistic one. As I shall later discuss more fully, the problem in epistemology that is involved here is that of *consensual validation*. Verbal communications are readily transcribed and shared with other researchers, and the recorded or transcribed verbalizations of one analysand can be compared with those of another. One might say that verbalization data are closer to material data, whereas affects and affective qualities are harder to capture on tape or paper. And the more subtle they are, the greater the difficulty. As on a curve of diminishing returns, gross affects in simple terms—"anger," "sadness"—are easily consensually validated, but become less and less so as they become more complex.

Consider, for instance, Mendelsohn's comment about Adam: "the therapist began to sense that the empty outer shell of Adam's mannerisms, behavior, and minimal sing-song vocalizations surrounded an inner perceptual experience that he was either unwilling or unable to communicate." Although many analysts would empathically recognize such an experience, I believe some would not, and the more controversial the point being made, the greater the index of suspicion. Nevertheless, the loss in omitting everything other than verbal expressions is great. Ricoeur's idea would be better phrased "what is *communicated* by the analysand," even with the ambiguities involved in using an interpersonal term—i.e., the receiver of what is communicated plays a part in the process. If the word "receiver" is replaced by "instrument"—something whose functions can be better defined and standardized—the statement presents less difficulty. The concept of the "analyzing *instrument*" (Isakower, 1939) would appear to be relevant here.

Ricoeur rightly characterizes the analytic experience as involving two parties. Perhaps more than any other author, Langs has pioneered in reminding analysts that their presence is felt and shapes the interaction, for better or for worse (see Langs, 1978, for the work I found the most illuminating). As part of this lesson, he has further reminded us of the dangers in relying too heavily on the concept of "transference" as that can be used by analysts to deny their "actual" participation. Mendelsohn seems exquisitely aware of the interactional aspects of his reported clinical experiences, and, in keeping with Langs, recognizes that the communications go in both directions. In other words, in assessing the two-person aspects of communication within the analytic experience, one has to acknowledge its reciprocity.

Ricoeur also places appropriate emphasis on the relevance of psychic over material reality. Perhaps more than any other aspect of the psychoanalytic situation this puzzles and confounds nonpsychoanalytic observers and critics of the process. But it is precisely the power of psychic reality that is the greatest discovery of psychoanalysis, there to be rediscovered by any one who is willing to learn how to be a psychoanalyst. Mendelsohn's paper, which reveals no compromise in his recitation of the central role of psychic reality, might therefore present problems to the psychoanalytically naive reader. Unfortunately we sometimes give ammunition to our critics by speaking primarily to ourselves, by believing and stating that a psychoanalyst can best understand psychoanalysis. What we mean by that is mainly that a trained and practicing analyst better acknowledges, understands, and perceives the impact of psychic reality. It is only a social convention that material reality is recognized as more "real" than the psychic; and this is buttressed on an individual basis according to the predominance of reactive character traits. The rigorous tripartite training of the psychoanalyst is designed well to offset both the cultural and the intrapsychic resistances to the awareness of the ubiquity and power of psychic reality.

Much could be said about Ricoeur's recognition of the importance of the eventual uncovering or formulation of a coherent life narrative. That storytelling in one form or another has been a part of all known cultures, past and present, must speak for some universal appeal and therefore for some basic human psychological given. Mendelsohn in his paper refers to a very esoteric aspect of this narrative—namely, perinatal ego developmental events—but he endeavors to evoke the need for narrative flow as part of his argument (i.e., that objectless differentiation must precede an undifferentiated state, or that there must be an early phase in which the self has object qualities). Admittedly, this narrative has a somewhat circumscribed audience to which it will appeal, but that should not necessarily take away from its validity.

Mendelsohn, then, would seem to have invoked appropriate data in his argument, albeit somewhat esoteric, abstract, and specialized data. The importance of valid data relates to *consensual validation,* perhaps the sine qua non of "scientific" thinking; that is, research methods must be capable of replication so that other researchers can see if they obtain similar results. It in itself is an interesting topic for discussion. One sees its beginnings in the early dyadic communications between mother and infant, in the "see the birdie" games that are such a meaningful part of the development of perceptual skills and self-actualization within the mother-child "dialogue," to use Spitz's term (1965). Mother's ritualized and unchanging confirmation of the child's early efforts at structuralizing his or her perceptions of the environment can be recognized as a prototype for the scientist's efforts at doing the same. It is also of interest that "science," the Protestant revolution, and the rise of the middle class are markers of the relatively recent shift from "truth" being determined autocratically by authorities to "truth" being something each of us establishes for ourselves. The basic means is consensual validation—i.e., "seeing is believing," something further elaborated and elevated into the material scientific method. In other words, the reliance on consensual validation in science is not an absolute, like the speed of light, but is also a part of the flow of the history of ideas, with individual intrapsychic determinants as well.

Mendelsohn refers in his paper to another type of consensual validation—namely, that which exists between the various perceptual modalities. The two would seem to exist in sequence in scientific inquiry. The hypothesis creator starts with an internal consensual validation derived from reviewing the data, their source, and his or her findings for internal consistencies; then the researcher strives to achieve an interpersonal or social one. There would appear to be considerable variation among researchers as to how much social consensual validation they seek for their propositions, relating to the degree to which they are comfortable with their internal validation and their self-assertion. As clinicians, we cannot blind ourselves to the obvious "symptoms"—to the overlengthy bibliographies, the excessive search for quotations from "established" authors (especially Freud) who have said the same thing, or whose words support at least a part of the author's argument. Indeed, I can think of very few analytic articles that omit the ritual of the bibliography—and those authors have all been senior, universally acknowledged authorities, with fully developed professional and personal self-confidence. It is surely easier to move the ball along an inch at a time, along established pathways; easier both psychologically for the author and for the science. It takes a certain kind of courage (or should one say "nerve"?) for the author to make a gigantic and unsupported leap. It is also harder for the scientific field to keep up with or to make practical use of such leaps. Here, then, it would seem that intrapsychic, individualistic caution works hand in hand with group inertia. Consensual validation can be viewed as the vehicle for countering this resistance to forward motion.

It is possible, finally, to elaborate a "scientific method" for psychoanalysis that in fact does not differ in form from that of the material sciences. This should not be surprising, for there are certain universal rules of logic that hold for both fields. First, the laboratory, the subject, and the data must be carefully defined in keeping with the specific task at hand. Just as the physicist and the chemist have their laboratories and equipment, so do psychoanalysts, and our requirements are no less stringent than theirs—especially as outlined by as rigorous a commentator as Langs. The training of the researcher and the required familiarity with the literature of the field are equally specific—i.e., once again, workers within any field are more knowledgeable innovators in and critics of that field. It is of interest that many criticisms of psychoanalysis by nonpsychoanalysts are accepted by the same general public who would laugh at similarly amateur criticisms leveled against one of the physical sciences. But is that not testimony to the universality of resistance against the acknowledgment of the power of the unconscious, of psychic reality?

The nature of the laboratory, the training of the researcher, and the characteristics of the subject all determine the peculiarities of the data obtained. For this reason, a similar setup should obtain similar data. Indeed, this has been the case with psychoanalysis, a field in which despite our many internecine squabbles, areas of agreement are the rule rather than the exception, primarily as a successful analysis generates fairly uniform information about the human condition.

And, as once again holds true for the physical sciences, psychoanalysis has its own vocabulary, its own basic concepts, its own abundance of variations on these basics, its own open-ended internal polylogue. We really need not apologize to those who criticize our scientific credentials; our laboratories can be just as proper, our research just as standardized, our data just as clean, our literature just as formalized as any other science.

Roy Mendelsohn, then, need not apologize either, even though his paper does verge on the edges of the psychoanalytic scientific arena. His laboratory—the psychoanalytic treatment of autistic or ego-defective children—is less familiar to some; his reliance on nonverbal communication a bit greater than some might accept; the area of theory to which he applies his data a bit more abstruse. His use of the term "speculation" acknowledges this. But his "method" remains essentially well within the scientific tradition: statement of the problem; discussion of the pertinent literature, in which his theoretical underpinnings are made clear; clinical (research) data; and final discussion in which the new formulations are offered and integrated with preexisting ones.

REFERENCES

Freud, S. (1920). Beyond the pleasure principle. *Standard Edition* 18:3–64.
Isakower, O. (1939). On the exceptional position of the auditory sphere. *Int. J. Psychoanal.* 20:340–348.
Langs, R. (1978). *Technique in Transition*. New York: Aronson.
Lewis, H. B. (1983). *Freud and Modern Psychology, Vol. 2: The Emotional Basis of Human Behavior*. New York: Plenum.
Ricoeur, P. (1977). The question of proof in Freud's psychoanalytic writings. *J. Amer. Psychoanal. Assn.* 25:835–872.
Spitz, R. (1965). *The First Year of Life*. New York: Int. Univ. Press.

14/
Narcissism, Object Relatedness, and Drive-Conflict Issues
James Beatrice, Ph.D.

The formulations of Kernberg and Kohut regarding the narcissistic personality are usually viewed as mutually exclusive and contradictory. As a result, psychoanalytic thinking in this area is divided. This paper attempts to bridge these positions by examining three distinct areas of human experience as they unfolded during the treatment of a narcissistic personality disorder. The case presentation reveals the progression from narcissism and self issues, to modes of object relatedness, and finally to drive-conflict issues relating to the structural aspects of the psyche.

The area of narcissistic personality disorders has been traversed from two distinct pathways. Kohut (1971, 1977) understands the specific transferences of this disorder, that is the empathically perceived fantasies, desires, needs, drives, and conflicts that patients present to the analyst, as the therapeutic revival of a normal, though arrested, developmental phase. In contrast, Kernberg (1975) concludes that the transference of the narcissistic personality is highly pathological. Each approach espouses such different psychodynamics and treatment recommendations that an either/or proposition confronts the clinician regarding the technical approach with such patients. However, each author approaches the narcissistic personality from different places of entry. Consequently, they travel a particular route that intrinsically reveals only those aspects and qualities that unfold along that respective path. Each contains value and meaning, yet they do not intersect to combine their knowledge.

In an effort to develop an integrated approach, it is proposed that there are separate but interrelated realms of human experience that unfold in the therapeutic interaction. Toward this end, clinical material will be presented, detailing the unfolding of three areas of human experience: issues concerning narcissism and the self; various modes of object relatedness; and the drive-conflict issues related to the structural components of the psyche. This clinical material will demonstrate the Kohut's interpretation of the function of narcissistic transferences to promote self cohesion actually represents an interpretation upwards. In response, the patient unconsciously perceived such interventions as depriving and incomplete. Consequently, interpretation in depth was necessitated, exploring and interpreting the libidinal and aggressive drives.

LITERATURE REVIEW

Kohut's (1971, 1977) studies of narcissistic personality disorders led to the development of self psychology. This metapsychology is conceived as independent of but complimentary to structural theory. The self, in its striving for cohesiveness, is placed at the forefront of the personality. Thus, libidinal and aggressive drives are replaced as the primary motivators of human behavior. This reformulation was deemed necessary for Kohut believed drive-conflict psychology could not adequately address the theoretical and technical issues evoked in the treatment of narcissistic personality disorders.

According to Kohut, narcissistic personalities suffer from a weakness in their ability to maintain a continuous and cohesive sense of self. Indeed, these patients are extremely vulnerable to failures, disappointments, and slights at the hands of others. Through careful, empathic listening to these patients' transference manifestations, Kohut formulated his concept of the selfobject. In his view, narcissistic personalities utilize the therapist to provide a psychological function that they are not as yet able to provide for themselves. The analyst, as a selfobject, is experienced by these patients as part of themselves. Predominant among the psychological functions to be provided by the therapist are those of the mirroring selfobject. In this transference manifestation, the selfobject provides responses to and confirmation of the patients' sense of vigor, greatness, and perfection.

Three clinical variations of the mirroring selfobject transference have been delineated. First, the merger transference consists of the most archaic constellation, whereby patients include the therapist as part of themselves without any differentiation between the two. In the second, twinship transference, the patient recognizes the therapist as separate only insofar as the therapist is perceived to be like the patient. Finally, the mirror transference in the narrower sense consists of a greater degree of differentiation between patient and therapist, in which patients recognize the therapist as separate but still need the therapist to mirror their narcissistic needs for continued self cohesion.

For the purposes of this paper, primary emphasis will be placed on the merger variant of the mirroring selfobject transferences. Kohut has also described idealizing selfobject transferences, whereby the therapist becomes an object patients can look up to and with whom they can merge as an image of calmness, infallibility, and omnipotence. In Kohut's formulation, the selfobject transferences, mirroring and idealizing, are the sine qua non of the narcissistic personality. Furthermore, these selfobject transferences are conceptualized as the therapeutic revival of a normal, phase-appropriate stage of development. Kohut conjectures that narcissistic patients suffered from nonempathic responses of an earlier selfobject, and that these early empathic failures led to fixation at archaic levels of narcissistic development.

Based on these assessments, Kohut views the therapeutic task as the rehabilitation of the weakened self. This is accomplished by the analyst's empathic acceptance and recognition of the patient's archaic needs for mirroring and for merger in order to stabilize the patient's faltering self-esteem. The patient then reexperiences the selfobject's acceptance of childhood grandiosity and the needs to merge with an idealized selfobject in a way that was not responded to early in life. If these needs are kept mobilized, showing patients that their demands stem from a sense of helplessness when their needs were unmet during childhood, then as the narcissistic demands are accepted, they will be transformed into healthy self-assertiveness and normal devotion to ideals.

According to self psychology, these selfobject transferences are not resistances to or defenses against the emergence of libidinal or aggressive drives. Rather, they are viewed as way stations leading to the acquisition of the psychic capacity to stabilize self cohesion. They are not regressive evasions from conflicts of object love or object hate. Indeed, it is asserted that the primary resistances to the full emergence of the selfobject transferences stem from fears of experiencing shame and embarrassment in the face of such primitive narcissistic needs, fears of further unempathic responses to these archaic needs, fears that fusion with the selfobject will precipitate loss of self, as well as disintegration anxiety when self-esteem falters. Failures in empathic responsiveness from the selfobject lead to narcissistic rage and destructive aggression. Hence, in this view, rage and destructiveness are the end products of a fragmenting self seeking to reestablish the selfobject transference. The primary anxiety is not due to primitive drives but to the anxiety of the self fragmenting as a result of the loss of an empathic selfobject.[1]

In contrast to self psychology, Kernberg (1975) views narcissistic disor-

---

[1] Support for and elaborations of Kohut's self psychology have been provided by a number of authors (Gedo and Goldberg, 1973; Ornstein and Ornstein, 1975; Stolorow and Lachmann, 1980; Goldberg, 1980–1981).

ders as organized around a highly pathological personality structure. Due to internal conflicts surrounding frustrated oral drives, heightened aggression and envy of others as well as the need to vigorously defend against envy and hate, the narcissistic patient is seen as insidiously devaluing any dependency needs mobilized in relation to the therapist. More to the point, for narcissistic patients, dependency on the therapist represents their greatest fear, for it rekindles feelings of hate, envy, fears of being exploited and manipulated. Selfobject transferences of the mirroring or merging variety are seen as defensive structures protecting these patients from dependency on the therapist by denying the therapist's independent existence. By seeking admiration or idealization from the therapist, these patients can safely bypass their hatred and devaluation of the therapist and keep this from being brought into focus. Kernberg (1975) emphasizes that the crucial resistance to treatment is this denial of dependency.

Supportive evidence for Kernberg's formulations comes from a number of authors. Earlier, Annie Reich (1960) described patients who utilized extreme forms of relating to others in order to secure their self-esteem, which was seen to be faulty due to heightened aggressive fantasies toward others, castration anxiety, as well as fears of homosexuality. Rosenfeld (1964) viewed narcissistic patients and their idealized self image as a pathological formation attempting to defend against aggression, envy, and paranoid anxiety. Altman (1975) presented a case history with evidence of defenses against merger fantasies with the analyst as well as homosexual fantasies, all of which prevented the establishment of a therapeutic alliance.

This body of work stresses the object relations and conflict-drive issues related to the structural components of the psyche. From this theoretical perspective, Kohut's self psychology has been criticized on a number of levels. Loewald (1973) states that Kohut's clinical material is overshadowed by theoretical discussion, making an evaluation of his case presentations difficult. Loewald also notes that resistance and defense issues are not developed, and analysis of ego defenses is neglected. Perhaps, he suggests, a subtle seduction of the narcissistic patient occurs with the use of mirroring, which then insulates the patient from unfolding aggressive fantasies about the analyst. From a different perspective, Schwartz (1974), while espousing self psychology, also criticizes Kohut's case material for overemphasizing manifest content and omitting associations that might confirm or deny the theoretical propositions. He calls for detailed clinical data of the treatment of narcissistic patients. Although this has been supplied by Goldberg (1978), the clinical material presents significant deviations in technique, such as direct gratification by visiting patients at their home, without a full recognition and analysis of the conscious and unconscious implications of such interventions.

Kernberg (1975) raises the concern that accepting the patients' needs for mirroring or merging fosters further splitting as these patients elevate their needs for an all-good object while keeping at bay their contempt and envy of the analyst. Additional criticisms have focused on evidence of libidinal and aggressive drive components within the selfobject transferences, thus suggesting a defensive function (Hanly and Masson, 1976), as well as evidence that narcissistic rage is equivalent to oral sadism (Hamilton, 1978) or that fears of merging with the therapist may be equated with loss of autonomy (Modell, 1978). Still others point to the avoidance of the potential multiple meanings in the patient's desire for mirroring (Saperstein and Gaines, 1978), and some have suggested that the selfobject transference may illustrate a regression to a pathologically distorted symbiotic phase (Giovacchini, 1979). Finally, in his overview, Wallerstein (1981) regards the debate as requiring a comprehensive approach to the narcissistic and self issues emphasized by Kohut and the object relations, structural issues outlined by Kernberg.

HEALTHY AND PATHOLOGICAL SYMBIOSIS

A review of the literature highlights the dichotomy in psychoanalytic thinking on the psychodynamics and treatment of narcissistic personality disorders. In an effort to develop an integrated approach, it is proposed that a qualitatively different object relationship presents itself within each respective variant of the mirroring selfobject transference. As the patient's experience of the analyst shifts progressively from one of merger with the analyst, toward viewing the analyst as separate but still a part of the patient, to eventually viewing the analyst as a distinct person, separate and apart from the patient, so too are there different levels of conscious and unconscious perception, fantasy, anxiety, needs, drives, and defenses. Kohut (1971) claims that the mirror transferences stem from the late symbiotic to the early phases of separation-individuation. Hence, each manifestation of the mirror selfobject transference may represent a specific subphase of development along the path of separation-individuation. Under this working hypothesis, Mahler, Pine, and Bergman (1975) may supply a theoretical bridge to link Kohut's narcissism and self issues with Kernberg's object relations and drive-conflict issues. This proposition arises from the fact that each phase of separation-individuation consists of specific goals, tasks, achievements, crises, and conflicts. As Kohut (1971) sets the boundaries of the selfobject transferences between the symbiotic and separation-individuation phases, attention will be given to the symbiotic phase.

The symbiotic phase is a state of object relations in which the child and mother function as an enclosed system with a common boundary (Mahler et al., 1975). At this stage children view mother and themselves as one; inside and outside are fused, with the "I," "not-I," and "we" yet to be differentiated. Within this symbiosis, mother supplies the child a "good-enough" hold to maintain the child's homeostasis and well-being. This hold takes the form of feeding, physically holding, mutually reflecting, and mirroring the child. These external functions place need-satisfying, pleasurable experiences in ascendancy, permitting healthy introjection of these interactions. Eventually, over repeated and predictable encounters, the child begins to gradually differentiate his or her body from mother, establishes a sense of self representations and object representations, and begins to structuralize the ego and its functions. All this takes place within the context of phase-specific psychosexual conflict and aggressive drives. The primary accomplishment here is the attachment of the child to the mother, thereby establishing the foundation from which all subsequent object relations will prosper. Kohut's formulation of the mirroring selfobject transference coincides with Mahler's depiction of normal symbiosis.

Concurrently, Mahler et al. (1975) discuss the consequences if the "good-enough" hold is not harmonious with the child's needs and reaches a point at which painful interactions predominate. Introjection of these painful interactions takes place, leading to feelings of worthlessness, inadequacy, and disturbances in the primitive sense of self. Specific anxieties such as fears of object loss, engulfment, and loss of the self are in evidence. Ego structuralization is impaired, fostering splitting defenses between "good" and "bad" self and object representations. This promotes heightened amounts of hatred, envy, and loss of identity, which are defended against by magical means of controlling and dominating others. In analysis this means of controlling others can be seen to provide a semblance of a desperately needed relationship, which, although denied by the patient—that is the dependence is denied—does bring some order to an acutely chaotic intrapsychic world. In sum, Mahler's description of pathological symbiosis stemming from absent or impaired mirroring culminates in severe narcissistic depletion with pathological consequences for object relations and drive-conflict issues. This, then, links with Kernberg's formulation.

From these conclusions, the occurrence of a mirroring selfobject transference represents a transference regression to the symbiotic stage. The therapist, then, must attend to a developmental deficit that engendered pathological defenses against relating to others due to fears and anxieties regarding dependence, hatred, envy, as well as damaged self-regulation. This raises the question of how to promote healthy symbiosis, with its resulting beneficial effects on ego development and self-regulation, while analyzing the pathological anxieties, drives, defenses, and object relations inherent in such a state.

MODES OF RELATING

One answer to the above question resides in the very nature of the psychotherapeutic relationship. Winnicott (1965) has demonstrated that the therapist should provide a "good-enough," hold, supplying for the patient a predictable and secure environment whereby the patient can utilize this much-needed symbiosis. More recently, Langs (1976, 1978) has shown the efficacy of a secure framework, which promotes the secure hold for the therapist and patient. He points to the therapist's appropriate management of the ground rules for treatment (such as the frequency of sessions and the fee), and the therapist's openness to receiving the patient's communication as well as basing interventions primarily on interpretation and reconstruction. The maintenance of a secure therapeutic frame implicitly supplies the patient the nonintrusive availability of healthy symbiosis. At the same time this represents only one type of object relatedness which can be experienced in a given therapeutic interaction.

In an attempt to classify the various types of object relatedness possible in a given therapeutic interaction, Langs (1982) has introduced the concept of maturational modes of relatedness. That is, by listening to patients' characterizations and implications of object relations in their associations, the therapist can ascertain and identify specific efforts toward the establishment of a particular mode of relatedness. This in turn must be assessed in terms of the patients' unconscious perceptions of the actual qualities of the therapeutic relationship. In viewing whether such qualities are present or not, the therapist can utilize these occurrences as important opportunities for interpretive work. The modes of relatedness Langs outlines are healthy or pathological autism, healthy or pathological symbiosis, and parasitic modes of relating. For our purposes, emphasis will be placed on the symbiotic and parasitic modes.

According to Langs (1982), healthy symbiosis for patients involves their acceptance of the therapeutic ground rules with the expressed wish to achieve resolution of their psychopathology through interpretation and reconstruction. For the therapist, healthy symbiosis means the renunciation of tendencies toward pathological modes of relatedness, gratifications, and defenses. This enables the therapist to be available for positive introjective identifications by the patient. In healthy symbiosis, the meaning of the patient's conflicts, drives, anxieties, and defenses is communicated to the therapist in such a way that they are readily analyzed and interpreted.

Pathological symbiosis is represented by pathological forms of merger oriented to action-discharge gratification rather than insight, understanding, and individuation. All efforts by the patient to modify the ground rules and to obtain gratifications beyond interpretation are signals alerting the therapist to the patient's attempt to establish a pathological symbiosis. The therapist may also participate in pathological symbiosis by offering noninterpretive interventions. Specifically, work proceeding solely on a manifest content level, without interpreting underlying unconscious derivative material, is a form of therapist-induced pathological symbiosis deterring insight and understanding.

Finally, there is the parasitic mode, whereby either the patient or the therapist expresses wishes and modes of relating that are exploitative, harmful, destructive, and belie misuse of the other person and his or her needs.

An integrated approach to the treatment of narcissistic personality disorders requires careful attention to three areas of human interaction. That is, I propose that within the therapeutic interaction issues related to narcissism and the self, issues related to modes of object relatedness, and finally drive-conflict issues related to the structural aspects of the psyche all unfold during the course of treatment. The therapeutic task must take the form of implicitly supplying the nonintrusive availability of healthy symbiosis, thus permitting the narcissistic needs to be recognized and interpreted. Concurrently, the accompanying fantasies, anxieties, drives, defences, and attempts by patients to gratify their narcissistic needs via pathological symbiosis must be analyzed. Finally, when the narcissistic and pathological symbiotic modes of relatedness are interpreted, material will unfold leading to interpretation of drive-conflict issues. The following clinical material illustrates these three areas as they unfold in the treatment of a narcissistic personality.

CLINICAL ILLUSTRATION

A 35-year-old male who suffered from a narcissistic personality disorder sought treatment with presenting complaints of boredom, a sense of tristesse, lack of meaning in life, and anger at his wife for her criticism of his habitual drinking. Furthermore, he was annoyed at his wife's suspiciousness about his promiscuity (which in fact was warranted). Psychoanalytic psychotherapy was conducted three times weekly. The sessions to be discussed occurred during the sixth month of treatment; the material is taken from clinical notes written after each session.

Before proceeding to the clinical data, however, a brief comment is in order regarding the status of this particular therapeutic frame. The patient was self-referred following recommendations from his legal colleagues regarding my professional services and qualifications. I had no personal contact with these colleagues, though they knew of my work through various sources. There were no third-party involvements such as insurance or contact with his wife. The fee was agreed upon between us, with the transaction of billing and payment occurring within the session. Indeed, his payments were prompt and in full monthly. The sessions were firmly adhered to, with no deviations regarding the time of beginning or ending the hour. Finally, the interventions before the sessions to be presented concerned my interpretation to the patient that he was increasingly aware of my importance to him, as indicated by his fantasies to take me with him wherever he traveled. However, I also interpreted how he quickly devalued me as soon as he verbalized these wishes. These interventions formed the adaptive context.

The first session of this sequence found the patient expressing interest in my opinion of him. He was having difficulty handling my not judging him. "You neither agree nor disagree," he complained. He again wanted me to visit his house and implored me to answer affirmatively. His house was described as a "monument to my success and something I'm proud of." He next desired me to accompany him to his next office party. Perhaps, he reflected, I would prefer to go with him on a ski trip, where he would buy me a drink. He stressed it was essential that I respond favorably for he could not understand how I could learn about him only in the therapy hour. He much preferred I see him in his "place in the sun." This also extended to his profession (law), where he wanted me to see him "handle" a court case, "dazzle" the jury, and "eloquently" state his argument. Only then could I appreciate him fully. Although he could tell me of his "exploits," only by my seeing him in "action" would I truly "know" him.

His manner implied a sense of conviction that once hearing his plea I would surely gratify his wish. He became more flustered and annoyed when I did not respond on his action level. I experienced his wishes as a continuous demandingness, whereby I felt he wanted to make me part of him. On the one hand, I conjectured, he was attempting to form a mirroring selfobject transference by my being with him and admiring him, yet he was expressing these desires with a demandingness for me to abandon my therapeutic stance and join him in pathological symbiosis geared to actual gratification without understanding.

The patient then associated to wishes not to talk. "To talk means we are separate, like living on two separate islands which can never be joined." References were made to a woman whom he desired and wanted sexually.

Specifically, he wanted to reach the level he perceived her on: not needing people's approval. Rather, he described her as taking what she wanted indiscriminately and without feeling for how she affected others. He viewed her as "psychopathic." He became annoyed at free-associating. He accused me of taking away his spontaneous thoughts which he enjoyed, such as his wanting me to be with him, and imagined I was solely interested in his "dark, psychopathic nature." His early self-assured affect and annoyance with me then shifted to a sense of concern and doubt as he worried about not wishing to "show" his "dark side." He spoke of his past employment as a probation officer, when he worked with "perverts like flashers, gays, and transvestites." He commented that he frequently saw them in "their element"; some he could help and some he could not. "Usually, I just tolerated these people; they were repulsive."

Initially I organized these associations as possible accurate commentary on and perception of my interventions and management of the frame. My only link to his themes of being separate from me, to his viewing me as psychopathic, as well as the issues concerning perversion, was that in the past sessions he had been groping to acknowledge my importance yet quickly devalued me and resorted to wishes to be self-sufficient. The reference to perversions initially raised in my mind the question of deviations in the frame. But this was not the case. Rather, I sensed the patient wanted me close to him but for some reason linked closeness to me with something "dark," psychopathic, and perverse. Perhaps, I hypothesized, his early wishes to engage in pathological symbiosis were now being amplified in derivative form as really destructive to him. Concurrently, he seemed concerned that if he could not merge with me, he would resort to parasitic modes of relating.

I interpreted that in the past few sessions he had expressed wishes to be close but quickly devalued me. Today he wanted me close to him but in ways that would disrupt his therapy and that he realized would be destructive. Perhaps, I added, his wish for me to be with him represented his concern about whether I could know and understand both his good and dark sides. I continued that he might be fearful that if he got close to me, I would be like he was as a probation officer: tolerant of him but repulsed by his dark side, so that I overlooked his goodness. His fear of this made him wonder if I could help him or not—in which case he would be left alone, wanting to take from others.

The patient responded that he still did not like talking. Words were depicted as "distancing, as always implying a gap." "They are just vehicles to contact another." He described how he would really like to say nothing. He then associated to his shoes and commented how extremely comfortable they were, asking if I would like to try them on. I remarked that maybe he wished for me to stand in his shoes and feel as he did. He then thought of "Mr. Spock and the Vulcan mind-meld," which was described as enabling us "to be one with one another, to be one together." (His allusion here was to a popular science-fiction character who possessed the ability to blend his personality with that of another in order to achieve understanding and knowledge about that other.)

Coming right after my interpretation, these associations were organized as reactions to my comments. At first it appeared I was off the mark, given his references to words as distancing. Therefore, I wondered if instead of bridging a gap, my intervention had created one. However, this appeared not to be the case, for my comment about his wish for me to feel what he feels led to material describing a positive symbiosis—that is, he wanted knowledge from me. As such, my interpretation of the pathological symbiosis, of his desires for me to be with him outside of treatment, maintain my implicit offer of healthy symbiosis. Concurrently, I hypothesized that his wish not to talk also had pathological elements in it, whereby we would merge and certain things would not be communicated openly and directly but rather obliquely and unconsciously. I therefore stated that his wish to be "one together" was the need to assure himself I would fully understand him without talking, thereby making us one. I added that he experienced words as frustrating to hear because they represented our separateness. Perhaps his insistence on not wanting to talk also related to wanting to keep his "dark side" separate from his accomplishments. He responded that this intrigued him, and the session ended.

This session depicted the initial development of a mirroring selfobject transference, albeit formed in terms of pathological symbiosis. My sense was that had I interpreted his need for mirroring and the wish for me to be with him, indeed had I centered my intervention exclusively on this, no material would have surfaced regarding his "dark side." Simply mirroring him would have sealed off acknowledgment that he did have a "dark side," which at this point remained just that. However, by intervening on the level of his desires for pathological symbiosis, with its accompanying gratifications and defenses against talking and self-revelation, healthy symbiosis was offered. In this way I was recognizing his need to merge while keeping mobilized the need to explore his "dark side." In fact, I believed that this first attempt at symbiosis had at its core a wish to subsume me within him, to silence me—that is, he and I would not talk—in the hope that his "dark side" could be avoided. At this stage, then, my working hypothesis was that his symbiotic needs were twofold: to be one together for understanding and to be one to avoid further self-revelation.

During the following session the patient spoke of his ski trip and expressed surprise that he had consumed no alcohol. He stated that he always felt the need for "peace of mind." The ski trip was an "anomaly" as he previously needed to "drink to achieve this." He felt he "lacked ecstasy" with his wife and that "external reality" always intruded on him. Then he recollected our last session and his image of the "mind-meld" with me. He felt this had a suggestion of peace and recalled how this had happened once when he was a teenager. He and a girl he knew would sit and rock on the back porch. They sang together and he felt "in harmony" with her. He described how he felt an "ecstasy, a bliss where there was no intrusion of external reality." Then he felt anguish and confusion. With her, it was all right, but to think that he felt this with me was "queer and fundamentally evil." Concerns about whether he was wrong to seek this with me or others became prominent, and he felt guilty that he did not feel "ecstasy and bliss" with his wife. His feeling of hatred toward his wife was then expressed. This feeling centered on his disdain of her for not being a "perfect female." Embarrassed at this remark, he stated the image of perfection sounded "Hitlerian." Indeed, he revealed he was fascinated with the Third Reich and wondered if some "deeper evil was lurking in his unconscious." He associated that whatever it was, he should keep it hidden; it was a "germ infecting his body." In turn, he was desperately trying to "form scar tissue to keep it from spreading."

I interpreted that his fantasies of "melding" with me on the one hand brought him peace, as he did not drink. On the other hand, I pointed out that in the last session I had raised the possibility that his desire not to talk was related to wanting to keep his "dark side" separate from me. Therefore, I wondered if my saying this and his present concern about being bad and queer meant that he felt closeness with me would result in his being infected by me because he perceived me as not perfect.

He responded that somehow I would make him adjust to external reality. He recollected Orwell's *1984* and the image of "Big Brother making you adjust." He worried that I might be colluding with his wife to make him adjust. Therapy, he considered, was a vehicle to adjust him so that he would see the world as everyone else did. His next remark was that he hated the idea that I had something he lacked. I was "all together, composed, and a wall of unassailable mental health." In contrast, he felt "out of balance," as he perceived me as "better" than himself. He next associated to his father as a "saint." He was angered by his father's ability to correct him: "Often it was so much better not to talk; it wasn't so much what I said to dad, he was more interested that I said it right." He believed this related to his need for perfection and then associated to his disdain of "disorderliness," adding, "yet I find I'm riddled with imperfections and evil."

I interpreted that with his growing sense of "melding" with me, as he felt with his teenage girlfriend, he feared I would view this as evil and therefore act like his father, critical and adjusting him, which would leave him out of balance with me, angry and in dismay. I suggested he needed to make sure I was in perfect order before he would share this "deeper evil lurking within."

He then recalled that his father was once proud of him for winning a fight. He was surprised that dad enjoyed his physical abilities. He had thought he would be criticized for fighting, but instead dad supported and encouraged him. This ended the session.

With this session, there is evidence of healthy symbiosis in the patient's not drinking. On the other hand, he viewed this development as evil, which in my mind pointed to homosexual anxieties accompanied by guilt and condemnation. He further revealed fears of being dominated and adjusted. It became evident that this stemmed from perceiving his father as critical of him and believing I would behave similarly. My stressing his fears of me seemed to aid him in differentiating me from father, as indicated by his comment on father's earlier pride in him. The reference to his wife adjusting him again alerted me to the possibility of frame compromises. In fact, I had had no contact with the wife, nor were there any third-party concerns in this treatment. Instead, I believed he perceived all relationships as fraught with fears of being dominated, criticized, shamed, and losing autonomy. It appeared the development of healthy symbiosis was slowly beginning to unfold anxieties, defenses, introjects, and past pathological object relatedness. In addition, there was a suggestion that drive-conflict issues—the homosexual fears related to me—were beginning to surface. Thus, as healthy symbiosis was established, the patient attained a stabilizing of self-esteem, as evidenced by not drinking. This development led to the suggestion, as yet still forming, of drive-conflict issues surrounding libidinal attachments to me. Closeness to me seemed to be associated with something evil and queer.

The next session the patient stated remorsefully that he "really screwed up." He had been drinking heavily and had intercourse with a woman he met at a bar. His drinking, he felt, must disappoint me. If I genuinely cared for him, I should punish him. He worried that I might view him as an "ugly guy," that I might find him "unworthy," "not good." He then voiced anger at me because he did not know how I valued him. He reflected on homosexuality, which was "fundamentally evil." "You must see it as evil and if you don't you are distorted and a liar," he declared. "If you accept homosexuality you either are a homosexual yourself or a supporter of it." Once, he recalled, he had looked up the term "homosexual" in the dictionary and read "abnormal." At the time he believed that the word would be "indelibly stamped in capital letters on my forehead."

With these associations, the patient seemed quite distressed. I experienced him as forcing me to agree that he should be punished for thoughts of homosexuality; if I did not, then I was perverted in his eyes. In either case, I felt he again was attempting to shift the relationship from exploration and analysis to action discharge with my criticizing him or else being rendered perverted. At the same time, with his association to abnormality and homosexuality, I conjectured that he might be attempting to unfold his dark side, which previously he viewed as infecting him. My earlier hypothesis of conflicts around libidinal attachment to me being equated for him with homosexuality appeared to be gaining credence. I then asked him what had occurred that prompted him to look up the word "homosexual."

He then felt terribly despondent. With much shame and embarrassment, he reported having homosexual encounters with his brother at age 13. They engaged in fellatio, with him first receiving and then performing the act. In his view this was "fundamentally evil and it's a lie if you try to turn something bad like this and twist it into good." He was utterly convinced that his father would also view him as "evil." He then discussed the "profoundest philosophical question of reality whereby two people can see the same thing differently; thus, you cannot prove it exists." He continued, "You see, I know I am evil yet I know you don't see it this way; therefore, we disagree so the case can be thrown out because I know I am not going to talk of this anymore." He told me that he frequently was "revolted" by his clients and advised that I should be "removed, tolerant, but dispassionate" toward him. To him, this meant whatever I said to him he was convinced I was actually revolted by him.

This material, I believed, confirmed my hypothesis, for he was viewing our relationship as akin to the homosexual encounter with his brother. Concurrently, he was convinced he was evil for this and expected me to play the role of his presumed punitive father, thereby punishing himself and stopping further analysis. In addition, he again attempted to create a pathological symbiosis, in which I should behave like he did with his clients: dispassionate, yet inwardly revolted. I sensed that he wanted to view my interpretations as a sham because he really preferred I criticize and punish. Nothing short of this would satisfy him, for he desperately wanted not to talk of homosexuality. Indeed, he had stated earlier he was trying to seal off an inner evil (now the homosexuality) behind scar tissue.

From this perspective, I interpreted that the evil within that he was trying to seal off seemed related to seeing our relationship as duplicating a homosexual tie with his brother. I stated that when I interpreted his wishes to be close to me, either his wish for me to go to his home or on a ski trip, this brought him relief, for he did not drink. Yet perhaps he saw my stating this as threatening and an attempt to dominate and subdue him, even though he seemed to see the benefit of the wish for closeness, for he recalled his enjoyment of his teenage girlfriend and his father's pride in him. Now, with homosexuality linked to closeness, he felt I, like himself or his father, should be only revolted and therefore should punish him. Unfortunately, I added, this would stop his understanding of our relationship and himself. Perhaps, I suggested, his renewed drinking and the sexual encounter with the woman were a way to dramatize his difficulties in expressing feelings toward me because he viewed this as evil and something to be punished.

His response was a desire to attend sessions every day. The idea that he wanted me to treat him punitively was precisely how he did treat himself. "I always wanted to create a philosophy that is devoid of the irrational, devoid of feelings," he continued. "It seems my whole life is to try to keep feelings out yet it really doesn't work, does it?" He recollected that he always tried to envision himself as sealed up in a box waiting for someone to pass by, toward whom he needed to reach out. He described always being fearful of reaching out, believing he would be harmed: "You see, here I'm beginning to feel myself coming out of my box, yet all these feelings of being queer, evil, and an ogre are constantly mixed together. Even the idea of coming out makes me feel I'm gay." The image of being in a box brought associations regarding his mother: "I felt boxed in by her. She never was really interested in what I said but that I said it correctly. Often it was better to say nothing." He was then anguished as he realized that maybe his need for a "perfect philosophy devoid of feelings" was what mom wanted, and what he now was trying to establish. "It's being caught between being perfect in language to maintain an illusion of being on top yet inside I feel hosts of feelings which to me are not perfect. I'm a riddle of contradictions trying to absolve, no resolve myself." He laughed at this slip and added, "You are trying to help me absolve myself but it seems I won't let it; it feels too threatening." The session ended with his saying it would be so much easier to relate to me if I were a woman.

The interaction from this session illustrated how his intense condemnation of closeness to me was connected with homosexuality. Thus, I believed that he needed to keep these drive issues out of our relationship through a pathological symbiosis, whereby he desired me to treat him as he would treat himself: either punish himor else abandon him as perverted. In other words, he wished to establish a specific mirroring selfobject transference, which would seal off exploration of his conflicted libidinal attachment to me. Once this was interpreted—by pointing out the pathological consequences of his defenses—material unfolded that, to my mind, brought into awareness his philosophy of warding off feelings and the pathological identifications with ideals of perfectionism. He even verbalized how he realized he was trying to re-create this in treatment, at the expense of what he actually felt. Poignantly, his closing statement regarding his wish for me to be female underlined his dilemma of wishing to relate to me but fearing my being a male because of homosexual fantasies.

Initially, the image of perversion suggested that he might be perceiving pathological elements in the therapeutic hold. Again, however, as I reflected on the frame issues, they all seemed securely held. The only indicator was the need to interpret directly his fear that I would subdue and dominate him and how this perception was linked to the encounters with his brother and mother. At this point, given his rigid insistence on being punished, his increasing awareness of linking closeness with homosexuality and being dominated, and his propensity to rely on pathological forms of symbiosis to avoid the fantasies, anxieties, and drives that threatened him, I sensed we would be in for quite an upheaval at any time.

My intuition was soon realized. The next session he was markedly despairing. His drinking had increased to the point where he was considering taking Antabuse. Suicidal ideation was prominent. He felt overwhelmed by guilt.

Given this material, I struggled with the possibility that I had not understood him in the previous session and was concerned that my interventions had had a disabling effect. Another alternative was to view the use of alcohol and medication as the use of external sources to promote pathological symbiosis and thus to avoid my interventions either as harmful or as leading to further revelations of unacceptable fantasies regarding his relationship to me. In any case, I was not sure what was happening but felt moved by his distress. Consequently, I asked what he felt caused his despair.

Still despondent, he struggled to share a nightmare that had terrified him. He then was silent and refused to discuss this further. At first I respected his silence, but he continued to shift in the chair, his hands were shaking, and he repeatedly hid his face behind his hands and sobbed. Given his intense distress, I reflected to him that perhaps he was worried about how I would react to this nightmare which caused him such discomfort.

After my comment, he severely criticized himself as being "filth, refuse, and the absolute dreg of humanity." He viewed himself as "totally unworthy" in comparison to his father, whom he held in "awe and esteem." Father was above reproach. "The man was a saint." As a child, he perceived his father as having "an absolute, unassailable sense of what was right and wrong." My patient desired to "possess, capture, and seize this philosophical system" yet he felt "unworthy" of it. He believed the values his father espoused were the "structure of all truth and knowledge; it is the foundation and basis for everything; yet he always wins because I don't measure up." He always sought this "system" yet described how it must elude him because he was "evil, queer, and a rampant homosexual." "If dad knew, I'd be rejected out of hand. As it is, just being me and thinking what I think is proof enough to me that I'm an outcast." Given that he was an outcast, he preferred to "drink myself to death." He saw no hope of being like father.

As all this followed my intervention, I organized his associations as reactions to and commentaries on my attempt to empathize with his distress. It was quite apparent that not only was he discussing feeling unworthy in comparison to his father, but that he also perceived my concern for him as a challenge in which I was the "saint" and he, an evil outcast. With this perception of me as beyond reproach, he saw himself as wishing to be like me but rejected because of his thoughts.

I therefore interpreted to him that when I expressed my desire to know what caused his distress, perhaps he perceived himself as unworthy and evil because he felt I was presenting myself as saintly and beyond reproach. With this perception, I sensed he felt I became like his father, possessing knowledge of what was right and leaving him feeling he was evil, wrong, and not worthy. I interpreted that he felt criticized because of his thoughts and wanted to drink, take medication, or commit suicide because he again felt he was evil for not measuring up to father's or my expectations. Given all this, I stated, it was no wonder he didn't want to share the nightmare.

The patient then related the nightmare: in it, he is performing cunnilingus on a woman he desires to "conquer"; suddenly her clitoris turns into a penis and he realizes he is performing fellatio on a composite figure of his father and me. He stated that he awoke terrified and felt he was "demented." In the session, he was visibly anguished. "This is proof of my insanity; I am homosexual and should be cast out," he declared. For him, the nightmare confirmed his fear of introspection. Never before, he claimed, had he had nightmares, nor did he previously recall his dreams. "I could always count on sleep and now that is threatened." He felt "despairing, hopeless, overwhelmed, with no way to escape myself." He believed the dream related to his "homosexual experience" with his brother. Yet he could not understand why I was in the dream: "You are not a woman." Here I recollected that he ended our last session by saying it would be easier to relate to me if I were a woman, and I shared this observation with him. In his view, that was "repulsive and sick." Further anguish and shame were expressed as he related a second nightmare, which had immediately followed the first. In it, he is performing autofellatio. He associated that he was repulsed by the idea of being sexual with me. For him, this was repugnant and he wanted to leave treatment. He would rather "cure and take care of myself" than face these feelings toward me. He desired to be "complete and perfect onto myself; 'I'll just therapize myself."

After I had interpreted his feeling unworthy because he believed I was beyond reproach and this perception prevented him from associating, I rectified the offer of healthy symbiosis. Again, in my mind, he wanted to use alcohol, drugs, or suicide as a pathological symbiosis to protect himself from his perception of me as beyond reproach and himself as unworthy and evil. Yet my interpretation did have a beneficial effect, for he did share the nightmare. This material indicated that his pathological symbiotic wishes defended against a blatantly expressed wish to perform fellatio on me and his father. When this material burst into his consciousness, it was thoroughly unacceptable to him. It seemed to me that his auto-fellatio dream was a way to establish a self-contained narcissistic position as a retreat from the anxiety and drive of object relatedness.

Given how quickly he was shifting his affect from despair, severe censure, and guilt, to attempts to be aloof and self-sufficient, I was impressed with the need to intervene with sensitivity and compassion. In the wake of such primitive drive material which repulsed him, leaving him desirous of punishment or flight, I elected to interpret upwards—that is, to at first interpret the more socially acceptable and adaptive functions of the dream. Thus, I pointed out that in the last session I had stated that perhaps his sexual encounter with the woman at the bar expressed feelings toward me. Furthermore, he ended that session by saying it would be easier to relate to me if I were a woman. In this light I suggested that perhaps his nightmare illustrated that his use of the woman sexually actually was an attempt to obtain support and comfort when he was distressed. At the same time it illustrated his need to conquer and take in parts of me and his father, which he felt were kept from him because he believed we were good and he was undesirable, making him feel lacking, criticized, and ashamed.

The patient began to cry intensely and related how he had always wished to "steal, seize, and take" his father's "power over right and wrong" yet he felt it was beyond his grasp and kept from him. As he perceived father as withholding, he believed he was not "worthy" of his father's "wisdom and strength." He then shifted, stating that he "really did not give a damn" about people and wished to take from them and leave. He spoke of his desire for physical perfection and thinking in others. Whenever he perceived this quality in others, he felt impelled to "divest" it from them. He viewed himself as "ruthless" and felt "desirous" of anyone whom he felt "had it all together." He then wondered why he had had the second dream.

Again, I organized this material as a commentary on my prior intervention. The patient unconsciously perceived that indeed I was withholding. In fact, I was withholding a full interpretation. In accurately perceiving this, he was left feeling unworthy. He then attempted to recover from my deprivation by a parasitic mode of relatedness, using others without concern in order to take what he needed from those who withheld from him.

With this in mind, I interpreted that he perceived me as not giving him enough, that he perceived I was withholding from him. When he sensed this, it left him feeling deprived, as if he had been found unworthy, which then impelled him to feel hatred and to take from others without concern for them. I continued by stating that he found his wishes to relate to me too threatening and repulsive because they took the form of fellatio fantasies. He felt revolted by this wish and believed it was better to comdemn himself and flee treatment because closeness for him and relying on another was intolerable. I added that he was so revolted by dependency being expressed via fellatio that his second dream, as his associations suggested, represented his desire to give to himself and feel self-sufficient to avoid depending on me, which had led to frustration, disapproval, shame, and rejection. Thus, when he feels rejected and senses that I am withholding, he either wishes to give to himself, to protect himself, or else seize from others what they withhold.

The patient's despair and hopelessness abated, and he associated to "needing seeds of knowledge, like advice and guidance." "When you talk," he explained, "it is as if you plant seeds inside me." Seeds made him associate to growth, development, and life prospering. With much embarrassment, he also associated seeds with semen. Again, he was convinced he was evil.

I stated he wished to receive "seeds of knowledge" from me or, as the dream portrayed it, semen, in order for him to grow. I reiterated that he felt revolted by these fantasies, feared I would reject him and deprive him, which would intensify his ruthlessness to seize from me or else be indifferent and take from others.

My comment, he stated, "really clicked and made sense." He saw therapy as a "help to see the meaning of symbols I always viewed as evil." He associated to a female client who had recently come to his office for legal help in resolving some financial problems. He related that he was direct and honest with how he would approach her difficulties and offered his opinions to her situation. He emphasized his need for her to be honest and to trust him, which enabled him to trust her. He was delighted with his directness and hers, and she accepted his services. He believed she would be pleased with his work. This ended the session.

This clinical material demonstrated the complexities involved in narcissistic transferences. Admittedly, I have highlighted only one link in an extremely complicated chain of transference developments with this particular patient. Indeed, I have brought the clinical material to a close just as one transference manifestation was understood, out of which another link formed, leading to further interpretive work. Thus, to amplify what has already been reported, I would like to comment briefly on subsequent developments.

I was aware of my irritation following the patient's derivative material describing his interaction with a female client. Despite my intellectual acceptance that this material validated my interventions, I was left with anger. Given this incongruity, I subjected my reaction to reflection. As a result of self-analysis, coupled with my pondering the patient's reactions to me, it became clear that the patient was reacting to my feminine surname "Beatrice." The patient's references to homosexuality, transvestism, and wishes for me to be a female were not indicative of his unconscious perception of my creating a deviant therapeutic frame. Rather, these references represented his conflicted elaboration of my feminine surname. When I then interpreted his perception of my name, material emerged in which he believed I epitomized his most anxiety-provoking conflict. As a consequence of my feminine surname, the patient perceived me as representing the devalued, humiliated, effeminate male, which he housed as a part of his self representation and which he now projected onto me. He was drawn to me because of these fantasies but also repulsed by them.

As he had done previously, the patient resorted to selfobject transferences, trying to merge with me to avoid exploration of these issues. However, he now feared if he merged with me, he and I would be so alike, so humiliated and effeminate, that no hope for resolution would be possible. In addition, he feared that depending on me would mean I would forcibly turn him into a femininized male or that simply by being with me, he would be magically transformed into the "she-male" he believed I already was.

After my self-analysis, I realized I was unable to hear his early associations as organized around his perception of my name and the conflicts this ignited within him. This inability was defensive on my part to keep at bay painful, personal memories of being criticized and devalued. Only once I was able to acknowledge within myself my reluctance to focus on my name as the adaptive context, could I interpret this as a source of the patient's homosexual anxiety. This step then led to exploration of his acute gender-identity conflicts.

DISCUSSION

My clinical illustration shows movement from issues concerning narcissism and the self to modes of object relatedness and finally drive-conflict issues related to the structural aspects of the psyche. In no way is this an attempt to say these are clearly graduated steps in the treatment of narcissistic personality disorders. Yet these issues cannot be separated and treated in isolation. Indeed, the clinical material highlights the interweaving of these issues in the therapeutic interaction. Consequently, technical interventions must address the various fluctuations and intensities of these issues as they arise during the course of treatment. As noted earlier, these issues have been sporadically documented (Altman, 1975; Hanly and Masson, 1976; Modell, 1978; Saperstein and Gaines, 1978; Giovacchini, 1979). My interest lies in organizing them into a unified statement.

The issues related to narcissism and the self were certainly underlined by the patient's expressed need for recognition and acknowledgment of his worthiness. Indeed, he very much needed to feel secure in the knowledge of being understood by me. This assured him that my warmth and genuineness were available to him without the threat of shame, embarrassment, and criticism. Here his wishes to find a healthy symbiosis with me were accepted and then interpreted in terms of their genetic links.

Concurrently, however, the patient attempted to engage me in specific mirroring selfobject transferences that did not serve the purpose of providing him with psychological help to bolster and secure healthy self-esteem. Rather, he attempted first to engage in a mode of object relatedness oriented to action without understanding and insight. This took the form of desiring me to visit his home, to accompany him on ski trips—in short, wishes to have me with him, but not in treatment. By not immediately recognizing and interpreting these wishes on their manifest level, but instead listening, containing, and awaiting further associations, I found that his mirroring wishes were defensive against self-revelation. My technical intervention was then one of interpreting the defensive aspect of this pathological symbiosis—the attempt to avoid exploration and unfolding of anxieties of being criticized, shamed, and dominated. The patient feared experiencing these issues in relation to me. Instead, he was attempting to split "good" from "bad" self representations. In response, my containing the patient's wishes and interpreting them offered the opportunity to partake in healthy symbiosis. This enabled him to reflect and understand himself without the necessity for quick use of pathological external support to split himself from his "bad" representation and have me respond only to his "good" representation.

Yet even this offer of healthy symbiosis was a source of apprehension for the patient. For him, relationships were equated not only with fears of humiliation, shame, and criticism (as was evidenced by material pertaining to his parents), but also with themes of domination, homosexuality, evil, and punishment. My interpretations gradually revealed the defensive aspects of his selfobject transferences, as well as his attempt to engage me in a pathological symbiosis whereby I would gratify his action requests at the expense of reflection and understanding. As he and I worked to analyze and understand this material, further anxiety and vulnerability emerged. The closer he felt to me, the more he was understood, the more he was also endangered by evil thoughts, fears of being infected, and desires to seal off further exploration.

Finally, it became apparent that his continued reliance on pathological symbiosis—whether with me, alcohol, medication, or sexual encounters—was an attempt to avoid acute homosexual anxieties from being revealed in the transference. The patient was defending against libidinal and aggressive drives—that is, structural conflicts—which in turn were adversely affecting and coloring his object relations. Thus, in contrast to Kohut's exclusive emphasis on the resistances to selfobject transferences being due to fears of humiliation, shame, fusion, and further unempathic responses from others, the clinical material presented shows that resistances may also be related to the structural aspect of the psyche. Once the latter were interpreted, healthy symbiosis was reestablished.

In Kohut's conception, the selfobject transference actually represents the need for the selfobject, in this case the therapist, to provide psychological functions patients cannot as yet provide for themselves. This view seems to argue for interventions designed to make patients aware of the healthy aspects of attempting to solidify their damaged self-esteem. I attempted such an intervention when my patient was highly distressed regarding his fellatio nightmare. I was aware of purposely sidestepping the more threatening and disruptive drive derivatives of the dream. That is, I thought it best to interpret the more sublimated and socialized meaning of the need to obtain comfort and security from me when he felt rejected and unworthy. I was attempting to be supportive when I perceived the patient as terrified and guilt-ridden concerning the more primitive elements of his personality. I feared if I interpreted them directly, more disorganization would result. Therefore, I interpreted the function of closeness, here expressed via fellatio, as an attempt to promote self cohesion. Yet such an interpretation does not appear to be a new psychoanalytic technique. Rather, I believe it can be formally classified as an interpretation upwards.

Moreover, what is rather striking in the clinical material is that my attempt to be empathic, supportive, and save the patient from further distress was actually perceived by the patient as my withholding from him. In this way I had failed him, for he fantasized resorting to parasitic modes of relating or else being self-contained (the auto-fellatio dream). In other words, with uncanny accuracy, he unconsciously perceived me as withholding, which fueled his sense of deprivation and rejection, and heightened his sadistic wishes to take from others indiscriminately. By adequately assessing and implicitly confirming his perception, I rectified my intervention. I next offered an interpretation in depth, which analyzed his wishes to take from me orally and his repulsion at this and his desire to be self-contained. His subsequent associations confirmed the appropriateness of my intervention. A healthy symbiosis was reestablished, leading to increased self-esteem.

Kohut's description of the selfobject transference is a valuable addition to our understanding of the transference possibilities for patients regressing to the symbiotic stage. His formulations, however, elevate the healthy, sublimated forms of this type of object relatedness while underplaying their drive-conflict underpinnings. As the clinical sequences suggest, a patient may be exquisitely sensitive to the therapist's exclusive emphasis on positive transference strivings and see this as representing further deprivation and the therapist's pathological needs to avoid interpretation in depth, which would include pathological object relatedness and drive-conflict issues. In other words, Kohut's assessments, in my opinion, avoid the complexities of healthy and pathological symbiotic relatedness as well as the drive-conflict issues stemming from structural aspects of the psyche.

Kohut's technical approach does not take into consideration the dangers of relying on incomplete interpretations. Chief among these dangers is the formulation of conscious fantasies, wishes, and expectations as reflective, in and of themselves, of the patient's general state of mind. By addressing such material solely on the manifest level, deeper, unconscious meanings and motivations are left unanalyzed. More to the point, such material needs to be organized around specific adaptive contexts (the therapist's interventions), and treated as accurate commentary on the perception of the therapeutic interactions before listening to the material as elaborations of the patient's anxieties, conflicts, drives, defenses, and pathological introjects.

A further precipitant of incomplete interpretations may be a defensive reliance on such interventions to avoid explorations of significant countertransference reactions to the patient's transference manifestations. In my situation, analysis of my anger led to the discovery of my patient working over his perception of my feminine surname. Utilizing this as the adaptive context enabled an interpretation, which facilitated exploration of homosexual anxieties and gender-identity conflicts within the transference.

Without exploration of one's countertransference reactions, reliance on interpretations upwards can lead to transference displacements away from the therapeutic interaction, with an increased likelihood of acting out. Inevitably, reliance on incomplete interpretations is a defensive reaction by the therapist that offers a pathological symbiosis to the patient whereby each participant avoids exploration, analysis, and interpretation of libidinal and aggressive drive derivatives.

Although I have spent considerable time assessing Kohut's views, a few comments are in order regarding Kernberg's ideas. Basically, I espouse Kernberg's psychodynamic formulations, but I find his technical terminology quite complicated to decipher and would prefer language with more immediate relevance to the therapeutic interaction. Similarly, Kernberg's clinical vignettes appear more demonstrative of pedantry than what I believe actually transpires between therapist and patient. To remedy this, I would like to see more exposition of countertransference reactions and how these are intimately linked to understanding our patients.

As I have indicated, the existing literature on symbiosis is useful in amplifying the more primitive form of the selfobject mirror transference. The ensuing phases of the separation-individuation process may illuminate further aspects of the two remaining variants of the selfobject mirror transference. I propose that the twinship selfobject transference involves object relations stemming from the differentiation subphase of separation-individuation. As Mahler et al. (1975) have described, this subphase entails the child's expansion beyond the optimal symbiotic phase. Although still fused, the child does differentiate his or her bodily existence from mother. There is a sense of recognizing another whom one feels separate from but still part of. Conflicts, anxieties, defenses, and accomplishments hinge on the management of relinquishing the symbiosis. Fear of venturing beyond this supportive base, fear of abandonment, and doubt regarding self-initiative and loss of object love are foremost. Thus, therapeutic technique in relation to a transference regression to the differentiation subphase would again include positive and negative elements.

I further propose that the mirror selfobject transference in the narrower sense may be reflective of the practicing subphase proper. At this stage children's greatest narcissistic investment concerns their bodies and bodily functioning as well as their objects. Kohut's belief that the mirror transference in its narrower sense is akin to a normal developmental stage and his recommendations for mirroring, reflecting, and echoing the infantile grandiosity are compatible with Mahler et al.'s (1975) findings on the practicing subphase proper.

CONCLUSION

My attempt has been to reconcile and integrate the contrasting views of Kernberg and Kohut regarding the understanding and treatment of narcissistic personality disorders. In this attempt, the work of Mahler et al. (1975) on the symbiotic stage of development and Langs's (1982) classification of modes of relatedness in the therapeutic interaction provide an organizing focus. From this perspective, as the clinical material demonstrated, technical interventions must account for and address issues relating to narcissism and the self, modes of object relatedness, and structural conflict-drive issues. It is my impression that Kohut's advocacy of interpretrations that promote self cohesion actually constitutes an emphasis on interpretation upwards. Interestingly, my clinical material indicated the patient viewed such interventions as the therapist's defensive attempt to avoid interpretation in depth—that is, directly dealing with libidinal and aggressive drive conflicts. Again, once the latter were interpreted, healthy symbiosis progressed.

The literature on developmental symbiosis and symbiotic modes of relatedness indicates that Kohut's variations of the selfobject mirror transferences have their developmental origins in the subphases of separation-individuation. In contrast to Kohut's descriptions, these transference variations are distinctly different forms of object relations with characteristic anxieties, conflicts, defenses, drives, and phase-appropriate developmental tasks and crises. The implication is that the three variations of the selfobject mirror transferences require therapeutic management different from what Kohut suggests. It is hoped that clinicians will be able to draw on the integrated approach I have attempted and supply the detailed clinical data to examine my hypotheses.

REFERENCES

Altman, L. L. (1975). A case of narcissistic personality disorder: The problem of treatment. *Int. J. Psychoanal.* 56:187–195.
Gedo, J. E., & Goldberg, A. (1973). *Models of the Mind: A Psychoanalytic Theory.* Chicago: Univ. Chicago Press.
Giovacchini, P. L. (1979). *Treatment of Primitive Mental States.* New York: Aronson.
Goldberg, A., Ed. (1978). *The Psychology of the Self: A Casebook.* New York: Int. Univ. Press.
────── (1980–11981). Self psychology and the distinctiveness of psychotherapy. *Int. J. Psychoanal. Psychother.* 8:57–70.
Hamilton, J. W. (1978). Some remarks on certain vicissitudes of narcissism. *Int. Rev. Psychoanal.* 5:275–284.
Hanly, C., & Masson, J. (1976). A critical examination of the new narcissism. *Int. J. Psychoanal.* 57:49–66.
Kernberg, O. (1975). *Borderline Conditions and Pathological Narcissism.* New York: Aronson.
Kohut, H. (1971). *The Analysis of the Self.* New York: Int. Univ. Press.
────── (1977). *The Restoration of the Self.* New York: Int. Univ. Press.
Langs, R. (1976). *The Bipersonal Field.* New York: Aronson.
────── (1978). *The Listening Process.* New York: Aronson.
────── (1982). *Psychotherapy: A Basic Text.* New York: Aronson.
Loewald, H. (1973). Review of H. Kohut's *The Analysis of the Self. Psychoanal. Q.* 42:441–451.

Mahler, M. S. Pine, F., & Bergman, A. (1975). *The Psychological Birth of the Human Infant.* New York: Basic Books.

Modell, A. H. (1978). The conceptualization of the therapeutic action of psychoanalysis: The action of the holding environment. *Bull. Menninger Clinic* 42:493–504.

Ornstein, A., & Ornstein, P. H. (1975). On the interpretive process in psychotherapy. *Int. J. Psychoanaly. Psychother.* 4:219–271.

Reich, A. (1960). Pathological forms of self-regulation. *Psychoanal. Study Child* 15:215–232.

Rosenfeld, H. (1964). On the psychopathology of narcissism: A clinical approach. *Int. J. Psychoanal.* 45:332–337.

Saperstein, J., & Gaines, J. (1978). A commentary on the divergent views between Kernberg and Kohut on the theory and treatment of narcissistic personality disorders. *Int. Rev. Psychoanal.* 5:413–423.

Schwartz, L. (1974). Narcissistic personality disorder: A clinical discussion. *J. Amer. Psychoanal. Assn.* 22:292–306.

Stolorow, R., & Lachmann, F. (1980). *Psychoanalysis of Developmental Arrests.* New York: Int. Univ. Press.

Wallerstein, R. S. (1981). The bipolar self: Discussion of alternative perspectives. *J. Amer. Psychoanal. Assn.* 29:377–394.

Winnicott, D. W. (1965). *The Maturational Processes and the Facilitating Environment.* New York: Int. Univ. Press.

15/
Discussion:
Is Narcissus a Myth?
Peter L. Giovacchini, M.D.

Drawing on James Beatrice's contribution, this paper shows how the treatment of patients suffering from structural defects highlights the contribution of early phases of development to psychopathology. Conceptualizations about sequences of structuralization and the establishment of object relations are critically reexamined in the light of clinical data derived from the transference-countertransference interaction. In particular, this paper questions whether fusion within a symbiotic union occurs regularly during normal development, and whether secondary narcissism is a very early stage of structuralization, following primary narcissism. In treatment the patient's fusing with the therapist while regressing to a primitive ego state is indicative of psychopathology. Narcissistic merger during later developmental phases, however, is often a sign of progressive integration and creative achievement.

STRUCTURAL CONSIDERATIONS

As our focus has shifted from an emphasis on oedipally based intrapsychic conflicts to an increased scrutiny of psychic structure, clinicians have come to assign considerable importance to early developmental stages. In our clinical formulations, Oedipus has frequently been replaced by Narcissus. Thus, in the light of all the recent attention it has received, the narcissistic phase of development, as postulated by Freud (1914), has to be soberly reexamined.

I do not wish to dwell on the significant recent neonatal research, which has in itself become an autonomous area. The findings of such investigators as Brazelton (1963), Emde and Robinson (1984). Freedman (1971), and Klaus and Kennel (1982), to mention just a few, are relevant to psychoanalytic formulations about the development of psychopathology. The role of early developmental stages in determining specific clinical pictures is highlighted, and intrapsychic processes, rather than being understood on the basis of conflicting drives, are perceived in terms of defects in psychic structure that are the outcome of traumatic interactions during early infancy or the neonatal period. At the same time the sequence of developmental stages postulated by Freud (1905, 1916–1917)—from autoerotism to primary and secondary narcissism to the psychosexual stages, beginning with the part objects of orality, anality, and the phallic phase, through the Oedipus complex, to the final, whole object orientation of genitality—has not been seriously challenged by the new data of the neonatologists.

Recent observations, however, have further stressed the influence of very early interactions on the formation of character, sufficiently so that it seems appropriate to extend and modify some of our concepts about pregenital phases. In particular, Tustin (1981), in her studies of autistic children, places them in a developmental conceptual framework that takes into account early cognitive abilities, which were not suspected before the systematic direct observation of infants. She has also demonstrated that mentation seems to emerge much earlier than we had surmised. Observations of the early exercise of cognitive capacities, greater sensitivities to specific interactions with the external world, and the bonding experience have changed or, at least, modified some of our conceptions about normal development and disturbances of emotional development as they lead to psychopathological adaptation and withdrawal, and structural defects.

In his paper James Beatrice, like Tustin, discusses these issues in a clinical psychopathological context, but unlike her, he derives his data exclusively from the one-to-one psychoanalytic interaction. He begins his discussion by reviewing the works of Kernberg and Kohut, two psychoanalysts who are representative of approaches that pay less attention to conflictual drives in favor of structural factors and developmental processes. This is especially true of Kohut, who gives an almost exclusive dominance to narcissism, whereas Kernberg, who also focuses on narcissistic phenomena, does not neglect drives, as he discusses oral destructiveness, envy, and rage.

I have written extensive critiques of Kohut and need not repeat them here (see Giovacchini, 1977, 1979). In fact, using Beatrice's paper as a point of departure to discuss my ideas about the psychopathological elements of early development, I wish to put the works of both Kohut and Kernberg to one side and emphasize Beatrice's contribution—which, in many ways, I find more clearly stated, clinically relevant, and useful than those of many authors who have received considerable recognition. My criticism of Beatrice is that he is going through the ritual of paying homage rather than expressing his own thoughts directly and autonomously. As many others have done, including myself, he has disagreed with these authors and used this disagreement to develop his antithetical thesis. By contrast, I shall use my acceptance of Beatrice's conclusions as the foundation for ideas I have formulated about patients suffering from severe emotional disturbances and fixations on early ego states.

I begin by questioning the primitive end of Freud's developmental spectrum: his ideas about primary and secondary narcissism. Our experience with patients who fall into borderline or psychotic categories, that is, patients who have characterological defects, has taught us that their psychopathology involves disturbances of these early phases. Clinical necessity has made us learn more about the quality of structural defects and how they affect adaptations to the external world and the development of object relations.

Freud's (1914) ideas about narcissism are not contradicted by the recent findings of neonatologists or those derived from longitudinal studies. But neither are they validated. This is understandable because the data that have been collected do not allow more than inferences about complex mental processes. Such data deal with actions and interactions and are of necessity limited to phenomenological sequences. Although these sequences may be suggestive of narcissistic attachments, fusion states, and, in psychopathology, of various regressive adaptations, in no way can they even approach conclusiveness. Studies derived from observations of the analytic process, however, permit us to make formulations about early mental processes. They also lead us to inferences about normal development that may differ, to some extent, from Freud's, at least in terms of the sequence if not the qualities of various stages. I believe the inferences collected from the psychoanalytic interaction—even if not more easily derivable than those from phenomenological data (which I believe they are)—prove to have greater plausibility in that they are clinically useful and help us understand our patients, as well as resolve transference-countertransference impasses, as Beatrice has demonstrated.

Focusing on Freud's sequence from autoerotism to secondary narcissism raises several questions. I shall not discuss autoerotism per se since this phase, as postulated by Freud, antedates psychological processes. I believe if it exists at all it would belong to what I have called a prementational phase (Giovacchini, 1979; Giovacchini and Boyer, 1983)—the earliest biologically based developmental phase, which precedes the construction of mentation and minimally organized affects. Instead, I shall concentrate on psychological processes in general and those involving narcissistic fusion states in particular.

Freud's model of emotional development, as is true of any developmental timetable, calls into question the inevitability of a particular preordained sequential scheme. Must one particular phase follow another? As the organism from a biological viewpoint progresses from less-differentiated organizations to better-differentiated organized states, does a similar or parallel organization occur in the psychic sphere? Certainly, we make such an assumption in that we view psychic states along the axis of a progressively structuralized hierarchy. Our concepts of regression and progression, so fundamental to our understanding of both psychopathology and the therapeutic process, depend on viewing development as a forward-moving differentiation both in a spatial (higher and lower levels) and temporal (archaic past and present secondary process) context.

Structural progression is well illustrated in the differentiation of the self and the outer world and the progressive structuralization of object relations. Consequently, it seems consistent to postulate an initially amorphous psyche that eventually becomes organized in a discrete manner, with well-delineated subsystems resulting in an integration of perception and adaptive behavior. The steps that lead to higher, complex differentiations vary according to different authors. Freud (1920) postulated an initial, undifferentiated id, which develops an embryonically organized core receiving modulated stimuli from the outer world that lead to higher psychic organizations. Hartmann (1939) wrote of an id-ego matrix as the beginning psychic state, whereas Glover (1930) described the coalescence of ego nuclei. Piaget (1937), Melanie Klein (1946), and many other investigators have introduced developmental sequences that vary, more or less, from one another but still depict a movement from the global to the structured. The latter has important implications for the development of object relations, the construction of the self representation, and the formation of ego boundaries.

In spite of what seems to be agreement about developmental progression and its inevitability, we can still question whether certain way stations, so to speak, are essential to the structuralizing process. For example, do we need to assume that the child hatches from symbiotic fusion as Mahler (1972) has postulated? Is there a movement from a global, amorphous, preobject psychic organization to fusion with the mother, followed by a gradual separation that results in individuation and the capacity to relate to external objects? To summarize, are we to accept that the essential way stations during these early phases are amorphous states, fusion, separation and individuation?

In a similar vein, we can ask whether secondary narcissism as a way station to the formation of object relations is an absolutely essential transition phase. Even though some authors have argued against postulating a phase of primary narcissism (see Balint, 1957), it seems to be much more consistent with biological maturation than secondary narcissism. The idea that psychic energy is focalized around that portion of the psychic apparatus that interfaces with the outer world just before there is an awareness of the outer world parallels what we know about the development of sensory systems. As they process external stimuli, they structuralize further so that, in a positive feedback sequence, they can relate with greater sensitivity and perceptiveness to the very same and other stimuli (Herrick, 1956).

In the psychic sphere, the stage of primary narcissism preceding an ego that will recognize and relate to external objects presents an analogous situation. The ego has to be sufficiently energized (cathected) so that it can direct itself to the external world, to the not-me, without being aware of it. As it does so, the ego's perceptive capacities expand and it becomes better able to process outer stimuli and recognize external objects in an ever-increasing totality. The ego has progressed from a primary narcissistic position, in which there is no distinction between the inner and outer world, to the establishment of object relations. The assumption of an in-between phase of secondary narcissism, with the construction of a selfobject and symbiotic fusion state, has no parallel in biological maturation.

Our need to understand patients justifies our preoccupation with what, on the surface, appear to be abstruse theoretical matters, an ivy-towered detachment from the hard and painful problems that clinicians face when dealing with overwhelming numbers of severely disturbed patients. Beatrice in attributing secondary narcissism to the practicing period described by Mahler (1972) differs significantly from Kohut, who places his different degrees of merger, the grandiose self, and the idealized parental imago at the level of primary narcissism. In this regard, Kohut shows a total disregard for theoretical consistency, since the accepted concept of primary narcissism is that it is a stage preceding any awareness of the external world that would include objects with which the infant can fuse. Still, the different developmental levels ascribed to fusion phenomena have important implications for how treatment should be conducted. Our understanding about such psychic processes will obviously affect the content of our interpretations and how we view the transference. Beatrice, again unlike Kohut, prefers at first to interpret the transference fusion at its highest adaptive levels rather than support it by mirroring the patient's grandiosity.

Kernberg's ideas about treatment are well known to differ considerably from Kohut's. Kernberg, as Beatrice describes, views merging phenomena or fusion states as being basically traumatic for patients with narcissistic personalities. Underneath their narcissistic orientation, these patients are covering up oral destructiveness, envy, and rage. Fear of despondency and of being exploited and manipulated stimulates the construction of specific defenses, which also serve to protect against merging. These patients use splitting mechanisms and projective identification—psychic processes described by Melanie Klein (1946) and her followers.

Because technical maneuvers may depend on whether certain pehnomena are considered to be developmental stages rather than the outcome of psychopathological defenses and fixations, I would like to amplify further where I believe secondary narcissism and symbiosis fit in the developmental scheme.

CLINICAL IMPLICATIONS OF HEALTHY AND PATHOLOGICAL SYMBIOSIS

Beatrice follows Langs (1982) in distinguishing between healthy and pathological symbiosis. Briefly, healthy symbiosis involves positive identifications in contrast to pathological symbiosis, which is action-directed and concerned with deviant acting out, drugs, alcohol, sexual perversions. Beatrice is describing self-destructive reactions that prevent fusion and highlight frustrated instinctual needs and rage. These reactions are difficult to conceptualize in terms of symbiosis, even pathological symbiosis—although these behavioral reactions, especially when they occur in the transference, can be understood as the outcome of a destructive symbiosis or, better stated, as the consequence of the fragmenting and disintegrative effects of a destructive symbiosis.

Although this is not their emphasis, both Langs and Beatrice are placing healthy symbiosis fairly high up on the developmental ladder when they describe it as a process that leads to positive identifications. In the hierarchy of psychic mechanisms, identification is fairly sophisticated. Selective aspects of the personality of the external object are incorporated in order to gain further cohesion of the self representation, giving it depth and dimension. The ego, to achieve this, has had to develop rather sensitive discriminations and perceives the external world in a structured fashion, far beyond what has been described as the ego state of the infant who is emerging from symbiotic fusion in order to first become aware of the external world as separate and distinct.

Is Freud's concept of secondary narcissism and the construction of the selfobject similar to healthy symbiosis? Inasmuch as secondary narcissism is a way station on the path that leads to the formation of object relations and the consolidation of ego boundaries, it would seem to be a nonpathological process. The question can be repeated whether it immediately follows primary narcissism. Or, to be conceptually consistent and clinically relevant, might it require further intermediary steps?

Before discussing this question further, I wish to return to pathological symbiosis in disorders of narcissistic equilibrium. This can best be done by introducing clinical examples—an obvious approach, but one I believe has advantages beyond those generally recognized. I am referring to the possibility that the treatment of narcissistic disorders, borderline states, and characterological problems in general resembles or becomes organized around the mother-child interaction, to a much greater extent than the treatment of better-structured patients.

Formulations about early fusion states have been made from the adult's viewpoint. During treatment the analyst relies heavily on his or her countertransference reactions to assess the patient's ego state and developmental level as it is reproduced in the transference. However, the patient is not a neonate; the patient's mental processes are based on the capacities and acquisitions of later developmental phases. If there is a symbiotic fusion between therapist and patient that is based on similar levels of ego states, it is the patient's ego state, as an adult who has regressed, that is represented and this differs markedly from what the neonate experiences. For the analyst, the patient's neediness and helplessness may evoke maternal and nurturing feelings.

The analyst may recognize that he or she is using fusing mechanisms in an attempt to respond intuitively to the patient to get in tune with primitive needs and despair. In turn the patient fuses with the analyst, and this constitutes a symbiotic union, although the analyst's needs—that is, the analyst's therapeutic intent—are at a higher level than those of the patient.

Something similar occurs in the mother-infant bond and interaction, although there must undoubtedly be vast differences as well. Winnicott's (1956) view of healthy mothers as being in a state of primary maternal occupation is compatible with the thesis that the mother fuses with her child so that she can anticipate infantile needs and provide optimal nurturing and soothing. She is constantly around, supplying, as does the analyst, her ever-hovering attention. This is how she feels and this is how we, as adults, view her. In this regard she is very much like the empathic analyst, although her dedication and devotion is total compared to the analyst's, whose involvement is time-limited. The infant, on the other hand, does not have the sophisticated mental mechanisms of the adult patient. The early ego states that have been traumatized during infancy, as our studies of psychopathology reveal, antedate the formation of object relations, and some patients' difficulties are the outcome of partial fixations at the prementational stage (Giovacchini, 1979). Secondary narcissism and fusion, in that they require at least a rudimentary percept of an external object, cannot occur with such amorphous psyches.

Even in the normal mother-infant relationship, it is not necessary to assume that the mother's and child's mental processes within the nurturing interaction are parallel to each other. The mother may perceive herself as being symbiotically fused with her infant and her intuitive reactions support her orientation, but the child does not reciprocate at the same level.

Here I am equating secondary narcissism and symbiotic fusion in that both are conceptualized in terms of a selfobject that represents a pathway to object relations. The term "symbiosis" can be questioned if we view the relationship as based on equal needs of the fused pair. The mother can obviously survive without the infant, whereas the reverse is not true. Still, there is a strong mutual dependency in a psychological sense that justifies the term "symbiosis." Regarding secondary narcissism, however, it is not an implicit assumption that the object the infant fuses with reciprocates in a similar manner and receives gratification of vital needs. Nevertheless, since it is the nurturing person, the mother, who is usually the object of the child's narcissistic attachment, she would also be involved in the fusion; thus, the interaction could be viewed as symbiotic.

There are, of course, many caretaker-infant interactions in which the caretaker is not symbiotically attached to the child. Undoubtedly, this is the basis of serious psychopathology. From a developmental viewpoint, the role of secondary narcissism can still be examined even when the child's nurturing source has not formed a symbiotic attachment. It is conceivable that the child could fuse with an external object without the object reciprocating and fusing with the child. However, is it likely, or are we dealing with a particular type of psychopathological merger that represents a deviation from or a distortion of normal development? During the phase of secondary narcissism described by Freud (1914), children enter the world of external object relations by first attaching themselves to the mother, at first viewing her as part of themselves. The devoted mother depicted by Winnicott (1953, 1956) does not disturb the illusion of her child, who feels in complete control and the source of his or her own nurture. Winnicott describes these interactions in terms of the transitional object, in the context of the mother's primary maternal preoccupation.

I repeat that I bring up these theoretical considerations because I believe that a further understanding or, rather, clarification of some of our concepts about the milestones of psychic development has crucial significance for how we understand and deal with severe psychopathology. Beatrice's paper is cogently addressed to this same issue. Here I am emphasizing that perhaps we can discard Narcissus as an important figure in the course of early emotional development. The implication is that when we find evidence in our patients' material narcissistic object relations, and if the external object is reciprocally fused (an example of symbiosis), we are usually witnessing the manifestations of psychopathology. There are, however, narcissistic and symbiotic elements that we clinically encounter that do not have serious implications for emotional disorders. I shall refer to such situations later, but now I wish to discuss further narcissistic attachments that run, so to speak, in one direction.

In treatment it is well known that during deep transference regressions, patients merge with the analyst. Beatrice discusses three types of selfobject transferences articulated by Kohut, which simply describe different degrees of merger. The degree of fusion has important technical implications, but the analyst's response is a decisive factor in determining the extent of the psychopathological significance of the patient's need to repeat infantile fusion states with the therapist. A spectrum of merger responses also emanates from the therapist. These responses may range from a minimal fusion, in which case there would be a relative absence of symbiosis; to almost total merger, which could result in a complex countertransference difficulties. Somewhere in the middle of this spectrum may be an optimal countertransference response, an optimal fusion, that can undo or, at least, help undo the effects of early traumas. *The analyst's orientation toward the patient can create a symbiotic transference that is not a repetition of the infantile setting. Rather, it represents a rectification of childhood deprivation.*

To summarize briefly, this discussion implies that there is both healthy and pathological narcissism, a formulation Federn (1952) made a long time ago. To carry this formulation just a little further, it also implies that within the state of narcissistic fusion, there can be both healthy and pathological symbiosis. The position of these phenomena on the developmental scale is a factor in determining what is healthy and what is the effect of emotional maldevelopment. I have already indicated that healthy narcissistic, and therefore symbiotic, attachments occur only when object relations begin to become fairly well established and ego boundaries consolidated. There is also considerable cohesiveness to the self representation. Earlier traumatic relationships, a consequence of the mother's pathological symbiotic needs, distort the infant's development so that when the child reaches later stages, narcissistic isolation becomes a defensive and psychopathological adaptation to maintain a false self (Winnicott, 1960). Now I am distinguishing narcissism as a psychopathological defense from the healthy fusion of secondary narcissism as part of a postindividuation developmental phase. In this instance, the patient, as Freud (1914) described, is withdrawing libido from the external object as a defense against fusion. Symbiotic fusion is experienced as terrifying. In analysis, such patients, during the transference regression, reexperience the assaultive maternal engulfment in the context of an early helpless and vulnerable ego state. I have placed this ego state at the primitive end of the developmental spectrum, where mentation is just beginning and before the external world is separated from the psyche.

The traumatic fixation point to which patients regress precedes the point of higher psychic organization when persons are capable of fusing with external objects or of being able to perceive, at conscious or unconscious levels, external objects fusing with them. Still, as we repeatedly observe in the therapeutic interaction, when patients regress they still retain many psychic mechanisms and adaptations that are characteristic of advanced developmental stages. Consequently, fusion and symbiosis in treatment can be experienced in the context of very primitive psychic organizations, something that cannot occur during the course of ordinary development. The amplification of these topics related to pathological processes can help in clearing up some inconsistencies and contradictions that have not been resolved in our understanding of how the psyche is progressively structuralized.

Two clinical vignettes will highlight disturbances of development during what usually is considered an early symbiotic phase. I believe, however, that these disturbances can be better explained in terms of disruptions of transitional phenomena.

CLINICAL ILLUSTRATIONS

The patients I have been discussing are puzzling in that they are difficult to classify. At times they seem to be psychotic, but they can also be eminently rational and capable of functioning at high levels. Frequently we call them "borderlines," but they do not precisely fit that category either. Still, clinicians are encountering this type of patient more and more frequently—the patient who, even when evaluated by an experienced clinician, represents an enigma because of his or her bizarreness. These patients are more likely to be thought of as crazy or queer than psychotic—that is, at times therapists drop their professional orientation when thinking about them.

Case Example 1

For example, I recently saw a middle-aged woman in consultation, a mother of 12 children who apparently lived her life in total chaos. I had learned from the therapist of the oldest daughter that the family never had organized meals, the beds were not made, and the house was filthy, with dirty clothes strewn on the floor of every room. Although they lived in an expensive and fashionable neighborhood, and their house was attractive, neat and harmonized with other expensive homes on the outside, it was a squalid, unkept hovel on the inside. The mother supposedly was oblivious to the surrounding disorganization; she never seemed to be involved with anyone and was unconcerned about what was going on around her. Still, unexpectedly, she would go into rage states, attacking the younger children to the point that she had to be physically restrained by either the older children or her husband. These outbursts could not be explained on the basis of a recognizable stimulus.

When I saw the patient, her behavior and appearance belied the picture that had been conveyed to me. She was mild-mannered, pleasant and affable, neatly if not fashionably dressed. She spoke in an animated, cheerful fashion, and my first impression was of a fairly integrated, moderately intelligent and educated woman. Her demeanor, however, was not appropriate to the content of her narrative. She spoke of a son's serious suicide attempt and the likely possibility that her husband would leave her and the children in a bland tone, as if these were not matters of any particular concern. Yet, this response was markedly different from the thought disorders and distortion of affect encountered in schizophrenics.

Perhaps the distinction between this woman and the psychotic patient is only a matter of degree, but I believe that there are important differences that are manifestations of particular defects in psychic structure. What impressed me was more a "flakiness" than a thought disorder. She seemed to have little or no capacity to get in touch with her feelings or to relate to others except on a superficial, nonfeeling level. What seemed most remarkable was her impression that there was nothing wrong with her life. I do not believe this was the outcome of denial.

I learned in a second interview that she believed she had had a reasonably happy childhood and that her mother and father had been average parents, without any unusual characteristics. However, I could gain no sense of what they were like. Since I knew that I was not going to treat her, I probed—but to no avail. Her mother was a nice woman and her father was "fine," but I could not gather any information about their relationship except that the mother was dominant. She was not a good housekeeper or cook, but these were inferences I made from pointed and detailed questions I asked about housekeeping and meals. I concluded that this woman's parental home was chaotic and disorganized, much as her present setting, but the patient accepted these environments as the norm. Two of her adult siblings still live with the parents because they are so incapacitated that they cannot function on their own in the outside world.

She could not give me any further information about her childhood or her relationships with siblings or parents. She emphasized that she was named after her mother's favorite doll, a doll that the mother still has. The picture I formed was that of a child who was never treated as an individual in her own right and with needs of her own. She was treated as a doll, as the mother's transitional object.

I have seen and heard of other women who were treated as transitional objects and named after the mother's favorite doll. They behaved as dolls and in some instances look like dolls. Superficially, they seem organized and well made up—often too much so, in that they appear as caricatures of attractive women, as dolls do with their brightly painted features and fixed expressions.

Returning to my consultation: the patient thrived in an atmosphere of chaos. It didn't matter if her world was crumbling around her, if her children were flunking out of school. One child even had violent episodes in which he would smash windows, break dishes, and wreck furniture. Moreover, her husband would leave for days at a time. Yet, she maintained her composure and behaved as if her house possessed the gentility of an English countryhouse afternoon tea. Throughout all this turmoil, I could envision her placidly sitting with a doll-like smile.

The reasons for the consultation are tangential to the purpose of this paper. I will simply mention that one of her children, an adolescent son, was becoming more and more unmanageable as his violent episodes were increasingly frequent. Paradoxically, the more upset he became, the calmer she felt. She maintained an amazing control in circumstances that would ordinarily be totally disruptive. At one level she appeared as the only sane person in the absolutely insane world.

I believe this woman illustrates two factors found in certain types of severe psychopathology that are relevant to the developmental factors being studied here. First, she was almost completely uninvolved with external objects; she had no sensitivity whatsoever to other persons' feelings. As individuals in their own right, they did not exist and she had no awareness of their needs. Second, in spite of, perhaps because of, her emotional nonparticipation, she was in control of her world.

Had this woman ever experienced symbiotic fusion? From what I could gather from her past history and my own reactions, I would conjecture that she had not. Her mother was never around, and her caretaker maids were usually indifferent and did not stay very long. There was discontinuity in the mothering she received. Not only was her mother actually absent, but she was probably withdrawn and depressed; most likely, she had been hospitalized during the first year of the patient's life. I, in turn, felt that I would find it very difficult to emphathize with this woman. Although she was pleasant and affable, the thought of my being able to fuse with her was completely out of the question. Moreover, she gave me the impression that she did not recognize my existence as an emotional being sufficiently for her to merge with me. As stated earlier, to fuse with an external object requires some recognition of another psyche beside one's own.

I was aware of the fact that we were not communicating with each other. We did not belong to the same species; we were on different planets. Our collective past experiences, which determine our values and norms, were so different that there was no basis for mutuality and understanding. On the other hand, I recognized that I was being manipulated in that she was thwarting my efforts to understand her on an empathic level through shared experiences.

There were moments, especially during our second interview, when I experienced some discomfort. I was mildly agitated because the session was not progressing the way I would have liked it to. I was put in the position of not knowing either what to say or what to ask her. One inquiry of mine did not smoothly lead to another that would have illuminated her emotional state. In retrospect, I can now understand how I was being controlled. In spite of this patient's structural incapacities to relate to anyone in terms of feelings, she was able to control her surroundings by her impregnable, insular attitude. An ego defect became a protective defensive modality.

It is plausible to assume that if her mother had had any relationship with her whatsoever, it was one in which she used her daughter as a transitional object. I have mentioned that she was named after her mother's doll and how I was impressed by her doll-like appearance. Yet, in contrast to other patients, I did not see her as a porcelain doll likely to shatter under the slightest stress, unprotected, vulnerable, and fragile. Rather, I saw her as invulnerable and myself as vulnerable. I was being controlled as transitional objects are. In my mind, she had defensively reversed the situation. As is so often the situation with patients, they tend to treat their therapists and other persons as they themselves were treated during their helpless infancy. She had been her mother's transitional object and now she controlled her world by relating to people as if they were transitional objects, nonhuman pacifiers. Whatever internal tension she experienced was absorbed by her environment, causing her husband and children to feel agitated and to act out destructively in order to seek relief.

I was not entirely aware of feeling agitated when I saw her. This is a retrospective reconstruction. However, I did feel impelled to be critical of her and had to restrain myself from being rude and probing. I believe that to defend myself, I may have become stiff and overprofessional. I was puzzled by my stance, once I recognized what I was doing, since she was not overtly unpleasant or obviously provocative. It was the subtle aspects of the relationship I was reacting to, as I felt myself increasingly dehumanized. To some extent, I was also absorbing some of her agitation and serving the transitional object's function of soothing. I was acutely aware, however, that I was being reacted to as if I did not exist and had no influence whatsoever on her.

That this patient did not want treatment could be explained by her feeling comfortable, calm and soothed, in a world that absorbed her agitation. I do not believe that she was projecting her inner disruption onto external objects. To project, as is true of both introjection and fusion, requires the acknowledgment of external objects. I conjecture that she was operating at a more primitive level, at the level of the transitional object. The transitional object is just that, a transition, and although it may, according to Winnicott (1953), represent the first not-me possession, it is, at the same time, part of the self. It does not reside in the space identified as the external world. During the transitional phase of development, that space has not yet been constructed. Rather, it resides in the transitional space, the space the adult perceives as part of the external world, but the infant feels as part of the internal world. Projection as such could not occur during this phase; rather, the infant transfers feelings from one part of the self to another and thus gains relief and satisfaction. This phenomenon is analogous to children believing that they are the source of their nurture, again as Winnicott stated.

Case Example 2

Another patient, a woman who was in treatment with me for many years, was unable to form enduring object relations that would absorb her inner disruption and soothe her. She had been married three times and had innumerable affairs, but all these relationships turned out badly. Because she is personable and intelligent, she attracted charming and successful men. However, much like her, they had difficulties in sustaining intimate relations. Apparently, they were highly narcissistic persons who used the patient to enhance their narcissism.

To summarize drastically, the first two years of her analysis were exclusively concerned with revealing how inadequate and empty she felt. Though she continued to function at high levels in her daily life, in the consultation room she regressesd to a state of helpless vulnerability, revealing a self representation consumed with feelings of worthlessness and self-hatred. She emphasized her lack of ego boundaries and the lack of cohesion of her identity sense. She exemplified this ego state by picturing herself as an empty bottle, buffeted around by both angry and capricious waves. She felt that, as a person, she did not exist; she was there just to be a slave, to do the bidding of others.

Her self-denigrating attitude was also quite visible in the transference. She idealized me and blamed herself entirely for her lack of progress as she viewed it, for her pervasive sense of misery. She frequently lamented that she was failing me in that I could not count her as one of my therapeutic successes. I would not be either personally or professionally enhanced because I had treated her. It was evident that she saw herself as having a definite role in the treatment, beyond the needs of a patient and the wish of the therapist to be helpful and a catalyst to the development process. Clearly, she expected me to use her. How was quite vague, other than gaining professional prestige. In any case, her needs would be totally subjugated to mine.

The patient often referred to herself as a dirty rag doll and frequently quoted the negative definition of a little girl: "a rag, a bone, and a hank of hair." This made me think of a much mishandled transitional object, and I felt impelled to reply "sugar and spice and everything nice." I did not, however, actually use this quote until much later in her treatment, when she was able to construct polarities. During this stage of therapy she could only deal with her dehumanized, manipulable self.

This period was followed by many sessions in which she experienced intense anxiety and despair. Finally, she started vociferously attacking me. She began by accusing me of exploiting her. In the first two years of our relationship, she had felt that I should treat her cavalierly because she was so unworthy. Now she felt I was manipulating and using her, that I insisted on treating her as a rag doll. In my mind, this represented a mother transference, but it was also evident that by attacking me, she was reversing roles and identifying with her mother, treating me as she felt treated as a child. Between attacks, I felt as if I did not exist—so much so that to some extent, I welcomed her abuse, because at least under these circumstances, I was being acknowledged and not simply ignored and controlled as a nonhuman object.

I was reminded of Modell (1968), who believes that the therapist being treated as a transitional object is the characteristic transference of borderline patients. In a positive sense, Feinsilver (1980, 1983) has written of transitional relatedness in treatment and Searles (1976) has addressed himself specifically to transitional phenomena in the context of symbiosis. I definitely felt as if I were being controlled as a transitional object as the patient, in reenacting the repetition compulsion in the transference regression, took the active role instead of being passively vulnerable—a reversal first described by Freud (1920). At this stage of treatment I did not feel at all fused with her and neither did she with me. In fact, she had never felt intimate closeness with anyone in her life. She was now, however, retrospectively aware of intense rage for never having been acknowledged as a person with her own needs and separate from others.

As in any analysis, there were, of course, many facets to the transference as it moved in different directions. To just focus on specific elements of the transference interaction may give the impression of a clear-cut continuity, which did not in fact exist. Nevertheless, I shall emphasize certain elements that can lead us to some conclusions about the symbiotic phase and its significance for psychopathological and normal development. I shall isolate them from the complex and varied reactions and feelings she had, as all patients have, toward her analyst.

Gradually, this patient began once again to have positive feelings toward me, but without the intense idealization that characterized her initial reactions in treatment. She felt that she had made considerable progress and had developed faith in herself as a person. She was proud of how she was able to do things in a self-assertive but not intrusive fashion and spoke of situations in which she managed quite effectively when previously she would have been overwhelmed by her vulnerability. She was especially proud of her ability not to be taken advantage of by men.

She also started reading some of my writings and adopted many of my viewpoints. She felt very much identified with my position and saw our closeness as mutually enhancing. Her asociations indicated concern about whether I found my relationship with her valuable—which, indeed, I did because of the pride I took in her progress and what I was learning from her. This sanguine state lasted six months, during which time she had at least a dozen dreams stressing that we were fused in a symbiotic attachment with each other.

Her comfort did not last; the analysis became an increasingly unpleasant experience for her. Her concern about whether I was getting something out of her treatment mounted and she finally concluded that I was exploiting her. At this point in treatment, I had become her paranoid object and she was reenacting her psychopathology within the transference context.

Through interpretations the patient was gradually able to understand how she was repeating certain maladaptive patterns and reexperiencing infantile relationships. The paranoid fervor completely subsided as we continued working in an atmosphere of mutual cooperation.

She repeatedly emphasized that she (and perhaps I) could not have survived the paranoid period if she had not built up her self-esteem when she felt herself symbiotically fused with me. She believed that she had gained a sufficiently stable sense of identity to enable her to maintain the integrity of her ego boundaries as she viewed herself in an unprotected state of helplessness, faced with my oppressive and exploitative onslaught. Furthermore, the treatment had provided her with a unique experience: the opportunity to fuse with a benign, helpful external object—something that had never occurred in her real life, as she put it. Although later she no longer responded to me as if I were benign, this represented a regression, as she was getting in touch with the more primitive levels of her psyche and revealing aspects of defective development.

DISCUSSION

The study of these two patients permits us to draw inferences about normal emotional development by emphasizing specific developmental phases. Psychopathological distortions highlight the existence of an underlying ego state, and working through these distortions can give us a picture of what the psyche may have been like had it not been pounded by infantile trauma.

Both these women were traumatized early in life; maternal caretaking was defective or nonexistent since birth. Instead of relating to them as individuating children, their mothers treated them as if they were transitional objects. Rather than being involved with them on the basis of the child's needs, they needed the relationship only insofar as they felt in control and did not have to give anything of themselves. It is unlikely that these mothers felt fused with their children in that they recognized them as separate and then merged with them. I am postulating that the patients, in turn, did not fuse with them. Secondary narcissism and fusion as psychic processes, were for the most part lacking in these women, and this was the outcome of their traumatic pasts and psychopathology. I do not mean to indicate that they were totally incapable of forming narcissistic attachments and fusion. I conjecture that the complete absence of a psychic mechanism is very rare, but these patients demonstrated its lack in the transference-countertransference interaction.

If we view the patients as fixated at the transitional phase of development—and Winnicott's implication that the transitional phenomenon occurs as a normal developmental stage makes sense—then we need to examine where this stage fits into the developmental timetable. The trauma these patients, or at least the second patient, suffered had its chief impact just before the child was beginning to form discriminating boundaries between the inner and outer worlds. From this sequence, we can infer that the transitional phenomenon, rather than fusion and secondary narcissism, is the intermediary pathway between the inner and outer worlds and the means of constructing external reality.

I repeat Freud's (1900) early caveat that it may be untenable to extrapolate from the study of psychopathology hypotheses about normal development. Nevertheless, he himself proved how useful this method can be, especially in his discussion of the psychology of dreaming. Granted that simply because these patients, the second patient in particular, indicated that they did not fuse during their infancy, we cannot generalize from their psychopathology, as Freud stated. Still, if during treatment, the developmental process is once again set in motion and symbiotic merger occurs, it behooves us to try to determine just where this happens in the developmental timetable.

In this instance, the second patient had already begun to feel she was an individual in her own right, having developed some aggressiveness and self-esteem prior to incorporating my values, beliefs, and attitudes. Merging seems to represent an advance in and enhancement of the individuating process. She then regressed to a pathological state of fusion in the transference, viewing me as the exploitative, controlling, destructive mother who used her as a transitional object. This feeling state had never been experienced before the transference regression in treatment. In fact, it was created by the therapeutic relationship. She stressed that I was fusing with her; she was not fusing with me—in fact, she was trying to escape my pursuit of her. She finally succeeded in maintaining separation by constructing a paranoid defense.

CONCLUSION

As Beatrice recognizes, symbiosis and fusion are complex processes that cannot be conceptualized on a simplistic basis as to whether they are defensive constellations, aspects of normal development, or manifestations of defective emotional development because of the impact of psychic trauma. To place such processes at the primitive end of the developmental spectrum is conceptually inconsistent and is not borne out by clinical data.

The nature of trauma is a subject that requires considerable exploration. We have moved away from Freud's (1905) early formulations of sexual trauma as the chief psychological etiological factor in the production of psychopathology. Although today we are faced with more and more examples of childhood sexual abuse, we are learning that there are many factors besides disruptive sexual assault that are responsible for the damaging effects of these early encounters.

The interaction between the caretaking adult and child can be considered from many perspectives. The axis that both Beatrice and I have been examining concerns the fusion or lack of fusion between parent and infant. The mothers I have been discussing treated their daughters as their transitional objects. They used them to maintain control of inner disruption, to soothe themselves so that they could maintain a tenuous connection with the external world. As a result, the infant does not develop a cohesive self-representation and a sense of aliveness, a true self with discrete boundaries.

The patients constructed characteristic defensive adaptations in response to being controlled and used as their mothers' pacifiers. They suffused the environment with their inner disruption—that is, they created external chaos and thereby gained relief from inner tension. This was especially true of the first patient. The second patient recapitulated the mother-infant relationship in her dealings with me. Her mother used her as a nonhuman object to support her narcissistic defenses. However, this patient, too, lived calmly in a chaotic world. Her professional life was highlighted by a continuous series of crises that she dealt with efficiently and calmly, but she always maintained her distance and never permitted herself to develop feelings about or reactions to her surroundings. In this instance, her attitude was advantageous because, as just about the only person who kept sane in a mad world, she could be effective and get the job done.

The second patient, in particular, illustrated a reversal of roles: she reacted to her environment as her mother had related to her. At the same time she continued the infantile relationship in which she was treated as a transitional object in current object relations. This repetition became the chief manifestation of her psychopathology and was so painful that it motivated her to seek treatment. She saw her numerous affairs as leading nowhere. By contrast, the first patient did not seem to be obviously repeating early infantile relationships with external objects. Perhaps, in subtle ways, she was, but the overriding situation was a reversal: using the world in the way she had been used. Consequently, the idea of treatment was as alien as her awareness of other people's feelings and needs.

This reversal of the early relationship, even though it is a defensive adaptation, suggests that the patient has been able to effect a fusion in adult life, something she was unable to do in early infancy. It is, however, a pathological state of fusion. The second patient indicated that in her work she often took segments of her environment and certain external objects, and treated them as if they were her possessions, as parts of herself. She then treated them mercilessly to gain her own ends. In treatment, when she was incorporating my values, the situation was different, in that she believed she was gaining something valuable instead of manipulating me. As stated, this was a new experience, which first occurred during treatment. Again, I believe this type of fusion was closer to that seen in normal development after some degree of individuation has occurred and ego boundaries are somewhat consolidated.

These conceptual reflections could be significant for our understanding of symbiotic psychosis in children, as described by Mahler (1952) and others. Child psychiatrists and social workers in residential treatment centers have reported data that do not support the thesis that these children are locked in a symbiotic fusion. Rather, the mother's propensity not to let the infant separate from her is prominent, but the reverse is not usually the case. In fact, I have been presented with examples that clearly indicate that these children have an incapacity to incorporate elements of the external world and make them parts of themselves, although they may demand the constant presence of the nurturing caretaking source. *In fact, it is this inability to survive without the actual presence of the mother that signifies that the child cannot fuse with her.* Apparently these children have not achieved the capacity for object constancy (Fraiberg, 1969); they cannot form and hold a mental representation without the reinforcement of the external object (Giovacchini, 1979). To fuse requires the establishment of an internal object representation so that the self representation can merge with it. In these cases, the mother in turn needs to be with her child at times when she feels agitated. However, she has more defenses available and can find substitute objects or even withdraw from her child as the child becomes inadequate to serve as an effective transitional object because of the intensity of the mother's painful and disruptive feelings.

As mentioned earlier, there are different types of infantile traumatic relations, which lead to various forms of psychopathology. I have described character defects that basically prevent patients from forming intimate relations because they have been raised as transitional objects. There are other types of mother-infant fusion, usually more primitive mergers in which the mother destructively fuses with her child, using her son or daughter as the receptacle for the hated parts of the self. This situation has been written about more frequently, especially by Melanie Klein (1946). These children go through life being panicked about fusing, about getting close to anyone, often using schizoid defenses to keep their emotional distance. In contrast, the patients I have described are not usually anxious. They are simply incapable of merging because of a developmental deficit. They have considerable rage, as my second patient did. But, with my patient, it first surfaced in treatment as she relived the early traumatic relationship with me.

These studies of psychopathology have implications for technique and the theory of emotional development. I do not wish to pursue treatment issues here since I cover this topic extensively elsewhere (Giovacchini, 1984). It suffices to point out that we are faced with transference reactions and elements of the repetition compulsion that have to be understood in terms of the unique features of infantile traumatic relationships. These aspects are different from what we are accustomed to in our usual treatment of patients. If we do not recognize these patients' needs to treat us as transitional objects or how angry they are at us for feeling we have reacted to them in a nonhuman fashion, then we are likely to have disruptive countertransference reactions, which could easily lead to impasses that eventually wreck the treatment.

With regard to emotional development, Winnicott's concept of the transitional situation gains much greater prominence. As structuralization takes place, from the prementational phase to beginning mentation, the child gradually becomes aware of the existence of a space that is separate from the self. This is accomplished by the construction of a transitional space, transitional in that the child perceives it as part of the inner world, whereas the adult sees it as a segment of the external world of reality. Objects within this transitional space are transitional objects, which children use to maintain control of inner tensions and to soothe themselves. Gradually, as children feel increasingly secure that tensions will be calmed and needs met, they are able to relinquish control over some of the objects in the transitional space and to begin to recognize them in their own right rather than as just the servants of their needs. Winnicott (1968) wrote about the use of an object as part of the process of relinquishing control over it as it moved from the transitional space into the outer world. Passing through the transitional space signifies the beginning of the recognition of the outer world and the establishment of object relations, or, at least, part object relations.

This process of emerging individuation does not require fusion mechanisms, but symbiotic attachments occur later as external objects become further differentiated. With increasing security that needs will be met and the growth of the sense of trust and confidence, children can allow themselves to become dependent and relax their ego boundaries in a fusion state, without feeling threatened or vulnerable. Disturbance of the earlier transitional phase will make the passage of objects from the transitional space into the external world traumatic and create disturbances in the establishment of symbiotic object relations.

Further examination of developmental factors and revision of concepts about emotional growth are important endeavors for the clinician. For the most part, we are dealing with severely disturbed patients who fill their world with misery. Knowing about the adaptive significance of their despair and how they are repeating dehumanizing experiences in their current life may enable us through our understanding and survival to help direct the developmental process in the right direction. Of course, we have to know what that direction is and where Narcissus enters the picture.

REFERENCES

Balint, M. (1957). *Problems of Human Pleasure and Behavior.* London: Hogarth Press.
Boyer, L. B., & Giovacchini, P. L. (1967). *Psychoanalytic Treatment of Schizophrenia and Characterological Disorders.* New York: Aronson.
Brazelton, T. B. (1963). The early mother-infant adjustment. *Pediat.* 32:931–938.
Emde, R. N., & Robinson, J. (1984). The first two months: Recent research in developmental psychobiology and the changing view of the newborn. *Basic Handbook of Child Psychiatry,* ed. J. Noshpitz & J. Call. New York: Basic Books.
Federn, P. (1952). *Ego Psychology and the Psychoses.* New York: Basic Books.
Feinsilver, D. (1980). Transitional relatedness and containment in the treatment of a chronic schizophrenic patient. *Int. Rev. Psychoanal.* 7:309–318.
—— (1983). Reality, transitional relatedness and containment in the borderline. *Contemp. Psychoanal.* 19:537–568.
Fraiberg, S. (1969). Libidinal object constancy and object representation. *Psychoanal. Study Child* 24:9–47.
Freedman, D. G. (1971). Genetic influences on development of behavior. In *Normal and Abnormal Development of Behavior,* ed. G. B. A. Stoelinga & J. J. Van der Werf Ten Bosch. Leiden: Leiden Univ. Press.
Freud, S. (1900). The interpretation of dreams. *Standard Edition* 4 & 5.
—— (1905). Three essays on the theory of sexuality. *Standard Edition* 7:255–268.
—— (1914). On narcissism: An introduction. *Standard Edition* 14:67–102.
—— (1916–1917). Introductory lectures on psycho-analysis. *Standard Edition* 15 & 16.
—— (1920). Beyond the pleasure principle. *Standard Edition* 18:3–66.
Giovacchini, P. L. (1977). A critique of Kohut's theory of narcissism. *Adolescent Psychiatry,* Vol.5, ed. S. Feinstein & P. Giovacchini. Chicago: Univ. Chicago Press. pp. 213–235.
—— (1979). *Treatment of Primitive Mental States.* New York: Aronson.
—— (1984). *Psychoanalysis of Character Disorders and Defensive Adaptations.* New York: Aronson.
—— Boyer L. B. (1983). *Technical Factors in the Treatment of the Severely Disturbed Patient.* New York: Aronson.
Glover, E. (1930). Grades of ego-differentiation. *Int. J. Psycho-anal.* 11:1–11.
Hartmann, H. (1939). *Ego Psychology and the Process of Adaptation.* New York: Int. Univ. Press, 1958.
Herrick, E. J. (1956). *The Evolution of Human Nature.* Austin: Univ. Texas Press.
Klaus, M., & Kennell, J. (1982). *Parent-Infant Bonding.* St. Louis: Mosby.
Klein, M. (1946). Notes on some schizoid mechanisms. *Int. J. Psychoanal.* 27:99–110.
Langs, R. (1982). *Psychotherapy: A Basic Text.* New York: Aronson.
Mahler, M. S. (1952). On child psychosis and schizophrenia: Autistic and symbiotic infantile psychoses. *Psychoanal. Study Child* 17:286–305.
—— (1972). A study of the separation-individuation process and its possible application to borderline phenomena in the psychoanalytic situation. *Psychoanal. Study Child* 26:403–424.
Modell, A. (1968). *Object Love and Reality.* New York: Int. Univ. Press.
Piaget, J. (1937). *The Construction of Reality in the Child.* New York: Basic Books, 1954.
Searles, H. (1976). Transitional phenomena and therapeutic symbiosis. *Int. J. Psychoanal. Psychother.* 5:145–204.
Tustin, F. (1981). *Autistic States in Children* London: Routledge & Kegan Paul.
Winnicott, D. W. (1953). Transitional objects and transitional phenomena. In *Collected*

Papers: Through Pediatrics to Psychoanalysis. New York: Basic Books, 1975, pp. 229–242.

——— (1956). Primary maternal preoccupation. In *Collected Papers: Through Pediatrics to Psychoanalysis.* New York: Basic Books, 1975, pp. 300–306.

——— (1960). Ego distortion in terms of true and false self. In *The Maturational Processes and the Facilitating Environment.* New York: Int. Univ. Press, 1965, pp. 140–152.

——— (1968). The use of an object and relating through identifications. In *Playing and Reality.* London: Tavistock, 1971, pp. 86–95.

III
CLINICAL TOPICS

16/
A Proposed Revision of the Psychoanalytic Concept of the Death Instinct
James S. Grotstein, M.D.

Whereas Freud emphasized two aspects of the death instinct—the drift of the organic to the inorganic state and the deflection of its force from the self to the outside world—Melanie Klein saw it as only destructive and conceptualized envy as its prime mental expression. This contribution suggests that the death instinct is spawned by the inherent preconception of death and danger, and that it is responsible for experiencing and expressing signal alarm anxiety about the danger of predators and other potential disasters. In this view, then, it is an adaptive, protective, life-supporting agency. Like the life instinct, the death instinct is seen as a semiotic signifier of the signified dangers inside and out.

CHANGING VIEWS OF THE DEATH INSTINCT

The concept of the death instinct has had a curious history in psychoanalysis. It was first proposed by Freud in 1920, allegedly due to the personal impact of World War I and his mouth cancer (Jones, 1955), although Hamilton (1976) has suggested other factors in Freud's life such as the death of his brother Julius. In any case, Freud may have been constrained to assign greater importance than before to destructiveness and/or aggression in his instinct theory, a trend adumbrated in *Mourning and Melancholia* (Freud, 1917).

Although Freud (1905) originally viewed destructiveness (in association with sadism) as a "component instinct" of the sexual instinct, he also stated, "It may be assumed that the impulses of cruelty arise from sources which are in fact independent of sexuality, but may become united with it at an early stage" (p. 193). Freud associated these independent sources to the self-preservative instincts and was later to link them with the instinct for mastery. When the independence of the ego's self-preservative instincts (instincts for mastery) was abrogated by Freud's theory of narcissism (1914), the independence of a destructive instinct had to await Freud's *Beyond the Pleasure Principle* (1920).

In that monumental work and in *Civilization and Its Discontent* Freud (1930) postulated an instinct independent of and earlier than the sexual instinct governed by the pleasure principle—a death instinct dominated by the constancy principle. Freud (1920) stated, "*It seems, then, that an instinct is an urge inherent in organic life to restore an earlier state of things* which the living entity has been obliged to abandon under the pressure of external disturbing forces; that is, it is a kind of organic elasticity, or, to put it another way, the expression of the inertia inherent in organic life" (p. 36). He linked the instinctual force behind this repetitive tendency with the death instinct, as the agency that restores the state of constancy.

It is important to note that Freud's conception of the death instinct is not so much one of a primary instinct of self-assertive aggressiveness as a principle of gratuitous destructiveness toward the organism itself. In his words:

> The hypothesis of self-preservative instincts, such as we attribute to all living beings, stands in marked opposition to the idea that instinctual life as a whole serves to bring about death. Seen in this light, the theoretical importance of the instincts of self-preservation, of self-assertion, and of mastery greatly diminishes. They are component instincts whose function it is to assure that the organism shall follow its own path to death, and to ward off any possible way of returning to inorganic existence other than those which are imminent in the organism itself [1920, p. 39].

The death instinct thus seems, to have had two distinct components in Freud's opinion: (1) a notion of biological entropy, with a drift from a higher state of vital energy to a lower one of death (the inorganic); and (2) destructiveness deflected outward as aggression. The latter aspect seems implicated by Freud as a defense against the emergence of the certainty of death within the organism as a result of the primary experience of this instinct.

The death instinct seems to have been the one theory Freud did not demand that his followers accept. He presented it almost diffidently, and this contribution has oftentimes been called biological mysticism rather than sound psychology or metapsychology. Ultimately, only a few were to accept it, particularly Melanie Klein (1933), Menninger (1938), Ostow (1958), and Eissler (1971). Some analysts rejected it altogether and considered aggression secondary to libidinal frustration (see Fenichel, 1945). Yet, most analysts today, particularly since the contributions of Hartmann, Kris, and Loewenstein (1949) and Jacobson (1950, 1964), do believe there is an aggressive instinct, although not one that is a death instinct. Klein and her followers have been the only major school to embrace the concept of a death instinct and extend it even beyond Freud's original conception.

Today, then, psychoanalysts generally seem to accept the instinctual nature of aggression. The ego psychologists in particular gave considerable regard to the function of aggression (Hartmann, 1939; Rapaport, 1958). Hartmann, et al. (1949) reformulated the theory of aggression, separating it from the biological mysticism of Freud's death instinct and realigning it with the vicissitudes of the libidinal instinct (repression, reversal into the opposite, turning around upon the subject, and sublimation). They further stipulated that aggression is the underlying force in all ego defense mechanisms, which differ mainly in terms of the degree of their neutralization. In sum they saw aggression as being equivalent in drive status to libido; it, like libido, is subject to a third force, neutralization, as well as a fourth force, instinctual fusion.

Recently, however, Kohut (1971, 1977) and the school of self psychology have reopened a dormant chapter in the history of analytic instinctual theory. For years, Fairbairn (1940, 1941, 1943, 1944, 1946, 1949, 1951) tried to do away with the separate status of the id and the ego. Instead he saw the id as an urgent aspect of the ego—one that in the trauma of infantile experience had been phenomenologically split off as unacceptable because of an unempathic environment. Aggression, in his view, was non-instinctual and secondary to libidinal frustration. At the utmost, in any case, he believed that instinctual urges were central to the ego and indivisible from it. Kohut has embraced this aspect of Fairbairn's conceptions virtually intact—with no modifications that I am aware of.

Kleinian Formulations

The Kleinians alone today seem to be adherents of the death instinct. Although their general views of aggression do not differ in any large measure from those of ego psychology and classical analysis, their theoretical and clinical use of the death instinct goes much farther and deeper. It is important to note that their conception of the death instinct is significantly different from Freud's insofar as they postulate an instinct of primary, inherent destructiveness, whereas Freud postulated that aggressiveness toward the external world was a defense against the operation of the death instinct on the self. There is also a relation to Fairbairn and Kohut insofar as Klein rarely spoke of an id in her later work.

I believe it is close to the truth to state that Klein—like Fairbairn, and Kohut considerably later—all but eliminated the differences between the ego and the id. Instead, she saw the death instinct as an inherent capacity of the primitive infantile ego to confront the experience of frustration. Yet she also saw the death instinct as one of the principal causes of that frustration. Klein first specifically mentioned the death instinct in "The Early Development of Conscience in the Child" (1933), but she had emphasized the psychological impact of destructiveness from the very beginning of her work (see Klein, 1921). Although she hinted that the death instinct had some adaptive purpose for the infant's survival, she nevertheless concluded that the end result of its use was the creation of even more persecutory objects, thereby paradoxically transforming the death instinct into a maladaptive defense. In her view, during the paranoid-schizoid position, infants project the death instinct outwards onto and into objects in order to diminish the pressure of experience. Objects are thereby transformed into persecutory objects. In the depressive position, on the other hand, infants must reconcile this projection of destructiveness into their objects and reown these feelings in an effort to "cleanse" the portrait of the object via reparation. The recall of destructiveness from the object back to the self is accompanied by amnesty from the now friendly object, which then helps the infant to sublimate his or her destructiveness.

Klein's formulations about the importance of destructiveness owe much to Abraham (1924), who, in establishing the pregenital autoerotic stages of development, had assigned parallel stages of object relations development to them along a dual-instinct track and in a biphasic mode. In other words, he had established the active and passive relationship of the infantile ego to its objects in each zonal stage of development according to the libidinal and destructive modes. He formulated the concept of a preambivalent stage, which was abrupted by the experience of teething and which eventuated in the infantile fantasy of cannibalistic anxiety.[1]

Klein accepted Abraham's denotations of aggression in the pregenital phases, but she differed with him by postulating that there was no preambivalent phase. Instead, she hypothesized that destructiveness exists from the very beginning (i.e., in the oral sucking phase preceding the oral biting phase). From this perspective, she developed her conceptions of greed and envy. Greed was a derivative of her idea of destructiveness by sucking. The infants' fantasy was that, because of an excessive sense of neediness, they would scoop out mother's breasts and incorporate them for themselves. In this case, the destructiveness was incidental and not

---

[1] The term "fantasy" is used here and elsewhere in the Kleinian sense of unconscious phantasy.

purposeful. Klein's (1957) formulation of envy was another matter. She began to think of envy as the mental representation of the death instinct, and she believed furthermore that all infants experience envy toward the breast and/or mother's derivative capacity to be nurturing and caretaking.

Klein's delineation of the destructiveness of greed and envy toward the breast inaugurated a significant new trend in psychoanalytic psychology. Before this, psychoanalytic formulations, even Abraham's pregential ones, had been couched in terms of infantile sexuality. The phenomenon of greed was rarely mentioned, and envy had been associated only with the small child's feelings of intimidation by the patriarchal penis (Freud, 1908). Klein redirected psychoanalysis away from an infantile sexual theory, inspired as it had been by a genital theory, to a nutritional theory, which Freud (1905) himself had adumbrated. Freud's statement was to the effect that infants experience disappointment at being deprived of the nurturing breast and find substitute sexual satisfaction with the autoerotic cathexis of their own bodies, thereby implying that infantile sexuality is secondary and defensive to the loss of the breast. Also implied is that the infantile sexuality is a defense, whereas infantile nurture is primary. This conception was solidly established by Klein and later elaborated by Fairbairn (1952), Winnicott (1958, 1965), and Balint (1959, 1968). Bowlby (1969) furthered the concept of infantile mental life as one of attachment behavior, and Kohut (1971, 1977) has generalized this whole trend in his concept of the selfobject—a notion that predicates that the boundary of the infant's self transcends the body boundary to include the nurturing object, who, during development, contains the infant's self functions, such as soothing, state regulation, self-esteem, etc.

Thus, Klein created a psychoanalytic psychology that reversed patriarchal hegemony in favor of a matriarchal one. She demonstrated that greed and envy were destructive manifestations of the libidinal and death instincts respectively, which attacked the maternal breast in the infant's fantasies. Klein (1933) also discovered that the child's conscience begins much earlier than Freud had thought and, consequenty, so does the Oedipus complex (which Klein posited as beginning in the oral-sadistic phase of development). In Klein's view, infants have an inborn knowledge of intercourse and are therefore predisposed to feeling rivalry toward anyone who interferes with their possession of the breast/mother. This rivalry becomes the forum in which self-assertion undergoes its fateful baptism. Thus, the first "oedipal" rival is the bad mother, who has been split off by the infant from the good mother because of frustration and made bad through projective identification. This bad mother then becomes the one who took the good mother away, because it could not be the good mother herself who went away on her own.

Klein then posited that infants have aggressive and exploratory fantasies in which they invade mother's insides to explore and destroy mother's internal (unborn) babies and father's penis (which is believed to be inside mother along with the internal babies). This last fantasy, which closely resembles the ancient Grecian myth of the labyrinth, was thought by Klein to arise from the infant's splitting off its greed and projecting it into mother. Then, once this greed is installed in mother, and under the domination of the early oedipal complex, the greedy infant aggressively introjects father's penis.

The intruding third party later becomes father and his penis and/or a sibling. A particular aspect of this disturbing thirdness is the phenomenon of envy, the infant's inborn hatred of being dependent. One must remember that Klein, in formulating the paranoid-schizoid position, gave metapsychological statehood to a stage of development that is at first entirely omnipotent. The schizoid mechanisms are like seraphim guarding the sanctity of omnipotence. They include splitting, projective identification, magic omnipotent denial, and idealization. Mother's nurture may thus at first be conceived by infants as maintaining their omnipotence rather than feeding their reality self. A breach in the caretaking function—caused, for instance, by mother's absence or delay in dealing with the infant's distress—makes the infant aware of his or her realistic helplessness and dependence on mother's caretaking and tension-relieving functions.

Reality, according to Klein, interferes with the infant's omnipotence and therefore precipitates envy, an affective denotation of rage and protest against mother for taking away the infant's omnipotence in order (in fantasy) to possess it for herself or to bestow it on those whom she prefers, such as father's penis or other siblings—particularly internal or unborn siblings. The infant forms a notion of unborn siblings as the preferred ones—those who are so good and so loved that they do not have to be born and experience frustration. Instead, they reside forever inside mother's womb.

The goodness of mother's breasts and of her capacity to take care of the infant thus inaugurates the feeling of envy and releases the destructiveness of the death instinct toward the breasts. This destructiveness toward the breasts creates, through splitting and projective identification, at least two different images of the maternal breast object: (1) a breast damaged by the hostile attacks, which is then identified with as an empty or destroyed aspect of oneself, and (2) a breast that is now fused and confused with the infant's envious destructiveness and is then internalized as a superego breast, which is experienced as being enviously critical, denigrating, and superior. Paradoxically, both the breast installed in the ego *and* the ego identified with it are attacked, corresponding to Freud's (1917) melancholia paradigm. The paradox is that the original unitary beast, having become frustrating, is split into two separate breast images initially, and the bad breast is then subjected to a further splitting between a *damaged* and a *damaging* breast; thus, paradoxically, one bad breast attacks another. Freud (1917) suggested this phenomenon when he posited a gradient in the melancholic's ego whereby an attacking object with an ego identified with it (ego ideal) attacked a damaged aspect of the object installed in the ego. The good object seems to be absent in the melancholic, or pulled into the victimized aura of the bad object, or, because of the transformation envy conveys upon a good object, it may become a victimizing object as well as a victimized object.

All in all, Klein's conception was of the early nurture-seeking infant attempting to minimize and master the sense of danger implicit in frustration by a needed object by utilizing fantasy. Hers was therefore an ego psychology employing primary process to minimize anxiety, only to create new anxiety as the result of these fantasies. The infant had to distribute the accumulation of instinctual danger through splitting and projective identification, a notion first employed by Freud (1920). Klein associated the development of a sense of reality with the attainment of the depressive position; she did not account for a sense of reality in the paranoid-schizoid position except as an intrusive force inaugurating fantasies.

Bion's Contribution

Bion (1958, 1959a) took up this slack in Kleinian theory by recognizing the importance of reality as well as fantasy in the infant's instinctual life. He was thus able to offer two significant contributions in regard to the infant's instinctual life. First, he proposed the theory of the *container* and the *contained*. In his view, infants realistically need the functioning of an external maternal container which is able to absorb and translate their cries and screams into meaningful communications important for their welfare. Bion's conception of the container and the contained corresponds to a mirroring function—also discussed by Lacan (1949), Winnicott (1952), and much later Kohut (1971, 1977).

Bion, however, added what I have come to think of as a prism or translating function. I use the term "prism" insofar as it receives a beam of light and refracts it into the various colors and hues of the spectrum (differentiating or sorting function) and therefore puts these differentiated elements into a gradient or a hierarchy of importance for operational use. Among the many meanings of the container and contained, the one that I should like to single out here is its communicative function.

Bion's conception of the container and the contained raises the infant's envious cries to the semiotic level of significance by virtue of there being a container to translate the infants messages. Thus, rage can be transformed by a suitable container into a message about urgent insecurity. In brief synoptic form: the infant is frustrated because of neglect and exeriences the irruption of feelings of being endangered. Mother, who has the capacity to give tension relief, is, by not being there, put into a category of an empty container and is then attacked. Thus, the infant's rage is not only a communication to mother as a distress signal but also the demonstration of an affective attitude toward mother for frustrating him or her. In the latter case, it is an attempt at rectification, a phenomenon I shall deal with later. Not only must the maternal container deal with the infant's physiological and secondarily psychological frustration, but it must also deal with the infant's affective responses to having been frustrated—envy.

Bion's second relevant contribution concerns the inherent preconception. Following Plato and Kant, Bion (1962, 1963, 1967) believed that thoughts are pure forms of things-in-themselves, which exist before there is someone to think them. He called these "thoughts without a thinker." They correspond to inherent preconceptions that each infant brings as his or her phylogentically honed bundle of "knowledge" (corresponding to DNA "knowledge"). Thus, for example, in lower species, the mouse "knows" the cat even before it has been properly introduced by experience. Bion did not explore this innovative idea of his beyond merely stating it and linking it to his grid. For example, he saw the experience of hunger as mobilizing the inherent preconception of something like a breast, which scans the external environment for its counterpart—realization—to mate with and, after successfully doing so, forms a conception of it, which then is internalized as a secondary preconception awaiting the next realization, etc.

Bion's idea of inherent preconceptions offers a new means of theorizing about aggression generally and about the death instinct particularly. Freud (1939) himself hinted at the idea of inherent preconceptions when he talked about the inheritability of the Oedipus complex and the unconscious memory of the primal horde that killed the primal father. Jung (1917) also conceived of racial memory.

In introducing this theme, I must call attention to my impression that psychoanalytic theory has historically shifted back and forth between rationalism and empiricism. Freud's first theory of psychoanalysis was one of a traumatic external reality that underwent amnesia. As such, it was an empirical theory of psychopathology, involving a tabula rasa or blank screen of innocent surprise to the unsuspected traumatic event. Freud's second theory of psychoanalysis, however, was a rationalistic philosophy—one in which the infant's biologically instinctual makeup provided an infantile psychosexuality that did indeed "prepare" the infant for trauma; this trauma was eroticized and then repressed.

The subsequent history of psychoanalytic theory has in the main been rationalistic, thanks to Freud's invocation of the biological principle. Nevertheless, in giving birth to dynamic psychology and psychiatry, psychoanalysis seems to have fostered an inadvertent return to the empirical mode of thinking: once again, the patient's problems are thought to be due to a bad external environment. Even classical analysts seem to accept this verdict more and more, although at the same time they have held onto the contribution of the instincts. Ego psychology, with its adaptive principle and idea of an average expectable environment, seems to have become more empirical even though it has never formally abandoned its allegiance to the biological infrastructure of psychoanalysis (Hartmann, 1939; Erikson, 1959). Self psychology, on the other hand, *does* seem to be abandoning its allegiance to the biological principle (Kohut, 1971, 1977).

Recent Contributions to the Concept of Aggression

Ostow (1958) invokes a biological approach to justify the existence of the death instinct. He states, "I should like to propose that death instincts in the human correspond to . . . our homologous width, the interspecific instincts of lower animals, predatory and counter-predatory, though death instincts are directed at human objects" (p. 5). Ostow's view is very close to my own insofar as he invokes the biological principle, not of primary destructiveness per se, but of destructiveness with a *purpose,* the protection of the self in the prey-predator series. Thus, aggression is invoked when the organism needs to know who the prey is toward whom aggression must be expended; at the same time, the prey must know who its predator is so that aggression can be employed to combat that predator or to escape from it. Ostow adds, "Sub-human animals suspend their predatory (encounter-predatory) instincts in intra-species behavior only with the aid of inhibitions. . . . I suggest that primitive interspecific tendencies constitute death instinct in man. These tendencies are normally controlled by the libidinization of their techniques, but occasionally the primary destructive tendency breaks through" (p. 16).

Ostow also links the death instinct with the second law of thermodynamics, the drift toward entropy. In his view, the organism's need to avoid the predator and to forage for the prey makes a virtue of necessity in complying with this law. As he states:

> It seems to me that it is the second law which requires that the degradation processes taking place in each living organism be compensated by the continual intake of sources of high grade (low entropy) energy. It is therefore in obedience to this law that foraging and feeding (and defense) are necessary. Since these are the primary expressions of the death instinct, we may say

that the death instinct is the response of living creatures to the demands of the second law, demands which they can never completely satisfy, but merely attenuate and defer by hastening the disintegration of other forms of life [p. 14].

From a different perspective, Katan (1966) contends that Freud's concept of the nirvana principle represents the regressive tendency to return to the state existing at the beginning of life, whereas the death instinct has a completely different goal, namely, to undo the source of life. He states, "We may express this as follows: the reality principle, as a result of resisting the nirvana principle, has a conflict with the pleasure principle on its hands" (pp. 101–102). Thus, Katan seems both to reavow a belief in the death instinct and to accredit the importance of the nirvana principle as the principal force in regression and the development of psychosis, one which must be resisted by the reality principle.

Rosenfeld (1971) has linked the life and death instincts to the problem of narcissism. He especially highlights the importance of fusion and defusion between the life and death instincts. In his view:

> . . . it is the destructive aspect of the death instinct which is active in paralyzing, or psychically killing, the libidinal parts of the self derived from the life instinct. I therefore think that it is not possible to observe an unfused death instinct in the clinical situation. . . . Some of these destructive states cannot be described as defusions because they are really pathological fusions, in which the psychic structure dominated by a destructive part of the self succeeds in imprisoning and overpowering the libidinal self, which is completely unable to oppose the destructive process. . . . It seems that certain omnipotent, narcissistic states are dominated by the most violent destructive process, so that the libidinal self is almost completely absent or lost. Clinically it is therefore essential to find access to the libidinal dependent self, which can mitigate the destructive impulses [p. 177].

Thus, in narcissistic disorders, according to Rosenfeld, the life and death instincts are fused, but the death instinct predominates. It is necessary to revive the libidinal aspect of the self so as to reverse subordination to the death instinct.

Eissler (1971) makes an interesting point, which is contrary to Freud's conception that the death instinct is mitigated by the development of civilization. Eissler believes that the death instinct emerges only with civilization. As he puts it, "It may be that the first murder constituted a great discovery: so long as man saw in his fellow man only a mirror image, he was unable to kill what was, after all, his own image. . . . If this construction should prove to be correct, it . . . would show that a higher development of ego structure does not necessarily lead to a pacification of aggressive-destructive manifestations; it may even lead to their intensification" (p. 75).

More recently, Parens (1979), through longitudinal clinical research on infants developing into latency, has evolved a clinically based theory of aggression, which supplants a theory of a death instinct with an epigenetic view of aggression corresponding to Mahler's (1968) schema for libidinal development. He summarizes his findings as follows:

> In the order in which these manifestations of aggression emerge into birth, we name them (1) *the unpleasure-related discharges of destructiveness,* (2) *the nonaffective discharge of destructiveness,* (3) *the nondestructive discharge of aggression,* and (4) *the pleasure-related discharge of destructiveness.* . . . The category [that] was so striking in our children's behavior—*nondestructive aggressive discharges*—describes a trend in the aggressive drive, the aim of which is to assert the self upon, control, and master both self and environment. In this trend we saw no aim to destroy structure. On the other hand, nonaffective destructive discharges (such as sucking and chewing) do evidence a trend deriving from *prey aggression,* a condition loosely demonstrated in carnivores, which is not, in origin, influenced by an affective state, and the aim of which is destruction of structure for the purpose of self-preservation [pp. 4–5].

At the beginning of separation-individuation, in the differentiation and practicing subphases, Parens indicates: "Hand-and-hand with maturation in ego and libido, we found a striking biological upsurge in the aggressive drive which showed itself in the three categories of manifested aggression already evident in the infants" (p. 9)—i.e., unpleasure-related discharges, nonaffective discharges, and nondestructive discharges. Parens connects this upsurge of aggression in the five-month hatching period with a concomitant maturation of the sensorimotor organization, which can now accommodate the toddler's greater locomotive efforts.

All in all, Parens seems to find that aggression is a normal, adaptive ego response in the development of self-assertiveness. He sees destructive aggression, particularly libidinized aggression, as secondary to environmental failures of nurture. Of key importance for this presentation, however, is Parens's emphasis on prey-predator anxiety in the infant, a thesis central to my conception of the death instinct.

A recent *Psychoanalytic Inquiry* issue offers additional perspectives on aggression. Rochlin (1982) restates the relationship between aggression and narcissism, whereas Gould (1982) stresses that aggression is the result of a reaction to interactions between the individual and the environment, so that it alters in different developmental phases and varies with the status of attachment. Freedman (1982), from his clinical research on blind children, concludes that drives cannot be separated from the influences of the environment. He thus seems to recommend a substantial alteration of the psychoanalytic theory of instincts. On the other hand, Ginsburg (1982) underlines multiple intersecting variables in his consideration of innate, gene-determined aggressive behavior. He offers a dual-track theory of aggressive display by emphasizing the importance of genetic and environmental factors, although he relates the latter to the "releasing" of the former.

In the same issue, Jaffe (1982) redefines the difference between instinct and drive. He proposes that the biological and evolutionary basis of the aggressive drive can be associated with the life-preserving, species-preserving, sexual and nutritional instincts, thereby bypassing the need for the conception of a death instinct. He suggests reserving the term "instinct" for "classes of functions, namely, the self-preservative and the species-preservative, represented respectively by the nutritional and reproductive functions. The drives can then be regarded as special components of the instincts, modifiable by learning and adaptive to special environmental demands. Behaviors vary in meeting the manifold pressures of drive adaptations in the course of carrying out the functions of the instincts and in response to environmental parameters" (p. 91). Thus, Jaffe seems to conclude that aggression is both constructive and destructive. It is not a primal instinct in the sense of a class of functions, but *is* nevertheless inevitable, innate, and constantly operative. As a drive, however, it is subject to modification and variability with learning experiences.

THE DEATH INSTINCT AND SYMMETRICAL LOGIC

Matte Blanco (1973) has submitted the death instinct to the unique scrutiny of a philosophical approach based on the antinomies of Hegelian dialectic, especially as applied to his own mathematical conception of the contrast between the symmetrical logic of the unconscious and the asymmetrical or bivalent (Aristotelian) logic of consciousness. In Matte Blanco's (1975) conception of the bilogical mind, one domain—the unconscious—dwells in the time-space continuum of infinity and is therefore symmetrical (no point of impact, no registration of experience). The other domain—that of consciousness—occupies time in space (with impact, temporal sequence, spatial measurement, and other qualities designating the properties of the third dimension of experience) it is thus a progressively asymmetrical domain. The antinomies Matte Blanco presents are:

First antinomy: . . . (a) life tends toward its conservation; (b) life tends toward its destruction. . . .
Second antinomy: (a) the destruction of life is at life's service; (b) life is at the service of the destruction of life. . . .
Third antinomy: (a) life evolves in the form of life movements; (b) life evolves toward the extinction (rest) of life movement. . . .
Fourth antinomy: Life is equal to death [p. 469].

According to Matte Blanco, the first three antinomies are Hegelian ones, but the last is a logical antinomy in the most rigorous sense of the word." He adds, however, "we are dealing with an *antinomy of the bi-valent logical system;* instead, *it is not so in the system of the symmetrical logic or the analytic logic. This is the central problem; unless we clear our ideas on the subject it will not be possible . . . to understand anything about the so-called death instinct.*" (p. 459). In the end, he believes, "all four antinomies are merely one: *life is equal to death*" (p. 459).

In order to understand Matte Blanco's logical leap, one must be familiar with his monograph *The Unconscious as Infinite Sets* (1975). If two qualities differ from each other as antinomies, they nevertheless belong to a series of infinite sets beyond the level of their own classification which can unite them. For instance, men and women differ but are united by a higher, species classification of humanness. I therefore believe Matte Blanco is stating that the death instinct is that aspect of life which *ap*poses life, *op*poses life, and is part of life. And, especially, death is that aspect of life relevant to symmetrical logic—that is, the logic of infinity, of boundarylessness, of the zero dimension (see Grotstein, 1978).

Perhaps another way to emphasize Matte Blanco's profound but recondite point is to analogize to Bion's (1962, 1963) conception of the grid. Here a definitory hypothesis of vertical column 1 (for instance, a spontaneous experience of a feeling) is "defined" by its negation in column 2, much like a figure-ground differentiation. In other words, death contrasts with life, gives a boundary to life, and therefore defines life. Perhaps there is no word in our language that can express Matte Blanco's point—a combination of life and death. Or perhaps "ultimate life" is a way of expressing it.

RECONCILIATION: THE DEATH INSTINCT AS A CLUSTER OF INNATE PRECONCEPTIONS (INNATE SCHEMATA)

Freud, in discovering the instinctual drives, may have uncovered but the tip of an iceberg, one that Bion's theory discloses more of. I believe that infants are born with inherent preconceptions, which constitute their preparedness for dealing with the rigors of the birth experience and all subsequent traumatic experiences. Elsewhere (Grotstein, 1977a, 1977b), I have discussed libido, not as a drive, but as part of an inherent libidinal organization whose aim is to keep the organism alive by reminding it of its need for nurture, comfort, tension relief, etc. I have also termed the death instinct the inherent undifferentiated defense organization whose job, like that of the libidinal organization, is to preserve the life of the organism, in this case by defending the life instinctual functions.

Thus, the tasks of the death instinct are defense, maintenance, and repair. In Bion's sense, I believe the death instinct has access to the inherent preconceptions of the prey-predator series as one of its priorities (J. Bowlby, personal communication), so that danger which can extinguish the life of the organism (and even the species) is known and knowable. Simmel (1944) seems to have had a similar view insofar as he posited that the death instinct is in the service of self-preservation. To me, instincts are inherent preconceptions equivalent to Lorenz's (1952, 1963) and Tinbergen's (1951) concept of innate schemata and innate releasing mechanisms. At the same time I agree with Schneirla (1959), who is critical of the biological instinct concept and prefers instead the notion of species-typical behavior patterns which, though based on innate foundations, are nevertheless subject to modification by experience.

I believe that the death instinct is a palimpsest of the suffering the species has undergone and a "recording" of all the classes of danger the species and the individual in the species have experienced since life was created. The death instinct appears to be a servant, always at our beck and call, to warn us about the possibility of danger to ourselves and to our race. Often the two can be in conflict, but more of that later. I believe that Abraham's (1924) notion of cannibalistic anxiety presaged the more profound psychology of Klein (1935), who, in delineating the phantasmagoria of the paranoid-schizoid position, was enlightening us about primeval fantasies that are "released" by the birth experience. These fantasies become epiphanies in the infant's mind until sufficient nurturing and caretaking are able to give the infant a sense of safety (object constancy) so as to effect primal repression and therefore to be able to push away (deconsequentialize) the full impact of these frightening, primeval fantasies.

Thus, greed and envy are but different affective expressions of a sense of danger that the life-support instincts (both the libidinal and the death instincts) offer to the infant in the experience of being a prey in the primeval rain forest of life. Greed then become the hypoertrophy of need, which the sense of danger of being the prey motivates. A consequence may be reversal into the opposite, with the infant transformed into a predator and the breast into a prey. Once our fantasies transform self into predator and breast into prey, then the next step inexorably follows: the breast becomes a terrifying victim of our predator feelings and is further transformed, via projective identification, into a persecutory predator toward the self, who has then been transformed into a prey. We are dealing then with an inchoately savage world of prey and predator, of victim and victimizer, in virtually endless spirals of transformations. Having established this dyad of prey-predator or victim-victimizer, we seek to reenact it so as to master it. To me, Klein's conception of the manic defense, which is one of triumph, contempt, and control over the object one depends on, is a reenactment of this anxiety and the desire to master it. It is particularly enacted upon an object of dependency because that object of dependency inspires our greatest vulnerability and therefore our greatest sense of danger.

It is therefore to danger, biological *and* psychical, that I wish to call attention as the prime motive for the operation of the death instinct. Anxiety, which Freud assigned first to an overflow of libido from the id and later to an ego signal betokening the advent of instinctual danger, should now be thought of as the property of the death instinct. In its raw ("uneducated" by experience), inchoate form, the death instinct presents primal organismic panic (Greenacre, 1941; Mahler, 1952). Mother's container capacity helps us to transform this organismic panic into signal anxiety (specific for individual dangers) and to transform the temporal locale of the sense of danger from a "panicky now" to a "localized danger in the future" so that a specifically anxious anticipation of danger can help us take proper steps to avoid its consequences. We cope with that danger by fleeing from it, attacking it, or rethinking it to make sure that it really is a danger rather than simply something strange, which we have not yet encountered but can safely try to master. Yet the preconception of danger must inescapably be in terms of the prey and predator. Both Bowlby (personal communication), in his ethological work, and Tustin (1980), from her long experience in the psychoanalytic treatment of autistically psychotic children, have come to this conclusion. Indeed, the play of children seems to reenact this fear and the attempt to master it in many different ways.

So far I have emphasized the death instinct as an adaptive, life-depending property of the human organism. I should like briefly to mention a third instinctual organization—the epistemophilic—which, although alluded to by Freud as a part instinct, never seems to have attained the enfranchisement in classical psychoanalysis that it has in Kleinian theory. I think of the epistemophilic instinct as combining the instinctual tendency to differentiate, to explore, to integrate, and to seek the future as well as to research the past. It sponsors constructiveness and reconstructiveness and, along with the death instinct and the life instinct, facilitates ambition, achievement, and restoration (reparation).

Put another way, the epistemophilic instinct, the libidinal instinct, and the death instinct are but three facets of a unitary, isomorphic *life instinct,* whose function is to keep us alive as individuals *and* as a group. The different facets are differentiated for varying functions—a phenomenon corresponding to a dual-track theory (see Grotstein, in press a).

THE DEATH INSTINCT IN THE SERVICE OF REPARATION

Once one begins to see the "intelligence traffic" of the internal world as information about states of safety or danger rather than gratuitous biological impulses, one can better comprehend an adaptive network of intelligence in which primitive sense receptors to internal stimuli can be evoked by the awareness of states of danger either within or without. Thus, an infant's "hostile impulses" are but desperate attempts to proclaim a message with urgency to the protective mother. The purpose of the hostility, I believe, is not only to call mother's attention to the state of danger, but also in fantasy (that is, magically) to contemplate the eradication of that danger through the employment of that destructiveness. The infant is thereby utilizing protective measures from the normal omnipotent immune frontier, which is associated with the developing skin-boundary frontier and the selfobject comfort loaned by parental objects. Once infants are confident that their destructiveness can "imagine away" the persecuting predator, a sense of relief is garnered from this benign, omnipotent postponement of confrontation with the real predators of external life.

The same is true of shame and other affects. When infants of children are ashamed of themselves because of some disappointment in their performance—or in the object's performance—the *experience* of shame, whether being ashamed of oneself or one's parents, has the same basic purpose: to "blame away the blemish." Probably at the root of depressive illness is the unmitigated hope that the perfect superego has the capacity, thanks to its perfection *and* sadism, to blame away any blemish in oneself and in one's objects.

Thus far I have been referring to the use of destructiveness as an agent of reparation in the symbiotic stage of the paranoid-schizoid position. Hostility, blame, shame, envious destruction, etc., are but magical attempts to reestablish a more suitable equilibrium of tolerability for the infant's welfare. The cries for help, however, are adaptively realistic and not necessarily magical. In the depressive position of separation-individuation, destructiveness may come to have, in addition to its commonly understood defensive meanings (such as manic defense or introjective identification), positive reparative aspects insofar as children may now feel inclined to protect their objects and themselves by asserting their own aggressive individuality. Hostility toward father by a male child in the oedipal phase, for instance, can be seen as the male child's attempt to defend mother against a predator father, and it is similar for the female child in terms of the Oedipus complex. It is thus very important to recognize the prime importance of the capacity to utilize destructiveness in the service of defense of valuable objects—including the self. At this juncture, appropriately defensive and constructive aggressiveness is not only self-appropriate but becomes a constructive "group instinct."

THE DEATH INSTINCT AND ENTROPY

I subscribe to Matte Blanco's advocacy of Freud's entropic conception of the death instinct. The model I would choose to illustrate this is the life cycle of the placenta. The placenta seems to be an intriguing, mysterious "third organism," regulating the relationship between the maternal host and the fetus. At the same time the placenta seems to have a built-in programming, which contains the knowledge of its life agenda. Its self-extinction is the signal for the act of birth to begin (Beaconsfield, Birdwood, and Beaconsfield 1980). It is quite probable that each organ system has its own built-in awareness of its life agenda.

Elsewhere (Grotstein, 1977a, 1977b), I have referred to René Spitz's 1954 lecture at the Pennsylvania Hospital, during which he showed slides of the "victims" of hospitalism he had studied. An extraordinarily high percentage had died before the age of four. The tissue pathology, according to Spitz, demonstrated advanced senile and arteriosclerotic changes as well as other advanced degenerative changes in many bodily systems. These four-year-olds were "dying old men and women," Spitz poignantly stated. I mention this touching episode to offer the notion that one's agenda may be predetermined by the genetic template but nevertheless hastened and precociously achieved in extreme states of stress. It may well be the death instinct's adaptive function to allow premature death to take place.

The passively adaptive aspects of the death instinct are of considerable importance in periods of overwhelming stress and catastrophic situations. (see Grotstein, 1977a, 1977b). In particular, I have in mind that aspect of the death instinct which, I believe, Freud (1925) hinted was associated with the mechanism of disavowal—allowing, not for the repression of impulses or the denial of reality, but for a disavowal of internal and external reality altogether. The defense mechanisms subsumed under repression seem to imply a postponement of the awareness of the repressed into a conception known as the "return of the repressed," which functions via the repetition compulsion. Disavowal, on the other hand, seems to be an eradication altogether of the mind and of the context of mind (Freud, 1925). I envision this aspect of disavowal occurring in active and passive aspects. Active disavowal entails the willful attacking of the links between percepts and the self in the very perception of these percepts, whereas passive disavowal involves mental disappearance, the abandonment of the embodied self.[2]

GROUP INSTINCTS

The Psychology of Human Sacrifice

We have looked at the death instinct as a biopsychological warning device, which acts like a strategic air command or radar system to scan the environment, both internal and external, so as to warn us of danger to our biological and psychological survival. Now, I should like to consider the death instinct as a racial instinct, in much the same way that Freud (1905) thought of the libidinal instinct as instituted to preserve the race, in contrast to the ego instincts, whose purpose was to preserve the individual. I believe that the death instinct also may function to preserve the race, especially the "horde," which is in itself a clustering together of individuals for their mutual welfare. Having acquired hordeship, however, the group also acquires an identity and psychology of its own (see Freud [1921] and Bion [1959b] particularly in this regard). Groups themselves are, for varying reasons, subject to dangers from individuals and/or other groups. At bottom, the psychology of the group may be predicated on a historical and mythic sense of danger in terms of the prey-predator series.

As Freud (1913) pointed out, the worship of totems was a way of trying to commemorate a savage event in the past—the killing (castration) of the primal father by the primal horde. Identification with a totemically symbolic residue of him was used to ward off dangers from his retaliation. I see this now in a somewhat altered way. I think the totem represents an animal, itself one's hereditary predator. Having been totemized, it has been identified with so as to give the group its sense of strength. The issue of the prey is yet another matter. Among animal hordes it is well known

---

[2] I have described the fate of these two selves, the disappearing self and the abandoned self, in other contributions, in which I connect disappearance with the origins of the belief in demoniacal possession (Grotstein, 1979a, 1979b).

that those who cannot keep up with the rest of the pack are left behind as stragglers to become prey to scavenger predators.

Space does not permit an exposition of research into history to demonstrate that practically every culture has had some practice of actual or symbolic human sacrifice (see Wilson, 1975; Lumsden and Wilson, 1981, 1983). The human sacrifice practices of the ancient Hebrew tribes became modified into the ritual of circumcision. This modification of a group ritual corresponds to the primary-process mechanisms of synechdoche and metonomy in which, for instance, one human being (Christ) may stand symbolically for everyone else, and part then of the self (the foreskin) stands for the rest of the person. Catholics today still observe the Eucharist, which has to do with the memory of the sacrifice of one for the many—of him who dies for the sins of all of us! In animal hordes, it is the weak, the young, and the lame—those who cannot keep up with the migratory horde—who become sacrifices to predators. Among humans it oftentimes seems to be the innocent who are sacrificed—the vestal virgins, or Christ, or Isaac, whom God initially demanded that Abraham sacrifice.

In another contribution (Grotstein, in press b), I profer the notion that the myth of Oedipus itself can be understood, not only as a universal myth of an individual, but also a group myth, in which the newborn member of the family-group is chosen either as the messiah (who will rescue the family from the results of its sins, errors, and failures), or as the scapegoat, the sacrificial lamb, the human victim who absorbs and condenses the group's sins. The myth of Oedipus seems to be the direct antecedent of the myth of Christ.

To explain such human sacrifice, we must again return to Bion's (1962, 1963) notions of the container-contained and inherent preconceptions. In his theory of the container and the contained, Bion states that the infant (facilitated by the containing mother) must be able to tolerate a gap in which there is a "no breast," an empty space, which can then be filled with the idea or conception of the breast that is absent (Freud's hallucinatory wish fulfillment). I believe that this empty container of the individual infant corresponds to the group's choice of an innocent or newborn child or youth (1) who, by virtue of this newness and innocence, is unspoiled and therefore a suitable gift to be sacrificed to a greedily and vengefully demanding god-predator, and (2) who constitutes, once again by virtue of newness and innocence, a suitable container, a holy container for the projective desecration of the troubles and agonies of the horde or group. As a container, the "innocent" collectively absorbs all the defects of the group, taking in the blame and blameworthiness, and then, through his or her own sacrifice, expunges and therefore protects the safety of the group.

Insofar as Christ is one of the most dramatic representations of human sacrifice in our time, I should like to use him as an example. According to one of the Apostles' creeds, Christ descended to hell after his crucifixion for three days and then rose to heaven, where he sat on the right hand of God. Yet, according to some scriptures, the archangel Lucifer himself once sat on the right hand of God before he fell.[3] What I am suggesting is that there are two images of Christ and thus of all human sacrifices. (1) there is the Christ who becomes the savior of mankind by absorbing unto himself the collective projective identifications of the weakness of the group; his sacrificial death thus collectively expunges the group and makes it safe. Moreover, he becomes divine, spiritually rising above the projections by being able to transform them rather than being transformed by them. (2) Yet there is also the Christ who has been overcome (transformed) by the projective identifications of the guilt and shame of the horde. His innocence is entrapped within the mire, and he thus becomes the Devil; here sin has become negatively holy, and Christ's innocence has become perversely redirected (see Grotstein, 1984).

In sum, my hypothesis is that the death instinct is a life-support defense organization not only for the individual but also for the species. As I hinted earlier, a human being in a group may encounter conflict between his or her own protective death instinct and that of the group. Human sacrifice seems to be one of the basic prescriptions for safety, both for the individual and for the group.[4] The choice of someone to be sacrificed is a "holy" modification of the prey-predator anxiety. The experience of blame, shame, and guilt seem to inspire weakness and thereby danger to a predator. These phenomena must be omnipotently expunged by individuals and groups who are still in the paranoid-schizoid phase of their development; a sacrifice seems necessary to cleanse and to protect the individual and the group. Klein's (1935) conception of the manic defense illuminates this holy phenomenon. Human sacrifice connotes the manic defense made sacred and a feeling of safety having been omnipotently secured.

In the depressive position—for the individual and for the group—there

---

[3] "Lucifer" (the "lightbearer") was the translation St. Jerome gave the metaphorical reference to the fall of the king of Babylon (Isaiah 14:12). When Jesus stated (Luke 10:18), "I saw Satan fall like lightning from heaven," it was interpreted by church scholars to be a reference to Lucifer. The legend became the basis for Milton's Lucifer in *Paradise Lot* (see *Encyclopedia Britannica*, 1972, vol. 4, p. 397).

[4] It is interesting that Wilson (1975; Lumsden and Wilson, 1981, 1983), speaking from the sociobiological point of view, strongly suggests that there is an altruistic instinct in the animal kingdom so that an individual member of a group seems to be willing to sacrifice its life in order to preserve the group.

is a realization that the parents must tolerate the child's working out his or her prey-predator anxiety on them so that they become sacrifices to the workings and practices of the child's anxiety. But the reverse is also true: the child becomes the sacrifice to the parents' working out their yet unresolved prey-predator anxieties on their infants and children—and so the race. In psychoanalysis, the analyst, like an exorcist, must, in his or her innocence, be the bearer of the patient's projections and therefore becomes the sacrifice. As we are now becoming more and more aware, however, the opposite may also be true—the patient may become our sacrifice (Searles, 1959; Langs, 1975, 1978).

Ethological and Ecological Considerations

A possible variant of the sacrifice motif can be seen in ethological and ecological life. Baldridge (1974), for instance, has found that sharks seem to patrol the sea much as macrophages patrol our hematic system and our connective tissue. When a fish demonstrates signs of trouble, the shark moves in to kill it almost as if (if not actually) to remove the now useless carcass from the environs. One can see numerous examples of this in wilderness life, where animals live together in a prey-predator relationship and yet seem to depend on one another to maintain the optimal size of their respective herds. We may then tentatively link this ecological balancing of animal hordes with Freud's (1920) nirvana principle for individuals. It is suggestive that both derive from a common source—the death instinct.

A NEW CONCEPTION OF THE DEATH INSTINCT

My contention is that the death instinct is a viable concept for psychoanalytic theory. To my mind, it represents a portion of a larger inherent-instinctual principle, which has been "programmed" into the DNA of our chromosomes—both literally and figuratively. In this sense, the death instinct may, perhaps, be better termed the inherent, undifferentiated defense organization in its inchoate form (Grotstein, 1977a, 1977b). Its emanations, warnings, impulses—until now called aggressive drives— are but RNA messengers dispatched from the DNA template to warn the organism of dangers in the external world *and* the internal milieu and to institute defensive tactics and strategies against them. The death instinct template contains a palimpsest of the history of the terrors all living and extinct organisms have endured. Current experiences resonate with the "wisdom" of this inherent template so as to evoke the signal of terror or danger in the organism. Organismic panic is thus the first inchoate response of the organism to danger. Maternal containment allows for the maturation of organismic panic into specific signal anxiety, which can more clearly specify the individuality of the danger and anticipatorily cope with it. It is my belief that Spitz's (1965) stranger anxiety is one of the first forms of the death instinct; the "stranger" evokes the frightening experience of the possibility of a predator in the infant's mind.

This hypothesis throws new light on Klein's paranoid-schizoid position. I see this phase of development (which I have termed "the symbiotic stage of the paranoid-schizoid position") as a staging area in which the infant attempts to cope with and master anxieties that are evoked by frustrations in the external world yet resonate with internal preconceptions of prey-predator anxieties. During the paranoid-schizoid position it is the infant's task—with mother's help—to sort out these terrors, to mythify them, to conquer them, and to mitigate their danger through a bonding alliance with mother (and father). I believe furthermore that all the variants of sadistic and masochistic behavior, let alone the so-called normal aspects of aggression in human sexual behavior, correspond to an attempt at mastery of the prey-predator anxiety, which the death instinct warns us about (see Stoller, 1979).

An even more speculative hypothesis is that the death instinct also constitutes a principle of behavior in groups and herds, with the aim of warning the herd about predators, alerting the herd to the presence of a prey, and offering sacrifices to the predator in order for the prey-herd to survive. These sacrifices may be of either defenseless victims or innocent members of the herd. It is my further contention that Klein's conception of the paranoid-schizoid position also applies to groups and herds. During that stage of development this group will try to work out its anxiety and theories of cosmic causalities by seeking to assign blame for all bad circumstances to the cosmic anger of a powerful predator god, whose wrath must be pacified by a sacrifice of an innocent member(s) of the group. If man's greatest sin is believed to be the sin of life—that is, the sin of accepting one's life by eating the fruit of life—then the punishment for this sin is the sacrifice of a relatively unlived life—that of an innocent child, ultimately the Christ child, or, more mercifully, the foreskin of Jewish male infants.

In the depressive position the guilt of being alive becomes compounded by fantasies of guilt in terms of anger toward the parental object. In the paranoid-schizoid position the maternal object was the infant's sacrifice or sufferer until a stage of reciprocity and interpersonal amnesty has taken place, not only in the mother-infant dyad, but in the family and in the group. The depressive position marks the end of persecution and the beginning of the recognition of real enemies in contrast to real friends.

Case Example

B. J., a 52 year old housewife and mother of three children has been in analysis with me for four years. She entered analysis because of feelings of low self-esteem and intermittent terror(the latter since her childhood). Before her analysis, she had been in psychotherapy for 12 years but had achieved little lasting benefit from it, she stated. She was critical of her husband's passivity and of his seeming indifference to her, although she did relate that she was sure of his love. She was also concerned that she had passed on her own dread of life to her children. When she related her family background to me, she portrayed a weak father who was seldom concerned with her, a strong and domineering mother who impinged into all her activities, a tyrannical older sister, and a "failure-to-thrive" younger brother who, to this very day, has not amounted to much—and was relatively less significant than the other family members as an influence on the patient's development.

In analyzing what appeared to be the patient's destructive impulses, particularly in the transference, I had reason initially to think of Klein's conception of the infant's envy of the breast and, consequently, of the patient's envy of the therapist. Gradually I came to realize that her destructive feelings toward me emerged, not only in response to empathic errors on my part, but also on occasions of separation from me and after she had attended my lectures, where my "exhibitionism" and capacity to leave her behind reminded her that she was no longer a member of a patient-therapist team, that there was no bonding or attachment at that moment, only dreaded isolation and aloneness. Thus, her destructive impulses emerged when the illusion of at-one-ment encountered jeopardy. In every instance, her anger and aggression seemed to be adaptive to states of distress and a belief in her being abandoned by me.

In those instances, and there were many, in which she directed her aggression toward herself, it was generally to attack herself for the possession of bad traits, the existence of which connoted danger for her in her world of objects. Although this use of destructiveness seemed to be maladaptive, it also seemed to have the teleological purpose of "blaming away her blemishes" so that she could be liked by herself and others. All her life she was afraid of being left behind, left out, abandoned, not being good enough. In several dreams this fear emerged as being left to the wolves.

Much of the early part of the analysis was dominated by the patient's hatred and fear of her mother. A third use of aggression emerged in this context—especially insofar as the patient began to understand her mother's alleged aggression toward her, the patient. One day, while discussing Holocaust victims, the patient related how she had heard from her grandparents about how they themselves had undergone a veritable holocaust with Cossacks in Russia. The patient was finally able to understand that her mother's domineering attitude, seemingly impinging into the patient's privacy (to her choice of dresses, friends, careers, etc.) was not merely the practice of a selfish, manipulating mother. It was also, she came to realize, the manifestation of a frantic mother, one who had been conditioned by her own parents' tales of horror from their lives in Russia that the patient, as well as her siblings, *had* to behave in a certain way, make certain choices of friends, be materialistic, make rich and successful marriages, etc., in order to ensure their survival. The patient, it turns out, believed she was chosen to be the "messiah" of her family—the rich, successful, well-married one who would bring good tidings to her parental family and relieve them of their hereditary panic. In contrast, her older sister, the ugly one, seemed to have been chosen to be the victim of the family, the focus for scorn and hatred by mother and father. When this understanding developed, the patient underwent a fundamental change in her attitude, not only toward her parents, particularly her mother, but also toward her sister, toward whom she had always had a deep antipathy and hatred.

THE DEATH INSTINCT AS A DIALECTICAL MOIETY OF LIFE

I have thus far approached the death instinct from the standpoint of biological inferential speculation in association with relevant clinical phenomena. I cannot close a discussion of the death instinct, however, without returning to Freud's metaphysical conception of it as an inborn destiny of organic life to return to inorganic matter. Whether or not one holds with Freud's belief, one must nonetheless recognize that Freud was, in this instance, approximating a theory of dialectics, in the legacy of Hegel; that is, he was constructing a natural, *seemingly* oppositional, reflexive component or moiety to its obligatory contrast. Psychoanalytic theory has developed along the lines of (1) Cartesian dualism, by which is meant the separation of observing subject from experienc*ed* object, and (2) the concept of psychic conflict (whether *intra*systemic or *inter*systemic), implying that each component of the conflict has an independent origin and then combatively, as it were, encounters an idea with which it is incompatible. The concept of a dialectic implies a common origin in the ancestral template of thought, much like Plato's *Androgyne*, which then, by prearrangement, separates and returns to keep its reflexive rendezvous with its counterpart—*seemingly* in opposition so as to discover its own full essence and uniqueness and the full essence and uniqueness of its counterpart, only then to reconcile into a higher form of synthesis, which then fatefully inaugurates the next dialectical sequence in turn. By this reasoning, the death instinct—or perhaps, better, the "principle of death"—can be understood as that dialectical counterpart to the "life principle" which gives the latter its meaning and its definition, especially in its creative thrust (see Ghent, 1984; Guravitz, 1984).

By the use of the dialectical perspective, we might more easily concur with Freud's thesis that there must be a governing principle within us counterbalancing states of excitation, arousal, tension, activity, ambition, progress, etc, to activate the opposite—a return to the resting state. This factor may help to account for what are otherwise called resistances and the negative theraputic reaction in analysis—phenomena can be that analogized to the tendency of certain "plastics with memory" to tolerate changes transitorally, only to return to their native form.

REFERENCES

Abraham, K. (1924). A short study of the development of libido, viewed in the light of mental disorders. In *Selected Papers*. London: Hogart Press, 1927, pp. 418–501.

Baldridge, H. D. (1974). *Shark Attack*. New York: Droke House/Hellus.

Balint, M. (1959). *Thrills and Regressions*. New York: Int. Univ. Press.

——— (1968). *The Basic Fault*. London: Tavistock.

Beaconsfield, P., Birdwood, G., & Beaconsfield, R. (1980). The placenta. *Sci. Amer.* 243:94–103.

Bion, W. (1958). On arrogance. *Int. J. Psychoanal.* 39:144–146. Also in *Second Thoughts*. London: Heinemann, 1967, pp. 86–92.

——— (1959a). Attacks on linking. *Int. J. Psychoanal.* 40:308–315. Also in *Second Thoughts*. London: Heinemann, 1967, pp. 93–109.

——— (1959b). *Experiences in Groups*. London: Tavistock.

——— (1962). *Learning from Experience*. New York: Basic Books.

——— (1963). *Elements of Psychoanalysis*. New York: Basic Books.

——— (1967). *Second Thoughts*. London: Heinemann.

Bowlby, J. (1969). *Attachment and Loss*, Vol. I. New York: Basic Books.

Eissler, K. R. (1971). Death drive, ambivalence, and narcissism. *Psychoanal. Study Child* 26:25–78.

Erikson, E. (1959). *Identity and the Life Cycle* [*Psychol. Issues*, Monog. 1]. New York: Int. Univ. Press.

Fairbairn, W. (1940). Schizoid factors in the personality. In *Psychoanalytic Studies of the Personality*. London: Tavistock, 1952, pp. 3–27.

——— (1941). A revised psychopathology of psychoses and psychoneuroses. In *Psychoanalytic Studies of the Personality*. London: Tavistock, 1952, pp. 28–58.

——— (1943). The repression and the return of the bad objects (with special reference to the 'war neuroses'). In *Psychoanalytic Studies of the Personality*. London: Tavistock, 1952, pp. 59–81.

――― (1944). Endopsychic structure considered in terms of object relationships. In *Psychoanalytic Studies of the Personality*. London: Tavistock, 1952, pp. 82–136.
――― (1946). Object relationships and dynamic structure. In *Psychoanalytic Studies of the Personality*. London: Tavistock, 1952, pp. 137–151.
――― (1949). Steps of the development of an object-relations theory of the personality. In *Psychoanalytic Studies of the Personality*. London: Tavistock, 1952, pp. 152–161.
――― (1951). A synopsis of the development of the author's views regarding the structure of the personality. In *Psychoanalytic Studies of the Personality*. London: Tavistock, 1952, pp. 162–182.
――― (1952). *Psychoanalytic Studies of the Personality*. London: Tavistock.
Fenichel, O. (1945). *The Psychoanalytic Theory of Neurosis*. New York: Norton.
Freedman, D. A. (1982). Of instincts and instinctual drives: Some developmental considerations. *Psychoanal. Inquiry.* 2:152–168.
Freud, S. (1905). Three essays on the theory of sexuality. *Standard Edition* 7:125–253.
――― (1908). On the sexual theories of children. *Standard Edition* 9:205–226.
――― (1913). Totem and taboo. *Standard Edition* 13:1–161.
――― (1914). On narcissism: An introduction. *Standard Edition* 14:67–104.
――― (1915). Instincts and their vicissitudes. *Standard Edition* 14:109–140.
――― (1917). Mourning and melancholia. *Standard Edition* 14:237–258.
――― (1920). Beyond the pleasure principle. *Standard Edition* 18:3–64.
――― (1921). Group psychology and the analysis of the ego. *Standard Edition* 18:67–144.
――― (1925). Negation. *Standard Edition* 19:235–242.
――― (1930). Civilization and its discontents. *Standard Edition* 21:59–148.
――― (1939). Moses and monotheism. *Standard Edition* 23:3–140.
Ghent, E. (1984). Masochism, submission, surrender. (Unpublished.)
Ginsburg, B. E. (1982). Genetic factors and aggressive behavior. *Psychoanal. Inquiry* 2:53–76.
Gould, R. (1982). Studies of aggression in early childhood: Patterns of attachment and efficacy. *Psychoanal. Inquiry.* 2:21–52.
Greenacre, P. (1941). The predisposition to anxiety. In *Trauma, Growth, and Personality*. New York: Int. Univ. Press, 1952, pp. 27–82.
Grotstein, J. S. (1977a). The psychoanalytic concept of schizophrenia, I: The dilemma. *Int. J. Psychoanal.* 58:403–425.
――― (1977b). The psychoanalytic concept of schizophrenia, II. Reconciliation. *Int. J. Psychoanal.* 58:427–452.
――― (1978). Inner space: Its dimensions and its coordinates. *Int. J. Psychoanal.* 59:55–61.
――― (1979a). Demoniacal possession, splitting, and the torment of joy. *Contemp. Psychoanal.* 15:407–445.
――― (1979b). The soul in torment: A newer and older view of psychopathology. *Bull. Nat. Guild Catholic Psychiat.* 25:36–52.
――― (1984). Forgery of the soul: A psychoanalytic inquiry into evil. In *Psychoanalysis and the Concept of Evil*, ed. M. Eigen & M. Coleman-Nelson. New York: Human Sciences Press.
――― (in press a). The dual-track theorem. (Submitted for publication.)
――― (in press b). The sins of the fathers: Human sacrifice from the group perspective of the Oedipus complex. (Submitted for publication.)
Guravitz, R. (1984). The meaning of the death instinct in psychoanalytic thought. (Unpublished.)
Hamilton, J. W. (1976). Early trauma, dreaming and creativity: The works of Eugene O'Neill. *Int. Rev. Psychoanal.* 3:341–364.

Hartmann, H. (1939). *Ego Psychology and the Problem of Adaptation*. New York: Int. Univ. Press, 1958.
────── (1948). Comments on the psychoanalytic theory of instinctual drives. In *Essays on Ego Psychology*. New York: Int. Univ. Press, 1964, pp. 69–89.
────── Kris, E., Loewenstein, R. (1949). Notes on the theory of aggression. *Psychoanal. Study Child* 3/4:9–36.
Jacobson, E. (1950). Contribution to the metapsychology of cyclothymic depression. In *Affective Disorders*, ed. P. Greenacre. New York: Int. Univ. Press, pp. 49–83.
────── (1964). *The Self and the Object World*. New York: Int. Univ. Press.
Jaffe, D. S. (1982). Aggression: Instinct, drive, behavior. *Psychoanal. Inquiry*. 2:77–94.
Jung, C. G. (1917). The archetypes of the collective unconscious. In *Collected Works*, Vol. 7. New York: Pantheon, 1953, pp. 88–111.
Jones, E. (1955). *The Life and Work of Sigmund Freud*, Vol. II. New York: Basic Books.
Katan, M. (1966). Precursors of the concept of the death instinct. In *Psychoanalysis: A General Psychology*, ed. R. M. Loewenstein et al. New York: Int. Univ. Press, pp. 86–103.
Klein, M. (1921). The development of a child. In *Contributions to Psycho-Analysis, 1921–1945*. London: Hogarth Press, 1948, pp. 13–67.
────── (1933). The early development of conscience in the child. In London: Hogarth Press, 1948, *Contributions to Psycho-Analysis, 1921–1945*, pp. 267–277.
────── (1935). A contribution to the psychogenesis of manic-depressive states. In *Contributions to Psycho-Analysis, 1921–1945*. London: Hogarth Press, 1948, pp. 282–310.
────── (1957). *Envy and Gratitude*. New York: Basic Books.
Kohut, H. (1971). *The Analysis of the Self*. New York: Int. Univ. Press.
────── (1977). *The Restoration of the Self*. New York: Int. Univ. Press.
Lacan, J. (1949). The mirror stage as formative of the function of the I as revealed in psychoanalytic experience. In *Écrits: A Selection*. New York: Norton, 1977, pp. 1–7.
Langs, R. (1975). Therapeutic misalliances. *Int. J. Psychoanal. Psychother*. 4:77–105.
────── (1978). *Techniques in Transition*. New York: Aronson.
Lorenz, K. (1952). *King Solomon's Ring*. New York: Crowell.
────── (1963). *On Aggression*. New York: Harcourt, Brace, & World, 1966.
Lumsden, C. J., & Wilson, E. O. (1981). *Genes, Mind, and Culture*. Cambridge, Mass.: Harvard Univ. Press.
────── (1983). *Promethean Fire: Reflections on the Origins of Mind*. Cambridge, Mass.: Harvard Univ. Press.
Mahler, M. (1952). On child psychosis and schizophrenia. *Psychoanal. Study Child* 7:286–305.
────── (1968). *On Human Symbiosis and the Vicissitudes of Individuation*. New York: New York: Int. Univ. Press.
Matte Blanco, I. (1973). Le quattro aninomie dell'istinto di morrte. Estratto da *Istituto della Enciclopedia Italiana*, 1973, pp. 447–460.
────── (1975). *The Unconscious as Infinite Sets*. London: Duckworth Press.
Menninger, K. (1938). *Man Against Himself*. New York: Harcourt Brace.
Ostow, M. (1958). The death instinct—a contribution to the study of instincts. *Int. J. Psychoanal*. 39:5–16.
Parens, H. (1979). *The Development of Aggression in Early Childhood*. New York: Aronson.
Rapaport, D. (1958). The theory of the ego autonomy: A generalization. *Bull. Menninger Clinic* 22:13–35.
────── (1959). A historical survey of psychoanalytic ego psychology. In *Identity and the Life Cycle*, by E. H. Erikson [*Psychol. Issues*, Monog. 1]. New York: Int. Univ. Press.

Rochlin, G. (1982). Aggression reconsidered: A critique of psychoanalysis. *Psychoanal. Inquiry* 2:121–132.
Rosenfeld, H. (1971). A clinical approach to the psychoanalytic theory of the life and death instincts: An investigation into aggressive aspects of narcissims. *Int. J. Psychoanal.* 52:169–178.
Schneirla, T. C. (1959). An evolutionary and developmental theory of biphasic processes underlying approach and withdrawal. In *Nebraska Symposium on Motivation*, ed. M. R. Jones. Lincoln: Univ. Nebraska Press, pp. 1–42.
Searles, H. F. (1959). The effort to drive the other person crazy: An element in aetiology and psychotherapy of schizophrenia. In *Collected Papers on Schizophrenia and Related Subjects*. New York: Int. Univ. Press, 1965, pp. 254–283.
Simmel, E. (1944). Self-preservation and the death instinct. *Psychoanal. Q.* 13:160–185.
Spielrein, S. (1912). Die Destruktion als Ursache des Werdens. *Jahrbuch Psychoanal.* 4:465–503.
Spitz, R. (1954). The general adaptation syndrome and its relationship to hospitalism. Presented to Philadelphia Association for Psychoanalysis, Philadelphia.
——— (1965). *The First Year of Life*. New York: Int. Univ. Press.
Stärcke, A. (1914). Introduction to *Civilized Morality and Modern Nervous Illness* (by S. Freud). Baarn: Hollandia Drukkerj.
Stoller, R. J. (1979). *Sexual Excitement: Dynamics of Erotic Life*. New York: Pantheon.
Tinbergen, N. (1951). *The Study of Instincts*. London: Oxford Univ. Press.
Tustin, F. (1980). Autistic objects. *Int. Rev. Psychoanal.* 7:27–39.
Wilson, E. O. (1975). *Sociobiology: The New Synthesis*. Cambridge, Mass.: Harvard Univ. Press.
Winnicott, D. W. (1952). Psychoses and child care. In *The Maturational Processes and the Facilitating Environment*. New York: Int. Univ. press, 1965, pp. 219–228.
——— (1958). *Collected Papers: Through Pediatrics to Psychoanalysis*. New York: Basic Books.
——— (1963). The developmental capacity for concern. In *The Maturational Processes and the Facilitating Environment*. New York: Int. Univ. Press, 1965, pp. 73–82.
——— (1965). *The Maturational Processes and the Facilitating Environment*. New York: Int. Univ. Press.

17/
Discussion:
Instinct, Structure, and Personal Meaning
Thomas H. Ogden, M.D.

James Grotstein's revised concept of the death instinct represents an important advance in developing a psychoanalytic instinct theory built on the foundation of a modern understanding of the relation between biology and mental contents. This paper suggests that Chomsky's concept of deep structure may provide a useful analog for understanding the mode of transmission of the experience of the species. Winnicott's work on the area of experiencing that lies between reality and fantasy offers a way of thinking about how impersonally structured experience (fantasy) is transformed into personal meaning (imagination).

A SEMIOTIC CONCEPTION OF THE DEATH INSTINCT

James Grotstein proposes that the death instinct be viewed neither as a well of destructive energy (Klein, 1952), nor as the psychological correlate of entropy, but as a system of schemata serving to orient the individual to potential danger. This system is based on a set of preconceptions through which the infant is constitutionally preprogrammed to interpret raw sensory experience in terms of possible danger of the prey-predator type. The death instinct is conceived as an inherent readiness to anticipate, seek out, and defend against danger, even before such danger is experienced. I infer that the experiential correlate of the infant's initial asymbolic anticipation of danger is Bion's (1962) "nameless dread"—a sense of formless, unlocatable danger that must be attended to (even before it can be symbolized and thought about) with the greatest sense of urgency. The intensity of the feeling of dread corresponds to Melanie Klein's (1952) conviction that the danger posed by the death instinct is far and away the most powerful motivating force in early development. Grotstein would modify the Kleinian conception of the death instinct by saying that the death instinct is not the origin of danger; rather, it is the facet of the psyche responsible for generating meanings relating to danger. To view the death instinct as the source of danger would be akin to killing the messenger bearing bad news.[1]

The infant's experience of "nameless dread" is subjected to two separate but interrelated influences: (1) the inborn organizing effect of the schemata associated with the death instinct and (2) the containing function of the mother. The preconceptions associated with the death instinct constitute a history of the experience of the species with danger. This "record" serves as a means of anticipating danger and of assigning meaning of the prey-predator type to experience. (As will be discussed later, I believe that Chomsky's concept of deep structure may provide a model for conceptualizing the relationship of inborn schemata to the act of construing experience in a particular way.)

In the infant, the operation of the death instinct occurs in the context of the mother-infant relationship. Diffuse awareness of danger is given symbolic meaning within the context of the mother's personality system and is thus rendered more manageable for the infant. A maternal failure in containment results in a stripping away of whatever meaning the infant had been able to attach to his or her experience and a return to the state of "nameless dread."

Once the death instinct is seen as a set of adaptive preconceptions of anticipated threats to the individual (accrued from the collective experience of the species), it can be understood as a component (along with the epistemophilic and libidinal instincts) of a unitary life instinct. Grotstein's conception of the death instinct is an expanded version of Freud's ego instinct. From an evolutionary point of view, it is very difficult to imagine the adaptive value of inborn, raw destructive energy (Klein's conception of the death instinct). In contrast, Grotstein's death instinct is the psychological systemization of the organism's constitutional readiness to manage danger. It is the origin of unconscious ego defenses as well as of many of the primary autonomous ego functions. Anxiety associated with the death instinct is understood to be an indispensable form of emotion, without

---

[1] I believe that a form of killing the messenger is resorted to in schizophrenic patients when they engage in attacks on their psychological processes of attributing meaning to experience. The upshot for these patients is a form of psychological deadness that I have termed a state of "nonexperience" (Ogden, 1980, 1982).

which we would be as vulnerable to the full spectrum of dangers as the person who cannot feel protective pain is to being burned.

The semiotic instinct theory proposed by Grotstein supplements impulse theory in viewing human motivation as more than the search for outlets for libidinal and aggressive energy. According to a semiotic model, all of us, as individuals, with our own system of meanings (some of which are shaped constitutionally), have *reasons why* we want to (need to, feel impelled to, feel we have no choice but to, feel with life-threatening urgency that we must, feel reluctantly that we should) act in a particular way. It is not the power of energic forces that constitutes motivation; it is the power of the logic of one's system of meanings.

The argument presented by Grotstein for a revised theory of the death instinct is extremely compelling. He turns the two major prior conceptions of the death instinct (Klein's cauldron of destructive energy and Freud's entropy theory) on their ears, replacing them with the theory that makes both evolutionary and psychoanalytic sense. It is a theory of adaptation and self-preservation, and at the same time a theory of unconscious meanings. Again, Klein's conception of inborn, raw destructive force makes no sense from an evolutionary perspective, while Freud's theory is strangely unpsychological in that it is exclusively a theory of energy distribution rather than a theory of meanings.

In the remainder of this discussion, I intend to comment briefly on three facets of instinct theory alluded to in Grotstein's paper: (1) the concept of preconception and the phylogenetic inheritance of knowledge, (2) the place of inherent systems of meaning in Freud's instinct theory, and (3) the relation of instinct to personal meaning.[2]

INSTINCT AND PRECONCEPTION

In this section I shall use a specific critique of Kleinian theory as a vehicle for exploring the concept of phylogenetic inheritance of knowledge. Kleinians are often accused of engaging in Lamarckian thinking when they talk about "phylogenetic inheritance of knowledge" (Klein, 1952, p. 117n). It is felt that Klein must be positing the inheritance of ideas when she envisions infants from the beginning as capable of fantasy that includes forms of experience to which they have never been exposed (e.g., the fantasy of tearing the breast to bits before the infant has ever experienced anything being torn to bits). Because, for the Kleinians, fantasy is the mental representation of instinct, instinct is the vehicle for the "inheritance of knowledge":

---

[2] I have addressed these topics at greater length in a separate contribution (Ogden, 1984a).

Such [inherited] knowledge is *inherent* in bodily impulses as a vehicle of instinct, in the *aim* of instinct, in the excitation of the organ, i.e. in this case, [the case of tearing the breast to bits], the mouth.

The phantasy that his passionate impulses will destroy the breast does not require the infant to have actually seen objects eaten and destroyed, and then to have come to the conclusion that he could do it too. This aim, this relation to the object, is inherent in the character and direction of the impulse itself, and in its related affects [Isaacs, 1952, p. 94].

So, for the Kleinians, knowledge is inherent in the instinct and actualized through the mental and physical activity associated with the instinct. But the Kleinians do not offer a model for the encoding and transmission of information from generation to generation. Grotstein points out that such information must be encoded in and transmitted by RNA and DNA, but he does not propose a model for the psychological correlates of this structuring and transmitting process.

I would suggest that instinct might be conceived as analogous to Chomsky's (1957, 1968) conception of linguistic deep structure. Chomsky contends that it is inconceivable that infants could learn any language if they had to deduce the grammar (the system of organization of symbols and meanings) of the language they were hearing from the phonemes (sound units of language) to which they were exposed. It is only because infants are equipped with a code, a deep structure, that is built into their perceptual and motor apparatuses that they are able to discriminate between groups of sounds and organize them into a system that becomes the syntactic and semantic structure of language. Infants are not born knowing how to speak French or English or Chinese, but they are born with a code that will enable them to do so given proper interpersonal experience.

The code is at the same time limiting and potentiating. The deep structure determines that infants will organize phonemes in a highly specific way and thus forecloses other possibilities. An example of the perceptual correlate of the inborn organizing function of deep structure is the way all human beings are "pre-wired" to discriminate between the phonemes "ba" and "pa." The human being is unable to discern any sound between these two phonemes (Eimas, 1975). On the other hand, without the organizing potential of an inborn code, language would not exist—language cannot be created afresh by each infant.

Instinct could be thought of as constituting a similar deep structure. It is difficult to imagine that language is the only psychological achievement safeguarded and organized in this way. The death instinct, for example, could be thought of not as a system of inherited impulses or inherited preformed ideas, but as a code by which *meaning is attributed to experience along highly determined lines* (for example, as Grotstein proposes, in terms of the relationship of prey and predator). The range of possible responses to actual experience is highly limited because all experience is organized along predetermined lines. Infantile mental processes could be thought of as operating according to a psychological reductionism that squeezes all experience into the procrustean beds of the codes associated with the life and death instincts. In other words, all raw experience is assigned meanings in terms of attachment (life instinct) or danger, especially danger in the form of attack and bodily damage (the death instinct). From this point of view, Bion's (1962) concept of preconception, Klein's concept of phylogenetic inheritance of knowledge, and Grotstein's concept of an inherited record of the experience of the species with danger can all be viewed not as theories of inheritance of preformed ideas, but as theories of inborn organizing codes by which meanings are attached to experience in a highly determined way. The assumption underlying this conception of development is that nothing is ever experienced absolutely freshly. Even at the very beginning, our perceptions are powerfully shaped by inborn codes that serve as the lens through which perception is attributed meaning. Without such linguistic and psychological codes, the infant would simply be buffeted by masses of disorganized and unorganizable stimuli, which would forever remain waves of unknowable things-in-themselves.

FREUD'S NOTIONS OF INHERITANCE OF KNOWLEDGE

It would be a serious error to view the proposals of Klein (phylogenetic inheritance of knowledge), Bion (preconception), and Grotstein (inherited record of the experience of the species with danger) as heretical departures from Freud's instinct theory. In fact, alongside his conception of instinct as raw, energic forces, Freud (1916–1917, 1918) viewed instincts as endowed with an inherent expectancy of an object. The sexual instinct for Freud (1905) is characterized by source, aim, and object, with the aim of discharge always dependent on an anticipated object as vehicle. The nature of the anticipated object is determined by the bodily source (erotogenic zone). For example, the oral component of a sexual instinct requires something to suck on and later to bite. Erikson's (1954) work on the relationship of erotogenic zones to specific modes of object relatedness has developed what was implicit in Freud's theory of sexual development.

In addition, for Freud there is an inherent expectancy of a specific form of danger built into each phase of sexual development. This expectancy of danger does not depend on actual experience. Castration anxiety and the Oedipus complex as a whole are not seen as sociological outcomes of actual threats and seductions encountered by the infant and child. Instead, the Oedipus complex, including castration anxiety, is conceived as a universal mode of organizing experience. Children will generate threats of castration by their acts of interpreting experience in a specific way that is determined by their instinctual endowment. Almost any set of life experiences will be utilized to generate this set of meanings. The Oedipus complex and castration anxiety are universal because they are reflections of the structure of the mind. Meaning is attributed to perception in such a way that no other outcome is possible except under conditions of extreme constitutional or environmental catastrophe.

For Freud, the Oedipus complex and castration anxiety are not simply the products of experience (although actual experience certainly contributes). The instincts seem to be the vehicle for a system of potential meanings that become universally occurring, actual meanings as living experience is interpreted along constitutionally predetermined lines: Freud asks: "Whence comes the need for these [universal] phantasies and the material for them?" And he answers:

> There can be no doubt that their sources lie in the instincts; but it has still to be explained why the same phantasies with the same content are created on every occasion. I am prepared with an answer which I know will seem daring to you. I believe these *primal phantasies,* as I should like to call them, and no doubt a few others as well, are a phylogenetic endowment. In them, the individual reaches beyond his own experience into primaeval experience at points where his own experience has been too rudimentary. It seems to me quite possible that all the things that are told us today in analysis as phantasy—the seduction of children, the inflaming of sexual excitement by observing parental intercourse, the threat of castration (or rather castration itself)—were once real occurrences in the primaeval times of the human family, and that children in their phantasies are simply filling in the gaps in individual truth with prehistoric truth. I have repeatedly been led to suspect that the psychology of the neuroses has stored up in it more of the antiquities of human development than any other source [1916–1917, pp. 370–371].

The primacy of the internal schemata over the actual event is unmistakable in Freud's thinking: "Wherever experiences fail to fit in with the hereditary schema they become remodelled in the imagination" (1918, p. 119).

It must be emphasized that the deep structure of instincts is a nonpsychological entity in the sense that it is not a thought, a feeling, or an action. The deep structure of instinct is unobservable, just as the deep structure of language is. We can see the organizing effect of the structure, but never the structure itself. Structure is the biological container for the ideational and affective contents of mind.

INSTINCT, FANTASY, AND PERSONAL MEANING

Deep structure (whether of language or instinct) is unlearned and impersonal. It is not a reflection of the individuality of a person; rather, it is part of the shared endowment of the species. Winnicott (1971) was the first to point out that fantasy, the mental representation of instinct, is itself impersonal. Fantasy is as external to the interpreting self as reality is. Winnicott makes a crucial differentiation between fantasy and imagination. The latter is the product of a self living between the impersonal external world of reality and the impersonal internal world of instinct-generated fantasy. Fantasy, as the psychic representation of instinct (i.e., a manifestation of one's biology), has a quality of automaticity and reactivity. It does not reflect an act of a self (with a personal history) interpreting and responding to experience. Fantasy and reality are the stuff that personal meanings are constructed out of by an interpreting self, but fantasy and reality in themselves are impersonal.

As I have discussed elsewhere (Ogden, 1984b), personal meaning becomes possible only when an interpreting self has become differentiated from one's symbols (e.g., one's thoughts) and the symbolized (that which one is thinking about). Only after subjectivity ("I-ness") has been achieved in this process can fantasies become experiences *of the self* that are interpreted *by the self,* since they are then distinguishable *from the self.* Before the differentiation of the self from one's symbols (one's thoughts), one is lived by one's fantasies. Following this differentiation, one becomes able to play with one's fantasies, thus endowing them with personal meaning. In this process the impersonal (fantasy) becomes personalized (imagination).

REFERENCES

Bion, W. (1962). *Learning from Experience.* New York: Basic Books.
Chomsky, N. (1957). *Syntactic Structures.* The Hague: Mouton.
────── (1968). *Language and Mind.* New York: Harcourt, Brace & World.
Eimas, P. (1975). Speech perception in early infancy. In *Infant Perception: From Sensation to Cognition,* Vol. II, ed. L. B. Cohen & P. Salapatek. New York: Academic Press, pp. 193–228.
Erikson, E. H. (1954). *Childhood and Society.* New York: Norton.
Freud, S. (1905). Three essays on the theory of sexuality. *Standard Edition* 7:130–248.
────── (1916–1917). Introductory lectures on psycho-analysis. *Standard Edition* 15 & 16.
────── (1918). From the history of an infantile neurosis. *Standard Edition* 17:7–124.
Isaacs, S. (1952). The nature and function of phantasy. In *Developments in Psycho-analysis,* ed. M. Klein et al. London: Hogarth Press, 1973, pp. 67–121.
Klein, M. (1952). The behaviour of young infants. In *Envy and Gratitude and Other Works, 1946–1963.* New York: Delacorte Press/Lawrence, 1975, pp. 94–121.

────── (1958). On the development of mental functioning. In *Envy and Gratitude and Other Works, 1946–1963*. New York: Delacorte Press/Lawrence, 1975, pp. 236–246.
Ogden, T. (1980). On the nature of schizophrenic conflict. *Int. J. Psychoanal.* 61:513–533.
────── (1982). *Projective Identification and Psychotherapeutic Technique*. New York: Aronson.
────── (1984a). Instinct, phantasy, and psychological deep structure: A reinterpretation of aspects of the work of Melanie Klein. *Contemp. Psychoanal.* 20.
────── (1984b). On potential space. *Int. J. Psychoanal.* (in press).
Winnicott, D. W. (1971). Dreaming, fantasying, and living. In *Playing and Reality*. New York: Basic Books, pp. 26–37.

18/
Recent Findings and New Directions in Child Psychiatry
Melvin Lewis, M.B., B.S., F.R.C.Psych., D.C.H.

Recent findings in child psychiatry have challenged some traditional concepts and opened up new areas of inquiry. New research has brought into question the thinking on continuity, infantile amnesia, fixation, dream formation, early infant development, attachment and regression, stranger anxiety, transitional objects, latency, and adolescent turmoil. Similar reconsiderations in the psychopathology of such conditions as bedwetting, obsessional neurosis, phobias, depression, and infantile autism are highlighted. Lastly, some issues confronting research in psychoanalysis in general are discussed, and some speculations are offered on possible future directions for child psychiatry.

Research in child psychiatry has changed enormously over the past 20 years. One result of this ferment is that new findings and new ideas present a challenge to some traditional concepts.

The bulk of new findings in child psychiatry today is clearly coming from the richness of biological research. Yet it is important to remember that Freud himself regularly thought about the biological contribution to human behavior, as the following quotations reveal:

> Even when investigation shows that the primary exciting cause of a phenomenon is psychical, deeper research will one day trace the path further and discover an organic basis for the mental event [1900, pp. 41–42].

First presented at the Hyman Caplan Memorial Conference on "Current Concepts and New Perspectives in Child Psychiatry," Royal Ottawa Hospital Department of Psychiatry, University of Ottawa, May 10, 1983.

all our provisional ideas in psychology will someday be based on an organic substructure. This makes it probable that it is special substances and chemical processes which perform the operations of sexuality [1914, p. 78].

Biology is truly a land of unlimited possibilities. We may expect it to give us the most surprising information and we cannot guess what answers it will return. . . .
They may be of a kind which will blow away the whole of our artificial structure of hypotheses [1920, pp. 3, 64].

In view of the intimate connection between the things that we distinguish as physical and mental, we may look forward to a day when paths of knowledge and, let us hope, of influence will be opened up, leading from organic biology and chemistry to the field of neurotic phenomena [1926, p. 231].

The future may teach us to exercise a direct influence, by means of particular chemical substances, on the amounts of energy and their distribution in the mental apparatus. It may be that there are other still undreamt-of possibilities of therapy [1940, p. 182].

The phylogenetic foundation has so much the upper hand over personal accidental experience that it makes no difference whether a child has really sucked at the breast or has been brought up on the bottle and never enjoyed the tenderness of a mother's care. In both cases the child's development takes the same path [1940, pp. 188–189].

One further point should be kept in mind: each form of research has its advantages and disadvantages. For example, epidemiological research, while meeting the test of scientific rigor from the point of view of statistics, is often at too great a distance from the individual person or subject, and so may lose in its value for an individual. At the other extreme, psychoanalytic research, which has the advantage of recognizing complexity and providing compelling, detailed explorations of a person's unconscious motives and feelings, does not meet current standards for scientific reliability. The analyst therefore sometimes has difficulty making scientifically valid inferences about, say, whole classes of people, such as infants or adolescents, and sometimes even about an individual. Other scientists then feel frustrated: it's as though a nonmusical scientist expected a musical person to explain the meaning or prove the beauty of a Mozart sonata through the use of multiple regression analysis—it cannot be done. The frustration by the way often goes both ways: some analysts become very bored and frustrated when they are confronted with what Ernst Kris used to call "counting papers." Clearly, we need both kinds of research, and I shall come back to this later.

Given these caveats, I shall now present some of the questions that have been raised by recent research and some new paradigms that have been offered. I shall only touch very briefly and highly selectively on a few areas in normal development and developmental psychopathology. In no sense is this intended to be a comprehensive review of all research. My purpose, rather, is to illustrate some changing viewpoints in the field, both in normal development and in psychopathology.

NORMAL DEVELOPMENT

The Idea of Continuity

Developmentalists have held on, with great tenacity, to the idea that there is an inherent continuity of development from the fetus through to old age and death, and that this continuity is all-encompassing. The concept of continuity is implied, for example, when psychoanalysts talk about transference and the compulsion to repeat in psychoanalysis (Freud, 1920). Of course there *is* continuity. Recent observations, however, have suggested that perhaps the concept of continuity is too global, that it may not be as all-encompassing as was once believed. Instead, there may be certain kinds of relative *discontinuities* that are important.

Kagan (1979), for example, has noted that the enhancement of memory between 8 and 12 months of age and the shift from a perceptual mode to a symbolic-linguistic mode at about 17 months may be related more to maturation of special areas in the central nervous system than to the mother-child bond. The significance of this, according to Kagan, is that not *all* the experiences of the average infant with his or her parents necessarily have a long-lasting, or cumulative, effect. The argument is an important one, since it suggests, among other things, that the present is as important as the past. It also suggests that an almost serendipitous, discontinuous emergence of new functions, related as much to current neurophysiological maturation as to past events, adds to the generous plasticity of the neonate and young infant, and that this plasticity allows for great leeway in early childrearing—in the end, providing further opportunity for later development to supersede, overshadow, or incorporate previous experiences. Kagan, then, raises the important issues of discontinuities and present development.

Infantile Amnesia

Few of us remember much, if anything, from our first years of life. Psychoanalysis has suggested the concept of infantile amnesia to account for this phenomenon, with the expectation that repressed memories, or what we call memories, will be recovered during analysis. An alternative hypothesis has now been suggested, derived from studies in cognitive development. Specifically, the observed behavior may now also be understood, in part, as the result of new cognitive and experiential schemata incorporating and superseding previous schemata. One further extension of this newer concept is the idea that what was previously thought of as relatively pure transference from very early periods may now equally be considered as later reconstruction, perhaps similar to what Elkind (1967) has called personal fables, or myths. Piaget, for example, has commented that we reconstruct the past as a function of the present and that there may be no such thing at all as pure memories; that is, all memories of early childhood, to a greater or lesser extent, may be "created" (reconstructed) from later material, with inferences and fantasies interwoven. Piaget once gave a fascinating example from his own memories of early childhood:

> I have a childhood memory of my own that would be absolutely splendid if it were authentic, because it goes back to an age when one doesn't usually have memories of childhood. I was still in a baby carriage, taken out by a nurse, and she took me down the Champs-Elysees, near the Rond-Point. I was the object of an attempted kidnapping. Someone tried to grab me out of the buggy. The straps held me in and the nurse scuffled with the man, who scratched her forehead; something worse might have happened if a policeman hadn't come by just then. I can see him now as if it were yesterday—that was when they wore the little cape that comes down to here (he motions with his hand) and carried a little white stick, and all that, and the man fled. That's the story. As a child I had the glorious memory of having been the object of an attempted kidnapping. Then—I must have been about fifteen—my parents received a letter from the nurse, saying that she had just converted and wanted to confess all her sins, and that she had invented the kidnapping story herself, that she had scratched her own forehead, and that she now offered to return the watch she'd been given in recognition of her courage. In other words, there wasn't an iota of truth in the memory. And I have a very vivid memory of the experience, even today. I can tell you just where it happened on Champs-Elysees, and I can still see the whole thing [Bringuier, 1980, p. 120].

This focus on the present is not, of course, to be construed as a discounting of the past; it merely serves to remind us, first, that there is a present during which development continues, and second, that although developmental processes may begin with genetic coding, the phenotypic expression is continuously modulated by interactions with the environment at each stage of development (Eisenber, 1977). For example, environmental variables may determine which identical twin develops schizophrenia (Kety, 1976), which children with neurological deficits at one year of age will subsequently show signs of an attention deficit disorder (Rutter, Tizard, and Whitmore, 1970), or which child who experiences a separation from parents will subsequently show a disturbance (Rutter, 1972b). Even the temperament of the child does not remain fixed, but varies with the successive environments in which he or she develops (Graham, Rutter, and George, 1973, Chess, 1978). In short, nowadays we attempt to see the child in his or her biological and social context as well as intrapsychically, and to see this whole within a developmental frame of reference that includes each step along the time line from past to present.

The Concept of Fixation

Is there such a thing as pure fixation? Again, findings from cognitive developmental research now suggest that each later stage of development supersedes all earlier stages and that constructs developed at a given stage appear to become an integral part of the qualitatively new constructs that follow in an invariant sequence. This suggests that the concept of a more or less unchanged past fixation may not necessarily be a viable concept in the basic structure of, say, a current phobia. Beyond that, it also may no longer be a *sufficient* explanation, since we now also have evidence for a biological component in certain phobias, which I shall come to soon.

Dreams

The neurobiology of dreaming at the very least raises new questions about the nature of dreams. Hobson and McCarley (1977), for example, have postulated that the giant neurons of the pontine reticular formation, the so-called frontal gigantocellular field (FTG) neurons, fire off during the desynchronized sleep state (D sleep) and bombard the forebrain, which then must make sense of the messages received, resulting in the "dreamy" quality of dreams. This FTG cells activity increases just before a REM period and peaks during REM sleep. The FTG cell activity also activates cells in other parts of the brain, including the visual centers and the vestibular system. Koukkou and Lehmann (1983) in Zurich have also proposed a physiological model for the biological significance of dreams, which suggests a physiological explanation for the psychological phenomenon of dream work.

With these findings and new theories, a new dimension must now be considered in our understanding of dreaming, if not our understanding of the role of the forebrain in a particular dream. What this may mean again is that an important set of developmental and neurophysiological variables now have to be taken into account in any comprehensive theory of the meaning of a dream. Put another way, the new struggle is no longer between nature and nurture, but between biology and meaning. At any rate, this newer work considerably broadens the basis for a more complete scientific understanding of dreams in general, and may in the future open up new possibilities for the understanding of a particular dream.

Infant Capacities and Behavior

What is striking is the wealth of new data on the earliest dyadic relationship and the astonishing capacities of the newborn. Feature perception and visual organization can be demonstrated at birth (Kessen and Bornstein, 1978). At one week of age, the infant can be attracted to strongly patterned stimuli, such as horizontal shapes, concentric circles, and facelike mosaics. Pattern is also preferred over color or brightness or size, again indicating some degree of form perception in the neonate. Infants also appear to be attracted by complex patterns rather than simple ones and by objects that are in motion rather than ones that are stationary. It soon becomes clear that the infant prefers to look at an object that (1) is in almost constant motion, (2) emits a great deal of highly varied stimuli, (3) appeals to several different sensory modalities, (4) is complex, (5) possesses a distinctive pattern, and (6) is responsive to the infant's own behavior (Fantz, 1975; Fagan, 1979). If we consider these characteristics, we see at once that they are all contained in the mother's face.

Thus, there is now satisfactory evidence for a strong developmental biological guarantee that, given a responsive adult, attachment will occur within the context of that dyadic relationship. Klaus and Kennell (1976) at one time carried this further and suggested that infants utilized *all* these capacities in their earliest bonding behavior. Here it is important not to go beyond the data. The development of the parent-child relationship is still a long-term, complex phenomenon; in this context, the concept of the critical importance or so-called sensitive period of the first minutes and hours of life goes beyond the data (Lamb, 1982a, 1982b; Korsch, 1983). Klaus and Kennell (1982) themselves retracted their extreme earlier position and recently noted that the human infant is highly adaptable and able to utilize any one of a number of fail-safe routes to attachment. Yet there is another point to note here: an original observation led to a hypothesis, perhaps an extreme one, which was then subjected to critical studies. Klaus and Kennell then acted as true scientists and were able to change their views on the far-reaching importance they initially attached to these early moments between parent and child.

Much of this research is consonant with the current tendency to include the dyadic relationship in all studies of infant development, a point emphasized by Schaffer (1977) and others. What is being suggested here again is that even within the dyadic relationship there is a complex biological component for the earliest adaptive behavior of the neonate and infant, and that this biological component probably plays an important part in the individual's subsequent formation of object relations (or attachments). And it may even be, in many instances, that the major thrust of the infant's genetic programming outweighs minor variations in parental behavior.

Emde (1981) recently reviewed a huge body of child development research (Clarke and Clarke, 1976; Bell and Harper, 1977; Clarke-Stewart, 1977; Kagan, Kearsley, and Zelazo, 1978; Osofsky, 1979; Sameroff, 1978), and he essentially noted what amounts to a number of challenges to clinical theory in psychoanalysis:

> 1. The infant constructs his or her own reality, and what analysts "reconstruct" for the patient in fact may never have happened. Analysts should therefore perhaps renew their emphasis on recent and current experience and not be so concerned to understand or modify early experiences. Analysts have identified, as it were, too much with the "helpless infant" who, it turns out, is not so helpless.
> 2. Discontinuities are prominent in development, suggesting that we modify the theory of so-called reorganization of experience that is said to take place, for example, at puberty. Discontinuities may occur not only during infancy, but also during so-called latency and, of course, at puberty, when new myelination arcs occur (Yakovlev and Lecours, 1967).
> 3. Because there is a strong self-righting tendency after deflection from a developmental pathway, a single traumatic episode is unlikely to be pathogenic.
> 4. The concept of irreversibility of adverse effects, such as major maternal deprivation, should be modified, since it has been shown that environmental changes can offer major compensation for early environmental deficits.
> 5. The term "object relations" is particularly unfortunate in the light of recent findings of social reciprocity and mutual interaction and change between infant and caregiver; the "object" is not simply the "target" of drives.
> 6. Psychoanalysts have not given sufficient attention to transactions within the family that determine which opportunities prevail and which early experiences endure. Psychoanalysts now should look to the environment as well as to the individual, to the interface as well as to the intrapsychic.
> 7. Developmental phases other than infancy are equally important, and subsequent experiences continue to modify early experiences.

Attachment Behavior and Regression

Studies on attachment (Bowlby, 1969; Ainsworth, 1973) also raise interesting questions about so-called regression. Consider attachment behaviors, such as crying and clinging, which become more prominent at times of stress, including separation, sickness, and death, particularly when there is no alternative solution. Clinically, one might ordinarily regard such behavior as regression. However, it is important to emphasize, as Bowlby does, that such behaviors may represent instead an intensification of attachment behavior, *not* regression. The significance of this difference is that intensification of attachment behavior must be recognized as a *normal* phenomenon and should be distinguished from pathological or pathogenic regression. This ethological approach to behavior is, I think, an important if circumscribed contribution to our knowledge, one that is worth noting in child psychiatry today.

Stranger Anxiety

The idea of intensified attachment behavior immediately raises the question of the meaning of "stranger anxiety" in six- to eight-month-old infants. Psychoanalysts emphasize the frailty of object constancy in its early stages of development, when object constancy is threatened by overriding drive needs and the anxiety precipitated by the danger of loss of the object when the familiar mother is replaced by the stranger.

Here too, however, we have several alternative hypotheses; one of these is derived from cognitive developmental theory. One could say, for example, using cognitive developmental terms, that the infant's behavior in reaction to the stranger is actually a reaction to a discrepancy that is beyond the infant's capacity to assimilate or otherwise respond to constructively (Kagan, 1976). More formally, the hypothesis would state that an event (such as the presentation of a stranger) that activates existing structures (the schema of a known person), but that cannot be assimilated into these structures, creates arousal. If the discrepancy and arousal are too great because of a failure of assimilation and accommodation, disequilibrium occurs and negative affect is experienced. Like the psychoanalytic theory of stranger anxiety, this cognitive developmental theory *too* remains to be tested. The point is: we now have competing theories that require empirical testing.

This newer theory, by the way, also suggests a biological maturational phenomenon, and as such raises new questions of the meaning of the experience for the future development of the infant. What may be important here is the infant's experience of being able, or not being able, actively to do something about the experience of discrepancy. Here then is another example of what is essentially a biological phenomenon confronting the infant, who now has to deal with it as a life experience and make his or her meaning of it.

Transitional Objects

Another trend in the field today is that child psychiatry is becoming more data-based and less speculative. That is, the data are better controlled and more reliable. For example, to tackle the question of transitional objects,

Sherman and her co-workers at Cornell University (1981) recently collected data from parents of 171 normal children between 9 and 13 years of age from the middle to upper socioeconomic class. Briefly, their study did not substantiate earlier theoretical formulations on the use of treasured objects in relation to psychological health or illness. In fact, they documented no significant differences between those children who *were* attached to a treasured object and those who were *not,* or between those children who continue to use a soft object after age 9 and those who *never* had a treasured object. These finding are interesting for two reasons: they underscore the necessity of testing a clinical hypothesis with the scientific method (in this case an epidemiological study) and highlight again "the diversity and richness of individual experience that falls within that larger category called 'normal' " (p. 383).

We need studies that establish what is normal behavior in a child, and much of this has recently come from Piagetian studies, as Elkind (1982) has elegantly pointed out. However, at the same time we need reliable data. A recent study by Mahalski (1982) illustrates this point. Mahalski studied 199 first-year psychology students by means of a questionnaire; 62 percent said that they had been attached to a special, soft object during childhood. When 80 mothers of the students were asked the same question, however, nearly one-fourth of the mothers' answers did not agree with those of their sons or daughters. What is more, nearly one-fifth of the students disagreed with their own answers one year later. The study clearly showed that retrospective questionnaire information about attachment to objects is unreliable. So we are still left with a question about the scientific validity of studies (at least of questionnaire studies) on the clinical significance of the transitional object.

A Period of Latency

The term "latency" is problematic at two levels: (1) at the level of the reliability of the observations and clinical data, and (2) at the conceptual level.

At the observational level, several empirical studies have shown, if anything, an *increase* in sexual activities during this age period (Broderick, 1966; Reese, 1966; Janus and Bess, 1976). That is, the sexuality is anything but latent; in fact it is often quite overt.

At the conceptual level, we can turn to the work of Shapiro and Perry (1976), who carefully and systematically reviewed three major areas of information about biopsychological events during this developmental period. Specifically, they reviewed the data on perceptual-postural maturation, temporospatial orientation, and cognitive change. On the basis of this very thoughtful survey, they concluded that the psychoanalytic idea of a biphasic growth of sexual drive is *not* the significant substratum on which the biological timetable for this period of development is based. Rather, they noted that processes within the central nervous system, together with cognitive strategies derived from maturation, probably provide the biological clock basis for this developmental period. Furthermore, they viewed this maturation as a significant *discontinuity* in behavioral development. But then Shapiro and Perry lost their courage: they attempted to incorporate all this new, multilevel, biopsychological information on the seven-year-old under the old term "latency." I think this was a procrustean effort, rather like fitting all our knowledge of modern neurochemistry under the old heading "alchemy." Psychoanalysts, it seems, are loath to discard a term. Yet the assumptions made when the concept of latency was first derived 75 years ago are no longer sufficient, particularly in the light of new epidemiological and biological knowledge. What is important here is that new data are enabling us to take a fresh look at an old concept, and that the fresh look now encompasses a biopsychosocial perspective within the context of a comprehensive developmental approach.

Adolescent Turmoil

Is adolescent turmoil a common, or even normative, phenomenon, as Erikson (1959), Anna Freud (1958), and Blos (1970) have asserted? One analyst even went so far as to state that she "would feel great concern for the adolescent who causes no trouble and feels no disturbance" (Geleerd, 1957, p. 267). What are some of the facts?

If we turn to the Isle of Wight Study (Rutter, et al., 1970), the data show that "alienation from parents is *not* common in 14-year-olds" (p. 40) and that most young teenagers in a general population in fact get on well with their parents, who in turn continue to have a "substantial influence on their children right through adolescence" (p. 54). Moreover, interviews with 96 boys and 88 girls revealed that at least half the group did not experience anything that could at all be called inner turmoil, and only a small minority appeared to be clinically depressed. Further, the data provided no support for the idea that psychiatric disorder is much more common during the middle teens; rather, most adolescents do not show psychiatric disorders (although the pattern of disorders shows a shift in terms of an increased prevalence of both depression and school refusal).

In short, Rutter and his colleagues convincingly demonstrated that the psychiatric importance of adolescent turmoil in normal adolescents, who constitute the majority, has probably been overestimated in the past—a conclusion based on sound epidemiological data. A subsequent study by Kaplan, Hong, and Weinhold (1984) confirms this view.

DEVELOPMENTAL PSYCHOPATHOLOGY

Let us now turn to just a few of the relatively recent ideas on some of the disorders we encounter in child psychiatry.

Bedwetting

Bedwetting hardly seems to be considered a psychological disorder anymore. Many of the beautiful anecdotal descriptions by Gerard (1939), Katan (1946), and others, in which bedwetting was attributed to psychodynamic conflicts, today might be considered instances of a general developmental arousal disorder (Shaffer and Gardner, 1981). In any event, attempts to operationalize these earlier hypotheses and test them in controlled studies (e.g., Achenbach and Lewis, 1971) have so far failed to produce evidence to support many of these psychodynamic hypotheses as of primary etiological importance. Once more, we are presented with a more comprehensive biopsychological basis for our understanding, in this case of bedwetting. And this new understanding has important treatment implications including, in certain instances of bedwetting, the use of imipramine (Martin, 1971).

Obsessional Neurosis

Even notions about the causes of obsessive-compulsive disorders are now being reappraised. For example, some evidence now supports a neurobiological hypothesis (Elkins, Rapoport, and Lipsky, 1980). The evidence—which includes twin studies, association with Tourette's syndrome, neuropsychological test data, psychosurgery reports, association with brain damage, and psychopharmacological effects—is only suggestive at this stage, but it is nevertheless of great interest. Rapoport et al. (1981), for example, recently reported on a group of nine adolescents with primary obsessive-compulsive disorder who had clear biological dysfunctions.

More specifically, a serotonin hypothesis has been suggested given the finding that clomipramine is more effective than a placebo in the treatment of obsessive-compulsive disorders (Marks et al., 1980; Thoren et al., 1980). In fact, correlations have now been found between a clinical response to clomipramine and changes in the cerebrospinal fluid levels of both 5-hydroxyindoleacetic acid (a serotonin metabolite) and L-tryptophan (a serotonin precursor) (Insel and Murphy, 1981).

All of these findings are tantalizing, and still inconclusive. But what they again suggest is the importance of remaining truly open to a biopsychosocial developmental viewpoint on human behavior and its disorders.

Phobias

Donald Klein (1964) recently postulated that some agoraphobic adult patients suffered from a disruption of biological processes that regulate separation anxiety. During childhood, these patients experienced panic and severe clinging, dependent behavior associated with separation. Both Propranolol®, a beta-blocker, and imipramine, a tricyclic, appear to prevent the unpredictable and spontaneous attacks in these adults which are apparently associated with an outpouring of catecholamines. Consequently, imipramine was tried in children with severe separation anxiety, e.g., "school phobia," with some startling, if transient, success (Gittleman-Klein and Klein, 1971, 1973). This biological component is now an important part of our understanding of certain kinds of severe phobias in children, which are beginning to be viewed from the multidisciplinary perspectives of what we now call developmental psychopathology. Recently, for example, Mikkelsen, Detlor, and Cohen (1981) suggested a role for catecholamines in the pathogenesis of phobic syndromes when they found that school avoidance developed in 15 patients with Tourette's disorder who were being treated with haloperidol.

What all this suggests is that we now need to include biological hypotheses, in addition to our intrapsychic and psychosocial formulations, as we try to understand phobias in children.

Depression

Depression is another area of psychopathology in which our thinking has undergone tremendous change over recent years. Not even 20 years ago some child psychiatrists and child analysts were saying that you couldn't have depression in childhood (Rie, 1966). At the same time, some other analysts, particularly Sandler and Joffe (1965), *were* presenting hypotheses about depression in childhood based on their psychoanalytic material (see also Laufer, 1976). These latter views continue to be of great interest, although they, too, remain to be confirmed by controlled studies.

Yet what is now of equal interest is the biological developmental knowledge of the disorder, based on controlled studies. For example, McKnew and Cytryn (1979)—in a controlled study of nine children, 6 to 12 years old, with diagnosed depression—suggested that a physiological counterpart to emotional "detachment" in children may be a suppression of the general arousal system, mediated through the noradrenergic network and centered on the locus ceruleus, resulting in a reduction in the level of 3-methoxy-4-hydroxyphenylethylene glycol (MHPG). Puig-Antich and his associates (1979) have demonstrated hypersecretion of cortisol in children suffering from a depressive syndrome. Puig-Antich essentially demonstrated that prepubertal children who fit the Research Diagnostic Criteria (RDC) for major depressive illness have a disturbance of the circadian rhythm of cortisol excretion similar to that of some depressed adults: in the evening and early morning, secretion ceases in normal (control) subjects, but continues in depressed patients.

Recently, Poznanski and her colleagues (1982) have provided preliminary data that suggests that the dexamethasone suppression test is significantly positive in children with major depressive disorder. Again, these findings suggest that an endogenous depression does occur in children, and that when it does occur such depression is clinically and neuroendocrinologically similar to the endogenous depression found in adults.

Also of interest from a biopsychological perspective is Brumback and Staton's (1981) hypothesis that dysfunctional aminergic neurotransmission associated with depression may unmask previously subclinical neurological signs. Signs of left hemiparesis (including pronation drift of the outstretched left arm, hyperactive left-sided tendon reflexes, and left extensor plantar responses) were found during a major depressive disorder suffered by the children they studied, but disappeared when the depression was temporarily relieved by treatment with tricyclic antidepressants (Staton, Wilson, and Brumback, 1981). In addition, they observed that in 21 children with major depressive illness, treatment with amitriptyline was associated with improvement in the results of right-hemisphere and frontal-lobe tests, including improvement in IQ on the WISC(R) Performance Scale (Brumback, Staton, and Wilson, 1980).

Recently, the suggestion has been made that there might be a specific genetic marker for depressive disorders. Weitkamp et al. (1981) initially reported that depressive disorders segregate along with HLA (human leukocyte antigen) in families, which suggested that a locus on the sixth chromosome might contribute to the risk factors for depression. Had this been confirmed, it would have been a very important finding because "linkage of depressive disorders to a specific genetic marker raises the possibility of discovering the gene product through techniques of molecular biology" (Matthysse and Kidd, 1981, p. 1341).

None of these findings explains depression in children, or describes what the experience feels like to the individual, but together they vastly broaden the basis for our understanding of the condition—far beyond the notions, say, of anger turned inwards, loss of self-esteem, or learned helplessness. Mandell (1976), for example, has hypothesized a psychobiological developmental theory of an altered biochemical state to explain the persistence of depressive affect even after the neurotic conflicts related to depression have been resolved. He suggests that this could conceivably arise because the developing nervous system of the young infant is particularly vulnerable to impingement on its biochemical balance. Thus, if a depletion of monoamine transmitters occurs in response, say, to an early and persistent psychological loss, *that* altered biochemical state may then become the "normal," permanent biochemical state for that individual throughout his or her life. Any subsequent return to a more gratifying environment, either temporarily during an interpretation, or for more prolonged periods as a result of psychotherapy or a changed social environment, still eventually would be perceived as though that, so to speak, were the "deviant" state of mind. That is, the prevailing tendency of the biochemical response would always remain in the direction of returning to the previously acquired and permanent "depressive" baseline state. Here, then, is an attempt to derive a superordinate developmental theory to account for both psychological and biochemical mechanisms of a disorder, in this case, major depressive disorder.

Infantile Autism

It's hard to believe that just 20 or so years ago some child psychiatrists and child analysts were still blaming mothers for childhood autism.[1] Recent studies on infantile autism now reveal, among other causes, evidence for at least one group in which there is a genetic factor (Folstein and Rutter, 1978; E. Ritvo, personal communication, 1979; August, Stewart, and Tsai, 1981). Infantile autism in many instances is also now considered by many scientists to be the result of a "central disorder of cognition" involving language (Rutter, 1972b); it is thought that the genetic influence "concerns some broader linguistic or cognitive impairment, of which autism is one result" (Folstein and Rutter, 1978, p. 220). CAT scans have also shown that some children with autism have a variety of abnormalities, often in the left hemisphere (Hier, Le May, and Rosenberger, 1979; Damasio et al., 1980; Caparulo et al., 1981; Campbell et al., 1982).

I mention this example of autism simply because I think it is humbling and important to remember how mistaken we can be in our views. The

---

[2] For example, Lippman (1962), a highly respected analyst and author of a book on treatment that was favorably reviewed at the time, after giving recognition to Leo Kanner for first describing the syndrome of infantile autism in 1943, then noted that Beata Rank felt that it was emotional illness in the mother that was primarily responsible for the child's pathology. He went on to say that "only when the parents have been in treatment . . . [does the] mother . . . gradually learn that she has rejected the child" (p. 305), and that presumably that was a major cause of the child's autism. It is difficult nowadays to realize that this was the prevailing view, at least among analysts, as recently as the early 1960s. It was not, of course, the view of Kanner and his colleagues, and of course it is not the prevailing view in child psychiatry today.

lesson, I think, is that we should be wary of any dogmatism in our views on any topic, including certain phobias, compulsions, and depressions.[2]

PSYCHOANALYTIC RESEARCH

Psychoanalysts doing research in psychoanalysis of course have formidable problems in establishing reliability and validity. Kaplan (1981), in his presidential address to the American Psychoanalytic Association, noted that the fundamental challenge to psychoanalysis was still "a much needed validation of . . . basic theoretical and clinical concepts" (p. 23). More specifically, he told analysts that " any progress in psychoanalysis must include an evaluation of the psychoanalytic process which involves making all of the data public by notes, tape recording, etc." (p. 19). This is a very difficult challenge. One consequence of the relative scarcity in scientific child psychoanalytic research is that many of the concepts in psychoanalysis are now considered by a number of analysts as descriptive metaphors rather than true theory. Most of the wealth of accumulated clinical experience awaits scientific validation through suitable methods, which still await invention. Validation is a major challenge for child analysis today.

Another challenge for child analysis is to relate itself to the ever-enlarging spectrum of biological sciences that now form such a formidable part of the foundation of human behavior. Neither psychoanalysis nor the neurochemistry of the synapse alone (nor perhaps even both together) is at present sufficient to explain all of human behavior. Behavior that may appear to have (and that may indeed have) strong psychodynamic determinants may also be associated with significant biological origins. At the very least, a rapprochement between the behavioral and biological sciences is needed. But, more than that, we may eventually need a superordinate general developmental theory that will incorporate knowledge from *all* the different fields we've mentioned.

What new directions lie ahead for psychoanalytic research proper?

At present the most popular and perhaps the best method in psychoanalytic research is the historical method, which essentially consists of using observation, circumstantial evidence, memory, reconstruction, and prediction to confirm or refute a hypothesis. As Waelder (1970) long ago pointed out, this is not a bad method, when one considers that the Rosetta stone was deciphered on the basis of reconstruction, or that

---

[2] Some time ago I think it was the dean of Harvard Medical School who said to a first-year class: "Gentlemen [in those days there were no women in the class] half of what you learn will in 10 years be out of date—and the trouble is, we don't know which half."

juries arrive at verdicts "beyond a reasonable doubt" through the use of reconstruction. The essential point is that if the reconstruction is correct, all future evidence will confirm that prediction and none will refute it. However, this historical method, as we know, is often fallacious.

The experimental method, on the other hand, is almost unknown among psychoanalysts, except when an experiment in nature affords an opportunity to observe what happens when a major variable is changed (e.g., Spitz' description of infants in institutions, or Anna Freud's description of children and their families when their lives were disrupted by war). Perhaps one might even say that experiment is an inappropriate method for psychoanalysis. In any case, just because something is experimental, scalable and measurable, does not in itself guarantee the importance of the findings: the finding that the tooth fairy or the Easter bunny is a common fantasy in a six-year-old may be demonstrated through impeccable methodology, but the finding will still be trivial in importance for a clinician dealing with a psychotic or violent adolescent. And of course subsequent research may always refute a previous supposed finding. That is one way progress is made in science.

Psychoanalytic research may nevertheless have to content itself with remaining essentially an observational and reconstructive pursuit. By that I mean it may never become an experimental science with a critical methodology. And that may be the ultimate limiting factor for psychoanalysis; the giant imaginative steps were taken by Freud, and those who follow him may have to consider themselves fortunate if they can merely follow, much less make truly substantive scientific advances in psychoanalysis.

Interestingly, according to Weizsaecker (1954), Freud himself thought in 1926 that psychoanalysis would have interesting material for about 50 years. To be sure, the 1970s marked a turn from the primacy of interest in psychoanalytic ideas to the present ascendency of biological ideas.

What is the future for psychoanalysis as a science? First, I shall define "science" here as an enterprise consisting of the interaction of all the following necessary components: observations, theories and hypotheses that have explanatory and predictive power and that conform to reality; and methods of critical testing, including access to data for purposes of verification and replication (Nagel, 1961; Pap, 1963; Popper, 1963; Medawar, 1982). Myths and religious beliefs, of course, may "fit" together, appear to make sense, explain, and endure, but they are not required to meet scientific tests of verification and replication. They may even comfort, soothe, and give meaning to life—but they are not scientifically true.

The measure of psychoanalytic theory as a science, then, is the extent to which *all* these necessary components are present. This means that an anecdotal report by an analysand that he or she feels better after analysis is not a *scientific* test of the results of psychoanalytic treatment: the relief may simply have been coincidental with the termination of the analysis rather than a result of the analysis (i.e.,*post hoc ergo propter hoc* reasoning is unscientific).

To gain some idea of the degree to which each of the above components is present in psychoanalysis, I recently reviewed three major psychoanalytic publications—the *International Journal of Psychoanalysis,* the *Journal of the American Psychoanalytic Association* and *The Psychoanalytic Study of the Child*—for the period 1972 to 1982. Although there was an abundance of observations, theories, explanations, predictions, and hypotheses, there was scant evidence of scientific testing. There were no reports of studies with adequate sample size, inclusion and exclusion criteria, matched comparison groups, minimization of observer bias, or tests of reliability. And none of the studies was replicated. Even the methodology of single-case design (Kazdin, 1982) was not in evidence.

It is possible that none of the available methods of science is suitable for the phenomena addressed in psychoanalysis. If this is so, a truly difficult problem is posed: If the definition of science includes an accepted critical methodology, and if psychoanalysis has *no* critical methodology, how will psychoanalysis achieve recognition as a science?

Several possibilities suggest themselves. First, a new generation of psychoanalytic scientists with appropriate training in scientific methodology as well as clinical experience may emerge, enabling the scientific investigation of psychoanalytic hypotheses to proceed. There are signs that this may already be taking place (Masling, 1983). Interestingly, the majority of the investigators engaged in research in psychoanalysis seem to be psychologists.

Second, psychoanalysis may move out of the sciences and into other areas. Certainly there is evidence of great interest in psychoanalysis among literature scholars, historians, lawyers, and others not usually considered to be scientists.

Finally, psychoanalysis as a science may become arrested and left behind as a stage in the history of ideas.

NEW TECHNOLOGIES

In contrast, one of the exciting things in child psychiatry today is that there are in fact new technologies on the horizon. Bax (1980) recently reviewed some of these new possibilities for research. For example, using a sophisticated combination of radioactive labeling of oxygen, carbon dioxide, and glucose with a computerized scanning technique (proton emission tomography, or PET), Lassen et al. (1977) have reported fascinating studies of cerebral blood flow during a whole range of normal cerebral activities. Phelps, Kuhl, and Mazziota (1981) have shown how "positron computed tomography can map the distribution of local cerebral metabolic functions in humans in a relatively safe and noninvasive manner" (p. 1447). The CAT scan of course has already demonstrated its usefulness in some children with a diagnosis of minimal brain damage (Bergstrom and Bille, 1978). Evoked potentials combined with computer technology have similarly given rise to a new technique for the study of children with learning disorders (John et al., 1977).

Perhaps even more astonishing is the nuclear magnetic resonance (NMR) technique, which may in the future yield information on tissue chemistry as well as provide images of the anatomy of the brain. The measures used involve the time required for atomic nuclei to lose the energy gained after being placed in a strong magnetic field (so-called relaxation time). One tentative finding is that relaxation times in the brains of patients with manic-depressive illness are longer than normal, but return to normal with lithium treatment.

DISCUSSION

Scientific research in child psychiatry, using sophisticated methods and technology, is on the threshold of giving us new windows on human behavior. In the light of these studies, some of our ideas have held up remarkably well; others have, well, withered a little. Given this multilevel and multidiscipline information explosion on child development and developmental psychopathology, in what directions are we going? Or, if we can project into the future at all, in what directions *should* we be going?

One direction is to continue to struggle, as we do now, with multiple theories, selecting whatever theory seems to work best clinically, regardless of its validity. In fact that is how clinicians must at times operate; for example, we do nowadays use multiple approaches in the treatment of anorexia nervosa; in the treatment of severe, major depressive disorders in children; and in the treatment of Tourette's disorder. Similar multiple approaches are now used in the treatment of certain severe phobic disorders and compulsive disorders.

Another direction is to lay the groundwork for some genius to come along, probably of the order of magnitude of a Copernicus, a Darwin, a Freud, a Watson or a Crick, to conceive of things in a radically different way to make the vital connection between experience and the synapse. Some fragile attempts have already been made to establish this bridge between psychological experiences and synaptic functions (Heilbrunn,

1979; Kendel, 1979). Correlations between psychological and neurological developmental sequences have also been suggested (Meyersburg and Post, 1979; Lewis, 1982), and specific biological foundations have been outlined (Rutter, 1981). Perhaps we might foster this process as we go about the business of formulating the psychopathology in a child or family, by regularly trying to hypothesize genetic, biochemical, and sociocultural hypotheses as well as psychodynamic hypotheses.

In conclusion I think we are on the threshold of exciting new directions in child psychiatry. We need to broaden the base for our understanding of both normal and abnormal behavior by including biological, psychological, and social factors, and eventually we may well have a new, superordinate, general psychobiological developmental theory in child psychiatry. At any rate, I think we need to recognize this possibility for a new theory, or theories, as we go about our day-to-day work with our patients. Chance, Pasteur once observed, favors the prepared mind.

REFERENCES

Achenbach, T. & Lewis, M. (1971). A proposed model for clinical research and its application to encorpresis and enuresis. *J. Amer. Acad. Child Psychiat.* 10:535.

Ainsworth, M. D. S. (1973). The development of infant-mother attachment. In *Review of Child Development Research*, vol. 3, ed. B. M. Caldwell & H. N. Ricciuti. Chicago: Univ. Chicago Press, pp. 1–94.

August, G. J., Stewart, M. A., & Tsai, L. (1981). The incidence of cognitive disabilities in the siblings of autistic children. *Brit. J. Psychiat.* 137:78–24.

Bax, M. C. O. (1980). Future trends and problems. In *Scientific Foundations of Developmental Psychiatry*, ed. M. Rutter. London: Heinemann, pp. 371–373.

Bell, R. Q., & Harper, L. V. (1977). *Child Effects on Adults.* New York: Halsted.

Bergstrom, K., & Bille, B. (1978). Computed tomography of the brain in children with minimal brain damage: A preliminary study of 46 children. *Neuropediatrie* 9:378–384.

Blos, P. (1970). *The Young Adolescent: Clinical Studies.* London: Callier-Macmillan.

Bowlby, J. (1969). *Attachment and Loss,* Vol. 1. New York: Basic Books.

Bringuier, J.-C. (1980). *Conversations with Jean Piaget.* Chicago: Univ. Chicago Press.

Broderick, C. B. (1966). Sexual behavior among preadolescents. *J. Soc. Issues* 22:6–21.

Brumback, R. A., & Staton, R. D. (1981). Depression-induced neurological dysfunction. *New Eng. J. Med.* 355:642.

——— & Wilson, H. (1980). Neuropsychological study of children during and after remission of endogenous depressive episodes. *Percept. Motor Skills* 50:1163–1167.

Campbell, M., Rosenbloom. S., Perry, R., George, A., Krichoff, I., Anderson, L., Small, A., & Jennings, S. (1982). Computerized axial tomographic scans in young autistic children. *Amer. J. Psychiat.* 139:510–512.

Caparulo, B., Cohen, D., Rothman, S., Young, G., Katz, N., Shaywitz, S., & Shaywitz, B. (1981). Computed tomographic brain scanning in children with developmental neuropsychiatric disorders. *J. Amer. Acad. Child Psychiat.* 20:338–357.

Chess, S. (1978). The plasticity of human development. *J. Amer. Acad. Child Psychiat.* 17:80–91.

Clarke, A. M., & Clarke, A. D. B. (1976). *Early Experience: Myth and Evidence.* London: Open Books.
Clarke-Stewart, A. (1977). *Child Care in the Family: A Review of Research and Some Propositions for Policy.* New York: Academic Press.
Damasio, H., Maurer, R., Damasio, A., & Chui, H. (1980). Computerized tomographic scan findings in patients with autistic behavior. *Arch. Neurol.* 37:504–510.
Eisenberg, L. (1977). Development as a unifying concept in psychiatry. *Amer. J. Psychiat.* 133:225–237.
Elkind, D. (1967). Egocentrism in adolescence. *Child Dev.* 38:1025–1034.
——— (1982). Piagetian psychology and the practice of child psychiatry. *J. Amer. Acad. Child Psychiat.* 21:435–445.
Elkins, R., Rapoport, J. L., & Lipsky, A. (1980). Obsessive-compulsive disorder of childhood and adolescence: A neurobiological viewpoint. *J. Amer. Acad. Child Psychiat.* 19:511–525.
Emde, R. N. (1981). Changing models of infancy and the nature of early development: Remodeling the foundation. *J. Amer. Psychoanal. Assn.* 29:179–219.
Erikson, E. H. (1955). The problem of ego identity. *J. Amer. Psychoanal. Assn.* 4:56–121.
——— (1959). *Identity and the Life Cycle* [*Psychol. Issues,* Monogr. 1]. New York: Int. Univ. Press
Fagan, J. F. (1979). The origins of facial pattern recognition. In *Psychological Development from Infancy: Image to Intention,* ed. M. H. Bornstein & W. Kessen. New York: Halsted.
Fantz, R. L. (1975). Early visual selectivity. In *Infant Perception,* ed. L. b. Cohen & P. Salapatek. New York: Academic Press.
Folstein, S., & Rutter, M. (1978). A twin study of individuals with infantile autism. In *Autism: A Reappraisal of Concepts and Treatment,* ed. M. Rutter & E. Schopler. New York: Plenum Press, pp. 219–241.
Freud, A. (1958). Adolescence. *The Psychoanal. Study Child* 13:255–278.
Freud, S. (1900). The interpretation of dreams. *Standard Edition* 4 & 5.
——— (1914). On narcissism: An introduction. *Standard Edition* 14:67–104.
——— (1920). Beyond the pleasure principle. *Standard Edition* 18:3–64.
——— (1926). The question of lay analysis. *Standard Edition* 20:179–258.
——— (1940). An outline of psycho-analysis. *Standard Edition* 23:144–207.
Geleerd, E. R. (1957). Some aspects of psychoanalytic technique in adolescence. *Psychoanal. Study Child* 12:263–283.
Gerard, M. W. (1939). Enuresis: A study in etiology. *Amer. J. Orthopsychiat.* 9:48–58.
Gittleman-Klein, R., & Klein, D. (1971). Controlled imipramine treatment of school phobia. *Arch. Gen. Psychiat.* 25:205–207.
——— ——— (1973). School phobia: Diagnostic considerations in the light of imipramine effects. *J. Nerv. Ment. Dis.* 156:199–215.
Graham, P., Rutter, M., & George, S. (1973). Temperamental characteristics as predictors of behavior disorders in children. *Amer. J. Orthopsychiat.* 43:328–339.
Heilbrunn, G. (1979). Biologic correlates of psychoanalytic concepts. *J. Amer. Psychoanal. Assn.* 27:597–626.
Hier, D., LeMay, M., & Rosenberger, P. (1979). Autism and unfavorable left-right asymmetries of the brain. *J. Amer. Devel. Disord.* 9:153–159.
Hobson, J. A., & McCarley, R. W. (1977). The brain as a dream state generator: An activation-synthesis hypothesis of the dream process. *Amer. J. Psychiat.* 134:1335–1348.
Insel, T. R., & Murphy, D. L. (1981). The psychopharmacologic treatment of obsessive compulsive disorder: A review. *J. clin. Psychopharmacol.* 1:304–311.
Janus, S. S., & Bess, B. E. (1976). Latency: Fact of fiction? *Amer. J. Psychoanal.* 36:339–346.

John, E. R., et al. (1977). Neurometrics: Numerical taxonomy identifies different profiles of brain functions within groups of behaviorally similar people. *Science* 196:1393–1410.

Kagan, J. (1976). Emergent themes in human development. *Amer. Sci.* 64:186–196.

——— (1978). *The Growth of the Child: Reflections on Human Development.* New York: Norton.

——— (1979). The form of early development. *Arch. Gen. Psychiat.* 36:1047–1054.

——— Kearsley, R. B., & Zelazo, P. R. (1978). *Infancy: Its Place in Human Development.* Cambridge, Mass.: Harvard Univ. Press.

Kaplan, A. H. (1981). From discovery to validation: A basic challenge to psychoanalysis. *J. Amer. Psychoanal. Assn.* 29:3–26.

Kaplan, S., Hong, G. K., & Weinhold, C. (1984). Epidemiology of depressive symptomatology in adolescents. *J. Amer. Acad. Child Psychiat.* 23:91–98.

Katan, A. (1946). Experiences with enuretics. *Psychoanal. Study Child* 2:244–255.

Kazdin, A. E. (1982). *Single-Case Research Designs.* Oxford: Oxford Univ. Press.

Kendel, E. R. (1979). Psychotherapy and the single synapse. *New Eng. J. Med.* 310:1028–1037.

Kessen, W., & Bornstein, M. H. (1978). Discrimination of brightness change for infants. *J. Exper. Child Psychol.* 25:526–530.

Kety, S. S. (1976). Studies designed to disentangle genetic and environmental variables in schizophrenia. *Amer. J. Psychiat.* 133:1134–1137.

Klaus, M. H., & Kennell, J. H. (1976). *Maternal-Infant Bonding.* St. Louis: Mosby.

——— ——— (1982). *Parent-Infant Bonding.* St. Louis: Mosby.

Klein, D. F. (1964). Delineation of two drug-responsive anxiety syndromes. *Psychopharmacologia* 5:397–408.

Korsch, B. M. (1983). More on parent-infant bonding. *J. Pediat.* 102:249–250.

Koukkou, M., & Lehmann, D. (1983). Dreaming: The functional state-shift hypothesis. *Brit. J. Psychiat.* 142:221–223.

Lamb, M. E. (1982a). The bonding phenomena: Misinterpretations and their implications. *J. Pediat.* 101:555.

——— (1982b). Early contact and maternal-infant bonding: One decade later. *Pediat.* 70:763.

Lassen, N. A., et al. (1977). Cerebral function, metabolism and circulation. *Acta Neurol. Scand.* (Suppl. 64).

Laufer, M. (1976). Attempted suicide in adolescence. Presented at the Yale Child Study Center, May 4.

Lewis, M. (1982). *Clinical Aspects of Child Development,* 2nd Ed. Philadelphia: Lea & Febiger.

Lippman, H. S. (1962). *Treatment of the Child in Emotional Conflict,* 2nd Ed. New York: McGraw-Hill.

Mahalski, P. (1982). The reliability of memories for attachment to special, soft objects during childhood. *J. Amer. Acad. Child Psychiat.* 21:465–468.

Mandell, A. J. (1976). Neurobiological mechanisms of adaptation in relation to models of psychobiological development. In *Psychopathology and Child Development,* ed. E. - Schopler & R. J. Reichler. New York: Plenum Press, pp. 21–22.

Marks, I. M., et al. (1980). Clomipramine and exposure for obsessive compulsive rituals, I. *Brit. J. Psychiat.* 136:1–25.

Martin, G. I. (1971). Imipramine pamoate in the treatment of childhood enuresis. *Amer. J. Dis. Children* 122:42–47.

Masling, J., Ed. (1983). *Empirical Studies of Psychoanalytic Theories,* Vol. 1. Hillsdale, N.J.: Erlbaum.

Matthysse, S., & Kidd, K. K. (1981). Evidence of HLA linkage in depressive disorders. *New Eng. J. Med.* 305:1340–1341.

McKnew, D. H., & Cytryn, L. (1979). Urinary metabolites in chronically depressed children. *J. Amer. Acad. Child Psychiat.* 18:608–615.
Medawar, P. (1982). *Pluto's Republic.* Oxford: Oxford Univ. Press.
Meyersburg, H. A., & Post, R. M. (1979). An holistic developmental view of neural and psychological processes. *Brit. J. Psychiat.* 135:139–155.
Mikkelsen, E. J., Detlor, J., & Cohen, D. J. (1981). School avoidance and school phobia triggered by haloperidol in patients with Tourette's disorder. *Amer. J. Psychiat.* 138:1572–1576.
Nagel, E. (1961). *The Structure of Science.* New York: Harcourt, Brace, & World.
Osofsky, J., Ed. (1979). *Handbook of Infant Development.* New York: Wiley.
Pap, A. (1963). *An Introduction to the Philosophy of Science.* New York: Free Press.
Phelps, M. E., Kuhl, D. E., & Mazziotta, J. C. (1981). Metabolic mapping of the brain's response to visual stimulation: Studies in humans. *Science* 221:1445–1448.
Popper, K. (1963). *Conjectures and Refutations.* London: Routledge & Kegan Paul.
Poznanski, E. O., Carroll, B. J., Benergas, M. C., & Cook, S. C., (1982). The dexamethasone suppression test in prepubertal depressed children. *Amer. J. Psychiat.* 139:321–324.
Puig-Antich, J., et al. (1979). Plasma levels of imipramine (IMI) and desmethylimipramine (DMI) and clinical response in prepubertal major depressive disorder. *J. Amer. Acad. Child Psychiat.* 18:616–627.
Rapoport, J., Elkins, R., Langer, D. H., et al. (1981). Childhood obsessive disorder. *Amer. J. Psychiat.* 138:1545–1554.
Reese, H. W. (1966). Attitudes toward the opposite sex in late childhood. *Merrill-Palmer Q.* 12:157–163.
Rie, H. R. (1966). Depression in childhood. *J. Amer. Acad. Child Psychiat.* 5:653–685.
Rutter, M. (1972a), Clinical assessment of language disorders in the young child. In *The Child with Delayed Speech,* ed. M. Rutter & J. A. M. Martin. (*Clin. Devel. Med.,* No. 43.) London: Heinemann/SIMP.
——— (1972b). *Maternal Deprivation Reassessed.* Harmondsworth: Penguin.
——— Ed. (1981) *Scientific Foundations of Developmental Psychiatry.* Baltimore: Univ. Park Press.
——— & Schopler, E., Eds. (1978). *Autism: A Reappraisal of Concepts and Treatment.* New York: Plenum Press.
——— Tizard, J., & Whitmore, K. (1970). *Education, Health and Behavior.* London: Longmans, Green.
Sameroff, A., Ed. (1978). Organization and stability of newborn behavior. *Monogr. Soc. Res. Child Devel.* 43:5–6.
Sandler, J., & Joffe, W. S. (1965). Notes on childhood depression. *Int. J. Psychoanal.* 46:88–96.
Schaffer, H. R. (1977). Introduction: Early interactive development. In *Studies in Mother-Infant Interaction,* ed. H. R. Schaffer. London: Academic Press.
Shaffer, D., & Gardner. A. (1981). Classification of enuresis. Presented at the 28th Annual Meeting of the American Academy of Child Psychiatry, Dallas, Oct. 15.
Shapiro, T., & Perry, T. (1976). Latency revisited: The age of seven plus or minus one. *Psychoanal. Study Child* 31:79–105.
Sherman, M., Hertzig, M., Austrian, R., & Shapiro, T. (1981). Treasured objects in school-aged children. *Pediat.* 68:379–386.
Staton, R. D., Wilson, H., & Brumback, R. A. (1981). Cognitive improvement associated with tricyclic antidepressant treatment of childhood major depressive illness. *Percept. Motor Skills* 53:219–234.

Thoren, P., et al. (1980). Clomipramine treatment of obsessive compulsive disorder: A controlled clinical trial. *Arch. Gen. Psychiat.* 37:1281–1289.
Waelder, R. (1970). Observation, historical reconstruction, and experiments. In *Psychoanalysis and Philosophy,* ed. C. Hanly & M. Lazerowitz. New York: Int. Univ. Press, pp. 280–326.
Weitkamp, L. R. et al. (1981). Depressive disorders and HLA: A gene on chromosome 6 that can affect behavior. *New Eng. J. Med.* 305:1301–1306.
Weizsaecker, V. von (1954). Reminiscences of Freud and Jung. In *Freud and the 20th Century,* ed. B. Nelson. New York: Meridian Books, 1957, pp. 59–75.
Yakovlev, P. I., & Lecours, A. R. (1967). The myelogenetic cycles of regional maturation of the brain. In *Regional Development of the Brain,* ed. A. Kinkonski. Oxford: Blackwell.

19/
Discussion: Psychoanalysis, Science, and Child Psychiatry
Joseph H. Beitchman, M.D.

Although this discussion agrees with Melvin Lewis that psychoanalysis needs revision in its methods and its theories, it emphasizes that psychoanalysis has also been the wellspring for many important ideas. There is a danger that if the pendulum moves too far toward the biological, the importance of psychodynamic factors may be overlooked. Though one must go beyond the strictly analytic method to test certain of its ideas, one must not be intimidated by the biological and statistical. Indeed, some of the ideas suggested by the empirical approaches do not on closer inspection have as firm a footing as may initially appear. Overall, the problem may be not so much with psychoanalysis per se, but with those who are sloppy in their thinking and in their methods.

Melvin Lewis's splendid paper is at once straightforward and complex. It is straightforward in that it points clearly to the need for new methods and new ideas if psychoanalysis is to remain relevant to the psychiatry of the 1980s, 1990s, and beyond. It is complex in that a vast array of biological and empirical data is brought forward to challenge traditional concepts such as fixation, latency, and adolescent turmoil. Revisions in our understanding of these concepts are offered and serve as the backdrop against which criticisms of psychoanalysis are made.

Lewis exhorts us to be scientific in our approach, laying particular emphasis on the need for psychoanalysis to develop a scientific methodology. Failure to do so will inevitably leave psychoanalysis behind as a stage in the history of ideas. Though its influence has been profound, the foundation on which it has been built has begun to crack. As a method of therapy, it has been found to be wanting; as a theory of personality development, it has also been shown to be faulty.

American psychiatry has shown a renewed orientation toward the medical, the biological, and the empirical. In part this may be a reaction to the armchair theorizing associated with psychoanalysis. This correction was needed, and the field should grow and mature because of it. But psychoanalysis and the psychoanalytic approach (in its broadest sense) still have an important role to play. It is right that psychoanalysis needs revision in its methods and theories; it is right that too often ideas become facts without any attempt at validation; but it is also right that it has been the wellspring for many important ideas and approaches. My concern is that in moving the pendulum too far in the opposite direction, we may overlook an important component in our inquiry into human nature.

It is also appropriate to distinguish between criticisms that apply to analysts and those that apply to the body of knowledge represented by psychoanalysis. In part, Lewis's criticisms of analysts may be taken as an indictment of the profession. Holzman (1973) states that analysts have inadequate clinical experience, poor scientific training, and a narrow concept of research tasks. Perhaps Lewis's criticisms are most applicable to sloppy-thinking analysts—those who have generated ideas on the psychodynamic determinants of bedwetting, or on the schizophrenogenic mother, for instance. It is worth noting here the comments of Anna Freud (1983), who decries those who take the mere fact of later pathology as evidence that the mother failed in her task of empathy with the infant. "I criticize above all the lack of data to support the concept of the unempathetic mother as a pathogenic agent," she states (p. 385).

Anna Freud's comments apply quite well to childhood autism. Not all analysts shared Lippman's (1962) views (referred to by Lewis); indeed, Lippman may be an example of those analysts who are quick to jump from speculation to fact without any intervening corroboration. Yet, despite the error of Lippman's views, and of the concept of the schizophrenogenic mother, one must remember that the larger concept of which it is a part—that environmental factors may be important in the causation or maintenance of the disorder—has not been disproved. One must keep one's mind open.

RECONSIDERING THE IMPACT OF BIOLOGY

Although it is now commonly accepted that autism is rooted in biology, I believe that it is wrong to think that parental attitudes and behavior play no role at all. Paul, Cohen, and Caparulo (1983) report that 50 percent of children with severe language deficits showed features similar to autism. The exact differences between autism and these language-disordered children remain to be established. There have been other reports of the autistic-like features of the receptive-language-impaired youngster (Berg, 1961; Wing, 1979). Clinical observation of these children suggests very strongly that their autistic features intensify when their environment is insensitive to their needs and fails to understand them (Beitchman, 1980). I do not mean to suggest that deviant parenting is a sufficient or even necessary cause of childhood autism. I am suggesting, however, that in some children with receptive-language impairment, insensitive parental and environmental handling leads to a picture that is indistinguishable from autism and that with appropriate intervention, the autistic features recede. In our haste to recognize the biological, we must not lose sight of the interplay of the psychodynamic factors.

A similar point holds true in relation to bedwetting. Specific psychodynamic determinants may not be the primary etiological agent. Nevertheless, psychological factors seem to be important at least for some children in the etiology of this syndrome. Thus, Shaffer (1980) cites Hallgren (1957) in noting that for 55 percent of secondary enuretics in unselected populations, bedwetting was precipitated by stressful events. Most of these children showed nervousness before the onset of the enuresis—a finding that was consistent with Rutter, Yule, and Graham's (1973) study. The point here is that even if specific psychodynamic factors have not been identified, psychological factors are indeed relevant.

The notion of discontinuities in development is an important one, with far-reaching implications for personality formation and growth as well as for therapeutic approaches. If it is true that the present is as important as the past, then therapeutic approaches may need to focus more directly on the current issues. The idea of discontinuity is consonant with some of Thomas and Chess's (1980) work and Sameroff and Chandler's (1975) discussion of the parent-child fit and the notion of the transactional mode. What is relevant here is that what occurs at one age may at a later age be undone because of changes in the parent-child relationship. This view may serve as an important corrective to those who emphasize too strongly the critical nature of early experience. Still, early experience can have long-lasting effects. Not many studies speak to this issue, but the one by Tizard and Hodges (1978) of children raised in institutions does. This study showed that effects on behavior and relationships were evident in children as late as middle childhood, several years after they had been removed from the institutions of rearing.

It is simplistic to speak of linear trends in development; discontinuities may be the rule rather than the exception. To search too strenuously for the single traumatic event that explains the neurosis or symptom is likely to be an elusive and frustrating goal. Perhaps it is only with extreme or prolonged stresses that later effects are manifest: because of the potentialities for self-righting, only the most severe effects are long-lasting. Again, it is worth quoting Anna Freud (1983):

> What worried us . . . is the present trend to place single pathogenic determinants at ever earlier phases of life—a quest which invalidates or ignores every element of Freud's original broad developmental point of view. It is the essence of this view that the onset of mental disturbance . . . has multiple causes; and that it can be located in all phases of development. In contrast to this view, many authors . . . inscribe to a single stage of development the power to determine on its own the individual's future health and pathology, thereby diminishing the importance of all further stages, preoedipal or oedipal, in this respect [pp. 383–384].

LIMITATIONS IN THE EMPIRICAL PERSPECTIVE

One of the major contributions of psychoanalysis is the notion of unconscious processes, and the idea that what may be similar on the surface may have different roots and meanings. This may seem to be a simplistic or naive assertion—yet it is fundamental. It is fundamental in that it reflects the polarization implied throughout Lewis's paper—the polarization between the methodologists and empiricists on the one side, and the theorists and depth psychologists on the other; the polarization between those whose first goal is reliability and those whose first goal is validity. One can hardly argue with Lewis's central point—that one must integrate the biological with the psychological. However, there is a danger in mindless empiricism, as the behaviorists themselves discovered after denying the existence of mental activity in years of strict black-box behaviorism; cognitive-behavioral therapy was born to answer the dissatisfaction with this too restrictive view.

The struggle between the methodologists and the theoreticians has been recently exemplified in the debate over the *DSM-III*, both the adult and the child portions. Compared to the *DSM-II*, *DSM-III* shows many improvements. It is fundamentally different from the Group for the Advancement of Psychiatry system; unlike the GAP system, which was shown to have low levels of reliability (Beitchman et al., 1978), *DSM-III* has operational criteria and moderate levels of reliability. The difficulty, however, is that the diagnostic categories are simply based on symptom counts, with inclusion and exclusion criteria. It does not permit the clinician any leeway in the interpretation of the meaning of the symptoms. Both Valliant (1984) and Michels (1984) have decried the lack of psychodynamic thinking in the current *DSM-III*. Its lack of a theoretical base relegates the clinician to the role of technician, not diagnostician.

It is easy to be awed by research in the biological sciences since their data seem "hard" in comparison with the "softness" of analytic material: there is something seductive about blood levels, factor analysis, and tests of significance. Yet asking the right questions is the essential precondition to testing theoretical notions, no matter which methods are used. The studies of the treasured (transitional) object are a case in point. Lewis cites Sherman et al.'s (1981) work, which showed no differences in the rates of health and illness among those who used or did not use a treasured object, thus casting doubt on the clinical significance of the treasured object. However, a subsequent study by Sherman and Hertzig (1983) shed further light on this issue. The authors found a dramatically reduced frequency in the use of treasured (transitional) objects among mentally retarded and pervasively developmentally disordered children in comparison with normals. The proportion of developmentally disordered children who ever form an object attachment (after age two) is significantly reduced and varies with diagnosis and IQ. Subtleties in health and illness may not be related to the use of treasured objects, but grosser levels of disturbance may be. It was only when this second question (relating to more severe levels of disturbance) was asked that a new, more complete answer was possible. Thus, an idea is tested and refined until it achieves status as the conventional wisdom of the day—this is the way scientific knowledge advances.

The notion of adolescent turmoil remains controversial. Although it may be true that some analysts have overstated the *Sturm and Drang* of adolescence, the evidence that adolescence is no different from any other developmental period in terms of the frequency of psychiatric disorder or emotional turmoil is not as clear-cut as Lewis suggests. For instance, the studies by Offer and Offer (1975) revealed that 21 percent of the adolescents they studied experienced tumultuous growth, and 35 percent experienced surgent growth with periods of turmoil and conflict. We also know that there is an increase in the incidence of psychiatric disorders among girls during adolescence. For example, the ratio of girls to boys receiving treatment for functional mental disorders in hospitals and outpatient clinics in the United States increased from 0.39 at 5 to 9 years of age, to 0.82 at 10 to 14 years of age, and to 1.10 at 15 to 19 years of age (Gove and Herb, 1974). A peak risk for suicide among males is also found in late adolescence, when death by suicide is exceeded only by death attributed to accidents and cancer (Kaplan and Sadock, 1981). Certain disorders are particularly common during adolescence, such as anorexia nervosa and bulimia. About 85 percent of anorectics develop the illness between 13 and 20 years (Kaplan and Sadock, 1981). Also, as Babigian (1980) notes, schizophrenia is unquestionably a disorder that afflicts adolescents and young adults; 70 percent of all new patients (in Monroe County) in 1970 were between the ages of 15 and 35 and the 15- to 24-year-old group accounted for 44 percent of all cases. Although some analysts may have overemphasized certain of the pathological aspects of adolescence, I do not believe that there is sufficient evidence to consider adolescence as a period without any increased risk to psychiatric disorder. In other words, a too narrow empirical view may lead to errors that deny important developmental and psychological issues.

Studies of the hyperactive child may be taken as another case in point. Most approaches to this syndrome simply deal with manifest behavior—the child is impulsive, aggressive, distractible, etc. The number of events per unit time is recorded, and the teacher and the parent may be asked to complete a questionnaire on the child. Despite the innumerable articles written on the subject, no one has studied the inner world of hyperactive children: how they think, how they explain their behavior, how they feel about things. Are there differences in these dimensions among hyperactive children? Are their ego defenses organized differently, for example? If so, what are the implications of these findings?

Some preliminary data (Beitchman 1982) suggest that some differences can be identified and are worth pursuing, both to understand these children and to help clarify treatment and prognosis. One group of hyperactive preschoolers showed evidence of brittle ego defenses: they were hypervigilant and tended to personalize events, so that these events were interpreted as a direct assault or insult. One youngster, for instance, took a momentary interruption in his therapy as an affront and with considerable agitation promptly devised poison potions, with which he would attack and destroy his therapist (persecutor). Are these reactions in some way the precursors of antisocial and aggressive behavior known to be found among older hyperactive children? A second group of hyperactive preschoolers, with evidence of significant delays in development, appeared to be as hyperactive and aggressive as the first group; but unlike the first group, their aggression was more impulsive and they were less likely to be angry and retaliatory.

One must have some notions of metapsychology and ego defenses to be able to conceptualize differences along these dimensions among hyperactive children. What is needed of course is some rigorous method of testing these ideas. The point I wish to stress here, however, is that the analytic mode of depth inquiry is almost totally lacking in the current literature on hyperactivity. The "counting papers" Lewis refers to have taken center stage. I believe that much can be learned about these children and the nature of hyperactivity, but those who would look at the metapsychology should not be intimidated by the rating scales, the questionnaires, and the blood levels currently in vogue.

The situation with regard to childhood depression remains controversial, with many questions still unanswered. Dogmatism of any kind is to be shunned of course, and the declaration that childhood depression *cannot* exist can only be considered to be a speculation, unsupported by the available data. Misery and unhappiness in childhood, however, are not to be confused with the adult form of major depression. It is therefore tempting to place great emphasis on biological correlates in children that seem to suggest a depressive illness. Halmi (1983) has cautioned, however, that too much faith may be placed in biological markers, and that the dexamethasone suppression test is not very specific. Rapoport (1983) has raised similar concerns and has sugested that even children with the *DSM-III* diagnosis of depression may have fewer vegetative signs than adults.

Rutter and Garmezy (1983), noting that depressed children differed from depressed adults in their sleep patterns, put forward the possibility that prepubertal and adult depressions constitute different conditions. A recent report by Werry et al. (1983) on 195 admissions to a psychiatric clinic failed to diagnose a single case of major depression in a prepubertal youngster, raising further questions about the nature of the major depression in childhood. We must of course continue our search for biological markers; in this way we may elucidate the pathophysiology as well as the psychopathology of depressive illness.

PSYCHOANALYSIS AS SCIENCE

We have seen that some analysts may be guilty of generalizing beyond their data and may thereby have given analysis a bad name. Strupp (1976), for instance, refers to the traditional psychoanalytic journals as ones preoccupied with clarifying esoteric theoretical issues, often far removed from empirical data. Perhaps Lewis is correct in stating that psychoanalysis may never become an experimental science with a critical methodology.

Psychoanalysis, however, can be understood in different ways, and it is useful to separate psychoanalysis into its different aspects: a specific therapy, a method of studying the mind, and a theory of the mind (see Wallerstein, 1980). To these one may add psychoanalysis as a theory of development and psychoanalytic psychotherapy, as an offshoot of psychoanalysis.

To some extent the role of therapist and the role of scientist show incompatibilities. The scientist must be skeptical, questioning, open to a variety of ideas in the pursuit of the truth. Certainly in the early stages of therapy, the therapist/clinician can and should be inquiring, questioning, and eager to seek the truth. At some point in the process, however, the therapist must take a stand, offering his or her ideas, interpretations, etc. For maximal effect, the therapist cannot be tentative. What one does not know one must believe. Effective and charismatic therapists may be successful for a variety of reasons; however, one important reason for their success is that they can persuade their patients to accept their beliefs—ones which are presumably more adaptive than the patients' own. It is axiomatic that one cannot be persuasive and convincing if one is tentative and uncertain. Taken in this context, Holzman's (1973) criticism becomes more understandable.

As a body of knowledge of development, the psychoanalytic method of historical reconstruction is limited, and Lewis may well be right in suggesting that most of what was to be learned has already been learned by this method. On the other hand, psychoanalytically oriented observations of infants and children seem entirely appropriate scientific methods of investigating developmental phenomena. The studies of Anna Freud at the Hampstead Nursery are examples of one highly successful approach. Thus, when Lewis states that psychoanalysis has no critical methodology, this is most true of historical reconstruction, which would seem to be the weakest link in terms of scientific testability. Observations of child development in nurseries are quite within the realm of proper scientific activity.

The efficacy of psychoanalysis and psychoanalytic psychotherapy has also been subjected to scientific study (Appelbaum, 1975, Luborsky et al., 1980). The results of psychotherapy in some instances have been surprisingly positive (Tramontana, 1980; D. Klein et al., 1983). Methodological concepts such as transference, alliance, and resistance also seem quite open to scientific testing (e.g., L. Horowitz, cited by Grinker, 1976). Marziali (1984), for instance, showed that there was a positive association between a more favorable outcome and the frequency with which the therapist's interpretations referred to emotions experienced in the transference relationship that were similar to those experienced with significant others. That control groups, chi squares, blind raters, and so on are missing from analytic reports is not necessarily the essential point—Konrad Lorenz, for instance, offered painstaking observations that led to fundamental truths, without the use of control groups or chi squares. Careful, meticulous description, as free from bias as possible, with the opportunity for replication would be sufficient. Although one must go beyond the strictly analytic method to test certain of its ideas, in doing so, one must not be intimidated by the biological and the statistical, just as one must also stay close to the data at hand.

It is not necessary that psychoanalytic ideas and theories be proved true or false in the psychoanalytic situation. The analytic situation may generate ideas, but the essential point is that they be put in such a way that it is possible to test them. For instance, when Einstein conceptualized his ideas on relativity, he did not and could not carry out experiments on the relation between the speed of light and the mass of an object traveling at that speed. Nor could he experiment with time or the effect traveling at the speed of light would have on time. In his biography of Einstein, Clark (1971) comments that inventiveness, imagination, and the intuitive approach played a serious part in his work. He did have recourse to mathematical equations to demonstrate his ideas, but the proof of his ideas has in part depended on new technologies. Thus, the invention of the atomic clock made possible the testing of the effects of high speed on time. In a like manner, the analytic situation can and should be a fertile ground for generating ideas on human nature—whether they are valid or not depends on the demonstration of their replicability and predictability.

CONCLUSION

What can we conclude from all this? One can hardly argue with Lewis's central point—that one must be open to alternative explanations of human nature and that one must consider the biological and sociological as well as the intrapsychic in any comprehensive general psychology. His discussion of several developmental concepts and the new light modern research has cast on them makes this point convincing. On the other hand, some of the ideas suggested by the biological and empirical approaches may not have as firm a footing as may seem. Moreover, they are limited in that a conceptual framework of the mind to guide research is lacking.

Lewis's criticisms about psychoanalysis as a science apply most directly to the use of the psychoanalytic situation to study development. This is not its strongest point; it is well suited to generate ideas and theories of development, but other methods are more appropriately used to test them. The techniques of analysis can be studied scientifically, and psychoanalytic ideas and principles can be used in the observations of infants and children. These can be as scientific as one cares to make them. The basic problem perhaps lies not with psychoanalysis, but rather with those who are sloppy in their methods and in their thinking. It is of course fun to speculate, but one must be cautious not to equate speculation with fact. Check your assumptions, review your data, and ask what evidence there is to support your ideas—these are truths for all psychiatrists, no less so for analysts.

REFERENCES

Appelbaum, A. (1975). Transactions of Topeka Psychoanalytic Society. *Bull. Menninger Clinic* 39:384–390.

Babigian, H. M. (1981). Schizophrenia epidemiology. In *Comprehensive Textbook of Psychiatry*, Vol. III, ed. H. I. Kaplan, A. M. Freedman, & B. J. Sadock. Baltimore: Williams & Wilkins.

Beitchman, J. H. (1980). Therapeutic considerations with the language-impaired preschool child. Presented to the Ontario Psychiatric Association, Ottawa, Oct. 25.

—— (1982). Familial and possible genetic transmission of language delay and hyperactivity in language-delayed preschoolers. Presented at the Canadian Academy of Child Psychiatry, Montreal, April.

—— Dielman, T. E., Benson, K., Landis, J. R., & Kemp, P. L. (1978). The reliability of the Group for the Advancement of Psychiatry Diagnostic categories in child psychiatry. *Arch. Gen. Psychiat.* 35:1461–1466.

Berg, I. S. (1961). A case study of developmental auditory imperception: Some theoretical implications. *J. Child Psychol. Psychiat.* 2:86–93.

Clark, R. W. (1971). *Einstein: The Life and Times*. New York: Avon.

Freud, A. (1983). Problems of pathogenesis: Introduction to the discussion. *Psychoanal. Stud. of the Child* 38:383–385.

Gove, W. R., & Herb, T. R. (1974). Stress and mental illness among the young: A comparison of the sexes. *Soc. Forces* 53:256–264.

Grinker, R. R., Sr. (1976). Discussion of "Some critical comments on the future of Spsychoanalytic therapy" by H. Strupp. *Bull. Menninger Clinic* 40:247–253.

Hallgren, B. (1957). Enuresis: A clinical genetic study. *Acta Psychol. Neurol. Scand. Suppl.* 114(32):1–159.

Halmi, K. (1983). Discussion of "Childhood depression," by D. P. Cantwell. In *Childhood Psychopathology and Development*, ed. S. B. Guze, et al. New York: Raven Press.

Holzman, P. S. (1973). Some difficulties in the way of psychoanalytic research: A survey and a critique. In *Psychoanalytic Research: Three Approaches to the Study of Subliminal Process (Psycholo. Issues*, Monogr. 30), ed. M. Mayman. New York: Int. Univ. Press, pp. 88–103.

Kaplan, H., & Sadock, B. J. (1981). *Modern Synopsis of Comprehensive Textbook of Psychiatry III*, (3rd Ed.) Baltimore: Williams & Wilkins.

Klein, D. F., Zitrin, C. M. Woerner, M. G., & Ross, D. C. (1983). Treatment of phobias: II. Behavior therapy and supportive psychotherapy: Are there any specific ingredients? *Arch. Gen. Psychiat.* 40:139–145.

Lippman, H. S. (1962). *Treatment of the Child in Emotional Conflict*, 2nd Ed. New York: McGraw-Hill.

Luborsky, L., Mintz, J., Auerbach, A., Christoph, P., Bachrach, H., Todd, T., Johnson, M., Cohen, M., & O'Brien, C. (1980). Predicting the outcome of psychotherapy. *Arch. Gen. Psychiat.* 37:471–481.

Marziali, E. A. (1984). Prediction of outcome of brief psychotherapy from therapist interpretive interventions. *Arch. Gen. Psychiat.* 41:301–304.

Michels, R. (1984). First rebuttal. *Amer. J. Psychiat.* 141:548–551.

Offer, D., & Offer, J. B. (1975). *From Teenage to Young Manhood: A Psychological Study*. New York: Basic Books.

Paul, R., Cohen, D. J., & Caparulo, B. K. (1983). A longitudinal study of patients with severe developmental disorders of language learning. *J. Child Psychiat.* 22:525–534.

Rapoport, J. L. (1983). Discussion of "Childhood depression," by D. P. Cantwell. In *Childhood Psychopathology and Development*, ed. S. B. Guze et al. New York: Raven Press.

Rutter, M., & Garmezy, N. (1983).Developmental psychopathology. In *Handbook of Child Psychology, Vol. 4: Socialization Personality and Social Development*, ed. M. E. Hetherington. New York: Wiley.

―――― Yule, W., & Graham, P. (1973). Enuresis and behavioral deviance: Some epidemiological considerations. In *Bladder Control and Enuresis (Clinics in Devel. Med., Monogr. 48/49)*, ed. I. Kalvin et al. London: Heinemann/SIMP.

Sameroff, A. J., & Chandler, M. J. (1975). Reproductive risk and the continuum of caretaking causality. In *Review of Child Development Research*, ed. F. D. Horowitz. Chicago: Univ. Chicago Press.

Shaffer, D. (1980). The development of bladder control. In *Developmental Psychiatry*, ed. M. Rutter. London: Heinemann.

Sherman, M., & Hertzig, M. E. (1983). Treasured object use: A cognitive and developmental marker. *J. Amer. Acad. Child Psychiat.* 22:541–544.

―――― ――――, Austrian, R., & Shapiro, T. (1981). Treasured objects in school-aged children. *Pediat.* 68:379–386.

Strupp, H. H. (1976). Some critical comments on the future of psychoanalytic therapy. *Bull. Menninger Clinic* 40:238–247.

Thomas, A, & Chess, S., Eds. (1980). *The Dynamics of Psychological Development*. New York: Brunner Mazel.

Tizard, B., & Hodges, J. (1978). The effect of early institutional rearing on the development of eight-year-old children. *J. Child Psychol. Psychiat.* 19:99–118.

Tramontana, M. G. (1980). Critical review of research on psychotherapy outcome with adolescents, 1967–1977. *Psychol. Bull.* 88(2):429–450.

Vaillant, G. E. (1984). The disadvantages of DSM-III outweigh its advantages. *Amer. J. Psychiat.* 141:542–545.

Wallerstein, R. S. (1980). Psychoanalysis and academic psychiatry—bridges. *Psychoanal. Stud. of the Child* 35:419–448.

Werry, J. S., Methven, R. J., Fitzpatrick, J., & Dixon, H. (1983). The interrater reliability of DMS-III in children. *J. Abnorm. Child Psychol.* 11:341–354.

Wing, L. (1979). Differentiation of retardation and autism from specific communication disorders. *Child: Care, Health, Devel.* 5:57–68.

20/
Murder, Frenzy, and Madness—The Logistics of Humiliations: Notes on Dostoevsky and *The Idiot*

M. Masud R. Khan

These "notes" on *The Idiot* evaluate experiences of murder, frenzy, humiliation, and madness as they appear in Dostoevsky's work. Humiliation—passive or active, being humiliated or humiliating—is seen as constituting the core of Dostoevsky's private self and his creations. Madness, on the other hand, provides the climate. In all this there is a "doubling," both between the characters in the novel and with Dostoevsky's own life and his epileptic illness.

MURDER

One definition of some murders could be: suicide through the Other. A person who has exhausted all his or her antics of self-sustenance and self-cure by external distractions or internal delusions needs to commit suicide but cannot. He or she then finds a "victim" to kill him or her and end the agony of non-being. This is why Nastasia Filippovna, all dressed and ready to go to church to marry Prince Myshkin, escapes to Rogonin and begs him to "save" her from the Prince. She knows the Prince will care *(agapē)* but not kill; while the passion of Rogonin in love *(erōs)* could be tantalized, humiliated, and provoked to the point where he would kill if not from jealousy or vengefulness then from a compelling mercy that knows what is being demanded of his love and must be done. This undoubtedly is the logic of Dostoevsky's narrative in *The Idiot* (1868).

Furthermore, for Dostoevsky, suicide "is the final stage of man's spiritual bankruptcy, the culmination of his ill being" (Jonge, 1975, p. 122). Nastasia Filippovna saves some of her "absolute beauty" from total moral bankruptcy through being murdered. This element of contrariness in Dostoevsky's concept of ideal beauty, which should harmonize the world but destroys it in fact, is an essential element in the logic of murder in Dostoevsky. In the total metaphor of Dostoevsky's vision, murder by Raskalnikov, the suicide of Prince Stavrogin and the being murdered of Nastasia Filippovna are all facts of the same dilemma: the human incapacity for the realization of "the final cause," "ideal beauty," and "the super-saturated moment" of Baudelaire's perfervid seeking. So murder in Dostoevsky is not just a random or vengeful or delusional criminal act but the ultimate result of a search for a finality and eternity of Truth and Beauty (as *erōs* or *agapē*) that inevitably ends in disillusionment to which murder as such or suicide or epileptic bankruptcy of self are the only answer (cf. Bakhtin, 1973).

FRENZY

Frenzy is a compounded ego state. Its phenomenology is as bizarre in Dostoevsky's work and sensibility as its etiology is unknowable. Its chief characteristics are a willful intensification of affects; be they love (Rogonin), agapé (Myshkin), vengeful wrath and frenetic egotism (Nastasia), or congealed and acidic contempt (Aglaya), etc., etc. One further outstanding feature of frenzy is humiliation, but of that later. What renders frenzy so melodramatic is its amplitude and the expression of that in behavior and relating (cf. Nastasia, Aglaya). I have said frenzy is a "compounded ego state." Perhaps it would be more accurate to Dostoevsky's sensibility and *écriture* to say it is an unintegrated ego state, in search of the Other, to render it into "absolute beauty," the "super-saturated moment" of Baudelaire's seeking, or the "final cause" of Dostoevsky's search. In frenzy, delirious unrealities feel like the *truth,* where hallucinatory sensations and images are mistaken for facts and actual perceptions (cf. Myshkin, Rogonin, even Aglaya!). Idealism is another component of the frenzied state, no matter in what context. It engenders an oversensitivity that renders the person like the chameleon in Jean Cocteau's parable, who died of exhaustion from changing colors when left in sunlight on a Scottish tartan rug. The acute and chronic exhaustion of the Prince and Aglaya derive from these gyrations of affectivity and hypersensitivity.

So it seems that frenzy is an unintegrated, conglomerate ego state composed of contrary, paradoxical, even incompatible and conflictual intrapsychic "events" that are merely triggered into action by some external circumstance or fantasy or suspicion. Paranoid self-vigilance is another element of the frenzied ego state. In spite of all his passivity ("the perfect man"), the Prince is always watching the slightest fluctuation in the nuances of the other's self-presentation. He does not talk about it but he *knows*. Hence the confusion in everyone as to whether he is really an idiot or just having everyone on. Aglaya notices it with an acute asperity of insight.

It would be a grave error to mistake frenzy, especially in Dostoevskian creations, for psychotic mania. His characters may behave in a deranged way but never really lose touch with their inner reality or external circumstances. The flight of Nastasia from marriage to the Prince to "save" herself and the refusal of Aglaya are proofs of this. Also the brutish and boozed passion of Rogonin is all in measure with his desires and character as well as with reality. Hence the melodramatic in Dostoevsky never degenerates into the farcical, only the fantastical.

What ensues from this frenzied ego state is even more perplexing and confounding. It can express and actualize through saintliness and martydom (Myshkin), or exhaust its relentless energy in an epileptic fit, or end in murder and/or suicide.

The person in frenzy seeks a "perfect" and whole, as well as an irreversibly absolute, experience that will cohere his randomized affectivity and wild contrary actions into a personalized continuity of self and being. In fact it never happens. Because the amplitude of mood and affectivity in frenzy renders it a very disruptive and violent force that the ego cannot substantiate psychically or integrate into purposeful behavior. Hence the acute sense of dismay and being doomed in Prince Myshkin, Rogonin, Nastasia, and Aglaya. The two types of mind that Aglaya talks of to the Prince (*The Idiot,* pp. 467–468) rarely become mutual and dialogic intrapsychically or through the Other.

HUMILIATIONS

Humiliations constitute the core of Dostoevsky's private self and that of his creations. Here I am deeply indebted to André Gide's profound essay on Dostoevsky's *Correspondence* (1908) and his work (1922). Unfortunately Gide's unmitigated Puritanism at crucial moments of insight confuses humility and humiliation: "humiliation damns whereas humility sanctifies" (Gide, 1967, p. 87). There is no humility anywhere in Dostoevsky's characters or in any of his creations. The only type of humility one encounters in Dostoevsky's *écriture* is in the resigned acceptance of poverty and the total incapacity to change its external circumstances. As, for example, the quiet humility of Ganya's mother, Mrs. Ivoglin. But even in her there is an unshakable pride and sense of honor which neither insults nor humiliations can destroy, as in her sudden and unexpected encounter with the outrageous Nastasia.

Perhaps the archetypal model for humiliation without shame, remorse, apology, or regret is Dostoevsky's parting from Turgeniev. Here is Gide's account of it. Dostoevsky had been on bad terms with Turgeniev for some time and then suddenly arrives one day to announce:

"Monsieur Turgeniev, I must tell you how deeply I despise myself . . ."
 He pauses again. . . . The silence remains unbroken until Dostoevsky, unable to contain himself any longer, bursts out in wrath "But *you* I despise even more! That is all I wanted to say to you" and off he goes, slamming the door behind him [Gide, 1967, p. 86].

Humiliation is of two types: passive or active. By which I mean, being humiliated and humiliating. The cathexes for this behavior derive from the state of frenzy but its idiom is confession. Gide very pertinently remarks that for the experience of humiliation to be absolute, the character seeks "to find the person before whom confession would cause him the acutest suffering" (1967, p. 85). It would be wrong to equate this suffering from humiliation with moral masochism, as Jonge (1975) implies. There are distinct elements of moral masochism in the ballistics of humiliations, which Dostoevsky narrates with such intensity and vividness in all types of humiliations in the first part of *The Idiot,* but essentially it is self-preservative.

What does the experience of humiliation achieve for the person, whether it is passive or active? It aims to give him a *personality:* an identity in the eyes of Others and a concrete shared experience for himself. One must never lose sight of the fact how utterly *lonely* all of Dostoevsky's characters are, like himself, in spite of his second wife Anna Grigoryevna's indefatigable love and devotion to him. He seeks and cherishes his loneliness and even nurtures it. In a letter to his niece Sofia Alexandrovna he wrote from Geneva while cogitating *The Idiot:* "All the time I was in such a bad temper and such continuous anxiety, that I needed to shut myself into myself and bear my woe in solitude" (January 1, 1868, in *Letters,* 1914, p. 141). So do his characters: above all the Prince and Aglaya in *The Idiot.*

Yet this is not sufficient explanation of the necessity and the need for humiliation in Dostoevsky and his characters. There is more to it: a pride that cannot be defeated by the utmost debasement of self or insult and humiliation by the Other. Ganya slapping the Prince at Nastasia's party, when she has humiliated him to the core, does nothing to change either of them. In this sense the experience of humiliation is never internalized and yet the paradox of it is that cumulatively humiliations engender frenzy, which in turn energizes the compelling need for humiliations. Nastasia is its most explicit exponent, both in its active and passive styles.

MADNESS

Madness is the all-pervasive *climate* of Dostoevsky's *écriture* and creations. It takes myriad forms of expression through his characters: the delirious state of Raskolnikov, the frenzy of Rogonin's passion, the quietism of the Prince's epileptic idiocy, the vehemence of Nastasia's awareness of non-being. She wrote to Aglaya in her last letter:

> But I have renounced the world. I expect you must think it funny that I should say so, meeting me covered in lace and diamonds and in the company of drunks and rogues? Don't mind that, for I have almost ceased to exist, and I know that. Goodness only knows who lives in me in my place [*The Idiot*, p. 495].

It can easily turn into insanity, as in the case of Stavrogin. Yet one must not be precipitate and confuse Dostoevskian madness with psychosis. There are no psychotics among Dostoevsky's characters. They are bizarre, eccentric persons outrageously negating reality and others; accusing each other of madness or prophesying it. The Prince's pity and compassion for Nastasia become absolute when he realizes she is mad. And madness for Dostoevsky is a creative as well as destructive human condition. In fact, it is that very private, hidden inner source of being from which all experiences of self, living, and others crystallize: no matter how absurd and reckless (Rogonin) or calculated and correct (Ganya, General Yepanchin). Being able to gain access to his madness renders a person individuated and "original" for Dostoevsky and separates him from "ordinary" persons. Dostoevsky considers even Ganya in the category of "ordinary" or "commonplace" people. (*The Idiot*, p. 500). But he does add that Ganya "belonged to the category of people who are much cleverer." Cleverness is not a virtue in Dostoevsky's vision. Hence his loathing for the sophisticated European society and the Russians who ape it.

Madness in Dostoevsky, like humiliation, has to do with pride, sincerity, and authenticity. (For a very instructive discussion of this, consult Mochulsky [1947], especially on *The idiot*.) A person in order to be true to himself must live from this core of madness in himself: like the Prince, Rogonin, Nastasia, and Aglaya—each in his or her frantic or muted style. Furthermore madness expresses itself in myriad forms of illness (physical or mental), as if such illness were the only way in which the past speaks to us. Again, Nastasia is its supreme exponent in her lifestyle and way of relating to others.

Lastly, madness is what frenzy, humiliations, murder, and suicide actualize, and exteriorize.

Yet once again one encounters a paradox here in Dostoevsky: none of his characters is ever really mad: they seek it, they behave madly but are not mad. This privacy of self (madness) every character retains even in his most extravagantly or exhibitionistic actions or confessions, through humiliations and insults, and all the weird antics of frenzy. Hence Dostoevsky rarely indicates *why* a person has become what he is. He restricts his insight to the *how* he is what he is. We do not know why Nastasia harbored such pungent contempt for Totsky or why Aglaya is encapsulated in a bitter silence and loneliness, which can be as biting and vindictive as it can be tender, compassionate, and forgiving. In Dostoevsky, people seek forgiveness only to refuse it; what they are always seeking is *a state of grace* that would be consentient with their madness.

In essence madness is that area in all of us which is unspeakably and unknowably private. Fortunately, in a vast majority of humans, whom Dostoevsky rather disdainfully calls the "ordinary people," it stays dormant and hence presents little problem. To a few it becomes a life task to render this "unlivable" area of madness into some form of personalized experience, intrapsychic or social, which can be identified by the Others and shared. General Ivolgin's outlandish confabulations about his past come into this category.

With the very few who have genius (or, to use Dostoevsky's favorite word, "originality"), it metaphorizes itself into language and imagery (literature, art); or collectively in the culture it becomes a myth or religion of which someone becomes the totemic mouthpiece—be it Moses, a Christ, a Mohammed, or a Buddha. But all these are derivatives of the unknowable area and the experience of madness. A few personalize the area of madness into eccentricity that is acceptable to the culture and even envied, as among the English. In Dostoevsky's characters eccentricity always borders on the absurd or the melodramatic. Furthermore, in Dostoevsky madness resulting in epileptic fits, whether in Prince Myshkin or in himself, is not merely a sick collapse of the psyche. The fits are also experienced as realizations of total experience, as outward thrusts of the most secret and central forces of life. In the moment of seizure the soul is liberated from the constricting hold of senses. Nowhere does Dostoevsky suggest that the "idiot" regrets his "hallowing affliction" (Steiner, 1960, p. 17; see also Lord, 1970). It can also be transformed by a person like Rousseau into the stance of an avatar. It can end in being taken for a heretic and possessed by the devil and hence burnt as a witch (cf. Foucault, 1972). Its last and most destructive permutation is that when a person tries to make this unknowable area of madness speak for him, it destroys the mental apparatus, and such persons we call psychotics. But each psychotic still retains his hidden madness in spite of the total derangement of psychic and affective structures.

20. Murder, Frenzy, Madness

Now I shall change my narrative and focus it more specifically on Dostoevsky and how subtly, as well as blatantly, he disperses his life experiences to crystallize some feature, nuance, or aberration even, of his sensibility and intellect, through one character or another (cf. Anna Dostoevsky, 1976). I have chosen *The Idiot,* as to me it reads as the grammer of the whole *écriture* of Dostoevsky and his life. He *speaks* himself candidly and without artistic guile. Lord (1970) argues that "this novel is primarily an exploration of the epileptic mode of being, which was also Dostoevsky's own" (p. 101). Little wonder that when he had started to work on *The Idiot,* he wrote from Geneva to his friend Maikov:

> Je ne vous parle pas de mon'travail, il n'y a encore rien à dire. Une seule chose: Il faut travailler intensément, très intensément. Mais les crises me mettent absolument à plat; il me faut quatre jours après chaque crise, pour reprendre mes esprits. Qu'on était bien au début, en Allemagne! C'est la faute de cette maudite Genéve. Qu'allons-nous devenir?—je n'y comprends rien! Le roman est l'unique salut. Le pire c'est qu'il doit absolument être très bon. C'est un *sine qua non.* Et comment pourra-t-il être bon, étant donné mes facultés bloquées par la maladie! Je possède encore de l'imagination, et pas mal: Je l'ai éprouvé dernièrement, sur le roman même. J'ai aussi du nerf. Mais pas de mèmoire. Bref, je plonge dans le roman *à l'aventure* la tête la première, j'ai tout misé sur cette seule carte, advienne que pourra! Mais suffit! [October 9–21, 1867, in *Correspondance,* 1960, p. 138].[1]

Yes, *The Idiot* is constructed like a *collage:* themes are superimposed on each other, persons double each other: Rogonin and Prince Myshkin, so different, yet two sides of the same coin—the metal of which is Dostoevsky. The same can be said about Nastasia and Aglaya. What is even more intriguing in Dostoevsky's creations is that it is not the same sex that "doubles." In many ways the Prince and Aglaya are two sides of the same coin (cf. Frank, 1977, p. 28), just as Rogonin and Nastasia are. What lends mystery to this "doubling" is that it never harmonizes. Rogonin declares love to Myshkin one moment and exchanges crosses, only to lie

---

[1] Of my work I will tell you nothing, for I have nothing to say about it as yet. Only one thing: I have to work at it intensely, very intensely indeed. My fits rob me of all vitality, and after each one, I can't collect my thoughts for at least four days. And how well I was, at first, in Germany! This accursed Geneva! I don't know what will become of us. I understand nothing of it. And the novel is my only means of salvation. The worst of it is that it must be absolutely the best. Nothing less will do. That's the indispensable condition. But how can it be, when all my capabilities are utterly crippled by my illness! I still have my power of vision intact, and imagination, and not poorly. I have proof of that from my last novel. I suffer from nerves still. But there is no memory. In short I must plunge into this novel by storm; fling myself on it head foremost. And I am staking everything on this one card, come what may! Enough of it!

in wait in his hotel to kill him. Similarly, Nastasia tries hard to bring the Prince and Aglaya together, but once she sees them in harmony she has to destroy it and grab the Prince. This final mad, frenzied, self-humiliating act decides Rogonin that death alone will give her peace, and he stabs her to death, with a ritualistic, almost mystical, reverence and love. The Prince doubles Dostoevsky himself, as Dostoevsky makes explicit by making the Prince describe how he had heard from a patient at Dr. Schneider's how he was reprieved from being shot at the last moment, and later the description of the onset of the epileptic fit is entirely Dostoevsky's experience of his illness. They are both ill and feeble in health, yet are titanic in their energy and capacity to live and influence others. Whoever encounters the Prince is changed, just as one is not the same person after reading *The Idiot* as one was before it.

The *personalization* of his literary creations is innate to Dostoevsky's mode of working. As Steiner (1960) pertinently points out: "He survived the agonizing experience of mock execution in front of a firing squad, he transformed the remembrance of that dread hour into a talisman of endurance and a persistent source of inspiration" (cf. Lord, 1970, and especially A. Dostoevsky, 1976).

In spite of his overt and apologetic passivity, Prince Myshkin never is at a loss or loses face in any situation. Even his epileptic fits are so effective in defeating the murderous malice of others, just as his "howlers" and clumsy body behavior—like smashing the precious huge vase at General Yepanchin's party—completely expose the *arranged* bourgeois decorum of intellectual pretentiousness and hypocritical good behavior to be seen for what they really are. Hence Aglaya's love of the Prince, because like Dostoevsky, he lives and speaks from "the essential mind" (*The Idiot*, p. 468).

I have deliberately called this article "notes" because it is impossible to abstract the massiveness and frenzy of Dostoevsky's life and work into a few abstractions (cf. Lord, 1970; Grossman, 1974; A. Dostoevsky, 1976). Dostoevsky was the first truly epic, purely Russian novelist. His work is universal, yet innately parochial Russian, and also fully cognizant of the European tradition, with all its decadence and mannerisms. Little wonder the hero he chose to portray "the perfect man," Prince Myshkin, is nurtured in Switzerland but actualizes his true self only in Russia. By ambiguously calling him "the idiot," Dostoevsky endows him with the native nonintellectual, unclever simplicity and a certain unmistakable religious quality of character and sensibility. Prince Myshkin is a true original Russian in the image of his creator.

REFERENCES

Bakhtin, M. (1973). *Problems of Dostoevsky's Poetics.* Ardis.
Dostoevsky, A. (1976). *Dostoevsky. Reminiscences.* London: Wildwood House.
—— A. G. (1978). *Journal.* Paris: Stock.
—— (1914). *Letters of Fyodor Michailovitch Dostoevsky to His Family and Friends.* London: Chatto & Windus.
Dostoyevsky, F. (1868). *The Idiot,* trans. D. Magarshack. London: Penguin Books, 1955.
—— (1960). *Correspondance de Dostoievski,* Vol. III. Paris: Calmann-Lévy.
Foucault, M. (1972). *Madness and Civilisation: A History of Insanity in the Age of Reason.* London: Tavistock, 1975.
Frank, J. (1977). *Dostoevsky: The Seeds of Revolt, 1821–49.* London: Robson Books.
Gide, A. (1967). *Dostoevsky.* London: Peregrine.
Grossman, L. (1974). *Dostoevsky: A Biography.* London: Lane.
Jonge, A. de (1975). *Dostoevsky and the Age of Intensity.* London: Secker & Warburg.
Lord, R. (1970). *Dostoevsky. Essays and Perspectives.* London: Chatto & Windus.
Mochulsky, K. (1947). *Dostoevsky: His Life and Work.* Princeton: Princeton Univ. Press, 1971.
Steiner, G. (1960). *Tolstoy or Dostoevsky.* London: Faber & Faber.

21/
Psychosomatic Symptoms and Latent Psychotic States
Herbert Rosenfeld, M.D., F.R.C.Psych.

Many variables enter into psychosomatic illness. This paper examines the impact in so-called normal patients of "psychotic islands," which may become lodged in a particular body part or organ. These psychotic aspects are walled off from the self, but may leak out in psychosomatic symptoms. As a detailed clinical example illustrates, once the psychotic island is dislodged in analysis, the underlying projective identification emerges. Although destructive impulses predominate in the psychotic island, creative aspects of the self may also be pulled in. Only gradually can linking interpretations be made, which assist the patient in slowly integrating the psychotic with the healthier parts of the personality.

The literature on psychosomatic illness has grown to such proportions that it is no longer possible to review, or even read, everything that has been written on this subject. Many authors have tried to describe specific psychic conflicts or character organizations related to a particular psychosomatic disease (Dunbar, 1938; Alexander, 1943). Some authors, such as Felix Deutsch (1939) suggest the strong interactions between body and mind in all psychosomatic states. Some have stressed multiple factors as the basis of psychosomatic illness, including genetic factors, the occurrence of traumas at a very early age, failure to solve the disturbing situation by behavior, symbolic representation, and even psychosis.

The ideational level may lead to direct pshysiological expression via autonomic pathways. In 1964 I suggested that mental conflicts such as early confusional states (which are particularly unbearable for the infantile ego) tend to be split off and evacuated into the body or body organs causing hypochondriasis or psychosomatic disease, or sometimes a combination of the two. Nevertheless, there are obviously many different factors that can cause psychosomatic disease. Only a detailed analytic investigation of a particular psychosomatic problem can clarify the factors leading to a psychosomatic problem in any one person.

In this paper I shall investigate the concept that when the anxieties of neurotic patients or of somebody undergoing analysis for professional reasons are touched on, they often have certain qualities we described as psychotic anxieties, to use Melanie Klein's terminology. Klein investigated and described in detail early infantile anxieties and mechanisms of the paranoid-schizoid and depressive positions. She particularly emphasized both the danger to the early ego in dealing with primitive destructive feelings and the defenses created early on to prevent the self from being overwhelmed by the derivatives of the instinct of destruction (the death instinct)—a problem that preoccupied Freud in his paper "Analysis Terminable and Interminable" (1937).

In our so-called normal patients, we often detect "psychotic islands," which are quite walled off or embedded in psychosomatic or other symptoms. One observes this wall because these psychotic areas are so firmly split off from the psychic self that one feels one has come up against an area that is completely inaccessible at first. At the same time however, the unknown psychotic problems seem to be lodged quite firmly in the body organs they have penetrated. So the walling off exists only insofar as the psyche is concerned—damaging influence is leaking out from the very destructive psychotic island into the body organs. The leaking, penetrating quality of the psychotic island seems to be related to omnipotent projective identification, probably deflected from an original attempt of projection into an external object. This problem becomes noticeable, and so can be investigated in analysis, only after the psychotic island is dislodged to some extent from the body organs and the conflicts appear in the transference situation. Then one can observe that the patient uses projective identification for communication but simultaneously tries to get rid of his or her unbearable psychotic problems by projection into the analyst.

When the area where the psychotic anxieties are located or encapsulated responds to analytic treatment, there is often an apparent cure, particularly if some aspects of the patient's anxieties have been clarified in the analysis. But often the "illness" or "psychotic anxieties" are displaced to an unknown area and the patient takes steps to ensure that this area is kept unknown. If patients believe themselves to be cured at such times because their symptoms have disappeared, and they discharge themselves from treatment, there is almost certainly a great danger that some illness will arise again in the future. I have found that hidden psychotic areas or "islands" are exceedingly common.

CLINICAL ILLUSTRATION

I shall use the case material of a young married woman, who came for analysis because of some depression following repeated miscarriages and a premature birth, which resulted in the baby's death. In this patient a psychotic island was lodged in her uterus. After giving a brief case history, I shall attempt, by the use of dream material and a description of the intense interaction between analyst and patient, to re-create how this developed during the analysis, from the first explosive appearance of the psychotic island in the analytic situation (which created a brief "transference psychosis"). When the psychotic island had been dislodged, the patient became able to conceive and have a healthy baby. In this case it was possible to bring the psychotic process more fully to the surface, where it could then be worked through in the transference situation.

In describing the psychotic island, I shall also attempt to differentiate the traumatic experiences of the patient from her deep-seated fear of genetically unacceptable and deadly destructive parts of the self, which had been almost completely walled off and hidden for most of her life. Attention will also be paid to clarifying the more or less successful attempt of the analysis to integrate the psychotic island into the patient's self.

From the history of the patient, I wish only to mention that she had a younger brother whom, as a small child, she completely ignored but afterwards felt very protective toward. The patient's mother had suffered for many years from heart disease, which made her very vulnerable, but she had also been experienced by the patient as vulnerable from very early childhood on because she seemed to be unable to stand any aggression or loud noise. Father made great demands on all his children to be first in school. My patient tried to satisfy him and did very well but felt that she could never satisfy her father's demands and give him real pleasure, even if she came top in her class. So there must have been a very pressurized and unaccepting atmosphere in the patient's home, which forced her early on to split off some of her intense desire to be herself and to express herself. She suffered from asthma and eczema in childhood.

In discussing her gynecological problem, the patient reported that the gynecologist believed that there was a physical defect connected with her losing her babies before they were ready to live. But the patient was quite aware that, apart from whatever physical weakness existed, she needed psychological help by the time she approached me. The patient was highly intelligent and very capable in her profession as a research worker. Although she appeared somewhat restricted and rigid in her preliminary interview, she developed very strong feelings from the very first session, after she told me of an experience that had moved her deeply: when she was in the hospital after the baby died, she felt despair and suddenly she had a very vivid fantasy of jumping into the breast pocket of the jacket of an admired, older male friend. This experience seemed to express her feelings for me at that moment, an almost instant transference; in fact, she cooperated both emotionally and intellectually in the analysis from that time. In this early session it became clear that she had been identified with her own unborn infant quite consciously, but apart from the anxiety and depression about the baby's death, she was also aware that she had been afraid of feeling restrained, controlled, and intruded on by the baby had it survived.

I shall now collect some fragments of the patient's analysis which are related to the problems I wish to discuss. The patient did not want to become pregnant again until she felt she had understood at least some of her problems. She reexperienced vividly rejection from her father at the height of her oedipal situation at the age of five, when her mother was pregnant with the patient's younger brother. It became clear that she had sworn to herself that she would never again be put into a situation where she could feel humiliated by a man, or by a mother and father who made her feel that she was *only a child, unable to produce a child herself.* Gradually she began to feel better toward her father and more hopeful, and she tried to become pregnant again. This had never presented any difficulty; on the contrary, she had complained that she conceived much too easily, which had led to some abortions earlier on. But in spite of trying quite hard and (later on) quite scientifically, with medical advice, she did not succeed. I suspected at that time that she had a hormone deficiency since infertility had never been a problem, and when she consulted a specialist it was found that the mucosa of her uterus was not growing sufficiently to make conception possible. After the significant improvement that had followed her reexperiencing her intense oedipal conflict with her father, I suspected a more deeply seated mental problem. During this time the patient had a very psychotic dream, which was ego-alien and destructive.

In the dream the patient was standing at the edge of a lake and she saw a man swimming in the middle of the lake. Suddenly she noticed that he was drinking from a large whiskey bottle and he was obviously trying to drown himself. She realized that by drinking he wanted to make quite sure that his attempt at drowning would be successful because he had a triumphant look on his face. The patient shouted at him to stop drinking, that she would help him, but he continued looking very triumphantly at her and began to sink deeper and deeper into the water. The patient, desperate, rushed to a nearby telephone kiosk to ring for the rescue service but found that all the telephone wires had been cut and she could not get through. Nevertheless, she thought that in the end somebody helped her to pull the man out of the water and he could be revived. The patient had no associations to the dream whatsoever, but I began to suspect that a very determined destructive and self-destructive part of her personality was at work and that she was desperate and trying to get some help from me.

A little later she had a dream that was similar but more focused and more clearly related to her uterus and her fear that she would not have a baby. In the dream there was a baby who was born so ill that it could not be cared for properly and did not develop normally. Eventually this baby had to be sent to a mental hospital in her home country where it received electroshock treatment. In her dream the alleged reason for this baby's illness was that his legs were bent in the womb.[1] Again she had no associations to the dream. I interpreted that she was afraid of having a severe depressive illness, which would not respond to analysis, and that she had projected her fear of mental illness into her uterus. I felt that the meaning of the baby's bending his legs in the dream was not clarified, apart from the fact that one felt that it was done deliberately and forcefully.

A little later, the patient reported a dream that she was staying in bed in the morning and her mother-in-law (who was with her in the house) had to do the housework. The patient felt bad about being in bed so long, so she got up at about 12 o'clock and attempted to assist her mother-in-law. Her mother-in-law, however, angrily informed her that she was tired and she was going away for a holiday. In fact, the patient's mother-in-law had a good relationship with her. The patient always got up early even on the weekend, while her husband often overslept; he often came late to his analysis but she was *always* on time.

Her behavior in this session was unusual. Although generally she gave few or no associations to dreams, here, after telling the dream, she remained completely silent to the very end of the session—even after I attempted to verbalize some of her feelings related to the dream. I pointed out the contrast between her behavior in the dream and her behavior in real life. After some time of complete silence, I pointed out that she was, on this day, rather inactive and (unusually for her) not doing anything to help me with the analytic work. From this I concluded that she was behaving in the analysis as in the dream, that she was afraid I would immediately get fed up with her and threaten to leave. I related the dream to her fear of my not being able to cope with her and to her difficulty in conceiving and her uterus behaving like a tired mother who could not cope with a baby.

In the next session the patient was a few minutes late. She said that she had just come by chance because she had decided, at first, that she would

---

[1] There was also an earlier dream of "crippled children," which she remembered in a session in which she suddenly developed a very painful cramp in her legs.

not come. She added that I had behaved in the last session in an incredibly clumsy way and she found this extremely infuriating. How could I, as an analyst, so completely lose my temper with her? She did not sound anxious but *extremely* cold and furious.

I had been aware that the patient had been almost too well behaved so far. So now she had allowed some of her aggressive feelings to appear in her dream and behavior. I myself had not felt any anger; on the contrary, the dream seemed very important to me. I pointed out that for some reason the dream of the previous day seemed on this day to have become a reality for her. I realized this was a temporary transference psychosis. In the session I said that she seemed to be absolutely certain that I had been furious and had lost my temper. She might have forgotten or not heard some of the things I had said, and I reminded her of them—for instance, my acknowledgment that she had always been well behaved in the analysis. At the moment, I stressed, she was *obviously* convinced that she was right and I was wrong but it might gradually become clearer what was going on. I asked myself what made her so convinced that her perception was true. At the time I felt that she probably wanted to attack me by being a miscarriage, but I also thought that *something specific* in the previous day's session had annoyed her, something she would not tell me.

For a few days the patient seemed to continue being icily angry and aggressive, but then she gradually felt warmer and said that she thought she might have been rather tense earlier and that she had probably made a mistake. Only very much later did she explain some of the reasons for her anger. She had not told me that in the dream the bedclothes were *rather strongly tightened* round her so that she actually felt tied in her bed, almost *as if the bed represented a womb*. She had also felt rather withdrawn on that day and had not wanted to talk; she did not want me to disturb her. This was a problem that she had often experienced with her husband, but it had not occurred in the analysis before.

So in that session she had strongly resented my talking, as if I had been intruding into her withdrawn state. This reaction reminded me of the dream of the baby bending his legs aggressively in the womb, for she admitted that her being in bed in the dream represented her withdrawal into the womb and a refusal to move forward. Many years afterwards the patient behaved in a very obstructive manner, which prevented the analysis from moving. So the intense blocking, representing a retreat into the womb, indicated her aggressive refusal to come alive and to be a dependent patient in need of me. It was this problem that she did not want to touch.

Retrospectively, it seems to me that in the dream of the tired mother-in-law the problem of the mother's incapacity to contain her was of central importance. In the transference psychosis she relived with me some of the intense rage and resentment against her parents; she had always felt that she had had to please her parents and she was afraid of her mother's violent rage if she (the patient) expected to be looked after and contained by her when the mother seemed unable to do so. But the transference psychosis also expressed the fact that anxieties from deeper sources were overwhelming her. Locked up in the womb, she felt an intensely destructive self which nobody could cope with; thus, she had to keep it locked up. With my "clumsy" interpretation about the womb, I had intruded into this dangerous area. She feared that I would open up an area that she was sure I could not contain because her feelings were too deadly and terrible.

The expression of her intense fury and resentment relieved her, and she did feel less blocked and was able to talk more freely. She was also surprised that I did not respond with anger and criticism to her revelations of her intense angry feelings. But several months later she reported a dream that had been rather disturbing to her. In the dream there was a carpet with a very thick pile and a horrid creature embedded in it. It was so horrid that she could not bear to look at it, but she knew it had a kind of greenish, deathly look. In spite of the horror related to the dream, I felt that this dream was very revealing but, again, she was not able to give any associations. I had a very clear picture in my mind of her uterus having grown a thick mucuous membrane and that she was ready to conceive. (This factor was not known to us at that time; the last physical examination had still been negative.) It was clear that she felt unable to look at her own horrid and deadly destructiveness, but the destructive influence on the uterus seemed to have diminished because there was an obviously healthy, thick carpet.

I think one should regard this dream as a remarkably clear revelation of her psychosomatic state, and of the psychotic violence (in her uterus). In spite of her reluctance in the dream to see the horrid creature, the psychotic state wass clearly represented as a psychogenic manifestation. So the walling off and the split between psyche and soma had diminished. It broke through in the transference psychosis when she felt very concerned about what was going on. The better functioning of the uterus, which had not been destroyed by the deadly creature, seemed to imply that she had not damaged me with her violent attack during and after the transference psychosis, and that she had confidence in my containing function. On the other hand, the persistence of the deadly creature, whom she did not want to look at, gave a warning of the problem we still had to tackle. I said nothing about this at the time. In this hour I simply interpreted that it seemed she wanted to inform me that her uterus was very much better and she was probably ready to conceive a baby, but she felt there was something horrid in herself that she did not want to see and I should not see.

The patient missed her next period, and the pregnancy test after four weeks revealed that she was pregnant. For the next nine months her whole attitude and behavior concentrated on following the advice of her doctors in keeping her baby safely inside her. She had to spend several months in the hospital because the doctors did not want to take any chances given that there was some physical weakness in the neck of the cervix. A healthy baby was born at the right time, and the patient was able to devote herself completely to her child for several months. She enjoyed her baby's behavior and communication and her own capacity to understand the baby so well. She told me everything about it in detail; her own problems seemed to have vanished.

I allowed this to go on for some time. It seemed natural that she was full of joy and happy to look after her baby and share her observations with me. But after a few weeks I pointed out to her how difficult it was for her now to bring herself to analysis. In response to this interpretation, she had a dream in which she was six weeks old, dressed in baby's clothes, and trying to walk and to talk. She had made it clear that she felt very understanding about her baby and liked to take care of her and observe her. But she also had projected her own baby self into her baby. This meant that for quite a time there was some difficulty in admitting her needs for analysis.

The other meaning of this dream revealed some of her psychopathology, her tendency to idealize herself, which was related to some pseudomaturity in which she tended to deny all her problems from time to time. The dream, then, could be seen as a kind of caricature of this situation, as if she saw herself as a six-week-old infant, who was growing up too fast and already pretending that she could walk and talk. This idealization of herself and superiority had always been noticeable, but it had never been very openly admitted. Now it had increased as she found herself able to be the ideal mother she had always wanted to be. This idealization of herself and the denial related to it soon began to cause considerable difficulties in the analysis. It was clear at the time that she had made considerable progress and now had much more confidence in herself and me. But it was also obvious that so far the analysis was only a partial success; there was a danger that whatever remained of the psychosis could remain hidden, perhaps for ever. It became particularly clear in the analysis that the patient was extremely intolerant of her own envious feelings and was always sensitive to the envy of others.

For example, the patient had invited a number of her colleagues to a house-warming party. One of them had, by accident, smashed a fairly large vase, which the patient was very fond of. This woman friend behaved in a very peculiar way because she did not say anything about this and the patient found the bits and pieces of the vase in a corner. Somebody else had to tell her about her friend's destructive behavior. The woman never apologized or said anything about what had happened. The patient only said she could not stand this kind of behavior. How could one go into a house, find something beautiful, smash it up, and not even admit that one had destroyed it? she asked.

At this time the patient was quite unable to accept any interpretation of projective identification. She reacted to interpretations of the split-off parts of herself she did not like with a sense of persecution, because she wanted to maintain the idealization of herself. While she was probably quite correct in judging the character of this friend, I was aware that she used this experience to project and disown any envious, destructive feelings she experienced toward me. They had appeared more openly in the analysis after the transference psychosis, when she felt envy about the framework of the analysis and when she had a dream of throwing a plate violently into a ship and making a hole in it. Now she claimed that she had a self she liked and she felt that I literally wanted to spoil her good self with my interpretations and make her feel uncertain and useless. She, however, constantly gave me associations of the destructive, spoiling character traits she observed in other people. At the same time she stated categorically that she did not believe in the validity of projection. She admitted that she was preoccupied with other people's destructive problems, but that had nothing whatsoever to do with her.

This loss of insight only lasted for a few weeks. I pointed out to her that she was provoking me, because she told me very little about herself apart from the fact that she felt all right and wanted to go on believing that this would remain so. On the other hand, she constantly invited interpretations from me about projective aspects of her own self by continuing to concentrate almost exclusively on her observation of destructive character traits in other people. I realized that sooner or later I would have to risk another paranoid flare-up.

At last I very cautiously made an interpretation about this problem, when it seemed particularly clear (she had been talking about rather mean and envious character traits in her brother-in-law for several days). She insisted that I was forcing bad character traits into her which had nothing to do with her. It seemed a rather nasty, spoiling attack on her personality and she was not going to put up with such analytic nonsense. For a few days she was enraged and withdrawn, and I feared that my cautious interpretation of projective identification had precipitated a transference psychosis a second time.

The patient was, however, annoyed that some slight doubt remained in her that there might be some truth in my interpretation. She complained that this made matters worse. She therefore decided to devalue everything I said. But a few days after visiting her older sister, who was rather depressed and obsessional, she decided she did not want to become like this sister; it was probably better to face any feelings that were part of herself. She then admitted that she was rigidly holding herself together and was afraid of allowing any unwanted feelings to arise inside her because this would make her feel weak, tired, and collapsed—she was *not* going to feel like that. This difficulty in bringing the destructive aspects into the open by interpretation of the splitting process is very typical of patients with split-off, psychotic, paranoid-depressive aspects in their personalities. It is the confusion of depressive-paranoid feelings that is particularly difficult for patients to bear, and it often creates psychosomatic or hypochondriacal symptoms, or severe splitting. At this stage the splitting process was more prominent than a physical state (which appeared later on).

During the summer holiday following this slow development in the analysis, the patient went abroad with her husband and child. Afterwards, she reported that she had had a difficult time. Every night she had had a very disturbing nightmare, from which she woke up exhausted and frightened. Sometimes the nightmare occurred twice in one night, and sometimes she was afraid to go to sleep. During the day she felt bored and empty and could not take any pleasure in what was going on. She felt unable to understand her own dreams and realized that she still needed a great deal of help. The content of the nightmares was very repetitive; they were generally examination dreams. For example, in most dreams she had started too late to prepare herself for a specific examination, which was not her real subject. As there was not enough time to learn enough before the examination, she was quite certain to fail. Obviously she felt the analysis as a critical examination where she would be rejected, and she feared she would be severely punished for her delaying tactics, which at that time were quite marked.

During the following year the patient's blocking and evading behavior came more into the open. She told me a dream about a two-ton truck that was stuck and could not move up a hilly road. The engine did not work at all. Two men, but particularly one, tried to push the truck up the hill with their shoulders, but the truck moved backwards and the man was pinned under it. In the dream the patient feared that he might be crushed. She got very anxious and rushed to a hospital in order to direct an ambulance to the road where the accident had occurred. She felt furious because the woman attendant in the hospital was rather casual in handing her the telephone, but when she talked with the ambulance driver she could not remember the road where she had left the truck with the man pinned underneath.

The dream had a similar structure to the drowning dream earlier in the analysis, in which the man had cut the telephone wires. I felt that there

21. Psychosomatic Symptoms and Latent Psychosis /391

was a split between her crushing behavior and her desire to do something quickly to help, but in this dream it was clear that *her disturbed linking function* had become the most pressing problem. It was not only the woman who was slow in handing her the telephone, but she herself did not remember the area where the blocking and crushing behavior had taken place. Nevertheless, it took a long time for her to admit that it was extremely difficult for her to think about anything when she came up against feeling that she did not want to be bothered or wanted to be left alone.

After a few months she told me that she had a very strong feeling that she could make herself so heavy and difficult that there was nothing on earth I could do to make her better and that I was more likely to be crushed by my desire to help her than for her to be driven or influenced by her appreciation of my help. During this period she had dreams of engaging in acrobatics in outer space. It was difficult to get hold of anything, but occasionally I was able to interpret that she was not only aggressive but withholding any clear appreciation of what was going on in her *particularly if it was positive and constructive.* She agreed with this and related an incident when she was 14.

At that time she was painting a water color picture of the sea with a very nice sky and clouds. A woman who was looking over her shoulder had admired the picture. The patient took it, crumpled it up, and threw it away, implying that she would never paint again. I pointed out that in her behavior she was not only throwing away what I or other people had given her and attacking her own artistic creative capacities when they aroused interest and admiration, but she was probably also *afraid again of envious attacks.* In the next session she said *she had nothing to say or only bits and pieces,* but after some delay she told me the bits because she had nothing else to say. She reported that in the morning she had gone to a store to give back some clothing which was too small for her. The woman serving her was particularly kind and helpful and replaced it with something that fitted much better. When she left the store, the woman held the door open for her, and she also felt that this was very kind because she had her little daughter with her. She also thought of a nice man, a builder, working in her house. At this time there was a great shortage of building material and he had to wait sometimes for several days until he had collected enough bricks and cement. She felt very touched by his patience, and she emphasized that she was very lucky to have such a man to help her with the rebuilding of her house.

The only disturbing situation had been an encounter that morning in the street with a woman, a psychologist, who had looked right through her, as if she had not seen her at all. This had been rather disconcerting. I then told her that the bits and pieces she had been telling me (which she wanted to throw away because they were meaningless and nothing) could be put together quite easily into a picture, which told the following story. There was an analyst mother who was helping her exchange her feeling of being stuck in a position of feeling small for one that allowed her the opportunity to grow and develop. She also felt that this careful analyst/mother was not possessively keeping her in the same position but allowing her to develop by making it easier for her to go out into the world. As the analyst/father, she felt I was patiently collecting the bits and pieces of her associations in order to build up the structure of her personality; she felt very grateful and lucky to have me but she still feared the persecuting figure, who represented not only the destructive, envious mother but also her own destructive, envious self. This figure would look at everything going on between her and me that she valued in the analysis, *but would simply say it was nothing, and throw it away.*

She was very thoughtful after this interpretation. During the following weeks there was evidence that her omnipotent attitude was beginning to collapse. She had a dream that a balloon broke and fell right on top of her. The material was thin and didn't hurt her. However, she started to develop serious headaches and felt physically rather unwell. One day she had such serious headaches that she could not come to her session, and when she tried to work, she felt so ill that she had to go to bed. On the following day she told me a story about people who were sailing off in a balloon. At first they did not know which way to go. Then one of them said he wanted to go to India rather than to a desert, because when he was flying a balloon he would try to bring it down to *earth where there would be people who would help him* so he would not be so isolated. This association seemed to suggest that her desire to fly away omnipotently was changing into a wish to get away from her destructive omnipotent self and her emptiness and isolation, to go to someplace where she was more able to make contact and receive help.

The next day the patient told me two dreams. The first she was not again a typical examination dream in which she was not sufficiently prepared and did not know how to find the way to the examination room, which made her worried and anxious that she might fail. In the second dream she was washing her laundry in the washing machine and the laundry was ballooning out from under the lid. It became clear that something was not properly closed. She thought that she might simply put the lid back and realized that would not work; she would have *to close the washing machine drum properly,* otherwise the laundry would go on ballooning.

In giving associations to this dream she complained that her blinding headache of the previous day, right on top of her head, was coming on again: so it was clearly related to the ballooning of the washing machine dream. The dream revealed her growing awareness that she could not just let her thoughts drift away into nothing, into space, but had to think clearly and use her head as a firm container for thinking her problems through. In other words, the headache was associated with the impulse to return again to the destructive tendency to disperse her ways of thinking by thinking of nothing and drifting away. But now this experience was causing her severe pain; so she was realizing that through this attitude she was doing herself damage—indicating that progress had been made in strengthening her ego by establishing better links.

After a bad summer, progress during the following year continued to be slow. Frequently the patient suffered from severe headaches, tiredness, or even exhaustion. The summer holidays that year were much better. On the first day of analysis after the holidays she reported the following dream. In the dream she was going up a spiral staircase, which became smaller and smaller; she had to hold onto the iron rails and realized that she would get stuck. She said, "Ironically, it was obvious to me that I was stuck in the end in some kind of domelike structure which looked very much like a breast." She then remembered a very nasty story. There was a man who was robbed while he was away from his house and he thought that it would be a good idea to wait for the robbers to return for another looting. So he built an iron structure over his house and waited for the robbers to appear. Sure enough, they came back and then he put the iron structure over the house and left the robbers alone so that they couldn't get out and would, of course, starve to death.

During the holidays I had moved into another house, but she denied any interest or intrusiveness. She felt my previous house had been interesting, but she felt rather critical about the new house. She thought she knew all about it so did not see why she should be excited or interested. I felt that here the patient was admitting the strength and reality of her fantasies, because she was letting me know to what extent she had felt she was greedily intruding into me to rob me of all the good things I possessed. So she knew all about the inside of me and my house, but she also saw me as being worn out and empty and depressed. She felt persecuted by her guilt and forced to be identified with me as an emptied-out breast, which she felt I was using as a trap for punishment and imprisonment. Her feelings of exhaustion and collapse related to this depression.

The next day the patient suddenly talked about the jacket of a large book on architecture in my consulting room. For a long time she said she had seen the jacket of the book as completely worn out, but now she realized this was entirely untrue. It was not worn out at all; in fact it was very colorful and looked new. She was surprised to realize that this worn-out state of the jacket was a completely inaccurate perception. But she still had difficulty pursuing any insight of this kind further. By the end of the session she felt that she was not really depressed but indifferent. She knew that her attitude was damaging because it was so boring and tedious and that changed and damaged my interest in her. She admitted that she was not only afraid of being criticized but was also very conscious of imposing or projecting her bored feelings into me, that this was causing the analysis to be very empty and pedestrian so that I would feel fed up about it. She added that she knew that I could not be bothered with her, that I was fed up when she was not interested enough to come and talk to me and give me the material I needed to get on with the analytic work. So it was not a question of *fearing* that I was bored—she was quite *sure* that I was bored with her. In other words, she was asserting that she was perfectly correct in her perception of me, that I had been changed into a bored and worn-out, colorless analyst by her boring behavior. She felt this as a very concrete projection into me.

The following Monday, the patient had an unpleasant dream. It seemed like a painting. There was a very strange place, filled with damp and fog, and it was rather dark. There were bits of rock sticking out, and these rocks were all isolated from one another; there was no connection or bridge from one rock to the next. She was also aware that it was extremely cold. It was like walking on a precipice; she felt very disembodied. She indicated that this dream had something to do with her inability to communicate, which increased her feelings of isolation, but the awareness and unpleasantness of this state had not been lost in the dream. What had become clear was that the patient was finding the connection, the bridge. She related this to her self-awareness because it had been her self-awareness, her capacity to understand and see herself, that she had cut out and lost, isolating her and making her feel that it was quite impossible *to know where she was and who she was*. The patient's difficulty (in the dream) of being stuck at one point and not connecting it with anything else, and therefore having a sense of falling, was very typical of her fear of collapse, which appeared quite clearly at certain moments and was usually related to a complete inability to think and use her mind. The patient's admission of her boring attacks on me was related to her fear of the real damage her envious feeling could do to me if she realized that the depressed state was inside her and that I was full of life and could help her. Instead of feeling relieved about this discovery, she felt annoyed and envious and tried to spoil my satisfaction at understanding and my feeling of pleasure.

After this, her dreams became more open in admitting her attitude to me. For example, she reported a dream in which she was leaning over a filing cabinet and talking to a Mr. B., whom she felt was quite a nice man. They were actually at a party—there were others about—and she felt she should be having a much more private talk with him instead of talking to him with all the others present. While she was talking to him, she dropped some notes she had in her hand rather casually into a filing cabinet, without any care where these notes should go. She admitted she felt rather haphazard, filing them away in this manner. Later on she was walking down a hill and she saw, a little further away, some people grouped in a semicircle, with a man talking to them in a rather animated way. In front of her was a tramp, who was walking rather quickly toward the group. Suddenly, he pointed a rifle at this animated man, and it seemed quite clear that he was out to kill him. She noticed this and rushed up to him and shouted: "Don't do it!" He then turned round and pointed the rifle at her, and then she shouted: "Don't shoot me!" He did not seem to do this but the whole of the group on the platform seemed to tumble over, as if it were a kind of cardboard picture.

I pointed out to the patient that she had made it very clear in the dream that she realized that she talked rather haphazardly and loosely in the analysis, which made it difficult to connect her thoughts clearly. In projecting and distributing her thoughts constantly into other people and situations, she felt her analysis went on in public. In the dream she experienced this as rather unsatisfactory; she could not find the connections or links she needed to make good contact with the analysis as a valuable experience. As this had become clearer to her when the links had been restored, she had seen that I was full of life and interest in others and in herself. But she had also been forced to recognize that there was still an omnipotent, envious feeling toward me and she had to bear the fact that she had murderous impulses to kill me at the moment of clearly seeing me and facing herself. It had been made quite clear in the dream that this attack was not only directed against me but against the part of herself that valued me and was trying to protect me. In the dream she was very clear about the way she dealt with her destructive attacks. So it seemed now that gradually the bits and pieces of her whole self were being brought together, in particular, the attacks on seeing, or connecting, or linking, were being clarified and made meaningful.

It is interesting that it was not only the feeling of persecution connected with her depression that made the patient so distressed, paralyzed, and often near a state of collapse, but also *her incapacity to think,* which was an attack on linking, as well as insight and understanding. The attacks on linking and the denial of reality are, of course, important aspects of the psychotic part of the patient's personality (see Bion, 1954, 1959).

The constant repetitive attacks on the linking of good and bad feelings in a meaningful way—combined with confusing, envious attacks on valuable external relationships, and aggravated by attacks on the capacity to see and understand—produced fears of permanent severe damage to the patient's self and her capacity for thought and even fear of madness. A psychotic state has many ramifications, but one of the most disturbing related to the patient's finding herself enclosed in a state of mind that imprisoned her and from which she could not find a way out by herself. It is this kind of "psychotic island" the patient had to face in the analysis. In cases of this kind, one has to do very patient work. Like the bricklayer in the dream, one gradually helps the patient to put the bits and pieces of her (or his) self and thinking together, but one has to be able to wait until there is sufficient evidence and material for understanding the whole structure of the patient's personality. One can then make detailed linking interpretations, which have an important therapeutic influence in helping these patients gradually integrate their psychotic problems with the healthier parts of the personality.

The analyst has to be on guard against idealizing these patients, who often have remarkable perception and creativity in their capacity for cooperation in the analysis. But one also has to be aware of the danger of being drawn into perceiving them as second-rate and undeveloped, instead of recognizing the great potential for creativity and development they tend to spoil when they lose awareness of the destructive parts of the personality. This is a painful process and has to be faced again and again until permanent progress can be stabilized.

DISCUSSION

With this clinical example, I have tried to illustrate the existence of encapsulated psychotic parts of the self, which I call "psychotic islands." These islands exist in many people who suffer from neurotic symptoms but generally appear to be not seriously ill. When these psychotic islands are completely split off, or walled off from the psychic self, they often become embedded in a body organ—the chest, the gastrointestinal tract, the womb, the skin, or some other parts of the body. I believe that these psychotic islands are often the cause of what we call "psychosomatic illness."

The content of the psychotic island varies greatly, but it is common that extremely destructive, unmanageable impulses and the anxieties and defenses related to them predominate in its structure. At the same time positive, creative parts of the self (which have become confused with the destructive self and can therefore no longer be differentiated from it) are often pulled into this psychotic island. This means, of course, that the whole of the personality may appear weakened or not fully developed, although this is frequently covered up by self-idealization and denial. Often, traumatic experiences in early childhood, and even later on, are reported by the patient or discovered in analysis. These experiences usually relate to the mother's difficulties in relating sensitively to the infant. In other words, one finds that the mother's holding and containing capacity was severely impaired or was even practically absent. Sometimes both the father and the mother had problems, which they imposed on their child (or children), but they themselves were unable to listen to, and take notice of, the child's real needs. The pressure exerted by this environment may be so great that the child gives up and completely adapts to this environment—a process Winnicott (1958) has called "the false self."

Bion (1963) has described a process which he calls "alpha function," which is necessary in normal capacity for thinking and functioning. He describes how infants project and evacuate into the mother impulses and mental content that they are unable to cope with. Through the mother's intuitive function (which Bion calls "reverie") the un-understandable impulses can become meaningful and understandable to the child, who then begins to feel accepted and acceptable. This situation creates a space in the external object for the child, where he or she can feel safe and held together. This space can then be introjected, forming the beginning of a space inside the infant where he or she can begin to think and observe, and gradually leading to the construction of a mental apparatus. In time the child learns to accept both good and bad impulses and a self develops, which can struggle with conflicts within the self and outside it.

Intense, overwhelming rage, however, may build up in the infant, and later on in the child, when the space for development is denied by the external environment. The child feels forced again and again to evacuate mental content, so no solution of mental problems is possible. They have to be dealt with by splitting and denial. But there is another problem, closely related to, indeed interrelated with, this situation. The genetic endowment of positive and destructive parts of the self varies considerably in different individuals. The stronger the child's destructive endowment, the greater the need for the environment's capacity to assist the infant in facing and accepting both the positive and particularly the negative self. In this way the child will be able gradually to face and overcome a deep-seated anxiety of being constantly overwhelmed and destroyed by his or her destructive impulses. If, however, these genetic destructive impulses are unacceptable to the environment and the self, they will be split off early in life and remain dangerous and overwhelming monsters. It is the interplay of these early, split-off and unmodified aggressive impulses, reinforced by later, overwhelming, frustrating experiences, that often forms the core of the walled-off psychotic island.

I used case material from a patient in whom the psychotic island became embedded in the uterus. In the analysis, the breakthrough to the psychotic island temporarily led to a transference psychosis, in which the patient was overwhelmed by destructive feelings that had been suppressed and split off all her life.

From her very first session, this patient seemed to feel at home in the analysis. She felt accepted and contained—an experience that I believe made it possible for her to produce the dream in which she stayed in bed, making the mother-in-law so fed up and tired that she left the patient for a holiday. It was this dream that became completely real in the transference psychosis, and it had probably, unconsciously, always been a real situation for her.

It took her a few days to overcome the shock of her belief that I had turned into the angry mother-in-law. Soon afterwards, however, the psychotic island became dislodged from the body organs, so that the psychosomatic state appeared to be cured. After this the slow process of working out all the details of the buildup of this psychotic island had to be faced and worked through in the transference situation. It appeared then that the early splitting off of envious, destructive feelings was an important aspect of the psychotic island (described as a horrid, greenish monster that had embedded itself in the uterus).

The attacks of the split-off, envious parts of the patient were expressed in dreams and actions for several years. Gradually the envious attacks against her own creativity and the annihilating, devaluing attacks on the analyst's function (which were mixed up with admiration and protectiveness toward him) could be disentangled. It then became clear that the destructive attacks on her linking functions had made understanding and reparation impossible. This discovery made it gradually possible to help her to integrate the horrid monster and the caring self so that she became more convinced of her capacity to love and protect her love objects, and to be creative herself.

REFERENCES

Alexander, F. (1943). Fundamental concepts of psychosomatic research: Psychogenesis, conversion specificity. *Psychosom. Med.* 5.
Bion, W. R. (1954). Notes on the theory of schizophrenia. Int. J. Psychoanal. 35.
——— (1959). Attacks on linking. *Int. J. Psychoanal.* 40:308–315.
——— (1963). *Elements of Psychoanalysis.* London: Heinemann
Deutsch, F. (1939). *The Production of Somatic Disease by Emtoional Disturbance.* Baltimore: Williams & Wilkins.
Dunbar, F. (1938). *Emotions and Bodily Changes.* New York: Basic Books.
Freud, S. (1937). Analysis terminable and interminable. *Standard Edition* 23:216–253.
Rosenfeld, H. A. (1964). *The Psychopathology of Hypochondriasis in Psychotic States: A Psychoanalytic Approach.* London: Hogarth Press.
Winnicott, D. W. (1958). *Collected Papers: Through Pediatrics to Psychoanalysis.* New York: Basic Books.

AUTHOR INDEX

Abraham, K., 302, 312, *323*
Achenbach, T., 345, *353*
Agel, J., 7, *22*
Ainsworth, M. D. S., 341, *353*
Alexander, F., 9, *22*, 190, *199*, 381, *398*
Altman, L. L., 250, 267, *271*
Anderson, L., 348, *353*
Appelbaum, A., 366, *368*
Arlow, J., 198, *199*
Auerbach, A., 366, *368*
August, G. J., 348, *353*
Austrian, R., 343, *356*, 363, *369*

Babigian, H. M., 363, *368*
Bachrach, H., 366, *368*
Bakhtin, M., 372, *379*
Baldridge, H. D., 319, *323*
Balint, E., 41, *59*, 226, *239*
Balint, M., 9, *22*, 158, *173*, 215, 235, *239*, 277, *294*, 303, *323*
Barad S. J., 120, *122*
Bax, M. C. O., 351, *353*
Beaconsfield, P., 315, *323*
Beaconsfield, R., 315, *323*
Beauvoir, S. de, 4, *22*
Beiser, H. R., 156, *173*
Beitchman, J. H., 361, 362, 364, *368*
Bell, R. Q., 341, *353*

Benergas, M. C., 347, *356*
Benson, K., 362, *368*
Berg, I. S., 361, *368*
Bergman, A., 211, 213, 229, 239, 251, 252, 270, 272
Bergman, P., 153, *173*
Bergstrom, K., 352, *353*
Berliner, B., 81, 85, 101, *116*
Bess, B. E., 343, *354*
Bibring, G., 37, *59*
Bieber, I., 37, 57, *60*
Bierer, J., 153, *173*
Bille, B., 352, *353*
Bion, W. R., 194, *199*, 213, 215, 226, 235, 239, 305, 306, 311, 316, 317, *323*, 327, 331, *333*, 395, 397, *398*
Birdwood, G., 315, *323*
Blackey, E., 153, *173*
Bleger, J., 157, *173*, 190, *199*
Blos, P., 344, *353*
Blum, H. P., 35, 41, 43, *60*, 64, 65, 66, *74*
Bornstein, M. H., 340, *355*
Boszormenyi-Nagy, I., 16, *22*
Bowlby, J., 303, *323*, 341, *353*
Boyer, L. B., 275, *294*
Brazelton, T. B., 273, *294*
Brenman, M., 85, *116*, 154, 155, *174*
Brenner, C., 36, *60*
Bringuier, J.-C., 338, *353*

Author Index

Broderick, C. B., 343, *353*
Broverman, D. M., 6, *22*
Broverman, I. K., 6, *22*
Brumback, R. A., 347, *353, 356*
Brunswick, R. M., 38, *60*
Burgner, M., 68, *74*

Campbell, D. T., 158, *174*
Campbell, M., 348, *353*
Caparulo, B., 348, *353*
Caparulo, B. K., 360, *368*
Carmichael, H. T., 156, *174*
Carroll, B. J., 347, *356*
Carter, D. K., 7, *23*
Chandler, M. J., 361, *369*
Chapman, J., 156, 160, *176*
Chesler, P., 6, *22*
Chess, S., 339, *353*, 361, *369*
Chodorow, N., 7, *22*
Chomsky, N., 330, *333*
Christoph, P., 366, *368*
Chui, H., 348, *354*
Clark, R. W., 367, *368*
Clarke, A. D. B., 341, *354*
Clarke, A. M., 341, *354*
Clarke-Stewart, A., 341, *354*
Clarkson, F. E., 6, *22*
Cohen, D., 348, *353*
Cohen, D. J., 346, *356*, 360, *368*
Cohen, M., 366, *368*
Cook, S. C., 347, *356*
Cooper, S., 158, *174*
Covner, B., 153, *174*
Cytryn, L., 346, *356*

Damasio, A., 348, *354*
Damasio, H., 348, *354*
Davis, L., 154, 156, *174*
DeRacker, C. T., 12, *22*
Detlor, J., 346, *356*
Deutsch, F., 381, *398*
Dewald, P., 36, *60*
Dielman, T. E., 362, *368*
Dixon, H., 365, *369*
Dobash, R., 77, *116*
Dobash, R. E., 77, *116*
Dollard, J., 155, *175*
Dostoevsky, A., 374, 377, 378, *379*
Dostoyevsky, F., 371, 374, 375, 377, *379*

Dowling, C., 79, *116*
Dunbar, F., 381, *398*

Edgcumbe, R., 68, *74*
Eichenbaum, L., 7, *22*
Eimas, P., 330, *333*
Eisenberg, L., 338, *354*
Eisenstein, S., 9, *22*
Eissler, K. R., 190, *199*, 300, 308, *323*
Elbow, M., 78, *117*
Elkind, D., 338, 343, *354*
Elkins, R., 345, *354, 356*
Emde, R. N., 273, *294*, 341, *354*
Endicott, N. A., 155, *174*
Erikson, E., 307, *323*
Erikson, E. H., 80, *117*, 331, *333*, 344, *354*

Fagan, J. F., 340, *354*
Fairbairn, W. R. D., 5, 9, 10, 13, *22*, 212, 213, 239, 301, 303, *323, 324*
Fantz, R. L., 340, *354*
Federn, P., 281, *294*
Feinsilver, D., 287, *294*
Fenichel, O., 301, *324*
Fink, G., 155, *174*
Firestone, S., 4, *22*
Fitzpatrick, J., 365, *369*
Fleming, J., 78, 101, *117*
Folstein, S., 348, *354*
Foucault, M., 6, *22*, 376, *379*
Fraiberg, S., 292, *294*
Frank, J., 377, *379*
Franks, V., 6, 7, *22*, 28, *32*
Freedman, D. A., 310, *324*
Freedman, D. G., 273, *294*
French, T., 190, *199*
Freud, A., 53, *60*, 65, 66, *74*, 344, *354*, 360, 362, *368*
Freud, S., 5, 8, 9, 13, *22, 23*, 34, 37, 41, *60*, 64, 70, *74*, 157, *174*, 189, *199, 200*, 211, 213, 239, 241, *246*, 273, 274, 275, 280, 281, 287, 289, 290, *294*, 299, 300, 303, 304, 305, 306, 315, 316, 319, 323, *324*, 331, 332, *333*, 335, 336, 337, 344, *354*, 382, *398*
Friedan, B., 4, *23*
Friedman, C. T., 154, 156, *174*
Fromm—Reichmann, F., 8, 10, *23*
Frosch, J., 37, 38, *60*

Gaines, J., 251, 267, 272
Gardner, A., 345, 356
Garmezy, N., 365, 369
Gedo, J. E., 249, 271
Geleerd, E. R., 344, 354
Gelles, R. J., 77, 78, 117
Gelso, C. J., 158, 159, 174
George, A., 348, 353
George, S., 339, 354
Gerard, M. W., 345, 354
Ghent, E., 323, 324
Gide, A., 373, 374, 379
Gilbert, L. A., 27, 32
Gill, M. M., 35, 60, 125, 127, 141, 150, 154, 155, 174, 177, 187
Gilligan, C., 6, 23, 120, 122
Gillman, I, S., 78, 106, 117
Gillman, R. D., 191, 198, 200, 201, 205, 207
Ginsburg, B. E., 310, 324
Giovacchini, P. L., 80, 81, 83, 89, 116, 117, 251, 267, 271, 274, 275, 280, 292, 294
Gitelson, M., 191, 198, 200, 202, 207
Gittleman-Klein, R., 346, 354
Glover, E., 34, 43, 60, 276, 294
Goldberg, A., 249, 250, 271
Goldberg, J., 39, 60
Gould, R., 309, 324
Gove, W. R., 6, 23, 363, 368
Goz, R., 40, 60
Graham, P., 339, 354, 361, 369
Greenacre, P., 34, 37, 38, 60, 66, 74, 158, 174, 313, 324
Greenson, R. R., 8, 11, 21, 23, 37, 38, 60
Grinker, R. R., Sr., 366, 368
Grossman, L., 378, 379
Grotjar, M., 9, 22
Grotstein, J., 81, 109, 117, 212, 228, 239
Grotstein, J. S., 311, 312, 315, 316, 317, 318, 319, 324
Guaravitz, R., 323, 324
Guntrip, H., 9, 23

Haggard, E., 156, 174
Hallgren, B., 361, 368
Halmi, K., 365, 368
Hamilton, J. W., 251, 271, 299, 324
Hanly, C., 251, 267, 271
Harmatz, M. G., 153, 174
Harper, L. V., 341, 353

Harper, R., 155, 174
Harris, I. D., 191, 198, 200
Hartmann, H., 211, 230, 239, 276, 294, 301, 307, 325
Heilbrunn, G., 352, 354
Herb, T. R., 363, 368
Herrick, E. J., 277, 294
Hertzig, M., 343, 356, 363, 369
Hier, D., 348, 354
Hiken, J., 156, 174
Hilberman, E., 77, 78, 117, 120, 122
Hobson, J. A., 339, 354
Hodges, J., 361, 369
Hoffer, W., 215, 227, 239
Hoffman, I. Z., 178, 184, 187
Holahan, C. J., 153, 174
Holzman, P. S., 360, 366, 368
Hong. G. K., 344, 355
Horner, A., 81, 82, 101, 113, 117
Horney, K., 80, 117
Hotaling, G., 78, 118
Howell, E., 4, 23
Hudson, J., 155, 174
Hughes, H. M., 120, 122

Insel, T. R., 345, 354
Isaacs, K., 156, 174
Isaacs, S., 330, 333
Isakower, O., 243, 246

Jacobson, E., 210, 211, 212, 213, 214, 239, 301, 325
Jaffe, D. S., 310, 325
Janus, S. S., 343, 354
Joffe, W. S., 346, 356
John, E. R., 352, 355
Johnson, M., 366, 368
Jones, E., 299, 325
Jonge, A. de, 371, 374, 377, 378, 379
Jung, C. G., 306, 325

Kagan, J., 337, 341, 342, 355
Kanefield, L., 7, 23
Kaplan, A., 7, 23
Kaplan, A. H., 349, 355
Kaplan, H., 363, 368
Kaplan, S., 344, 355
Karme, L., 41, 42, 58, 60, 63, 74

Karpel, M., 16, *23*
Katan, A., 345, *355*
Katan, M., 308, *325*
Katz, N., 348, *353*
Kazdin, A. E., 351, *355*
Kearsley, R. B., 341, *355*
Kemp, P. L., 362, *368*
Kendel, E. R., 353, *355*
Kennell, J., 274, *294*
Kennell, J. H., 340, *355*
Kernberg, O. F., 80, 81, 82, 103, *117*, 213, 214, 233, *239*, 247, 249, 250, 251, *271*
Kessen, W., 340, *355*
Kety, S. S., 338, *355*
Kidd, K. K., 347, *355*
Klaus, M., 274, *294*
Klaus, M. H., 340, *355*
Klein, D., 346, *354*
Klein, D. F., 346, *355*, 366, *368*
Klein, M., 13, 14, *23*, 35, *60*, 213, 235, *239*, 276, 278, 292, *294*, 300, 302, 303, 312, 318, *325*, 327, 328, 329, *333*
Kogan, L. S., 154, *174*
Kohut, H., 80, 81, 89, 90, 93, 100, 103, *117*, 190, *200*, 212, *239*, 247, 248, 251, *271*, 301, 303, 305, 307, *325*
Korchin, S. J., 153, *174*
Korsch, B. M., 340, *355*
Koukkou, M., 339, *355*
Krichoff, I., 348, *353*
Kris, E., 301, *325*
Kubie, L. S., 37, *60*
Kuhl, D. E., 352, *356*
Kulish, N. M., 63, *74*

Lacan, J., 305, *325*
Lachmann, F., 249, *272*
Lamb, M. E. 340, *355*
Lamb, R., 154, 156, *174*
Landis, J. R., 362, *368*
Langer, D. H., 345, *356*
Langs, R., 8, 11, 12, 14, 19, 21, *23*, 30, *32*, 35, 36, *60*, 125, 126, 129, 133, 137, 141, *150*, 155, 157, *175*, 189, 190, 191, 198, 199, *200*, 201, 206, *207*, 217, 231, *239*, 243, *246*, 253, 270, *271*, 278, *294*, 319, *325*
Lassen, N. A., 352, *355*
Laufer, M., 346, *355*
Laufer, M. E., 27, *32*

Lecours, A. R., 341, *357*
Lederer, W., 79, *117*
Lehmann, D., 339, *355*
LeMay, M., 348, *354*
Lerner, H., 120, *122*
Lerner, H. E., 79, *117*
Lewis, H. B., 242, *246*
Lewis, M., 345, 353, *353*, *355*
Lippman, H. S., 348, *355*, 360, *368*
Lipsky, A., 345, *354*
Little, M., 8, 10, 11, 20, *23*
Loewald, H. W., 70, *74*, 250, *271*
Loewenstein, R., 301, *325*
Lord, R., 376, 377, 378, *379*
Lorenz, K., 312, *325*
Lubin, M., 180, 184, 186, *187*
Luborsky, L., 366, *368*
Lumsden, C. J., 317, 318, *325*

Mahalski, P., 343, *355*
Mahl, G., 154, 156, *174*
Mahler, M. S., 65, 66, *74*, 211, 213, 229, *239*, 251, 252, 270, 272, 276, 277, 291, *294*, 309, 313, *325*
Malone, R. P., 9, 20, *24*
Mandell, A. J., 347, *355*
Marcuse, F. L., 159, *175*
Marks, I. M., 345, *355*
Martin, D., 77, 78, 101, *117*
Martin, G. I., 345, *355*
Martin, H., 80, *117*
Marziali, E. A., 366, *368*
Masling, J., 351, *355*
Masson, J., 251, 267, *271*
Matte Blanco, I., 310, 311, *325*
Matthysse, S., 347, *355*
Maurer, R., 348, *354*
Mazziotta, J. C., 352, *356*
McCarley, R. W., 339, *354*
McDevitt, J. B., 65, 66, *74*
McKnew, D. H., 346, *356*
Medawar, P., 350, *356*
Menaker, E., 101, *117*
Menninger, K., 300, *325*
Methven, R. J., 365, *369*
Meyersburg, H. A., 353, *356*
Michels, R., 362, *368*
Mikkelsen, E. J., 346, *356*
Miller, J. B., 4, 7, *23*
Millett, K., 4, *23*

Milner, M., 157, 175
Mintz, J., 366, 368
Mitchell, J., 4, 7, 23
Mochulsky, K., 375, 379
Modell, A. H., 157, 175, 251, 267, 272, 287, 294
Mogul, K., 42, 60
Mollinger, R. N., 81, 85, 117
Munson, K., 120, 122
Murphy, D. L., 345, 354
Muslin, H., 127, 150

Nagel, E., 350, 356
Newman, R., 125, 150, 155, 174, 175

O'Brien, C., 366, 368
Offer, D., 363, 368
Offer, J. B., 363, 368
Ogden, T., 81, 90, 109, 113, 116, 117, 328, 329, 333, 334
Orbach, S., 7, 22
Ornstein, A., 249, 272
Ornstein, P. H., 249, 272
Osofsky, J., 341, 356
Ostow, M., 300, 307, 325

Palombo, J., 90, 117
Panken, S., 81, 85, 88, 90, 117
Pap, A., 350, 356
Parens, H., 309, 325
Paul, I. H., 155, 174
Paul, R., 360, 368
Payne, E., 57, 60
Perry, R., 348, 353
Perry, T., 343, 356
Pfouts, J. H., 78, 117
Phelps, M. E., 352, 356
Piaget, J., 276, 294
Pine, F., 211, 213, 229, 239, 251, 252, 270, 272
Pizzey, E., 77, 117
Popper, K., 350, 356
Post, R. M., 353, 356
Poznanski, E. O., 347, 356
Puig-Antich, J., 346, 356

Racker, H., 158, 175
Rangell, L., 65, 67, 74

Rapaport, D., 301, 325
Rapoport, J. L., 345, 354, 356, 365, 368
Rawlings, E. D., 7, 23
Redeheffer, M. A., 80, 117
Redlich, F. C., 125, 150, 155, 174, 175
Reese, H. W., 343, 356
Reich, A., 250, 272
Renz, C., 78, 117
Renzaglia, G., 158, 159, 175
Ricoeur, P., 242, 246
Rie, H. R., 346, 356
Roberts, R., 158, 159, 175
Robinson, J., 273, 294
Rochlin, G., 80, 81, 103, 117, 309, 326
Rogers, C. R., 153, 175
Rohrbaugh, J. B., 6, 7, 23
Roose, L. J., 158, 175
Rosenbaum, M., 191, 198, 200
Rosenberger, P., 348, 354
Rosenbloom, S., 348, 353
Rosenfeld, H., 250, 272, 308, 326
Rosenfeld, H. A., 381, 398
Rosenkrantz, P. S., 6, 22
Ross, D. C., 366, 368
Ross, J. M., 68, 74
Rothman, S., 348, 353
Roy, M., 77, 117
Rutter, M., 338, 339, 348, 353, 354, 361, 365, 369

Sadock, B. J., 363, 368
Sameroff, A., 341, 344, 356, 361, 369
Sampson, H., 88, 117
Sandler, J., 35, 60, 346, 356
Saperstein, J., 251, 267, 272
Sauer, R. C., 159, 175
Schaffer, H. R., 340, 356
Schneirla, T. C., 312, 326
Schwartz, L., 250, 272
Searles, H., 8, 13, 14, 16, 17, 20, 24, 155, 157, 175, 287, 294, 319, 326
Segal, H., 5, 14, 24
Seiden, A. M., 39, 60
Settlage, C. F., 66, 74
Shaffer, D., 345, 356, 361, 369
Shainess, N., 78, 118
Shakow, D., 153, 156, 160, 175, 176
Shapiro, T., 343, 356, 363, 369
Shaywitz, B., 348, 353
Shaywitz, S., 348, 353

Sherman, M., 343, 356, 363, 369
Simmel, E., 312, 326
Simon, T., 155, 174
Singer, R., 14, 24
Slaikeu, K. A., 153, 174
Sloane, P., 195, 196, 200
Socarides, C., 69, 75, 90, 101, 102, 118
Sommers, M., 125, 150, 155, 174
Spark, G., 16, 22
Spitz, R., 215, 227, 239, 244, 246, 315, 320, 326
Stanley, J. C., 158, 174
Staton, R. D., 347, 353, 356
Steiner, C., 6, 7, 24
Steiner, G., 376, 378, 379
Steinmetz, S., 77, 118
Stern, M. M., 153, 160, 175
Sternberg, R. S., 156, 160, 176
Stewart, M. A., 348, 353
Stoller, R. J., 320, 326
Stolorow, R. D., 101, 118, 249, 272
Stone, L., 41, 60, 63, 75, 158, 176
Strachey, J., 158, 175
Straus, M., 77, 78, 101, 118
Strom-Olsen, R., 153, 173
Strouse, J., 4, 7, 24
Strupp, H., 158, 176, 365, 369
Sullivan, H. S., 8, 10, 24
Symonds, M., 78, 82, 118
Symonds, P. M., 153, 176
Szmarag, R., 42, 60, 63, 75

Tanney, M. F., 158, 159, 174
Thomas, A., 361, 369
Thomas, S. A., 7, 24
Thompson, C., 39, 61
Thoren, P., 345, 357
Ticho, E. A., 38, 61
Tinbergen, N., 312, 326
Tizard, B., 361, 369
Tizard, J., 338, 344, 356
Todd, T., 366, 368
Tramontana, M. G., 366, 369
Tsai, L., 348, 353

Tudor, J. F., 6, 23
Tustin, F., 274, 294, 313, 326
Tyson, P., 43, 58, 61, 66, 68, 73, 75
Tyson, R. L., 66, 68, 75

Vaillant, G. E., 362, 369
Van Atta, R., 159, 176
Viderman, S., 157, 176
Vogel, S. R., 6, 22

Waelder, R., 349, 357
Walker, L. E., 78, 118
Wallerstein, J., 120, 122
Wallerstein, R. S., 251, 272, 365, 369
Weil, A. P., 66, 75
Weinhold, C., 344, 355
Weiss, J., 88, 117
Weizsaecker, V. von, 350, 357
Werry, J. S., 365, 369
Whitaker, C. A., 9, 20, 24
Whitmore, K., 338, 344, 356
Wilson, E. O., 317, 318, 325, 317, 318, 326
Wilson, H., 347, 353, 356
Wing, L., 361, 369
Winnicott, D. W., 9, 12, 13, 14, 15, 16, 24, 80, 118, 157, 176, 190, 200, 226, 239, 253, 272, 279, 280, 281, 286, 293, 294, 303, 305, 326, 333, 334, 397, 398
Woerner, M. G., 366, 368
Wolberg, L. R., 38, 61
Wolkon, G. R., 154, 156, 174

Yakovlev, P. I., 341, 357
Yamamoto, J., 154, 156, 174
Young, G., 348, 353
Yule, W., 361, 369

Zelazo, P. R., 341, 355
Zetzel, E. R., 8, 24, 38, 42, 61
Zitrin, C. M., 366, 368

SUBJECT INDEX

Adaptive contexts, 128–132, 136–137, 140–142, 180
Adolescence, 27–28
   turmoil of, 344–345, 363–364
Aggression, issues and theory of, 79–116, 301, 302, 307–310, 397 (*see also* Instinctual drives)
Amnesia, infantile, 337–339
Anxiety, 53, 137, 161, 164, 287, 305
   stranger, 342
Audiorecording, in psychotherapy, 151–173, 177, 184–187
Autism, infantile, 209–210, 216–217, 217–220, 238, 348–349

Bedwetting, 345, 361
Bipersonal field (*see* Interpersonal dimension, in therapy)
Body ego experience, 209–216, 227, 235

Capacities, innate, 340–341 (*see also* Preconception, innate)
Communication, unconscious, 125–128, 140–142, 144–146, 148, 157–159, 162, 164–165, 167–168, 192–199 (*see also* Perception, unconscious)
Container/contained, 305–306, 317, 328

Contexts, adaptive (*see* Adaptive contexts)
Continuity, in development, 337
Countertransference, 8–11, 31, 269, 285–286 (*see also* Therapist, errors of)

Death instinct, 299–323, 327–333 (*see also* Aggression, theory of)
   adaptive aspects, 299, 311–315, 318–320, 327
   and separation, 314–315
   and entropy, 310–311, 315–316
Defect, ego (*see* Ego defect)
Depression, 14, 161, 318
   childhood, 318, 346–348, 365
Development, early, 5, 15, 65–67, 77, 80, 121–122, 209–239, 273–278, 278–282, 289–293, 302–305, 309–310, 337–349
Discontinuity, in development, 337, 361–362
Divorce, 120
Dreams, 54–56, 71–73, 92, 189–199, 201–207, 263, 384, 385, 386–396
   in childhood, 339–340

Ego, body (*see* Body ego experience)
Ego defect, 273
Empathy, 224–226

Subject Index

Envy, 68, 299, 302–303, 304, 312, 321, 398
Errors, of therapist (*see* Therapist, errors of)

Females
  and Freud, 4–5, 8–9
  and therapy, 3–22, 37–40, 63–64
  development of, 4, 5
Feminist views (and movement) 4–5, 6–8, 10, 25–32, 78
First session (*see* Session, first)
Fixation, 289, 339
Frame (*see also* Ground rules)
  deviant, 129, 135–136, 137, 142, 145, 146–149, 151–173, 189–199, 206
  secure, 129, 133–134, 137, 141, 146–149
Frenzy, 372–373

Genetic factors, in therapy, 63–68, 133, 135, 192, 193, 273–278, 278–282, 289–293
Gender, and therapy, 33–59, 63–74
Ground rules, of therapy and analysis, 129–132, 132–137, 138–146, 146–149, 151–173, 178, 189–199 (see also Frame, secure and deviant)
Group instincts, 316–319, 320

Homosexual issues, 37, 44, 48–59, 72–73, 254–270
Humiliations, 373–374

Individuation, 16, 53, 270, 276, 309
Instinct
  aggressive (*see* Aggression, theory of)
  death (*see* Death instinct)
  life (*see* Life instinct)
  group (*see* Group instincts)
Instinctual drives (sex and aggression) 35, 230–232, 248, 266, 271, 299, 310, 331, 333 (*see also* Aggression, issues and theory)
Intimacy, 80–82
Interpersonal dimension, in therapy, 8–11, 25, 30, 35–37, 125–149, 177, 216–217
Interaction, therapeutic, 8, 9, 35, 125, 153–160, 179, 182–185, 217, 237, 243, 254–266, 281, 282–289, 383–396
Interventions
  of therapist, 46–57, 69–71, 72–73, 126–132, 136–137, 138–146, 149, 166–167, 180, 185, 209, 217–224, 256, 258, 262, 263, 265, 266, 288
  valid, 143–146

Latency, 343–344
Life instinct, 299, 308
Love, 3, 25

Madness, 135, 147, 375–378
Manifest content, in psychotherapy, 177–187, 189–199
Masochism, 80–82, 85, 101–116
Method, scientific, 241–246 (*see also* Psychoanalysis, as science)
Murder, 371–372

Narcissism, 48–49, 89–106, 133, 135, 212, 247–253, 254–266, 266–270, 273–278, 278–282, 301, 308
Neurosis
  infantile, 63–68
  obsessional, 345
Nontransference, 10–12, 140

Object
  background of primary identification, 228–229, 238
  constancy, 292
  relations, 5, 26, 63, 80–82, 135, 212–217, 248, 250–251, 266–270, 273, 286, 303–305, 309–310
  with self qualities, 234–236
Objects, transitional (*see* Transitional objects [phase])

Patient
  as therapist to therapist, 5, 13–17, 27–32
  borderline, 38, 92, 107, 113, 287 (*see also* Patient, regressed)
  curative capacities in, 12–21, 27–32
  narcissistic, 38, 89–106
  psychotic, 209–210, 216, 217–224, 291, 363–364, 381–398 (*see also* Madness)
  regressed, 282–289
Perception
  unconscious, 20, 30, 127, 137, 140–142, 144–146, 206, 209–239, 256
  of self and object world, 210–217

Phobias, 346
Preconception, inherent, 306, 311–314, 317, 328, 329–331 (*see also* Capacities, innate)
Process, therapeutic, 6–22, 25–32, 126–137, 138–146, 179–185, 383–396
Projective identification, 81, 106–116, 389
Psychiatry, child, 335–353, 359–367
Psychoanalysis, 9–12, 25, 33–43, 63–74, 126, 286–289, 321–322, 349–351, 365–367, 383–398
  as science, 241–246, 349–351, 362–367
Psychosomatic symptoms (*see* Symptoms, psychosomatic)
Psychotherapy, 6–22, 25–32, 43–59, 70, 87–88, 90–91, 92–93, 94–95, 96–97, 97–98, 98–99, 103–104, 107–108, 110–112, 112–113, 113–114, 114–115, 125–149, 151–172, 179–185, 189–199, 201–207, 209–210, 216–224, 254–266, 282, 285, 321–322, 366
Psychotic islands, 382, 396–398 (*see also* Patient, psychotic)

Rage, narcissistic (*see* Narcissism)
Rapprochment, 81 (*see also* Individuation)
Real relationship (*see* Therapy, reality in)
Recording, in psychotherapy (*see* Audiorecording, in psychotherapy)
Relating, modes of, 133–135, 169, 253–254, 266, 278–282
Relationship, psychotherapeutic, 6–22, 33–59
  real (*see* Therapy, reality in)
Reparation, 18–19, 27, 312, 314–315 (*see also* Patient, as therapist to therapist)
Research, studies and issues, 152–160, 186–187, 273–278, 335–353, 360–367
Resistances, in patients, 127, 137, 201–207

Self (*see* Narcissism)

Self, nuclear (core), 81, 89–106, 211–217, 226–228, 229, 232–236
Selfobject, 303
  transference, 248–251, 251–253, 267–271
Self-psychology (*see* Narcissism)
Self-representation(s), 232–233, 234–236
  of goodness, 229–231, 238, 252
  of badness, 109, 230–231, 252
Self, with object qualities, 234–236
Separation-individuation (*see* Individuation)
Session, first, 103, 125–149, 161, 177–178, 181–184, 255, 282–285
Sexuality, infantile, 303–305
Splitting, 81, 106–109, 214, 233–234, 252, 389, 398
Symbiosis, 16, 68, 81–89, 193, 209, 251–254, 259, 267–268, 270, 276–282, 284, 290
Symptoms, psychosomatic, 381–398

Tape recording, in psychotherapy (*see* Audiorecording, in psychotherapy)
Technique, in psychotherapy and psychoanalysis, 68–71, 125–149 (*see also* Interventions, of therapist)
Therapist
  errors of, 21, 30, 57, 141, 269 (*see also* Countertransference)
  manifest in dreams, 190–199, 201–207
  selection of, 37–40, 46–48, 51
Therapy, reality in, 11, 36, 41, 63, 73, 191–199
Transference, 8, 10–12, 31, 33–59, 63–74, 205, 252, 257, 267–270, 281, 287–288
Transitional object (phase), 286, 289, 342–343, 363

Validation, of interventions and theory, 126, 157, 170, 179, 243–246, 260
Values, feminist, 4–22, 28–29
Violence, adult, 77–116, 119–122

THE YEARBOOK OF PSYCHOANALYSIS AND PSYCHOTHERAPY

Adopted by The Society for Psychoanalytic Psychotherapy as its official journal, *The Yearbook of Psychoanalysis and Psychotherapy* is an all-new publication designed to focus on issues of concern to today's practicing psychotherapists. The spirit of *The Yearbook* is originality, clinically documented debate, and pertinence—an annual summation of the best work available in the field of psychotherapy that advances The Society's dedication to the development, teaching, learning, and researching of sound psychotherapeutic modalities. Readers interested in membership in the Society should write to Audrey McGhie, Executive Secretary, *The Society for Psychoanalytic Psychotherapy*, c/o The Lenox Hill Hospital Psychotherapy Program, 100 East 77th Street, New York, New York 10021.

YEARBOOK POLICY

The Yearbook publishes clinical papers that present original views on the technique of psychoanalytic psychotherapy, the nature of the therapeutic interaction, and the understanding of many forms of psychopathology, as well as contributions that touch on psychotherapeutic research, current debates in the field, and communicative studies of the therapeutic interaction and experience. Discussants are selected at the discretion of the Editorial Board.

Please submit manuscripts in triplicate and double-spaced on quality bond paper. The title page of each article must contain the author's full name and address, academic affiliation, date of submission, and a 150-word abstract. Footnotes should be numbered consecutively and double-spaced. Both footnotes and references (also double-spaced) should be listed separately at the end of the article and should follow the format recommended in *The Chicago Manual of Style* (13th ed.). Charts and tables must be on separate pages keyed to the manuscript. Manuscript submissions or inquiries should be directed to the Editor-in-Chief, Robert Langs, M.D., 300 East 75th Street, Suite 3M, New York, New York 10021.